D1547502

IRISH CATHOLIC WRITERS
and the INVENTION *of the* AMERICAN SOUTH

SOUTHERN LITERARY STUDIES

Fred Hobson, Series Editor

IRISH CATHOLIC WRITERS

and the

INVENTION

of the

AMERICAN SOUTH

Bryan Giemza

LOUISIANA STATE UNIVERSITY PRESS)((BATON ROUGE

Published by Louisiana State University Press
Copyright © 2013 by Louisiana State University Press
All rights reserved
Manufactured in the United States of America
First printing

DESIGNER: Michelle A. Neustrom
TYPEFACE: Ingeborg
PRINTER: McNaughton & Gunn, Inc.
BINDER: Dekker Bookbinding

LIBRARY OF CONGRESS CATALOGING-IN-PUBLICATION DATA

Giemza, Bryan Albin.
  Irish Catholic writers and the invention of the American South / Bryan Giemza.
    pages cm. — (Southern literary studies series)
  Includes bibliographical references and index.
  ISBN 978-0-8071-5090-0 (cloth : alk. paper) — ISBN 978-0-8071-5091-7 (pdf) —
ISBN 978-0-8071-5092-4 (epub) — ISBN 978-0-8071-5093-1 (mobi) 1. American
literature—Southern States—History and criticism. 2. Authors, American—Southern
States—History and criticism. 3. Irish American Catholics—Southern States.
4. Southern States—Civilization—Irish influences. 5. Southern States—Intellectual
life. 6. Southern States—In literature. I. Title.
  PS261.G54 2013
  810.9'975—dc23

                                                                    2012048402

In loving memory of my grandfather,
John Andreas Kearney,
a gentleman and a scholar.
Wasn't it awful, being Irish?
And wasn't it awfully good?

CONTENTS

ACKNOWLEDGMENTS

In one form or another, this book has been nearly a decade in the making. In preparing it I was faced with the classic paradox: any time one sets out to do something, something else must be done to get halfway there. Without the help of many others, I could not have taken up a task that seemed to veer to infinitude. And so goes my gratitude. It extends to the many unmentioned and to those whom in carelessness I may have forgotten to mention, but I wish to express it specifically to those named below.

—The many friends and colleagues who read and commented on drafts of this study, offering crucial support along the way, including: Fred Hobson, for his guidance, for suffering my drafts gladly, and for his love of writing; Farrell O'Gorman, whose knowledge of the southern Irish experience is bone-deep; Richard Russell, whose friendship has sustained and inspired my work in many ways; Linda Wagner-Martin, for her truthful criticism, her sense of the important, and her unfailing advice; Joe Flora, a brother in spirit and father in wisdom; Tom Inge, for unreasonable generosity; Bill Andrews, for true encouragement; Bland Simpson, for friendship and swamping; Connie Eble, for meticulous proofreading and enthusiasm; George Lensing, a constant and generous ally; Patrick O'Neill and Nicholas Allen, for good humor; Rick Wallach, my friend-o; Donald Beagle, for sharing his knowledge and writing gifts; Jimmy Buttimer, for opening his hand and his home; and Weldon Thornton, the finest teacher of Irish literature I will ever know.

—Those who consented to interviews and correspondence and gave me generous access to their time and resources, including Bruce Bickley, Ashley Brown, Horace Butler Jr., Jimmy Buttimer, Robert Coles, Pat Conroy, Bob Gentry, Patricia Persse, Anne O'Brien Rice, Louis Rubin, Patrick Samway, SJ, Valerie Sayers, Bill Sessions, and John Sullivan.

—The institutions who furnished inspiration, underwrote costs, and provided other material support. These include The Institute for Southern Studies at the University of South Carolina and the Watson-Brown Foundation for a wonderfully well-appointed postdoctoral fellowship and for research support, without which the book might not have been completed; for the initial support that gave it life, the University of Notre Dame's Cushwa Center and the Ancient Order of Hibernians (Hibernian Research Award), along with the University of North Carolina's Center for the Study of the American South and UNC's English department (Frankel dissertation fellowship and travel grants); Amy Goodwin, Dal Wooten, and Randolph-Macon College's English department for providing unstinting support, with additional support from the College (Rashkind Grant for Advanced Research and Walter Williams Craigie Research Grant); Wake Forest University's English department (William C. Archie Research Grant); the Jessie Ball DuPont Fund; Loyola's Center for the Study of Catholics in the American South; the American Conference of Irish Studies; and finally, the Buttimer family and the Savannah Irish Festival for doing much to support and promote the book.

—The archivists and librarians at the thirty or so institutions who threw open doors, tracked down ephemera, and answered myriad queries. They are directly responsible for bringing so much of what is new to these pages. Ginger Young and her wonderful staff obligingly obtained every text I needed, however obscure. Donald Beagle, David Berg, Gillian Brown, Tommy Mixon, and Katie Salzmann are typical of those who went above and beyond the call of duty in alerting me to new discoveries indispensable to the writing of this book.

—The students of the University of North Carolina, East Carolina University, Wake Forest University, the University of South Carolina, and Randolph-Macon College. I have done my best to transmit something of their creativity, intelligence, and friendship to this project.

—David Gleeson and James Woods, for generously permitting me to reproduce tables from their research; and Andrew Giemza and Sarah Huber, for helping to prepare the figure included in these pages.

—For providing encouragement and contributions too various to name: Andy and Marcella Barrett, John Blevins, Bob Brinkmeyer, Tad Brown, William F. Buckley Jr., Maura Burns, Carlo Caruso, Joan Conners, Marisa Cull, Don Doyle, Walter Edgar, Paul Elie, Bob Ellis, Ayse Erginer, Barbara Ewell, Bill Ferris, James Flannery, David Gleeson, Michael and Hampton Ford, Bill Franz, Scott Frederick, George Garrett, Nora Green, Cathy Hankla, Justin Haynes, Harris Henderson, Noel Ignatiev, Barlow Jacobs, Bill and Susan Johnston, Steve Juras, Sean Kirk, Phil Kowalski, Barbara Mangione, Brad McDuffie, Eileen Murray, Chris Newton, Tim Owen, Tom Peyser, Tara Powell, Paul and Mindy Quigley, Jim Rogers, John and Dale Reed, Woody Register, Adrian Rice,

Lain Shakespeare, Dave Shaw, Julia Ridley Smith, Graham and Jane Snyder, Kenneth H. Thomas Jr., Andrew Utschig, Sue and Ritchie Watson, Amy Weldon, Mel Williams and the Watts Street family, Diane Woodbury, and the Woodsides.

—Amanda Urban, for reviewing the material on Cormac McCarthy.

—Mary Flannery O'Connor, who taught me that mother is the necessity of invention, and Cormac McCarthy, who taught me to judge not lest ye be Judged.

—Wyatt Prunty and the Sewanee Writers' Conference, for a new lease on writing life.

—The staff of the LSU Press, especially Fred Hobson, John Easterly, and Margaret Lovecraft for unflagging good cheer and their help, at every stage, in seeing this book to print. Thanks are also due to Lee Sioles for her guidance and Joanne Allen for her excellent work.

—My parents, Ray and Mary Ann, my stepfather, Jimmy Griffin, my brothers, Paul and Andrew, my family first and last. Those who have a writer in the family know that "the book" becomes a member of the family, if not always a welcome one. For their forbearance, for the joy of each day, my heart sings for my wife, Kristi, and our children, John Paul and Vera Rose. They are, as I once wrote, all I will ever have or stand to lose. A.M.D.G.

IRISH CATHOLIC WRITERS
and the INVENTION *of the* AMERICAN SOUTH

INTRODUCTION
Mavericks of Religion

They say we aren't Irish; God knows we aren't Scotch.
—JOHN BOYLE O'REILLY[1]

The Irish exile, whether he was Presbyterian, Catholic, Quaker, or Noncon-
formist of any kind, sought for freedom of soul and body.
—FR. WILLIAM TOBIN

I think there was more real sentiment for St. Patrick along
the banks of the Mississippi than in the East.
—T. P. O'CONNOR, *My Beloved South*

When the bestselling humorist Irvin S. Cobb (1876–1944) stepped to the podium before the Catholic-leaning American Irish Historical Society in January 1917, he flashed some of the familiar chutzpah that would make him a crowd favorite. He began with a curious blend of southern and Irish nationalism:

Always it was to the south of Ireland . . . that one must turn to find the dreamer and the writer, the idealist and the poet. It is to the south of Ireland also that one must turn to seek for a people whose literature and whose traditions are saddened by the memory of the wrongs they have withstood and the persecutions they have endured and still endure, and yet whose spirits and whose characters are uplifted and sanctified by that happy optimism which seems everywhere on this footstool to be the heritage of the true southerner.

In a measure these same things are true of our own country. The North excels in business, but the South leads in romance. The North opens wide the door of opportunity to every man who comes to its borders with willing hands and eager brain. The South opens a door, too, but it is the door of hospitality, and it bids the stranger enter in, not so much for what he can give, but for what he can take in the way of welcome. I think there is a reason, aside from topography and geography and climate and environment, for these differences between the common divisions of our great country.[2]

The reason, it turns out, is the Irish. With an impresario's glee, Cobb shredded cherished notions of Anglo-centric southern identity, launching into the turning tale of his family's origins: his mother, "of the breed of Black Douglas of Scotland, as Scotch as haggis, and rebels, all of them, descendants of men who followed the fortunes of Bonnie Prince Charles, and her mother lived in a county in North Carolina, one of five counties where up to 1820, Gaelic was not only the language of the people in the street, but was the official language of the courts." His father's line "ran back straight and unbroken to a thatched cottage on the green side of a hill in the Wicklow Mountains, and his people likewise had some kinsmen in Galway, and some in Dublin." It seemed he "descended from a group of men who went from New England to Kentucky and the names of these men were Lyon and Cobb, which is a Danish corruption of O'Connor, and Machen, and Clendenin, and O'Hara, and Glenn, which is a corruption of Glynn." "What a hot bunch of Anglo-Saxons!" he declared, to the laughter of his audience.[3]

In his memoir, *Exit Laughing,* Cobb noted also a family patriarch who had been "reared in the Catholic fold" and subsequently had become a deacon "at a dissenters' meeting-house." "Deacon Henry must have had a Celtic sense of humor," he added: "by two wives he begat thirteen children and named the last one 'Experience.'" Remarkably, Cobb acknowledges the play of Catholicism throughout his lineage: "At intervals since then, some of us have returned to the Ancient Faith. I have a cousin who is a nun and I had a great-uncle, who, though outwardly a pious Episcopalian for all his days, on his deathbed sent ninety miles for a priest to come and shrive him, much to the astonishment of a soundly evangelical household."[4] His southern descendants, he reluctantly owns, may have been slave runners.[5] In exploring his family's deep history, he points to an often overlooked chapter of the American Irish experience: "I tell you that fifty percent, at least, of the dwellers of the mountains of the South and notably of Kentucky and Virginia are the lineal descendants of runaway indenture men, Irish rebels mainly, from the Virginia plantations."[6]

Today remembered as a poor man's Mark Twain, Cobb does not let the facts get in the way of a good story—yet he had put his finger on a topic that historians continue to tease out. The notion that the Appalachians are somehow a bastion of purest "Anglo-Saxon" culture has been thoroughly debunked. Meanwhile, new attention has turned to indentured colonials in books such as *White Cargo,* Don Jordan and Michael Walsh's well-received study.

In fact, runaway notices for indentured servants in colonial-era southern newspapers make frequent mention of the Irish. Two 1785 notices, published within weeks of each another in the *Virginia Journal,* reveal that differing pictograms were employed to represent runaway indentured servants and slaves. In one, Thaddeus McCarty of Alexandria called for the return of a mulatto named Harry Jackson, who is depicted wearing a loincloth and carrying a walking stick. David Kennedy sought the escaped Philip Lougherey, "an Irish servant lad," represented in European breeches and hat. Both refugees merit an eight-dollar bounty, and both, the advertisements say, are fond of liquor. But only Philip Loughery would be described as "very impertinent, and very much given to swearing."[7]

Elsewhere, the Charleston *Gazette* gives ample evidence that indentured Irish did sometimes hie to the hills, and on its pages one also finds notices for the sales of imported servants, with shipments originating in Ireland.[8] Expatriation of religious rebels and Jacobites accelerated in the 1680s, with many exported to Carolina to work as indentured servants.[9] And in the Virginia of Cobb's forbears, between 1736 and 1768, 37 percent of indentured servants were identified as Irish, compared with 49 percent of English descent."[10]

Black and Irish fortunes too were entwined from the beginning. "Remarkably," writes Kerby Miller, "the records of almost every major slave revolt in the Anglo-American world—from the West Indian uprisings in the late 1600s, to the 1741 slave conspiracy in New York City, through Gabriel's Rebellion of 1800 in Virginia, to the plot discovered on the Civil War's eve in Natchez, Mississippi—were marked by real or purported Irish participation."[11] Suspicions of Irish insurrection can be explained partly by Anglo and Anglo-American colonial prejudices, for "as early as 1800 frightened Virginians had accused Irish republican émigrés of involvement in Gabriel's slave rebellion (allegations later repeated in Mississippi and elsewhere)."[12] The fact remains that southern politicians and slaveholders who depicted southern Irish as friendly to blacks deployed a grain of truth in service of propaganda.

Indeed, the Irish are deeply implicated in southern thinking about race, in part because of the transnational practice of indenture in the colonial mid-Atlantic, South, and Caribbean. Though this study considers in passing the complexities of interrelationships between black and Irish southerners, it is a topic that might easily fill the pages of another volume.[13] Suffice it to say that like most southerners of his time, Cobb preferred to frame his family's experience with slaves in terms of ownership, not kinship (though his views of race seemed to change over the course of his life, as when he gave a speech pouring praise on black veterans of World War I, objecting to crap-shooting, buck-dancing caricatures, and saying "The Negro is great in every way except complaining").[14] In observing that credulous southerners had been sold a bill of Anglo-Saxon goods, Cobb also touched on how the construction of northern and southern "races" helped catalyze the Civil War.

This sort of rhetoric was often ginned up to promote warmaking agendas, and it succeeded to an astonishing degree in naturalizing differences that were only the lately conceived chimeras of polemicists. Ritchie Watson records the case of the unnamed *Southern Literary Messenger* writer who "articulated an even more nuanced definition of the Yankee race. While the blood that flowed through southern veins was largely of Norman origin, he believed that the great majority of northerners were products of the unfortunate union of two racial strains notable for their proclivity for intemperance and violence: the Saxon and the Celtic."[15] And the results of infusion? "Wherever there is Celt there are revolutions, disorders and violence," answers the writer of "Northern Mind and Character." In fact, for this (qualified) proslavery and pro-Union writer, the "reckless" southern Irish enthusiasm for the dissolution of Union was grounds for taking caution. Cromwell was of Norman descent, notes the writer, and a glance back to Britain's rulers suggests that "they *have* controlled them there, and we *may* control them here, IF WE WILL."[16]

The *Messenger* essayist faced a problem in promoting this view, since *Celtic* might include the Irish, Welsh, Scots, and Scots-Irish, with the latter groups increasingly well respected for their contributions to southern culture. Acknowledging belatedly the presence of "a certain *Celtic* element . . . among us," the author "neatly finessed this potential racial complication with the facile assurance that Norman blood had always dominated the South," explains Watson.[17] If the idea that northerners and southerners were made up of distinct races was naturalized with remarkable swiftness, the attendant idea that to be Irish was to be somehow "unsouthern" endured with remarkable tenacity as well.

Knowing that he was pushing against this idea, Cobb simply turned it on its head: as a rule, he argued, southerners were more Irish than English. So he offers an overarching theory that he was neither the first to invent nor the last to employ: "The soft speech of the Southerner; his warm heart, and his hot head, his readiness to begin a fight, and to forgive his opponent afterwards; his veneration for women's chastity and his love for the ideals of his native land—all these are heritages of his Irish ancestry, transmitted to him through the generations."[18] Only five years before Cobb delivered his speech, the Hibernian Society of Savannah celebrated its centennial with a lavish banquet whose attendees included President William Howard Taft (keynote addresses in later years would be given by the likes of Harry Truman, Fulton Sheen, and Jimmy Carter). The speeches were charged with the high patriotic rhetoric of the time, delivered in a Confederate register, with special plaudits for James Ryder Randall and Abram Joseph Ryan, Irish American war poets of the South, Roger B. Taney (for his "forceful mind and philosophic thoughts") and William Henry Elder, the unreconstructed southern archbishop.[19]

To hear echoes of Cobb's triumphalism resounding in a posh banquet hall in 1912 Savannah is not just to perceive the large motifs of southern Irish literature —race, religion, and social orders—but to hear the earliest murmurs of a forming trend. Cobb delivered his speech around the high-water mark of historians' reclamation of the Scots-Irish, whose previously low standing in the American order would be rescripted, via the frontier thesis, to portray them as the avatars of American exceptionalism. Thus it is revealing to note where Cobb lays emphasis in offering an "Irish" Irish counternarrative: the winning of the Northwest Territories was accomplished by Irishmen, "not Scotch-Irish, nor English-Irish, but plain Irish-Irish men who were rebels and patriots by instinct." Six years later, in his famous "Sahara of the Bozart" essay, Mencken would join Cobb in claiming, "The chief strain down [South], I believe, is Celtic rather than Saxon, particularly in the hill country."[20] It was a vision refracted and reprised by W. J. Cash, another great upsetter of southern myths.

Why begin with Cobb, a blowhard and curmudgeon, whose work a *New York Times* critic described dismissively as "kindly, slangy little tales"?[21] Precisely because Cobb is perfectly emblematic of the southern Irish in literature. As a latter-day southwestern humorist, Cobb counts as a late exemplar of the Irish influence on that genre, an influence that touches on William Gilmore Simms, Joseph Field, William Caruthers, George Washington Harris, and Mark Twain, all southern writers who either claimed Irish descent or brought an Irish presence to their humor writing. In his ability to divide critics on whether he offered a "real" portrait of the South, in his enormous popularity, in his apprenticeship as a journalist, in his awareness of Catholic skeletons in the family graveyard, even in his resurrection of the wily (and flawed) notion that the Irish invented the South, Cobb is, above all, a reminder of the complexity of Irish identity among southerners.

Cobb's theory notwithstanding, the critical record suggests that southern literary history takes a selective view of the Irish, and so it is necessary to consider both the ways that these writers were classified as southern and Irish and how what would eventually be called the "Celtic thesis" affected these classifications. Perhaps a majority of white southern writers of note—and quite a few black southern writers as well—reflect the legacy of the Scots-Irish in their work, through social attitudes, dialect, and folkways. And it is something of a commonplace among white southerners that Scots-Irish folkways became the widely acknowledged bedrock of southern culture. Or did they? And how do we know? What about Irish Catholics? A lively historical debate swirls around this topic. There is no scholarly consensus on the meaning of such superficially straightforward terms as *Scots-Irish, Scotch-Irish, Irish American* (usually implicitly Catholic), *American Irish,* and *Irish Catholic* (sometimes unfairly held to be the "Irish" Irish) or, for that matter, on whether such terms are useful. (Kevin Kenny and others have suggested replacing them, in American historical reference, with a single term: *America's Irish.*)[22] Nor is there any consensus on how many Irish Catholics came to the South for most of the region's early history. Frequently the numbers are argued from absence, deduced from economic and political conditions with the assumption that hard times breed migration.

The evolving understanding goes something like this: (1) *Scots-Irish* and its permutations (e.g., *Scotch-Irish*) reflect real migrations and cultural associations in history but (2) are simultaneously terms of art that evolved in tandem with the dominant themes of American history, pronounced by Frederick Jackson Turner and others, in which a wily and untamable people proved equal to the task of taming a frontier. (3) These identities were more mutable, on either side of the Atlantic, than suggested by the "two traditions" model (a binary way of viewing Irish historical experience simplified into two camps: Irish Catholic and Scots-Irish).[23] (4) The number of Irish Catholics in the South is probably greater than has been acknowledged in the past. The historian Kerby Miller affirms that

> among poorer migrants, the relative frequency of intermarriage and conversion reflected a pragmatic understanding that ethnic and religious affiliations were not absolute but contingent on local economic and social circumstances. Early Irish emigrants appear to have been relatively nonchalant about what subsequent generations would regard as religious apostasy or ethnic treason. The result . . . was the absorption of nearly all early Irish Catholic (and also Irish Anglican) emigrants into the Presbyterian faith of the great majority.[24]

In the meantime, it took little more than a single generation of historians to hallow the "Scotch-Irish." R. D. W. Connor, a Scots-Irish historian from North Carolina, noticed this tendency to fulsome praise in 1920: "There is perhaps no virtue in the whole catalogue of human virtues which has not been ascribed to [the "Scotch-Irish"]; no great principle of human liberty in our political and social systems which has not been placed to their credit; no great event in our history which they are not said to have caused."[25] If one talks to southerners about the "Scotch-Irish" today, the song remains much the same.[26] Though American Irish history is not a limited good, the preeminence of the Scots-Irish in southern history might well overshadow Irish Catholics' part in that history.

Then there is the related difficulty of retrieving a clear picture of Irish Catholics, whose story has been fragmented by assimilation and sometimes simply subsumed in the larger tale of southern history. While assimilation worked to efface the Irish Catholic presence in southern history, in some cases that presence was simply written out. The story of the first British colonial governor of South Carolina, James Moore Sr., is illustrative. As Kerby Miller noted in *Irish Immigrants in the Land of Canaan,* "Royal officials of Irish origin were common to the southern colonies," especially in an era when the English and Irish governing classes were highly interrelated.[27] Moore's story is in some ways typical: As a young man he remigrated to South Carolina from Barbados and made out handsomely in trading with Indians.[28] To the victors went the spoils: following a political shift and series of realignments that played to his favor, he was appointed governor in 1700. As one might expect of the chosen agent of the Lords Proprietor, Moore was an Anglican.

But his family's complete tale, often expurgated from southern histories, points to a different story. The consensus holds that Moore was the son of Rory O'Moore, remembered as an Irish Catholic stalwart and one of the chief architects of the Irish Rebellion of 1641. With the fugitive family's fortunes in tatters, young Moore was whisked away to an outpost of empire, with an anglicized identity and enough of his family's political capital to make the best of an unfortunate situation. (Meanwhile, the family bided their time with generation-spanning loyalties; O'Moore's grandson Patrick Sarsfield became a renowned Jacobite leader who fought at the battle of the Boyne.) When Paddy Larkin performed in an 1838 New Orleans stage adaptation titled *Rory O'More,* the entire Hibernian Society turned out to see it. And Mary Chesnut would recall how John England, Charleston's Irish-born bishop, would bring a visiting train of priests who sang of Rory O'Moore.[29] *Moore* became eponymous with the "best families" of South Carolina.

Kevin Kenny submits that "because the 'Scotch-Irish' ceased to be Irish (in their own estimation as well as that of others) in the early nineteenth century, the story of American Irish thereafter is largely if not exclusively a Catholic one."[30] In this way, he explains, we might understand how it came to pass that John F. Kennedy, not Andrew Jackson, was regarded as the first Irish president. Historians who, like Timothy Meagher, are skeptical of assimilation point to the persistence of Irish Catholic ethnic identification, which endures across generations, suburbanization, and economic comfort. The deliquescence of southern Irish Catholics, who could effect a kind of ethnic disappearing act by means as simple as dropping the *O'* before a surname—as did the families of Henry Grady (the editor of New South fame) and James Moore—could give rise to the false assumption that they had abandoned any meaningful Irish identity.

It also gives rise to an apparent paradox: these "invisible" Irish proved to be energetic chroniclers of their adopted region, largely by holding fast to a sense of ethnic and religious outsiderism. Every study begins by setting boundaries (unless it is very tiresome indeed!), and in this one I propose to limit the field of southern Irish writers by focusing primarily on the Catholic ones. In so doing, I do not wish to perpetuate the religious divisions underlying the ethnic divisions that have washed Irish history in blood. Certainly one must begin by acknowledging that *Catholic* itself can become an artificial label, especially given a troubled history of appropriation by a nationalism that presses religious practice into serving the fine distinctions of "racial" purity. We should remember that the "natural" conjunction of the terms *Irish* and *Catholic* is itself a fairly recent historical invention. While there are venerable evidences of Catholic piety in Ireland's unique relationship with the Roman faith, the notion of Ireland as a uniquely and innately devout country is of demonstrably recent coinage, stemming in large part from Ireland's mid-nineteenth-century devotional revolution.

Another difficulty hovering over this project is that parsing ethnic identity becomes more important for what it shows than for what it tells. Irish Catholic and Scots-Irish distinctions can become something of a historical fog bank or else fade into latter-day boutique Irish distinctions; the number of southerners who self-identify simply as "Irish" on the census has risen dramatically in recent years. And the artificiality of such distinctions as *Celt* and *Anglo-Saxon* have only become more pronounced as geneticists take up the issue. As the *New York Times* reported recently, British historians "teach that [people from the Isles] are mostly descended from different peoples: the Irish from the Celts and the

English from the Anglo-Saxons who invaded from northern Europe and drove the Celts to the country's western and northern fringes." The article continues:

> But geneticists who have tested DNA throughout the British Isles are edging toward a different conclusion. Many are struck by the overall genetic similarities, leading some to claim that both Britain and Ireland have been inhabited for thousands of years by a single people that have remained in the majority, with only minor additions from later invaders like Celts, Romans, Angles, Saxons, Vikings and Normans. The implication that the Irish, English, Scottish and Welsh have a great deal in common with each other, at least from the geneticist's point of view, seems likely to please no one.[31]

That these folk have mingled since time out of mind should not come as a surprise. Perhaps everything old is new again. In his 1877 history, *The Irish Race in America,* Edward Condon rejected the use of the terms *Anglo-Saxon* and *Celt* as historically "groundless," suggesting that "Celtic Britons" had been the majority all along.[32] Nevertheless, the idea that the Irish are racial Others has proven remarkably durable, as evidenced by the commonplace belief that red hair is an Irish trait (as opposed to British or, for that matter, Norman, Scandinavian, etc.). Joel Chandler Harris, most remembered for his Uncle Remus tales, was teased mercilessly about his red hair. This salient fact, combined with the modest circumstances of his upbringing, made it easy for a biographer to sell the notion that his absentee father was an Irishman, despite the lack of any substantive evidence in the matter. (Studies suggest that brown is in fact the most common hair color in Ireland, with red being the least common—but this is mere hairsplitting.) Nineteenth-century writers elaborated a racial divide between Anglo-Saxon and Celt that continues to impress the modern mind, DNA evidence notwithstanding.

But it is also important to understand, as Matthew Jacobson argues, that the Irish themselves subscribed to the existence of such a "racial" chasm, even when they rejected its corollary assumptions about Irish inferiority. In other words, the typical Irishman of the nineteenth century would likely tell you, with some pleasure, that he was a specimen of the Celtic race. Hugh Quigley, a nineteenth-century priest-author-émigré who had once worked with Chippewa Indians, wrote proudly, "The modern Irish are the most genuine, unmixed, and unchanged Celtic people that exist on the globe."[33] Operating in the mode of those who framed the Civil War as a conflict between Norman and Saxon civilizations, Abram Ryan wrote in one of his postbellum newspaper columns,

"Like individuals, races differ from one another in temperament," and asked, "Who cannot distinguish a Celt from a Saxon?"[34]

It goes without saying but should be said again: as the purebred is to the artificial universe of vaporous racial typology, so is the Irish Catholic (and Scots-Irish) to the Irish. That is to say, if one looks deeply enough in the family lineage of Irish, both Catholic and Protestant, rare is the soul who comes from an "unadulterated" line. From the perspective of religious and ethnic identification, since Catholicism preceded schism in time, *all* Christian Irish were once Irish Catholic (with the implicitly curious features of this stripe of Catholicism). In some cases the term *Scots-Irish* denotes a specific historical migration of people to Ireland, but in many other cases an ideological divide was politically levered into service as a race marker—especially since the Irish looked to Scotland as an ancestral homeland. The process is analogous to the way in which Confederate ideologues attempted to invent the "southern race," a hastily conceived attempt to build at once nationalistic pride *and* an enemy, its usual complement.

Regrettably, Irish nationalists in both America and Ireland have tended to exclude the Protestant Irish from their definition of Irishness, with pernicious results to show for it. Equally provincially, many "Scotch-Irish" came to embrace that term to set themselves apart from their Catholic countrymen, who, just arrived, looked a lot like the wretched refuse from yon teeming shore. In the South, *Scotch-Irish* also served both as a kind of mental partition and as a term of convenience: Catholic Irish immigrants were to be found in the Northeast, the Midwest, and the West. The South, so the line went, was an Anglo-Saxon redoubt and as far as the Irish were concerned served as the natural habitat of the displaced "Scotch-Irish," the indomitable carriers of what the southern author Ellen Glasgow called a "vein of iron." Glasgow of course did not mention that William Byrd II, one of her literary predecessors and the original Virginia patrician, regretted that these lately arrived and heedless folk "swarm like the Goths and Vandals of old, & will overspread our continent soon."[35] As with the Irish Catholics who came later, it took a while for the Scots-Irish to be epitomized as red-blooded Americans. After all, they were not English, and, writes Kerby Miller, "belying their eulogists' claims of inherent superiority, by 1900 the 'Scotch-Irish' of the southern states were generally poorer and less-educated than the Catholic Irish who had settled in the urban-industrial North during the previous century."[36]

If sectional-identity politics worked to efface the Catholic side of the southern Irish story, this was owing partly to a need for crisply drawn categories: in the overwhelmingly Protestant South, it was simply easier to shrug off the Irish Catholic outliers. It did not help that they were guilty by association with northern manufactures, Yankee conscription, and the sort of urban ethnic complexities that extended beyond the South's tidier black/white binaries. Certainly Irish Catholic emigration to the South, the region that George B. Tindall memorably termed "the single biggest WASP nest this side of the Atlantic,"[37] has been historically light, particularly in comparison with other American regions.

Light, but significant. While few would challenge Tindall's argument in the main, a few have been attuned to the exceptions to his rule. David N. Doyle reckons that at the time of the 1790 census over a quarter-million southerners were of Irish birth or descent.[38] The estimates vary widely, but as many as fifty thousand to eighty thousand Irish Catholics came to the colonies in the eighteenth century—only to be "lost," both to history and to their families. Upon arrival, the indentured Irish certainly faced "poverty, bond service and the recruiting agent," as Kerby Miller puts it, and gave up more than their Irish language as they acculturated.[39]

Historians have started to rediscover some of them. A smattering of primary eighteenth-century documents appear in *Irish Immigrants in the Land of Canaan,* chronicling the lives, for example, of Denis Driscol, Ædanus Burke, and John Daly Burk. Though few left any scratch on the literary record (in the sense of *belles lettres*), one might recover the stories of some of these lost Irish in the correspondence of immigrants like John O'Rawe (d. 1841), one of the "nameless" poor, a Catholic who fought in the 1798 Rebellion at Antrim. Captured and "brought to be hanged in his mother's doorway," O'Rawe had the good fortune to escape and sailed for America in 1806. He had the bad fortune, alas, to be on board a ship where six of the passengers were immediately "pressed" and put on board British ships, the extra bad luck to be shipwrecked some fifty-nine days after leaving Belfast, and the Irish luck to survive—by bushwhacking in scorching Bermuda. Repeatedly summoned to appear before "the governor and his secretary" on the island, he prudently laid low, "as I understood it was their intention to reel me on board a man of war." Repairing to "obscure and remote parts of the island" where he "couldn't sleep," he spent seventy-six days on the island, "almost reduced to a skeleton by the flue." He subsequently made his way to Charleston, went on to Savannah, Augusta, and finally, Newbury, South Carolina. After all, a Carolina acquaintance had bought 130 acres of land for three hundred dollars, and as O'Rawe boasted to his parents in correspondence, "He will in a short time be rich which he never would have been in Ireland."[40]

Recovering the traces of these lost Irish in turn becomes the province of the literary imagination. In a period earlier still, the Pulitzer Prize–winning Irish poet Paul Muldoon, aware of Sir Walter Raleigh's penchant for putting down Irish rebellions and his love of courtly poesie, reimagined the possibility of an Irish presence in the earliest colonial American past:

> We are some eighty souls
> On whom Raleigh will hoist his sails.
> He will return, years afterwards,
> To wonder where and why
> We might have altogether disappeared,
> Only to glimpse us here and there
> As one fair strand in her braid,
> The blue in an Indian girl's dead eye.[41]

Curiously, a group that was in many respects lost to historical view could be counted, by the mid-nineteenth century, "as the largest white ethnic group in the Confederacy."[42] The following century brought new changes and reversals, as Kerby Miller notes: "Despite the size and significance of this early Irish emigration to the Old South, by the late 1830s and 1840s most Irish-born men and women were avoiding the southern states, primarily for economic reasons that included a reluctance to compete with slave labour." Whereas 1.6 million Irish-born Americans comprised approximately 6 percent of the nation's white population in 1860, "only 11 per cent of these emigrants—fewer than 200,000—resided in the slave states, where they comprised merely 2.25 per cent of the South's white population. Moreover, nearly 70 per cent of these Irish-born southerners were concentrated in a handful of exceptionally urbanized 'border states.'"[43]

James Woods points out that the Irish population of the southern states actually declined by some twenty thousand between 1860 and 1870, a fact no doubt partly attributable to the toll of war. In states such as Alabama, South Carolina, Tennessee, and West Virginia, Irish-born Americans accounted for 40 percent or more of the foreign-born.[44] Even so, by Woods's count, in 1870 "only 6 percent of the total Irish-born population resided in the fourteen southern states and the District of Columbia, and only 7 percent of the immigrants lived in the South" (see tables 1 and 2).[45]

So the Irish in southern states remained more the exception than the rule, especially if one excludes the murky eighteenth century. By 1870 Catholic churches (the actual physical buildings) accounted for an anemic 2.3 percent of the southern total.[46] Patrick Griffin deems these "Catholics in so-called Scots Irish enclaves," however, "the exceptions that disprove the rule."[47] By the mid-twentieth century, despite a growing (and false) consensus among scholars that Irish immigrants were all but exclusively a northern phenomenon, a few remained attuned to the presence of ethnic minorities within the South, among them a colorful history professor named Ella Lonn. A *Time* magazine reporter writing in 1944 described the quirky Goucher College teacher as "in her middle 60s, unmarried, friendly, animated," and "traveling paths of history no one had traversed before."[48] The indefatigable Lonn, who once lost her book notes to a fire and promptly started all over again, had a habit of poking into unexamined corners, leading her to produce, for example, a study devoted to the importance of salt during the Civil War. Lonn's singular *Foreigners in the Confederacy* (1940), still in print and, according to University of North Carolina Press publicity, still "the only work on the subject," exploded the "long cherished belief

TABLE 1. Irish-born to foreign-born population in the southern states and the District of Columbia, 1870

	IRISH-BORN	FOREIGN-BORN	IRISH PERCENTAGE
Alabama	3,893	9,668	40.2
Arkansas	1,428	4,885	29.2
Florida	737	4,662	15.8
Georgia	5,093	10,753	47.3
Kentucky	21,642	63,346	34.1
Louisiana	17,068	60,615	28.1
Maryland	23,630	83,259	28.3
Mississippi	3,359	10,981	30.5
North Carolina	677	2,980	22.7
South Carolina	3,262	7,773	43.2
Tennessee	8,048	19,189	41.9
Texas	4,031	61,484	6.5
Virginia	5,191	13,701	37.8
West Virginia	6,832	17,032	40.1
District of Columbia	8,218	16,171	50.8
Total	113,109	386,499	29.2

Source: Reprinted with permission from Woods, *History of the Catholic Church* 347.

TABLE 2. Irish population of the South as a percentage of the total and white populations, 1850 and 1860

	1850		1860	
	IRISH % OF TOTAL POPULATION	IRISH % OF WHITE POPULATION	IRISH % OF TOTAL POPULATION	IRISH % OF WHITE POPULATION
Alabama	0.47	0.85	0.59	1.08
Arkansas	0.24	0.31	0.30	0.40
Florida	1.00	1.86	0.59	1.06
Georgia	0.35	0.61	0.62	1.11
Louisiana	4.69	9.50	3.98	7.89
Mississippi	0.32	0.65	0.49	1.10
North Carolina	0.06	0.10	0.09	0.14
South Carolina	0.60	1.48	0.71	1.70
Tennessee	0.26	0.35	1.12	1.51
Texas	0.66	0.91	0.57	0.82
Virginia	1.02	1.28	1.35	1.57
South	0.78	1.26	0.98	1.56

Source: Reprinted with permission from Gleeson, *Irish in the South* 26.

Note: James Woods offers similar calculations for 1860 but includes more southern states (Kentucky, Maryland, etc.) and the District of Columbia, the population of which was 11.9 percent Irish-born in 1860. As to the Irish percentage of the white population in southern states in 1860, Woods arrives at an even 2 percent.

that the Southern armies were composed of men of the 'purest Anglo-Saxon blood,'" as a contemporary reviewer put it.[49] Observing that Germans and Irish made up the bulk of the foreign-born (as well as the venerable exception of Texas, where one in five had "German blood" in 1860), Lonn also pointed to French, Italian, Scandinavian, Jewish, Swiss, Mexican, and Portuguese immigrants in Confederate ranks. Acknowledging that these foreign-born southerners constituted only 13.5 percent of the national total, she argued that "in a foreign population the size of that in the United States . . . 13.5 percent must still constitute a very appreciable and important number."[50]

According to Woods's *History of the Catholic Church in the American South, 1513–1910,* the foreign-born made up just 4.9 percent of the white populace of the South, including the District of Columbia, in 1870.[51] Not everyone was persuaded that these numbers were appreciable, in part because they did not accord with race-based assertions concerning the superiority of southern civilization. True to her efforts to justify the ways of Irish southerners to history, Margaret Mitchell advised her friends to read Lonn's book.[52] In the decades following Lonn's "outlier" study, scholars of the American South[53] have reconceptualized the region in more global and meridional terms, giving currency to her forward-looking work. Some historians have pointed out that the themes of southern history, especially in the colonial phase, share more in common with those of Caribbean history than with those of the history of other states, a point that has won converts among economic historians.

Taken in this light, the famous San Patricios—the mostly Irish soldiers who "infamously" defected to the Mexican side during the Mexican-American War— seem less an anomaly than an extension of the pan-ethnic and "treacherous" provinces of southern/meridional Catholicism. Indeed, some Irish Catholic Confederate stalwarts imagined a South that would annex Latin America and the Caribbean. They included the poet-politician Theodore O'Hara, an Irish Catholic southerner from Kentucky who filibustered in Cuba. Meanwhile, the past few decades have seen an outpouring of interest in the Confederados of Brazil.[54] While they were not originally Catholic (they clung to an evangelical Protestantism), they represent the last fragment of O'Hara's unusual vision, an ethnically mixed, pan-Catholic deep Deep South. After all, in the first part of the nineteenth century the American South seemed best positioned to become the seat of American Catholicism, politically and demographically, and to receive a stream of ethnic immigrants in turn. Irish immigration, among other factors, would change the tide.

To some degree, well into the twentieth century Lonn's polyethnic vision of southern history was muted by racialist prerogatives tacitly accepted by Lost Cause ideologues who eventually abandoned earlier apologist traditions and took up the rosier hues of high Cavalier (and hence "Anglo-Saxon") codes of honor.[55] Despite alert skeptics like Lonn—and W. J. Cash and H. L. Mencken, who both placed come-lately Irish southerners at the "center" of the southern plantation—Catholic Irish Americans have been counted anomalous in the South. No less an authority than Louis D. Rubin Jr., a Jew from Charleston and a founding scholar of southern literary studies, told me, tongue in cheek, "You're not supposed to write about Irish Catholics in the South. That's not Southern." In Rubin's time, the authors of *Southern Literary Study: Problems and Possibilities* (1975) were concerned to ask, "Is the introduction of 'alien' philosophical concepts into recent southern literature—O'Connor's Catholicism, Percy's existentialism—indicative of a significant change in the orientation and motivation of southern writing?"[56]

Yet if one considers a short list of prominent southern writers with southern Irish Catholic associations—Joel Chandler Harris, Kate O'Flaherty Chopin, Lafcadio Hearn, John Kennedy Toole, Flannery O'Connor, and Cormac McCarthy—it soon becomes apparent that the "change" was in perception and that the alchemy of Irish historical identity, southern nationalism, and Catholic ideology exerted quite a force on the literary imagination. Indeed, Flannery O'Connor seemed to anticipate the "problem" of "alien philosophical concepts" by explaining that Catholicism and mainline southern culture were not only compatible but strangely amicable: "The Catholic novelist in the South will bolster the South's best traditions, for they are the same as his own."[57] Writing about "Agrarian Catholics," the post–World War II southern writers who investigated Catholicism and were sometimes converted to it (with Allen Tate and Caroline Gordon among their number), Thomas Haddox suggests that "the historically dubious notion that Catholicism may be the most authentic southern religion originates in the efforts of white southern Catholics . . . to reassure their fellow southerners of their regional loyalties," including their implicit support of slavery.[58] The fact remains that southern intellectuals who "willed" themselves (as the Southern Agrarians would put it) into a unitary political and theological complex bore an understandable attraction to Catholicism. Catholicism and southern politics historically complemented each other in their implicit acceptance of social hierarchies, their rejection of modernism, and their advocacy of precapitalist economies.

And this created anxiety. In the nation at large, as Timothy Meagher explains, "the two fears, fear of slaves and fear of Catholic immigrants, were in fact related." Following Eric Foner, he notes that northern antislavery activists were concerned as much with the notion of a "corrupted" South/fallen nation as with the hard treatment of blacks.

> They saw it as a root of the South's backward civilization and the ruin of
> southern whites: it sapped their initiative, hindered education, bred lazi
> ness and petty sensitivities to honor and violence, and dragged people down
> into reactionary decadence. The South, they believed, looked backward—not
> forward, as the North did, to industry and the economic development that
> free labor would produce. Kevin Kenny [another scholar of Irish American
> history] suggests that this image of the South was easy to transfer to Irish
> Catholics. . . . Irish Catholics, then, were not merely temporary allies of
> Southerners but products of similarly flawed cultures.[59]

Indeed, the reticence of the church, and particularly southern churchmen, to declare against slavery made it easier to blur distinctions between Catholics, the Irish, and southerners—all could generally be counted on to oppose enlightened New England political attitudes. For example, the confusingly named John England, the Irish-born bishop of Charleston, mounted a tepid defense of slavery and complained that the anti-Catholic southern press was eager to brand him an abolitionist when he was appointed papal legate to Haiti.[60] In theory, the slave trade was a prohibited evil *(malum prohibitum),* not evil in itself *(malum in se).* In practice, southern Catholics steered an uneasy course, accepting the status quo. Even though southern Catholics fell in line with the peculiar institutions of the region—in essence, by playing the race card and embracing the Democratic Party to become "natural southerners"—they were still perceived as an outside force.

And despite the common ground of the Roman Catholic Church and some shared political alignments, in crucial respects the southern Irish were not interchangeable with their counterparts in the North. For one thing, they were set apart by their manners, or so it would seem to the North Carolina novelist Thomas Wolfe (1900–1938) when he encountered the Boston Irish, who were "utterly different from all the Irish he had known before."[61] When Eugene Gant/Wolfe goes to Harvard, he boards with the Irish family Murphy, finding them "hard, sterile, arid, meager, and cruel: they were disfigured by a warped and infuriated Puritanism, and yet they were terribly corrupt" (181). There was in them "none of the richness, wildness, extravagance, and humor of such people as Mike Fogarty, Tim Donovan, or the MacReadys—the Irish he had known at home" (181). On reflection, the southerner advances a theory for the nastiness of the urban Irish: "It seemed to him that they belonged to a grander and completely different race; or perhaps, he thought, the glory of earth and air and sky there had kept them ripe and sweet as they always were, while their brothers here had withered upon the rootless pavements, soured and sickened in the savage tumult of the streets, grown hard and dead and ugly in the barren land" (186).[62] Wolfe deems Boston Irish Catholics, shackled in religious ignorance, the living embodiment of Yankee anathema. By contrast, Eugene Gant's obstreperous and exceedingly idiosyncratic Uncle Bascom Pentland—a southern sentimentalist, religiously obsessed failed preacher and general crackpot— defends *his* Irish ancestors in a "fierce distemper": "*Scotch! Scotch*-Irish! Finest people on earth. No question about it whatever" (187).

Whereas many studies have considered the finest "Scotch-Irish" of the South, few have suggested looking at southern Irish Catholic writers as a discrete group, and the few that enter this territory obliquely, such as Thomas

Haddox's *Fears and Fascinations: Representing Catholicism in the American South* (2005), have tended to come to it in pursuit of Catholicism rather than by following Irish tracks. The handful that consider Irish Catholics in the South, such as Kieran Quinlan's *Strange Kin: Ireland and the American South* (2005), have tended to construe *Irish* (meaning "those from Ireland") broadly. This approach usefully questions, in Faulknerian terms, the "old verities" of Scots-Irish and white southern identity that colluded to produce the glories of Appalachia—and, for that matter, the specters of Thomas Dixon's version of the Klan, shrouded in misty Scottish nationalism. Surely the Scots-Irish are complicated in ways that Jacksonian legends fail to acknowledge. These settlers were indeed shaped by conflict, as James Webb's popular *Born Fighting* (1995) describes, but there was more to their accomplishment and politics than the beating of the war drum. Moreover, the Scots-Irish deserve to be liberated from overextended pan-Celtic notions that sweep past cultural distinctions.

Just as surely, the process of considering their Irish Catholic companions needs to be initiated, in part because the failure of literary scholars to see them this way—as a distinct group writing from within an ethnic subculture, steeped in ethnic nationalism –shows how completely their Catholicism and Irishness were, at times, subrogated to southern identity, not to mention the "imaginative category of discourse," as Jenny Franchot termed it, of anti-Catholicism as a means to "voice the tensions and limitations of mainstream Protestant culture."[63] Properly revealed, the presence of these Irish Catholics belies the conventional belief that Catholicism is an alien influence within the region. And it makes a larger comment on the plasticity of American identity. Irish Catholic literary accomplishment has been absorbed into the larger species of southern literature in a process analogous to the simplifying of the historical narrative. In essence, writes Patrick Griffin, only those few self-described Catholics (such as Charles Carroll of Carollton) were apt to be deemed Irish. As to the rest, he observes without much exaggeration, "if they came from Ireland and achieved any sort of prominence—even if they were not dissenters in Ireland or descended from Scots—they are Scotch Irish."[64] Southern literary studies has been reluctant to move beyond the one-dimensional Scots-Irish model.

In any case, this study picks up where the Scots-Irish left off and takes a look at Irish Catholics as insider outsiders. Thus, for the purposes of this study Catholic is implicit in the (shorthand) term *Irish southerners,* even though the vast majority of Irish in the region came to be called Scots-Irish or Scotch-Irish. Irish Catholics have never been wholly "alien" to the South or to southern literature. Nor is Irish Catholic writing exceptional in its location of southern literary themes. It is not exceptional precisely because southern Irish writers gave full-throated voice to many of the conventional southern tropes contested by the new southern studies: Who evinces a stronger sense of place than Gerald O'Hara in his "love of the land" soliloquy? Whose writing better demonstrates the Janus-faced union of race and class than Kate O'Flaherty Chopin's? Who understands the roots of southern defiance and violence better than Cormac McCarthy?

On the contrary, Irish American writers in the South have been highly influential in shaping the perception of the region in much the same way that Anglo-Irish arguably shaped the canons of the Irish literary renaissance. Individually invisible, they take on a new significance when viewed as a group. In his groundbreaking study *The Irish in the South, 1815–1877,* David T. Gleeson argues that Irish Catholic emigrants to the South fell out of view because they had achieved more or less complete social integration by the time of Reconstruction, assimilating fully enough to be considered generically southern rather than Irish. During the Middle Ages, the apothegm *Hiberniores Hibernis ipsis* (More Irish than the Irish themselves) expressed the truism that foreigners and invaders were most often "converted" to Irish customs, and, notes Kieran Quinlan, "it has even been argued, a little tongue-in-cheek perhaps (though Margaret Mitchell concurred), that the Irish were so anxious to fit in that they eventually became more southern than the southerners themselves."[65] Perhaps southern literary studies has not considered southern Irish American writers as a group because, ultimately, many of them ceased to see themselves as such, preferring to become *southerners first.*

Putting all presuppositions on the table, Irish Catholic identity is best understood as a complex of identities that often embraces (1) elements of Irish nationalism and regeneration, (2) a religious ideology informed by place, (3) larger associations and disassociations with other Catholic ethnicities, and (4) sensibilities of union and disunion particular, if not exclusive, to Irish historical experience. Southern Irish identity adds a layer of regional complexity to Irish Catholic ethnicity that sometimes subverts the expected order of Irish Catholic sympathies. For example, Fenianism, which plays on the aforementioned elements of Irish Catholic identity, found wide support among Irish Americans throughout the United States in the nineteenth century. Frequently Fenian notices ran in Father Abram Ryan's New Orleans newspaper, where they jockeyed with the volatile politics of the Redeemers. But as the Fenians staged a series of unsuccessful antebellum raids into Canada with the hope of bargaining for Irish independence, they filled their ranks with former Union soldiers, thereby alienating many would-be southern supporters.[66] One southern Irishman wrote to Ryan's newspaper to chide the hypocrisy of those who had helped put down "Southern Irishmen" and "self-government in the South."[67] (Of course, the Union soldiers might fairly have pointed to soft, unofficial British support for the Confederacy during the war years.) For his part, Ryan could never be accused of cheerful consistency. The self-styled Reb and Irish nationalist would later stand before Canadian parliamentarians and counsel deference to the Queen![68]

Whereas many Irish American histories make little mention of the South, this study questions notions of southern ethnic homogeneity and aspires to tug the center of gravity in Irish studies southward by helping to show that the Irish diaspora in the South were no less inventive than their relations to the north and west. Some might wish for a book that would do more than illuminate the Irish and Catholic elements in a southern writer's work, that would offer a grand theory, in other words, about the *why* of these things. Only books and lawyers do we fault for not making argument. Yet this invites reductionism, as the influences of Irish Catholic ethnicity are as variable as the writers and the manifestations of the culture in which they write. Moreover, the point of this book is not to offer another affirmation of Irish exceptionalism. This study happens to limit its scope to Irish Catholics, but this fact should not be taken to suggest that Irish Catholics were the drivers, the sole inventors, or the proprietors of a regional literary imagination. Important, perhaps, and even influential—but what's to say that German immigrants to the South or later-arrived Koreans were not pioneering figures too, even if we have not looked at them as a group?[69] Only relatively recently have critics started to appreciate how black southerners have helped to define a regional mythos, by both rejecting and affirming aspects of the southern mystique. As to the Irish, in rethinking influence we might begin by seeing it as a process far from unilateral, since propagandists have often been quick to extoll an Irish influence on the South, from the time of the American Civil War until the present. Influence implies commonality, and commonality follows various avenues (see fig. 1).

Note that these are mirroring processes, so that perception may lead to assumptions of commonality. Too often, the irresistible southern-Irish analogy has served political ends and been based on superficial appearances. To take an example from the other side of the Atlantic, one need only look as far as the

Israeli and Palestinian flags displayed in Belfast neighborhoods to understand how quickly—and how blearily—causes can be joined and deployed to signal political fealties. Or consider the Belfast murals, some of them recently effaced, depicting pantheons of southern Civil War heroes purported to descend from Ulster immigrants. Or take the Belfast murals that juxtapose imagery from the American civil rights movement with scenes from the Irish civil rights move-

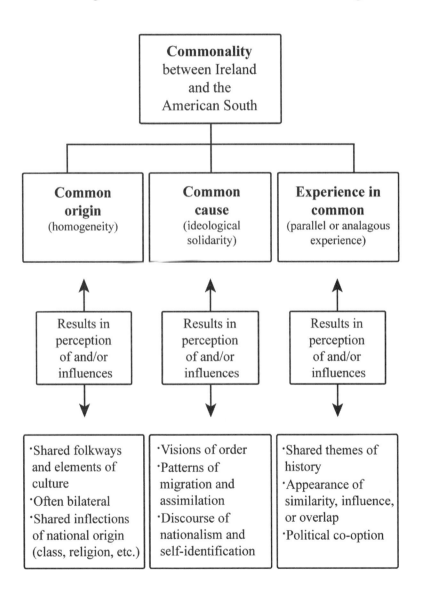

ment. History seems to teach that it is difficult to discern, in the present moment, how far cultural parallels truly extend, since we are so often fixated on things of the moment, yet cognition longs to find the analogy. Cleanth Brooks, writing in the Southern Fugitive-Agrarian vein, quotes Sean O'Faolain's observation that between Ireland and the American South one finds the "same oscillation between unbounded self-confidence and total despair."[70] It might be pointed out that the word *same* announces in advance the danger of generalization—but it's not clear that the more nuanced *similar* would serve here either, for the first register of that word, per the *Oxford English Dictionary*, is "of the same substance or structure throughout; homogeneous." Who would be so bold as to claim that the two groups, across the space of the Atlantic, were meaningfully homogeneous? If we resort to etymology, can we really say that the two groups are of the same "genus" without entering the thickets of racial mythology? And whither this (white) southern despair if not in civil rights and the tumult of the times?

Far from being "natural," rather, the Irish presence in the region is something that is historicized, unstable, and shifting. The observation of things is sometimes the wherefore and why of them, and in taking a second look at Irish Catholic writers of the South I do not wish to suggest that I have perceived a revisionist truth that others have overlooked—along the lines of what John McGowan facetiously calls the "heroic individualism" model of academic enquiry. In sum, I am not the farsighted wanderer who returns with a new vision; I am pointing to what was there all along. If there is profit in this, it might be in praxis: How can we pursue a more collaborative and transnational investigation of the American South in Irish studies? What can we learn of the Irish in the context of southern studies, and how do we get past the idea that "un-American" Irish southerners could not be Irish American southerners? Instead of deeming southern Irish writers a subfield of southern or Irish American writing, we might see them as crucial to understanding both.

For the southern Irish are indeed fascinating, offering a case study in how literature's potential energy vibrates in the invention of regional cultures, political ideologies, and ethnic identities. Because exile is indeed the cradle of nationalism, and because they were practitioners of a minority faith marginal to the region, these keen-eyed southern Irish Americans were at once creators of the region and its creation. They participated in southern ethnogenesis even as they became invisible within the larger social fabric. It follows that Catholic Irish Americans—by nature somewhat outside the American cultural mainstream—helped invent for the South a regional mythos, an enduring literature, and a national image.

An explanation of how the subjects of this study were vetted also serves to set boundaries. How Irish, how southern, and how Catholic need they be?

The answer to all three questions, some might say, is, not very. But each category is so important in identity formation that a small part might color the tincture of perception, and furthermore, the idea of purity in any category is itself an artifice, a chimera of identity construction. Therefore the terms *Irish, Catholic,* and *southern* are construed broadly, recognizing that the valence of each varies according to the writer. Starting with the category southern, it should be pointed out that the notion that southerners must be hip deep in native-born generations or else FFV (First Family of Virginia) or from a "three ships" family in Charleston (descended from original colonists) is one that W. J. Cash spectacularly skewered in *The Mind of the South.* It runs contrary to the immigration pathways of southern history, and it is, in any event, a mirage of Confederate nationalism. Those who are of this mind-set are wont to intone, "Just because a cat has kittens in the oven doesn't make them biscuits." One would think that southerners had been in the region since time immemorial—a convenient prerogative.

Southern parochialism adds another stipulation: "real southerners" must emerge from a southern port to be properly credentialed, a "touch-base" test closely related to the Reconstruction-era fear of the carpetbagger. Flannery O'Connor's origins could be imputed on that theory: she was the descendant of displaced Catholic Marylanders gone to Georgia. The likes of Cormac McCarthy could be rejected out of hand; if he is southern, it is truly by the grace of God. After all, he had not the good grace to be born on southern soil; his family did not arrive in Knoxville from Rhode Island until he was four years of age, with the frost of the North still clinging to his play-pretty.

Of course, there are other southern litmus tests: Jerry Leath Mills waggishly proposes that there is a "single, simple, litmus-like test for the quality of southernness in literature. . . . The test is: *Is there a dead mule in it?*"[71] The mule rule vindicates O'Connor and Hearn, who was rather carried away with carrion (his novella *Chita* is choked with dead ruminants). Cormac McCarthy zestfully decapitates a few of them in *The Crossing.* If Kate Chopin did not dispatch with her mules, she, like Abram Ryan, fails a strict southern nativity test: both were essentially Missourians who migrated farther south. Lafcadio Hearn was born in Greece, thence to Dublin, Cincinnati, and New Orleans. Yet there are strong arguments that each was southern where it counts: within the landscape of the mind. And so, with apologies to the new southern studies, I own that when

I use a term like *southernness,* I mean the quality of subscribing to a regional ideology, however mythic, and its innate protonationalism.[72]

Looking to other tests of southern ideological identity, such as Sheldon Hackney's suggestion that "a sense of grievance" lies at the core of southern identity, southern Irish writers pass easily, since a sense of grievance is part and parcel of Irish Catholic identity as well. The comedian Stephen Colbert, bestselling author and Charleston native, explained the sensibility recently in a genealogy documentary with Henry Louis Gates Jr. Summarizing the impact of British colonialism on the "Irish public record, especially that of Catholic citizens," Gates explained that "not only were many records destroyed, but Penal Laws restricting the civil rights of Catholics, from the late 1500s until well into the 1800s, served as a powerful disincentive to keep records in the first place." Colbert explained how the incidents lingered in his family's memory:

> When I met my wife, who is Presbyterian, we went to visit her sister, and her sister was living at Oliver Cromwell on 72nd Street in New York. And I thought, I can't tell my mom that anyone lives at the Oliver Cromwell, because Cromwell is like saying "Satan." He drove our family west of the river Shannon to farm rocks—300 hundred, 350 years ago—and yet I was raised with that story. That has not gone away. Part of being Irish is, even to this day, not liking the English. They've probably gotten over it better over there than we have over here because we're an isolated genus.[73]

Likewise, the Kentucky writer and editor John Jeremiah Sullivan, the son of an Irish Catholic sportswriter from Ohio and a Kentucky mother of debutante lineage, recently wrote in his *Paris Review* blog about his father's one-man boycott of BP: "It was a common (because essentially effortless) Irish-American affectation. He'd pass up a roadside exit, with the needle squarely on E, if the only station there were a BP. So at the risk of walking with the can, we'd wait to patronize a benevolent establishment such as Sunoco."[74]

In addition to having some awareness of ethnic grievance, even if its expression is purely gestural, almost every writer in this study reflects on the self-abnegating qualities of an Irish Catholic upbringing, either in a concern for the last things of life—death, salvation, and so on—or in the commonly expressed sense of participation in a religion that hovers behind consciousness, or indeed serves as a second consciousness, minute by minute. In *South of Broad* Pat Conroy describes the inburnt, even self-abasing worldview of a Catholic upbringing in protagonist Leopold Bloom King. The character's experience tracks closely with comments Conroy has made concerning the difficulty of leaving the faith: "I think I hold tightly to my religion with the same rigorous inflexibility as I hold the sacredness of my laughable marriage. The form of my faith appreciates the hardness and unapologetic rigidity of my church. It gives me rules to live by, and it demands I follow them twenty-four hours out of every day. It offers no time off for good behavior."[75]

Pat Conroy does not like to be called Irish Catholic or labeled as an Irish American, though he acknowledges that the ethnicity and his difficulty with religion are related. So how "Irish" need a writer be to be considered here? Charles Fanning excludes Flannery O'Connor from his study of Irish American writers because she "[chose] not to consider Irish ethnic themes"—or none that he noticed, in any case. There is no such prerequisite here: Irish Catholics were regarded as a white Other in the South, and based on this theory a single ancestor could influence a southerner's identity. One could as well object to the term *African American* because little of Africa remains. In point of fact, though Irish Catholic ethnicity figures explicitly in just one of her stories, Flannery O'Connor did have a sense of Irish ethnic awareness, right down to the fine grain of the Jansenist influence on Irish Catholicism. O'Connor told the critic Richard Gilman that she could hardly take Mary O'Connor for her name as a writer: "Who was likely to buy the stories of an Irish washerwoman?"[76] Her ethnicity was partly inherent in the pride she took in her Catholicism, and it showed in the way she muted it too, broadcasting her southern credentials even as she cracked jokes about Irish priests and touring Ireland.

By the twentieth century, and with some amount of "ethnic fade," the importance of Irish identity was already receding for many southern transplants, a process facilitated by their assimilation. Yet important markers remained. The Saint Patrick's Day parade in Savannah might be seen, in the parlance of theory, as "performing" Irishness, but this must be set against the fact that a recent survey of Irish Savannahians revealed that they place more emphasis on being Irish than on being southern, even after generations.[77] Regardless of how persistent Irish identity is for the southern Irish, there is an additional reason for lowering the bar as far as who qualifies for consideration here: when the term applies, the *Irish* and *Catholic* of *Irish Catholic* are in a sense inextricable. Catholicism remained the enduring signifier of Irishness long after immigrants had abandoned any sort of self-conscious ethnic identity. In other words, where Irishness drops off, Catholicity very often persists.

So how Catholic need a writer be? At one extreme is the ultra-Catholic Father Ryan, who authored polemical Catholic tracts and apologetics, editorialized for turning the South into a Catholic state, and assailed the Protestant ministers who crossed swords with him. At the other is Lafcadio Hearn, who openly repudiated his Catholic education and yearned to become a Buddhist. But it is no accident that late in life he professed his great admiration for the Jesuits ("The Rottweilers of Catholic boys' education," Pat Conroy calls them), whom he had so often spurned, fantasizing a life not lived as a priest.[78]

For this study, at least, a Catholic writer need not be terribly concerned with Catholic themes or theology, nor is a sophisticated theory of Catholic aesthetics needful. Synthesizing a number of such theories, Farrell O'Gorman usefully suggests that Catholic writers share "a common emphasis on the concrete and a faith that the world itself holds mystery and a meaning that does not have to be imposed by the artists but is already present, if only recognized."[79] For example, Lafcadio Hearn was quite convinced that religious mysteries literally grew and moldered in New Orleans's soil, there to be sacramentally discerned. Cormac McCarthy writes scenes that some have been deemed antisacramental, yet his liturgical mode of writing shows how deeply informed his writing is by the rites of the church. A writer may in fact write in a very Catholic mode even when Catholicism is not a central concern of his or her work, or indeed, when he or she repudiates it.

Sometimes Catholicism is difficult to recover. There are quite likely many writers who could have been included in this study if their families had not elected a Protestant identity. John Pendleton Kennedy's *Rob of the Bowl, a Legend of St. Inigoe's* (1854) evinces enormous sympathy for the early Catholic settlers of Maryland, yet his family acknowledged none but Anglican roots. Then there is William Gilmore Simms, an irregular churchgoer who sometimes attended St. Paul's Episcopal Church in Charleston. It is widely known that his freewheeling father was "Irish." But what sort? He immigrated to Charleston, a southern Irish redoubt, before heading to the frontier. Simms's writings evince unusual sympathy for the Irish, attributing Francis Marion's recruitment success around Charleston to "settlements . . . originally founded by the Irish," whose "bitter hatred of the English, which they brought with them to America, was transmitted with undiminished fervor to their descendants."[80] He observes the colonial Irish presence in many of his frontier novels, having published, at age twenty-two, a poem called "Song of the Irish Patriot." The Simms scholar James Everett Kibler suggests that Simms's family were refugees of the Rebellion of 1798, and Simms himself claimed that his father was "of Scotch-Irish stock."[81]

The fact that the author's father was born in Larne, (now Northern) Ireland, hardly settles the issue. Where he appears in Simms's fiction he speaks with an Irish brogue, which in contemporaneous writing was most often employed to flag Irish Catholic identity.[82] Simms, after all, is a variant of Semmes, a resounding name in southern Catholic history. Raphael Semmes, the celebrated admiral of the Confederate navy, was a cradle Catholic by way of Maryland colonists, and Flannery O'Connor's aunt was married to one of his nephews. Could the Simms trace their roots to the same Anglo-Catholic sources as the Semmes? Or were they Anglo-Irish?

Given the paucity of biographical information and the fact that no Irish Simms today claims consanguinity with him, this study, which has a threshold requirement of some meaningful remnant of Catholicism, passes Simms by. If Kennedy and Simms knew of Catholic ancestors, they would hardly be the last American writers to let go of Irish Catholic roots. To find a prominent example one need go no further than F. Scott Fitzgerald, of an Irish Catholic father and a shabby-genteel Maryland Catholic mother. Culturally a southerner through his family history, aware of Baltimore's southern dimensions (as his story "The Curious Case of Benjamin Button" proves), and indisputably married to the South, he qualifies for consideration in these pages, if only narrowly. Culturally southern, Irish, Catholic, Fitzgerald really *wasn't* a Princeton man. Even if one heeds Alfred Kazin's warning not to find more in "Fitzgerald's Catholicism than he ever put into it," one is struck by a kind of Catholic Gatsbyism at play in a country where power consolidates around Waspishness.[83]

Certainly it can make difficult the task of identifying southern Irish Catholic writers. Writers who embraced Catholicism are more easily brought into this study, obviously; they share an extra layer of regional consciousness because of their minority religion. Yet even self-identifying southern Irish Catholics can elude the eye of the critics who classify them, as will be seen, and mere designation as a Catholic can change the critical fortunes of a writer's career. Flannery O'Connor was not just one of the first-rank southern writers of the twentieth century; she is internationally recognized as one of the leading *American* writers. Some thirty-five years would pass before the publication of a biography that earned critical sanction.

How to account for it? Canonical prerogatives, issued by those who "claim" authors, decide not only who will be admitted but by what means. In *Bright Book of Life* Alfred Kazin grudgingly acknowledges that O'Connor "was one of the few Catholic writers of fiction in our day . . . who managed to fuse a thorough orthodoxy with the greatest possible independence and sophistication as an artist."[84] A deep-seated and often tacit bias in academe suspects that Catholic scholarship might be poisonously tainted by dogmatic prerogatives. Even today, many Catholic scholars are cringingly aware of the church's reputation for anti-intellectualism, a self-image problem little assuaged by a church that published the *Index Librorum Prohibitorum* until 1966. Understandably, then, many Catholic academics seem to straddle two camps, caught somewhere between self-awareness and embarrassment.

Ralph Wood recounts the question that an "eminent author" put to Robert Giroux when O'Connor was posthumously honored with the National Book Award: "Do you really think Flannery O'Connor was a great writer? She's such a Roman Catholic."[85] John Kennedy Toole reportedly conned a line from the writer Peter Viereck when he went to his classroom and chalked on the board, "Anti-Catholicism is the anti-Semitism of the American intellectual."[86] Yet there are signs of change as scholars reexamine canonical writers through the Catholic lens. Tracy Fessenden's *Culture and Redemption: Religion, the Secular, and American Literature* is a promising step in this direction. The proposition that our most canonical writer may have been a secretive Catholic has been gaining support; Shakespeare's "outrageous fortune," one reading goes, was the regime change that outlawed his family's faith. The presumption that any discussion of religious affiliation clouds rational academic enquiry seems all the more perverse in a time when sexuality has become something of a holy grail to literary critics. If sexuality is the lost codex by which an author's life might be understood, what can be made of religion? In the past, writers who raised sexual themes found that their sexuality immediately became their most salient quality among critics.

The same analysis might apply to religion: we generally admit an author's religion only if it was of significant and *visible* import within that author's opus. Otherwise religious orientation is seen as simply irrelevant, a strange result considering that a religious or even irreligious worldview becomes a gateway through which subsequent ideologies must pass. As long as Catholicism is regarded as innately anti-intellectual, "the last acceptable prejudice" may continue to operate, and Catholic culture—not just Catholic belief—will remain a lost province of American, and southern, literature.[87]

Three years after Cobb's speech, Eamon de Valera, president of the Irish Republic, stood at the so-called four corners of law, at Broad and Meeting in Charleston, and declared that the Irish cause was similar to that of Revolutionary-era South Carolina, motivated not by "religious struggle" but by the thirst for independence.[88] In an interview with William Ferris, Eudora Welty remarked that southern writers "have some of the same background of those Irish. . . . The family tales while away a long winter evening, and that's what they have to draw on."[89] Faulkner craned his neck to glimpse Joyce in Paris, and Joyce's influence no doubt worked to, if the term may be pardoned, "Celticize" Faulkner's work. Quentin Compson ("I don't hate the South I don't I don't") is, in a sense, an empathetic dead ringer for Stephen Dedalus ("History is the nightmare from which I am trying to awake"), and Patrick Samway, SJ, has shown how Quentin's last walk in Boston is much in step with Leopold Bloom's. Cleanth Brooks pointed to specific parallels between the southern and Irish literary renascence in a number of essays, including "Regionalism in American Literature." "Any Southerner who reads Yeats' *Autobiographies,*" wrote Brooks, "is bound to be startled over and over again at the analogies between Yeats' 'literary situation' and that of the Southern author." Among these similarities Brooks cites "the strength to be gained from the writer's sense of belonging to a living community and the special focus upon the world bestowed by one's having a precise location in time and history; the penalties and gains connected with his being in a minority position vis-à-vis the dominant cultural pattern."[90]

But the devil is in the details, and a number of paradigms have foundered on the shoals between Irish and southern experience. The old-is-new spin on the Irish-southern question advanced by Forrest McDonald and Grady McWhincy in *Cracker Culture: Celtic Ways in the Old South* enflamed an academic debate that at first shed more heat than light.[91] The historian Rowland Berthoff denounced, and many would say roundly discredited, McWhiney's "Celtic-southern thesis" in a rather tart essay that appeared in the *Journal of Southern History.* Rejoinders and rebuttals followed. Some scholars deplored what they saw as a rhetorical feint. By reconceptualizing southern history in "Celtic" terms, suggests Michael Newton, McDonald and McWhiney effectively "turn the Civil War into an ancient blood feud between ethnic peoples with irreconcilable differences rather than a conflict over slavery," something that southern propagandists had already had a go at.[92] A series of stock criticisms of the Celtic-southern thesis took shape: it was overbroad and nebulous, it relied on terms that were archaisms (not least of which was the word *Celt* itself), its all-encompassing definition of *Celtic* threw together such unlikely countrymen as Midland Englishmen and Donegal Irishmen, it was blind to the ways in which these identifications changed through time and political agency, it was colored by sweeping statements suggestive of racial essentialism, and so on. And it was tainted by its entanglement with white supremacy, from the time of the Klan onward. Tony Horwitz explained how neo-Confederates adopted the argument in the 1990s: "Most . . . neo-Confederates I'd met were romantics. The South they revered was hot-blooded, Celtic, heedlessly courageous; their poster boy was the Scottish clansman played by Mel Gibson in the splatterfest *Braveheart*. In their view, rationalism and technological efficiency were suspect Yankee traits, derived from a mercantile English empire that had put down the Scots and Irish."[93] Viewed in a more hopeful light, the debate surrounding the Celtic-southern thesis, saddled though it is with ideological baggage, has served a useful function in reorienting the academic exploration of the interplay between Irish and southern culture, or, if you like, discerning the ways in which the Irish retained Irish culture in their new environs. Factors such as "Ireland's history of failed rebellion, her agrarian economy, and economic colonization" made such comparisons virtually inevitable on some level.[94] Even the usages of Irish and American causes—(Irish Republican) Confederates, (Irish) rebels, (Irish and English) Union, (Irish) Secession, (Irish Catholic) Emancipation— invited a blurring of ideologies. Nevertheless, the implicit essentialism of Forrest McDonald's assertion that the "entire history [of the Celts] had prepared them to be southerners" has not held up well to scrutiny (the circularity of it requires no explanation), and many of the superficial similarities between the two cultures require so much qualification that they quickly lose meaning when placed in more nuanced contexts.[95] That Irish and southern writers share many affinities, especially in the twentieth century, is certainly true, but it would be a tautology to assume on this basis alone that Irish culture was a prime shaper of southern literature, notwithstanding James P. Cantrell's sometimes insightful work on this subject.[96]

Instances of cross-pollination are better considered in the particular than in the abstract, and the backlash that the McWhiney-McDonald Celtic-southern thesis generated among historians illustrates the perils of going too far too fast. The evocation of "Celtic" nationalism among ideologues past and present, as well as politicians such as James Henry Hammond, who as early as 1833 tied southern and Irish causes together in an Independence Day speech, serves to illustrate how ideas may be co-opted by ideologues who manufacture a sense of shared origin and hence identification. Better to say that the process of influence between the two places is recursive, evolving, and far from unilateral. John Burrison acknowledges Irish contributions as one of four "cornerstones" of southern culture.[97] Though he looks only at the Scots-Irish in that chapter of his study, his terminology offers a useful way of reframing the southern Irish: we might think of them in terms of diffusion, recontextualization, and synthesis.

Recognizing that I am likely to introduce errors of my own, and that not all stereotypes are without some basis in reality, there are a few mistakes that I hope to avoid. Assertions of Irish triumphalism are as passé as they are condescending. And if one takes an approach based in racial essentialism—for example, the suggestion that Irish writers tended to write a certain way because of the peculiar chemistry of their "racial" makeup—it opens the floodgate to more flawed generalizations. It is one thing to stake out "Irish themes" by connecting them to their cultural mooring; it is quite another to suggest that the Irish and their ilk *think* a certain way (just try telling them that). On the other hand, it is reasonable to test the proposition that Ireland's fissured national identity might give rise to a longing for wholeness in her literature, or that a socially oriented culture favorably disposed to shame-based coercion might develop an extraordinarily well articulated tradition of satire. These things go to Irish culture and history, not "race."

Unavoidably, if generalizing about cultures is a risky business, generalizing about writers is equally so, especially if one groups them by ethnicity. As one considers the field of eligible writers for this study and their commonalities, a ticklish stereotype might emerge. One cannot ignore a leitmotif in their lives: these writers seem, in varying degrees, to grapple with conflicting impulses urging them simultaneously to strenuous social rebellion and to less admirable forms of conformist prostration. Rebelliousness, a trait stereotypically ascribed to Irish people, characterizes many of the writers of this study, but then it is also the artist's prerogative. The idea that the Irish—like another "troublesome" people, African Americans—are particularly fractious has been used to distort and manipulate their image for centuries. These themes in turn connect powerfully to the traditional metanarratives of southern history, in a region at times spectacularly independent (to the point of obstinacy and recklessness) and at others viciously conformist (witness the Solid South). As mentioned earlier, some of the speculations attaching to Irish-southern affinities are ill-defined, widely discredited, or, as in the case of such loaded terms as *union* and *disunion,* elements of shared but distinct histories.

What makes them so thorny is that like so many stereotypes, they contain just enough truth and just enough contradiction to sow the seeds of their own destruction. Some of the subjects of this study are collaborators in what might be termed the Irish Empire, quickly transferring their nationalistic zeal to their new section. For example, Father Ryan, Flannery O'Connor, Kate Chopin, and Joel Chandler Harris all stood accused at times of being a shade too loyal to the South. Yet upon closer inspection each also stood up for the dispossessed and the powerless. The apparent oxymoron of the party-line rebel should be set against a body of evidence that Kerby Miller advances, which "suggests that—because of a complex of sociocultural, political, and psychological factors, individuals of Irish Catholic birth or descent (along with Irish Protestants who shared similar perspectives) may indeed have been disproportionately prone—relative to other 'British' migrants—to interact with native or subject peoples overseas on comparatively equal terms, to empathize with their plight, and even to support their struggles for liberation."[98]

Sympathetic conquerors in the march of empire? Oppressed turned oppressor? Kieran Quinlan has the right answer: "Whether, and to what extent, Ireland has been a colony of England is an extremely vexed [question], as is the case also of the American South vis-à-vis the United States. It may even be the wrong question to ask since it forecloses nuanced interpretations of complicated facts."[99] The blame game serves mainly to support a presentist sense of moral superiority, but in these contradictions we find something essential about the Irish American experience in the South. It becomes possible to understand how Father Abram Ryan came to stand before the White League, an organization that functioned as something of a Klan rump in Louisiana, declaring, "I am not a Democrat. I am not a Republican. I am a Southern man. That means all." Beyond the obviously troubling issue of a Catholic priest maneuvering for a bully pulpit among vigilantes—a stance that ultimately alienated Ryan from some of his parishioners and caused not a little consternation among his religious superiors—Ryan's speech demonstrated how readily southern nationalism blended with Irish distrust of centralizing authority in a tale of a "fresh" Irish American voter:

> He did not know much about the politics of this country, but he knew a great deal about the politics of his own country. He was about to cast his vote. One man belonging to our party took him by the arm, and another belonging to the other said, "Vote for me," and the other said, "Vote for me." The poor man was bewildered, and said to one of them, "Who are you?" and the other gave him the name of his party. At last they asked him, what are you then? And the Irishman answered: "I am against the government."[100]

Cobb could report on his Confederate ancestors, not to mention "three great-great grandfathers, two of them Irish and one of them Scotch, who were Revolutionary soldiers." "And of these facts, too, I am quite proud," he explained, "for I find that my strain, being Irish, is always intent either on trying to run the government or pull it down."[101] Demonstrating similar independence of mind, Father Joseph Breen, a well-loved priest in his eighth decade, born and raised in Nashville, Tennessee, recently made national headlines by calling into question church teachings on papal authority, priestly celibacy, and birth control.[102]

Simultaneously, many southern Irish writers experienced pangs of class yearning, reached for access to social influence, and yet remained cautiously aloof from such pomps. For decades Joel Chandler Harris rivaled Mark Twain in popularity, a status he enjoyed in spite of his purported "Irish" bastardy. As a society man, he admitted that he failed to "draw an impartial picture of Southern civilization, its lights and its shadows," but he nevertheless audaciously questioned southern social norms in his fiction and journalism. Lafcadio Hearn loathed the phoniness of the "parlor"—the soulless, Americanized imitation of a much richer Latin institution—and yet he yearned desperately to enter the inner circles of New Orleans society, from which he was firmly precluded. Kate Chopin, widely viewed as an early paragon of feminine nonconformity, gained social cachet by downplaying her Irishness and playing up her Gallic *je nais sais quoi;* the Irish did not fare well before her pen.

The theme holds among the later writers too. Mary Flannery O'Connor embodied audaciousness in her fiction, which expressly called forth a grotesque menagerie of rebels and conformists. In her own life, O'Connor happily groomed her image as a daring, sharp-witted woman, but to some extent she subscribed to the racial orthodoxy and proclaimed her southernness rather more loudly than her Irishness. Cormac McCarthy styled himself a kind of social dropout, breaking from the church and decrying a culture increasingly opposed to individual autonomy.

Perhaps conflicting impulses are to be anticipated, since southern Irish already felt themselves estranged from a culture in which Catholicism was deemed a foreign influence. In any case, the felt sense of distance among southern Irish heightened their perception of southern norms. The idea that they were positioned to have special insight is borne out by more than anecdotal or theoretical evidence. The sociologist John Shelton Reed's penetrating observations of southern identity formation apply here: "Those who are somehow marginal to the South seem to be more likely to *think about it* than those who are more comfortably and unquestionably Southern. This proposition has the paradoxical corollary that the most self-conscious Southerners are often the least typical, men and women whose backgrounds and experiences put them somehow on the edge of the regional group."[103]

As Robert Penn Warren put it, a fish doesn't think about the water until it's out of it. Reed illustrates his theory with Eudora Welty—"the Mississippi daughter of a West Virginia mother and Ohio father"—and the twelve white southerners who authored *I'll Take My Stand* (1930). Pursuing this point, he adds, "It's striking how many Southerners who write about the South have come from the edges of the region, from Texas or Arkansas or Tennessee or Kentucky—parts of the South remote from the region's cultural heartland."[104] In a nutshell, Reed's findings are that regional consciousness is heightened (1) by urban upbringing and residence, (2) by education, (3) by exposure to the national mass media, and (4) by travel and residence outside the South. The figures of this study bear this out very closely. For example, Abram Ryan's life began in the conurbations of Maryland, and he grew up in Saint Louis—both parts of the Outer South, in areas often called upon to prove their southernness—at the furthest reach of his regional group. Much in keeping with Reed's model, Ryan was highly educated and "became urban" by living in Saint Louis and, later, by teaching at Niagara University. It may seem strange that a Catholic fringe southerner would become a darling of Southern Nationalism, yet it is precisely the result that Reed's model predicts. Suddenly Irvin S. Cobb seems less of an outlier.

The concept may be enlarged to include the greater part of southern Irish Catholic writers. "The Irish experience in the Old South," writes David Gleeson, "was primarily urban."[105] Almost all of the writers treated here received considerable education, the sine qua non of belles lettres; most traveled or lived outside the region and had significant exposure to the mass media. Indeed, many of the principals of this study *were* the media, working as journalists or writing for magazines. Some of them kindled a vocation and an avocation. Moving from journalism to more creative projects was an accepted, even expected practice in the nineteenth century (as Howells, Twain, and countless others demonstrated), and strikingly many of the southern Irish writers in this study keep to the trend. John Kennedy Toole and Cormac McCarthy both took military jobs early on. On this score, Flannery O'Connor has perhaps the best claim to being exclusively and professionally a writer.

Many, too, were self-made arrivistes. Ryan's immigrant family migrated from shanty to lace-curtain Irish status; his white-collar job completed the transformation. Hearn came to the country penniless and earned a literary reputation so estimable that he felt comfortable both consorting with and sending up his Irish type. E. P. O'Donnell quit a factory job and, against the odds, set out to become a self-taught writer. The rest were removed, by a generation or two, from the challenges endemic to entry-level immigrant life, writing instead from newly achieved middle-class security of both haute and petit bourgeois persuasions. These include Flannery O'Connor, Cormac McCarthy, and Kate O'Flaherty Chopin. Even when they seemed distant from their roots, they kept their family histories near. It is not an accident that Catholics have a reputation for keeping the dead alive through their votive administrations, and in this their worldview meshes neatly with southern ancestor worship.

A yearning for acceptance, along with simultaneous pride in their distinctness, is largely to be expected. To some extent, they are all "displaced persons," as Catholics and southerners, an embedded minority at a double remove from the American cultural main line. Their outsiderism made them born South-watchers, aware of the ways in which they fit in (e.g., in the politics of self-defense and self-reliance) and the ways in which they were set apart (e.g., class stigma and religious identity). They exhibited a high degree of racial consciousness. Many of them hungered for a place on earth, making regionalism attractive. Their conflicting impulses of conformity and rebellion fueled their need to tell about the South. Many wrote with underdog heart. They shared in a sense of social conservatism predicated by Catholic sensibility. A friend of Margaret Mitchell's once observed of her, "Peggy was a maverick because of religion."[106] The same might be said of these Irish Catholic writers from the South: they were all mavericks of religion, naturalized rebels of their section, outliers of place, Americans twice removed.

They shared a common desire to imagine the American South as well, and in the way of writers they dreamed their way into it. These dreams took on their own reality, as dreams will do. The images flicker before us still, and the smithy where they were forged continues to animate the regional imagination.

I

GOSPELS
of
WAR
and
PEACE

NEW IRISH, OLD SOUTH
Revolution and Its Discontents

Such were the sensations experienced by the hero, and heroine,
of this tale, that their transition [to America] was rapturous; and these
two noble [Irish] minds, which were so well suited for each other, found that in
Columbia alone there was true liberty, except in one instance, which it is true
was a disgraceful one—that a part of the human species are held in bondage,
and that of the most ignominious description, merely in consequence of
their differing in color from their own fellow creatures, and being
much less refined than they who pretend to Christianity,
but still vindicate the base doctrine of slavery.
—ADAM DOUGLASS, *The Irish Emigrant*

I should say it (now at least), with the strongest self-reproach—but *à marveille*,
it is impossible for me to get up even a respectable counterfeit of penitence,
while I confess that the name of rebel has no terrors whatever for me.
—A. M. KEILEY, *In Vinculis*

Cruel, bloody war! Little did they know who wished for this!
—JOHN DOOLEY, in his war journal

T he very first Irish American novel was published in the American South, and it was the product of a failed revolution. It issued not from the crowded, ink-stained chambers of some gritty center of northern manufactures but from—of all places—Winchester, Virginia. *The Irish Emigrant, An Historical Tale Founded on Fact,* published in 1817, was signed by an unnamed "Hibernian," who has subsequently been identified as one Adam Douglass (1790–1847). It was Douglass who registered the book with the Virginia state clerk in Winchester, a town at the throat of the established pathway of Scots-Irish immigration that trickled down the Shenandoah Valley.[1]

Douglass's father, William (1746–1832), was born in Killinchy, County Down, the son of a Scottish immigrant to northern Ireland. He served as a

"Captain of the Irish Rebellion of 1799 under Theobald Wolfe Tone."[2] His son Adam is said to have come to America in the company of his uncle, also named Adam Douglass. The young revolutionary would return to Ireland in 1812, where, sharing his father's revolutionary ardor, he joined the Irish regiment and was twice wounded at the Battle of Waterloo. He then returned to America and settled at New Market, Virginia, where he worked as "a school master and surveyor."[3] On 27 April 1819, he married Nancy Pennebaker, from Pine Forge, just a few miles south of New Market. His bride was the sister of a state senator from Virginia and the granddaughter of Captain Dirk Pennebaker, who fought in the Revolutionary War.[4] With a new bride, a new book, and new connections, Douglass had good reason to savor what his protagonist called the "sweets of freedom" in his new country. It was indeed a fresh beginning, a place where he might luxuriate "on the bank of the majestic Potomack" and permit the "degradation" of "Irish bondage" to fade into memory.[5]

Douglass came to his new country prepared to measure it against Revolutionary tumult, action, and rhetoric. Little wonder that he could say, as did the Confederate partisan A. M. Keiley in later years, that "the name of rebel has no terrors whatever for me." Like many of the Ulster Irish who immigrated during his time and shortly before, including many of the families who produced the Confederate leadership—Davis, Lee, Stuart, Jackson, Polk—Douglass was a nervous, almost tentative undersignatory to the social contract, ready to exit at the first sign of despotism and equally ready to take up arms. As it happened, Douglass found the first breach in American acceptance of slavery.

Others of his countrymen would come to see slavery as a necessary evil, or else to view the Irish experience in terms akin to that of the American slave. The moral hazard was that the Irish, who did not emplace the American system, might join the Irish-born Charleston bishop John England in viewing slavery as an evil "which Britain has superinduced." And they might even be willing to subject others to shackles from which they had only recently escaped. James Henry Hammond's famous mudsill speech evoked the Irish factory "operative" as the prime exhibit in the industrial hall of shame. Could this be preferable to slavery? he demanded.[6]

From the skeletons of landlordism in Tipperary to the ghosts of Shane's Castle, the experience of subjugation and revolution ran deep in Irish experience. Though they came from different generations from the Federal period to the Jacksonian and beyond, Adam Douglass, Abram Ryan, and Richard Wilde all turned to account their common inheritance of revolutionary displacement. Their will to power, characterized by the attendant violence of nation making, ethnic warfare, and religious fundamentalism, helped catalyze a body of wartime propaganda that took such diverse forms as Irish anti-Tom novels, the wartime journal of Rose O'Neale Greenhow, and a seething pro-Catholic, pro-Confederate novel aimed at Irish sympathizes in the Isles written by a Louisianan named Florence M. O'Connor. Many if not all of these Irish southerners came from families with histories deeply entwined in war and revolution.[7] All were masters of warfare, of both the declared and silent varieties, as they forged new ideologies of conquest and racial status. All would at times play the race card to their advantage.

And all were aware of a card that could be played against them. Tracy Fessenden has argued that Protestantism emerged as an "unmarked category" in American religious and literary history, and she writes to show "how a particular strain of post-Protestant secularism, often blind to its own exclusions, becomes normative in that history."[8] Protestantism became southerners' unmarked category for interpreting the late unpleasantness and enshrining the ideology of the Lost Cause. But this was not yet a settled issue for the nineteenth-century Irish, who participated in shaping the discourse and indeed driving on the dogs of war. The inclination of southern Irish writers for fomenting gospels of war and indeed for shaping southern identity endured even when their Catholicism was effaced by normative Protestantism.

If the Lost Cause became the dominant paradigm for interpreting southern history in the twentieth century—seamlessly interlaced with larger narratives of defeat and redemption—scholars now labor to detect the silences signaling its presence. In *Poet of the Lost Cause: A Life of Father Ryan,* Donald Beagle and I framed the question, "What . . . are we to make of southern histories that depict Catholics as cultural outsiders, when southern Irish Catholics such as Father Ryan and Margaret Mitchell participated in the very *invention* of southernness?"[9] In asserting their *pietas* for their new country, they had to stand down the nativist elements that would brand them as Irish Others and accuse them of "papolatry." In the analysis of Gerald Fogarty, SJ, during the Civil War "Virginia's Catholics would rally to the Stars and Bars, perhaps to prove the loyalty that had been so severely challenged during the Know-Nothing campaign."[10] There was an unexpected twist, in this regard: the southern Irish had to face the fact that many of their northern immigrant brethren were fighting for Union even though they were often the scapegoats of New England nativist and Protestant scorn. When he confronted a "Yanko-Irish" conscript in the hospital, the Confederate soldier John Dooley would write that the Irish in Union ranks, "invigorated and under infamous leadership, have now done far more than the envenomed *puritan* to rob us of our property, devastate our lands . . . and crush out completely our identity as a free people."[11] *Puritan* was a watchword for anti-Catholic, abolitionist extremists, and a term widely employed by southern Catholic apologists.

Rhetorical parallels between Ireland and the American South, deployed by the likes of the Irish revolutionary John Mitchel, who served for a time as a Confederate propagandist, had real traction among the southern Irish ascendant. Partisans on either side of the war had long been vying for Irish hearts and minds, and their tactics found expression in some surprising avenues. The southern Irish facility for *ethnogenesis,* the invention of an ethnicity, permeates the literature of writers who weathered the century's many revolutions, whether Irish, American, or regional. They were looked to as a test case in acclimation, both within the South and outside of it, but they were hardly passive in the assertion of their belonging, selectively embracing and pushing against Anglo-American standards. Sons and daughters of revolution became agents of rebellion and arbiters of conformity, responding to a powerful matrix of racial, religious, and nationalist polemics. In rescripting their roles in American life, they informed the creation of a *southern* ethnicity with distinctive normative racial and political views.

This section considers a time of international revolutionary ferment, when refugees from Irish revolutions and their descendants met with the revolutionary spirit of the new world. At the start of the nineteenth century the religious distinctions mattered perhaps less than simply being Irish, as Adam Douglass's *Irish Emigrant* makes plain. The partitioning of Irish Catholic and Scotch-Irish would entail some additional force: the political tumult of the 1780s and 1790s, combined with class tensions, pushed the Irish into new ethnic postures. The later arrival of Famine immigrants and Daniel O'Connell's celebrated repudiation of slavery also would catalyze this process. For his part, Douglass pointedly does not align himself with either group. If the protagonist of *The Irish Emigrant* "sees" with Douglass's eyes and memories, then the author likely shipped to his new country via the Delaware Bay, since Philadelphia is the first destination noted in the book. It would be consistent with the course he followed. The preponderance of Scots-Irish settlers in those areas, combined with Douglass's lineage, suggest that he was almost certainly a Protestant. The territories canvassed in the book follow the Great Wagon Road (known variously as the Irish Road and the Valley Road) as it crosses the Potomac at Watkin's Ferry, winding through the Great Valley of Virginia, and on to Winchester, essentially where Douglass initially settled and where the book would be published. Douglass wrote at a time when Irish immigrants, both Catholic and Protestant, were more likely to refer to themselves simply as "Irish." His preface gives simply, "An Irishman, he glories in the idea of being so."[12]

At the same time, as Kerby Miller, David Doyle, Kevin Kenny, and other historians of the American Irish have pointed out, even these first-wave Irish immigrants had significant numbers of Catholics in their midst.[13] David Doyle, a historian of the American Irish, suggests that by the year 1790 perhaps one-fifth of the white population of the southern states had come from Ireland or descended from Irish immigrants. Of these he surmises that perhaps a third were or had been Catholic.[14] Put differently, a ship that sails from Ulster does not an Ulsterman make. In fact, Douglass's generous definition of *Irishman* comes closer to the prevailing attitude of his time. So it is that Douglass might choose a Catholic protagonist for his baggy four-hundred-page, two-volume novel, which fulminates against the cruelty of British rule as it follows the career of Owen M'Dermott, a fugitive of County Antrim.

The romantic plot of the book follows an old standard: Owen falls in love with his neighbor, Emma Oniall, whose people fought on the side of William of Orange at the Battle of the Boyne, their family fortunes buoyed by the Protestant Ascendancy. This complicated love can only be properly resolved in the sweet land of liberty, in a novel that gives equal play to sectarian fealties while propounding a free Ireland agenda. Various details of the failed Rebellion of 1798 are thinly fictionalized, and others are reported in a factual way, including the grisly details of Lord Edward Fitzgerald's arrest, a tale no doubt heard as an eyewitness account at Douglass's father's knee. The blurring of fiction and history is especially pronounced in Douglass's treatment of the Onialls (O'Neills) of Shane's Castle. It would be difficult to find a family whose history is more riven by complicated political realignments, fratricide, and dynastic strife, making the O'Neills perfectly representative for Douglass's book—and symbolic of the outrageous fortunes of experience in an America where, Douglass fancied, there might be an end to old vendettas.[15]

But there was already a serpent in the bosom. Douglass laments a blemish in his American experience: nominal Christians who "vindicate the base doctrine of slavery."[16] One wonders whether this detail originated in family schism. Records show that his uncle who remained in Shenandoah married one Ann McMullen and did reasonably well in business, acquiring land in

Loudon and Hardy Counties in northwestern Virginia (Hardy County is now part of West Virginia). It is possible that the Douglasses, having acquired property in land, began to acquire human property.[17] The 1820 census lists a freed slave named Adam Douglass, aged somewhere between forty-five and fifty-five, presiding over a household constituting eight free people of color in Lexington, Rockbridge County, Virginia.[18] And the 1830 census for the western district of Shenandoah shows a white Adam Douglass, perhaps the writer's cousin, in his twenties, with a slave of like age, presiding over a family of nine.[19]

In the meantime, census records reveal that by 1830 Adam Douglass the writer had moved with his family of five to Indiana.[20] Though it is difficult to say to what extent his Virginia relatives became entangled with slavery, for his part, Douglass appears to have stayed true to the revolutionary principles of his age. By extolling a platform of freedom for all peoples, he honored the spirit of the United Irishmen, his book a kind of manifesto for their cause. In the same vein, Thomas Addis Emmet, the exiled leader of the United Irishmen, had waved away the invitation of an Irish friend in Georgia who urged him to move south, "refusing on principle to reside where his family would be dependent on coerced labour."[21] In so doing, they joined the like of Daniel O'Connell (1775–1847), "The Liberator," whose American support, especially in the South, largely evaporated when he decried the evils of African slavery. (Irish Catholics in Savannah immediately accused O'Connell of having "learned his lessons on southern institutions from Northern Abolitionists, the dire enemies of real liberties, and the notorious enemies of Ireland's religion.")[22] O'Connell was the polemical ally and inspiration for another Douglass as well—one Frederick Douglass.

Kerby Miller points out that "Emmet's scruples were not widely shared, and other Irish political exiles managed to accommodate republican principles and American slavery."[23] As a new Virginian, Douglass held himself apart from a southern culture that was rapidly developing its "peculiar institution" even as other systems of indenture, including its Irish variant, receded. For Irish who were heading south, racial codes would serve as the litmus test of sectional loyalty.[24] There would be no reprieve from the difficult politics of ethnic identity in America, as the literary record shows. William A. Caruthers (1802–1846), a pro-Stuart Virginian, helped to invent a mythic regional type based in stereotype with his early novel *The Cavaliers of Virginia*. The novel features a comic Irish "retainer," one Brian O'Reily, who serves mainly to illustrate Anglo-American values by clashing with them. O'Reily is later revealed to be the childhood savior of Nathaniel Bacon, leader of Bacon's Rebellion. In one scene O'Reily carries on his back the body of Jamie Jamieson, a fisherman killed by Indians. There could be no better symbol of the Irishman as the bearer of colonial progress—at once victim, hero, and architect—as O'Reily strides boldly into the new ranks of the manifest American expansion. J. Robert Baker reads the scene as Caruthers's assertion "that Bacon's Rebellion was a rehearsal for the American Revolution and that both were part of the providential destiny of the country."[25]

In this same spirit, one of the earliest southern Irish American writers, Richard Henry Wilde—like Adam Douglass a displaced child of Irish revolution—would go to the halls of Congress in 1829 to assert the rights of colonists before those of Indians, declaring, "We cannot alter the laws of Providence, as we read them in the experience of ages. . . . The gift was not to the red, or to the white, but to the human race—and the inscription was, to the wisest—the bravest—to virtue—and to industry!"[26]

From an early stage biographers would labor to preserve Wilde (1789–1847) to the Cavalier southern ideal by exorcising any taint of Irishness, and frequently Catholicism, from his biography, providing a textbook illustration of the Fessenden thesis: if a writer achieved canonical success, he could always be recast as an Anglo-American after the fact. Such was the case for Margaret Mitchell's ancestry, suggests Patricia Homer. The surname of Roger Brooke Taney, of Dred Scott infamy, is from the Irish language. He was once esteemed as the very flower of reasonable Anglo-American (not Irish American) jurisprudence, and his biographers tended to cast him as Anglo-American even though Taney himself wrote unambiguously of his father's forebears, "They were Roman Catholics."[27] Taney's Irish and Catholic sympathies were soft-pedaled by admiring biographers, and in an interesting parallel, some Catholic scholars have attempted to bring Oscar Wilde—purportedly related to Richard Henry Wilde—back into the Catholic literary canon on grounds that his attraction to Catholicism and family ties to it have been muted by biographers.[28] As to the southern poet R. H. Wilde: "His family are of Saxon origin," proclaimed Rufus Griswold confidently in his 1843 study, "and their ancient name was De Wilde."[29] (Wilde himself investigated this matter and believed the name "Dutch" but admitted that he had not gotten very far with it.)[30] Other scholars have gone along with the notion. The eminent Irish Catholic jurist John T. Noonan Jr. declares simply that Wilde was "Anglo-Irish."[31] Edward Tucker tellingly paints Wilde as a "Catholic throughout his life, though not an ardent one."[32] He cites no specific source for this assertion, inserting it following a discussion of Wilde's apparently non-Catholic ancestors.

Loose affiliations that might later be deemed apostasy were far more common during a period in which many were indifferent churchgoers. Though the devotional revolution that transformed the face of Catholicism in the United States and Ireland had yet to transpire, a careful reading of Tucker's own text might call into question his claim that Wilde was but an indifferent Catholic. Even in the pages of his brief (98-page) account of Wilde's life—the only scholarly biography of record—one finds a smattering of Catholic allusions, though no single one of them proves the case. They are nevertheless suggestive: the "Deo Gratia!" that concludes his manuscript treating Dante; difficult travels in North Carolina, where "the prayers of the Church" are needful; in New Orleans, a residence chosen where there is "'a little Catholic chapel not far off, a thing not without its influence' on the purchase he made"; and fellow travelers on the packet to London, "all *great* folks and good *Catholics*," Wilde exults.[33] In any case, Wilde's posthumously published epic poem, *Hesperia,* signals Irish Catholic sympathies in ways that scholars have entirely overlooked, while affording him a chance to style himself as the new Byron. Consider, for example, these passages from Lord Byron's *Childe Harold's Pilgrimage* (1812) and Wilde's *Hesperia* (1867), respectively:

> Sylla was the first of victors; but our own
> The sagest of usurpers, Cromwell; he
> Too swept off the senates while he hewed the throne
> Down to a block—immortal rebel! See
> What crimes it costs to be a moment free
> And famous through all ages.
> (Byron, 4.85)[34]

> Strange fate of men and realms!—the rise and fall
> Of that brief Commonwealth, so sternly made,
> Hung upon him, who, towering above all,
> With sceptred truncheon Europe's balance sways,
> Usurper and Protector;—yet how small
> The seeming chance that Cromwell's flight delayed;
> Had he, self-banished, the Atlantic crossed,
> Albion her freedom ne'er had won or lost!
> (Wilde, 4.70)

In fact, Wilde attempts to resituate the center of a Catholic New World in the imagined South of his New Hesperia, a South of "Saint Juan's orange-groves,—

Dominga's smiles" (1.25), where seamen listen for "the distant vesper-bell" announcing "The Virgin Mother's twilight hour of prayer" (4.1), a place where a poet might genuflect to "Holy St. Louis! Best of sainted kings . . ." (4.60).[35] *Hesperia* is dedicated to "La Signora Machesa Manfredina di Cosenza"; Wilde's biographer Edward Tucker makes an airtight case that the *signora* is Ellen White-Beatty, the wife of Wilde's business partner. This ascription is confirmed by family lore (including a historical romance, *The Floridians,* written by a descendant, Margaret Anderson Uhler), and the intrigue is heightened by a note in the Library of Congress manuscript: "Is it possible he can have suspected?"[36] Wilde's own son would at one point wonder whether his father was trying to steal away his girlfriend.

A fun-loving, irreligious playboy? Wilde's biographers cannot be altogether faulted for choosing to see Wilde as he himself wanted to be seen. He seems not to have made a show of his religion, as he styled himself a new American and demonstrated his mastery of his new country's politics. Though he lived in Ireland until he was nearly teenaged, accounts of his life make no mention of an Irish accent. He had secured a seat in Congress by the time he was twenty-six. He would habitually protest the crassness of the financial pursuits to which he dedicated most of his life. Nor would power satisfy the poet as he reinvented himself as a member of the ruling classes: "Spurning restraint, disdainful of the crowd, / Statesman I am not, and never will be, / For rule too indolent, for strife too proud," he once sniffed.[37]

Certainly his brisk political rise supports the kind of "Irishman-made-good" vision of the Cavalier myth that W. J. Cash sketched in *The Mind of the South.* By 1827 Wilde had every reason to be sanguine about his future prospects. He was sufficiently established in real and political capital to have a go at the most conspicuous form of southern success, the ultimate mark of regional assimilation: the acquisition of a plantation and slaves. He entered into a business partnership with the lawyer Joseph M. White, a Florida congressman, establishing a sugar plantation in Florida to be overseen by White's brother. About this time a revenue officer impounded a Spanish ship carrying slaves off the Florida coast, touching off an ownership dispute that stretched out for seven years, eventuating in a Supreme Court decision and a windfall of the "cargo" to Richard Henry Wilde. The *Antelope* incident, known mainly to scholars of slavery's legal history, culminated in a case that "became the province of the famous and powerful," writes Chuck Mobley, "a veritable who's who of what was known as the Era of Good Feeling."[38]

The subsequent congressional maneuvering to capture the *Antelope*'s prize of human cargo had more to do with good stealings, with much of the boot going to Congressman Wilde. This was not the only debate surrounding the meaning of freedom in which the poet participated. His moment of glory on the congressional floor came during the debates surrounding the Indian Removal Act of 1830, when he filled the record with a chapter-and-verse overview of Indian treaties and cases. He had recourse to the same ancient principles of law that supported adverse possession: land belongs to those who improve it. "Before we indulge our tears at the extinction of the Indian race," begged Wilde, "let us inquire what it is we lament." Wilde argued that they purposed not to extinguish the "race," but to convert Indians to the dominant culture. "What is it, then, that constitutes Indian individuality—the identity of that race which gentleman are so anxious to preserve?" asked the acclimated Irish American on the congressional floor. "Is it the mere copper color of the skin, which marks them—according to our prejudices, at least—an inferior—a conquered—a degraded race?"[39]

If it comes as a surprise that the first Irish American novel was published in the South, there are other twists in the tale: we might now add that one of the first Irish American poets of reputation was a conservative southerner who defended "southern rights" in Congress. Ultimately, Wilde's status can be likened to that of the poet to whom he is most often compared: Thomas Moore, the first Irish writer to enjoy an international reputation. Wilde emulated Moore, a Dublin-born Catholic who enjoyed fair access to Anglo-Irish political capital and had been permitted entry to Trinity under the Catholic Relief Act. Moore married Elizabeth "Bessy" Dyke, a Protestant, but remained nominally a Catholic and an Irish nationalist. The Dubliner born and bred prospered by bending to Anglo-Irish norms.

In a sense, so did Wilde—no Irish nationalist he, but a player of Anglo-American society. Were it not for his origins, it is doubtful that he would have achieved as much, or insisted upon epic reinvention. His father was a refugee from Irish rebellion, a conflict eclipsed in his son's mind by the American revolution of a prior generation. So, too, first novelist Adam Douglass, who passed away the very same year. But Douglass had taken up arms at Waterloo—how could he abrogate his principles without making a sham of everything? Having barely missed revolutionary bloodshed, Richard Henry Wilde could sing it more freely.

Wilde's self-reinvention serves as an object lesson in how the southern Irish might become enthusiastic southern partisans in the generation to follow. Like the good-natured and willfully purblind captain of Herman Melville's *Benito Cereno* (1866), this man who was eminently the product of revolutions seemed incapable of seeing the one in which he was most directly an agent and unwitting participant, the one that played out before his unseeing eyes. The polemics surrounding who should receive American freedom eventuated in a war deemed by some to be civil, by others, rebellion, and still others, revolutionary.

In the runup to the American Civil War, Irish Catholic propagandists would play a part in dramatizing and manufacturing consent for the conflict. Turbulent times made for some unlikely alliances. Even as Catholic numbers in the South increased, the visibility of English abolitionists in the halls of Parliament and in popular culture would in some respects chill southerners' love of all things English. Henry A. Wise, of Virginia, redoubtable in his defense of southern rights, worried that Know-Nothingism concealed the "plans of Exeter Hall, in old England, acting on Williams Hall, in New England, for a hierarchical proscription of religions, for the demolition of some of the clearest standards of American liberty, and for a fanatical and sectional demolition of slavery."[40] The southern Irish were quick to see New England's shadow in acts of nativist bigotry, as Wise struck an Anglophobic chord that resonated profoundly among the southern Irish.

On the eve of the war those Irish numbered perhaps eighty-four thousand.[41] Although distinctly a minority in Dixie, they flocked to the war footing, both for the high stakes of warmaking and sometimes on the principle, in response to anti-Catholic nativism, that "the enemy of my enemy is my friend." The anti-Catholic rhetoric in the wake of the Kansas-Nebraska Act proved remarkably supple. As Jenny Franchot points out, "New England nativists allied themselves with antislavery forces against Irish Catholic immigrants while siding with southern planters who attacked German Catholic immigrants in Kentucky."[42] Catholics responded in kind. For example, Mary Austin Carroll (1835–1909) immigrated to help establish the Sisters of Mercy in the United States and was initially dispatched to New England. Yet she would develop strongly southern sympathies, writing in one of her books,

> We hear a great deal about the march of intellect, but which party gave greater evidence of common sense and humanity—not to speak of religious toleration—the Orangemen of the last quarter of the past century, who refrained from molesting an institution erected in defiance of existing laws, or the enlightened Yankees of Massachusetts, who, under a Constitution that

guarantees religious toleration, burned, in 1832, a convent which was built without infringing on any law?[43]

Though she was a proponent of peace throughout the war, and though her astonishingly productive literary work was overshadowed by men like Father Ryan, Carroll never wavered in her defense of the South.[44] Nor did most Irish: John Mitchel suggested that forty thousand southern Irish Catholics fought for the Confederacy, a number that must be inflated, since it would have meant that they fought to a man (not to mention a boy). Gleeson halves that number to the more plausible twenty thousand. If this figure is accurate, it means that "around 70 percent of able-bodied Irish men served in the Confederate armed forces"[45]—a significant number, at any rate. Despite the perception of Catholics as outsiders in the South, Civil War records demonstrate that as a percentage of the whole, more priests served as chaplains in Confederate ranks than in northern ranks.[46]

In the run-up to the Civil War, while Irish American immigrants contended with nativism and calibrated their politics to regional pieties, they became shills for the rhetorical posturing of politicians, northern and southern. For example, in 1844 the *Southern Quarterly Review* held out the Irish in a Malthusian nightmare scenario, contrasted with the assumed munificence of southern planters:

> What does the landlord in Ireland more than others to alleviate the famine of the people? But should it please Divine Providence to inflict the same calamity of scarcity and famine, on the slaveholding States, which now prevails in Ireland and a part of Scotland, it would be the duty of the master—a duty growing out of his position and belonging to it—to exhaust his fortune and his credit, in procuring subsistence for his slaves. . . . Here only exists that combination of labor with capital, which insures to the first, in sickness and in want, as well as in health, competent supply of clothing and food.[47]

The comparisons had been in the air for some time. One of the earliest comes from James Henry Hammond in 1833. A South Carolinian whose ascendant political career was later ended by revelations that he had fondled his teenage nieces, he was then little more than a fresh-faced twenty-five-year-old officer with great ambition. His Fourth of July address added recent charges to a long list of British wrongs. In a likely allusion to the Coercion Act of 1833 he alleged that the Parliament had turned its back on freedom and consigned the

Irish people to "absolute & unmitigated slavery."[48] The next step in this analogy, naturally, was to compare Irish enslavement with its southern counterpart—British tyranny contrasted with southern benevolence.

Hammond's sleight of hand gives us one of the very earliest examples of what would become a stock argument for later proslavery ideologues (and the implicit backdrop for his infamous mudsill speech). As Edward Rugemer explains, "Hammond's portrayal of Britain as the brutal enslaver of the Irish hinted at one of the most important planks of the emerging proslavery argument: the contrast between the oppression imposed upon free white laborers and the alleged ease of life enjoyed by southern slaves."[49] The South Carolina bishop John England was among those who remonstrated with Daniel O'Connell—his old friend—when the Irish hero came out in favor of abolition. He wrote to O'Connell, "With every Carolinian I know, I lament an evil [slavery] which Britain has superinduced. . . . And I pray that you may succeed in raising the ruined population of Ireland to the level of the comforts of the Carolina slave."[50]

This idea was already in chrysalis in 1833; by 1850 the Irish analogy, comparing the comforts of slaves and the Irish, was so ubiquitous that an exasperated Frederick Douglass would seek to counter it bluntly in his lectures: "There is no analogy between the two cases. The Irishman is poor, but he is not a slave."[51] About the same time, John Mitchel, of the United Irishmen, who would later work as a Confederate propagandist, would first glimpse slavery from a literally shuttered perspective whilst a shipboard prisoner sent to Tasmanian exile. He had no qualms about conflating slavery with Irish serfdom: "Slaves in Brazil are expected to work moderately, but are not treated with contumely. They are often admitted to the society of the families they serve, and lead in some measure the life of human beings. Is it better, then, to be the slave of a merciful master and a just man, or to be serf to an Irish land-appropriator? God knoweth."[52]

In the war for hearts and minds, Irish-slave comparisons soon found their way into fictional representation and allegory. Anti-Tom novels became a primary means of returning fire to Stowe's *Uncle Tom's Cabin* (1852), and though most are of doubtful literary merit, some came from bestselling authors of the day. William Gilmore Simms, who wrote a handful of abortive states'-rights dramas, fired an early salvo in *Woodcraft* (1852), and so did Mary Eastman with her popular *Aunt Phillis's Cabin; or, Southern Life as It Is* (1852).[53] Some would make the Irish analogy central to their claims. Florence J. O'Connor, of Louisiana, the Irish Catholic author of a one-off wartime propaganda novel titled *The Heroine of the Confederacy* (1864), pitched the argument to readers in the British Isles and Ireland during wartime exile in London. In a fairly standard slavery apologetic, she employs the language of "white slaves"—among Irish propagandists a term with a troubled history too tangled to be unwound here. "Go to the Five Points of New York [where Irish immigrants thronged with Germans and African Americans] and glance at the miserable hovels on the shore of the Bay of Brooklyn," the novel's Catholic heroine urges readers, "and tell me then if you can find a negro in the whole South who would change quarters with the poor white of your cities."[54]

Some years before Florence O'Connor, Delaware-born David Brown (b. 1786) became a slavery apologist who invoked the Irish after his travels to Charleston convinced him of slavery's benevolence. *The Planter: or, Thirteen Years in the South* (1853) attempts to rehabilitate slavery's reputation by setting it next to Irish degradation. Scripted largely as a dramatic dialogue, it opens with a talk between the Doctor and his family at the breakfast table. In the adjoining kitchen sits their domestic, "a neat handed and newly and warmly clad Irish girl,—a good natured and faithful creature. She was one of the survivors of a packed cargo of emigrants from the almost desolated Connaught;—the daughter of a family, by oppression separated for the ever of this world." In the ensuing conversation, The Doctor's winsome daughters feed him questions such as, "Are the negroes starving to death, like the poor people of Ireland and Scotland? and even of England and Germany? . . . Or are they turned out of their cabins, and hunted away from their homes, as our good Peggy says the poor Irish women and children are, by thousands upon thousands; and that they may never get back to them, their poor hovels are all burnt down to the ground?" (The answer, quite naturally, is no.) Brown devotes an entire chapter to Ireland, of which this sort of observation is typical: "Poor unhappy Ireland! O that thy oppressors, by whom thy wisest sons have been maddened, would withdraw their pseudo-sympathy from our happy negro slaves, and extend to thee a true and efficient Christian sympathy, that should elevate thy children to the condition of happy freemen!"[55]

Of more interest here are several other proslavery anti-Tom novels that incorporate Irish examples. John Page's *Uncle Robin, in His Cabin in Virginia, and Tom Without One in Boston* (1853) coaxes an entire chapter from this rather parched ground. It finds one Dr. Boswell, scion of "one of the oldest and most influential families of Virginia," graduated from William and Mary College and married to a Pennsylvania lady who must be disabused of her Yankee prejudices against slavery. Dr. Boswell's benign tour of slavery, put on for the benefit of his wife, brings him to a demonstrative encounter with the Irish in Virginia.

> "We are now at the turnpike, and there are the Irish shanties."
>
> "What are they, my dear?"
>
> "Shanty, my dear, comes from two Irish words, which mean an old dwelling; but with us, they mean what you now see before you: huts for human beings to live in. The women and children occupy them in the day, and the men who work on the public road, join them at night."

The family squatting within the hovel includes six shivering "half-naked" children, a long-suffering mother, and a witless alcoholic father who will not brook comparison to blacks:

> "Now, your honour shouldn't compare your nigger slaves with white people, onyhow; we go when we plase, and stay at home when we please; and your honour knows there's a warld of difference between free people and slaves."
>
> "If slaves have more learning than free people, more religion than free people, and have better houses to live in than free people, I think the difference is in favour of slaves."
>
> "But, your honour, there's something in liberty better than the like of onything else in the warld."

The horrid encounters are later summed up by the good doctor and his wide-eyed wife, who exclaims, "My dear, I can't hesitate in assigning to the cabin of Uncle Robin a vastly greater amount of every procurement of real happiness in this world, than is to be found in the shanty of Dennis Flinn."[56] A contemporaneous reviewer in *Southern Churchman* began a (predictably) approving review of this pap by building Page's ethos: "The author is a pious and intelligent layman of the Church of Virginia, who, for many years has sustained the relation of master with Christian fidelity and benevolence."[57]

Mercifully, *Uncle Robin* appears to be Page's only contribution to American literature. The author of *The Cabin and Parlor* (1852), another Dickensian anti-Tom novel with Irish themes, achieved considerably greater notoriety. Charles Jacobs Peterson (1819–1887), a Philadelphian of *Peterson's Magazine* fame, wrote the book and published it under the pen name J. Thornton Randolph. Part of the ironic beauty of Peterson's story is in his Anglicized name. As his biography in *Appleton's Cyclopædia* records, "He was a descendant of Erick

Pieterson, who came to the Delaware with a colony from Sweden in 1638."[58] The Swedish American latterday slavery defender was one of the coterie of editors clustered around *Graham's Magazine* and at one point its financier.[59] Peterson and his circle of middling literati aspired to be the Brahmins of the mid-Atlantic, a pretension that Poe enjoyed deflating. Like most notables in Philadelphia's literary circles at the time, Peterson befriended Poe and was later de-friended by him.

Both geographically and politically, Philadelphia found itself caught between North and South, with its commercial interests in many instances favoring the latter. The city's position made it ground zero for the ideological battle before the impending conflict. Even as Friends spirited escaped slaves across the Delaware, Philadelphia witnessed the 1853 debut of a play by Sam Sanford's uncreatively titled *Southern Version of "Uncle Tom's Cabin"* replete with a "Happy Uncle Tom."[60] Fittingly, Mason Stokes takes *The Cabin and Parlor* for the first work of discussion in *The Color of Sex,* a book that attempts to explain how whiteness as a racial category arose from gender and class crises in the antebellum period. The City of Brotherly Love was a flashpoint for the rhetoric of racism.

In proslavery polemics, Peterson's novel follows Hammond's proslavery line exactly, with cradle-to-grave paternalism: "We, at the South, buy our operative outright, giving him food and clothing, and providing for him in youth, sickness, and old age. In return, we appropriate his labor, during the years of his maturity. This is, I don't deny, the rudest shape which these relations assume; but then our operative is the rudest of all, and fit, as a general thing, for no higher relation."[61] The plot devises that in Philadelphia a southern planter's son, Horace, displaced by economic circumstance, encounters appalling poverty, labors for a Scrooge-like taskmaster named Mr. Sharpe, and finally contracts the wasting disease that polishes him off. Before his death Horace is taken in by a destitute Irish immigrant family in a decayed tenement. His wholesome ways and winsome work ethic are vouched for by his adoptive Irish matron, who delivers a rattling monologue to a slaveholder named Walworth. Walworth inherited his human "stock" brought from Africa, "which was done by England, against the wishes of the colonists" (168). The poor Irishwoman is convinced that Horace "caught the fever by working like a naygar." When Walworth engages Mr. Sharpe, a profiteer of child labor, in a debate over slavery, he opines, "The worst huts I ever saw human beings inhabiting, in this country, I saw, some years ago, at the Summit Hill coal-mines. We have nothing so bad at the South" (186). The example is a pointed one: the hardscrabble area around the Summit Hill coal mines was a breeding ground for the Irish miners' vigilante group, the Molly Maguires, either inspired by or derived directly from earlier underground Irish Catholic groups that resisted British landlordism, such as the Whiteboys. Mr. Sharpe's reply draws a rebuke from Walworth suggesting that the Irish, however low, are at least white. Not accidentally, the question of who will be counted white is tied to anxiety over labor.

Walworth later wanders into a dangerous scene with rioters, evidently based loosely on one of the innumerable Philadelphia riots of the period, pitting nativists against Irish and the Irish against all comers, not infrequently including black Philadelphians.[62] He cannot suppress his horror when he encounters a mob intent on incinerating "a nigger meeting-house" (198) in response to a perceived slight from blacks. Facing them down, he is at once branded a race traitor. As he backs away, he is trailed by "the two rioters following him threateningly, with their eyes, and the red-shirted ruffian muttering something about 'the white nigger, who ought to be thrown alive into the burning meeting-house'" (200). The propagandist's lesson, of course, is that racial hatreds burn more brightly in Philadelphia than in the old cotton fields back home.

Anti-Tom novels were soon joined by anti-Tom plays. Remarkably, the famed Irish dramatist Dionysius Lardner Boucicault would have a hand in the dramatic interpretation of the southern racial caste system. Born of Irish parents and classed by posterity as an Anglo-Irish playwright, Boucicault would pursue a career that included work as a playwright and actor in America. His life as an actor in that time had typically transatlantic dimensions, taking him to London, Dublin, Philadelphia, Washington, Boston, New Orleans, and New York. But it was his brief foray to the South that inspired one of his most popular and divisive productions. *The Octoroon* (1859) was set in Louisiana and based on *The Quadroon* (1856), written by Thomas Mayne Reid, an Irish immigrant who sometimes caroused with Poe.[63]

Boucicault's timing in debuting the play could not have been more inauspicious, as it fated him to be an Irish ingenue who wandered headlong into America's seething obsession with race. Or perhaps that was what he wanted. His play seemed star-crossed from the beginning, embroiling Boucicault in a legal dispute over rights and royalties that soon degenerated into skullduggery.[64] New York was on edge: rumors flew that the play would be picketed or worse, as scarcely a month had passed since John Brown's raid at Harper's Ferry. And the Boucicaults' reputation preceded them. The interracial heroine Zoe was to be played by Agnes Robertson, Boucicault's much younger Scottish bride, with whom he had eloped to general scandal. She purportedly received a death threat in advance of appearing in the play, which one Boucicault biographer suggests her husband contrived as a publicity stunt.[65] Notwithstanding the whiteness of the actress, advance rumors of miscegenation scandalized New Yorkers. As a tragic heroine of mixed blood, Zoe is ripped away from her lover and fated to be sold into slavery, partly through the machinations of a whisker-twirling, dastardly overseer named Jacob McClosky.

The stock villain is a Snopes incarnate, and indeed there are some fascinating parallels between the play and particularly Faulkner's *Absalom, Absalom!* (1936), with its unnamed "octoroon," incestuous flirtations, and menacing Continental Catholicism. A carpetbagger some years before the term would be coined, Boucicault's McCloskey arrives from Connecticut to insinuate himself in the financial affairs of Terrebonne Plantation. The arriviste is stingingly aware of his distance from the "quality": "Just because my grandfather wasn't some broken-down Virginia transplant, or a stingy old Creole, I ain't fit to sit down to the same meat with them."[66] The idea of the plantation aristocracy was taking hold of the popular imagination, and another of the play's innovations— the use of a photographic camera to produce damning evidence—showed that it was on the cutting edge of regional invention.

Enter the Irishman. Through a number of cues the play suggests that the murderous scoundrel McCloskey is pedigreed Irish: he breakfasts on a "julep . . . and a bit of cheese," he is quick to cry for a lynching, and his dialect blends Irish pronunciation with the American idiom ("consarn," "whar," "ye," etc.). Illustrating once again the dangers of Irish and "impure" races in proximity, Mc-Closkey has a more than avuncular interest in Zoe, whom he has picked out for concubinage. As he salivates in the shadows when she meets her true love, he mutters an aside that speaks volumes about the unfettered sexuality associated with blackness: "She loves him! I felt it—and how she can love! That one black drop of blood burns in her veins and lights up her heart like a foggy sun."[67]

Despite intense public interest and some acclaim, the curtain had barely fallen before the one reviewer accused Boucicault of "tak[ing] advantage of the existing anti-Southern excitement . . . to bring out a play, which, for all practical purposes, is more pernicious than anything which has heretofore been conceived in the spirit of sectional hate."[68] The *New York Herald* scented abolitionist insubordination in it all. Having decried "negro worshipping mania," the editorialist indicted a familiar unholy alliance of antislavery societies, whose "philanthropists were in close correspondence with their British brethren, and stood in higher favor at Exeter Hall than at home." The paper implored Boucicault and his ilk not to touch the question of slavery "in any way": "[It] will carry with it the abolition aroma, and must be classed with the sermons of Beecher and Cheever and the novels of Mrs. Stowe. It will tend still further to excite the feeling which now threatens to destroy the Union of the States and ruin the republic."[69]

By that time, stage adaptations of *Uncle Tom's Cabin* had proven enormously popular, with at least nine on offer within a few years of the book's release, and shades of the novel clearly inform Boucicault's play.[70] An unabashed plagiarist, Boucicault had read the book and found it wanting in verisimilitude, as his impressions of slavery in Louisiana had been mostly positive.[71] Still, Stowe's Simon Legree furnishes a transparent prototype for Boucicault's Simon McCloskey: Legree comes from the North, is most generous when drunk, may by implication be a papist ("like most godless and cruel men, [he] was superstitious"; and later, "How I hate these cursed Methodist hymns!"), is sensually depraved, a cursing tippler, and a murderer. Of Legree's past we know that he worked as a sailor for a time, and his colloquial mixture of American eye dialect, like McCloskey's, has a suggestively Irish ring to it ("Ye could n't [*sic*] treat a poor sinner, now, to a bit of sermon, could ye,—eh?").[72] Stowe's book contains a smattering of Irish references (e.g., to Curran), but of course the skulking Irishman is under the reader's nose the entire time.

Stowe had little good to say about Irish domestics, as is widely known; she felt that they "enslaved" their mistresses. But "if slavery was to be condemned in all its forms . . . both 'blackness' and 'Catholicism' were for Stowe the sites of more reluctant disavowals," argues Fessenden.[73] Like Hawthorne and others, Stowe balanced what she called specifically Yankee determination to squelch "everything unique and poetic" in their world against her need to refashion Catholicism into an acceptably neutral fetish of antiquarianism, a process well documented in Franchot's *Roads to Rome*. For his part, Boucicault merely stirred what was already in the pot, thus alienating partisans on both sides. The play hints at incest—again reminiscent of *Absalom, Absalom!*—as Zoe's true lover, George Peyton, is likened to her father, suggesting that he is something more than the nephew advertised in the dramatis personae.

Surprisingly, in light of its southern sympathies, the *New York Times* took a more sanguine view of things. Across the span of several reviews it deemed the controversy to be a case of much ado about nothing, pronouncing the improbable, crudely drawn melodrama "a cleverly constructed, perfectly impartial, not to say noncommittal, picture of life as it is in Louisiana."[74] *Noncommittal* was also the word used by Joseph Jefferson, whose opinions on the subject probably come closest to the truth. Jefferson, a celebrated stage actor of his day, appeared in *The Octoroon.* His first stage performance had him singing T. D. "Daddy" Rice's eponymous "Jump, Jim Crow"; Rice reprised the Jim Crow character only after discovering that it rivaled his Paddy routines in popularity. In any case, Jefferson recalled his audiences cheering for both the South and the North at varying crucial moments of the performance—a sign, perhaps, of the tragedy that lay in store. "There were various opinions as to which way the play leaned," he acknowledged. "The truth of the matter is, it was non-committal. The dialogue and characters of the play made one feel for the South, but the action proclaimed against slavery, and called loudly for its abolition."[75]

Evidently stung by criticism, or perhaps enticed by the publicity, in January 1860 Boucicault published a discreet rejoinder in the *New Orleans Picayune* that was eventually picked up by the New York papers. His carefully hedged loyalties ran to the usual Irish package: "As for my political persuasion, I am a Democrat, and a Southern Democrat, but do not mix myself up with politics in any way; still when I found myself under an imputation of writing anything with the smallest tendency against my convictions, I withdrew the work not because I disowned it—I withdrew it to send it down South that you might see for yourselves whether even inadvertently I could prostitute my abilities, my convictions and my feelings."[76]

Intending to put an end to two years of itinerant stateside thespianism, Boucicault then betook business, bride, and a newborn son briefly to New Orleans. He bought the Varieties Theatre and rechristened it the Gaiety but could not keep it solvent.[77] And he faced an uphill battle in trying to get New Orleans to warm to the play. As early as 1852, when an apoplectic writer for the *Daily Picayune* learned of a stage adaptation of *Uncle Tom's Cabin,* he predicted that such would be "the source of innumerable horrors to both sections and both races."[78] No fewer than three locally produced plays were contrived in quick response. These included an entry by an Irish American southerner named Joseph M. Field. His *Uncle Tom's Cabin; or, Life in the South As It Is* (1854), attributed to "Harriet Screecher Blow," ran for a week at Dan Rice's Amphitheatre in New Orleans. Like most of Field's dramatic efforts, this one is lost to history, apart from what can be reconstructed from newspaper accounts. Field's anti-Tom play finds Uncle Tom "shivering and forlorn amid the inclemencies of a Canadian winter," pining for the old folks at home. The curtain closes on "a gang of plantation negroes dancing 'Juba' and singing 'Old Jawbone.'"[79] A separate effort titled *Amalgamation; or, Southern Visitors* took northern abolitionists to task.

If the southern press was preemptively defensive about amalgamation and Tom plays, it was "immediately, even prematurely, enthusiastic" about anti-Tom

productions, which drew "thousands" of viewers.[80] The trouble was that Boucicault's play was hardly in step with the anti-Tom blandishments calculated to
please spectators in New Orleans. Anxious to show his loyalty, Boucicault sent
the governor of Louisiana a copy of *The Octoroon* dedicated to him, pledging
that "Southern families of distinction" had embraced the play. The actor seemed
to know that his career in the region was prematurely finished; he told the
Picayune: "It is not probable that I shall ever visit the South again, so I am doubly anxious to retain the good opinion of the friends I made and left there."[81]

Boucicault once advised young students at the Madison Square Theatre
School, "Always put your foot down as if to say, 'This spot is mine!'"[82] True to
his word, when the play debuted in London after folding in New Orleans, he
stepped into the role of Salem Scudder, the typecast shrewd and systematizing
Yankee inventor who is a fixture in Tom and anti-Tom plays. The American
version of the play ended with a Hollywood-like finale: a fight and stabbing, a
collapsed heroine, and an exploding steamship. By contrast, the English version's muted, happy ending was tailored to audiences who would not flinch at
seeing an interracial marriage represented on stage.[83] Boucicault also courted
the papers in London, where he was called to account for his true feelings
on slavery. In a letter to the *Times* he averred that "the slaves are in general
warmly attached to their masters." But, he added, "behind this there are features in slavery far more objectionable than any hitherto held up to human
execration, by the side of which physical suffering appears as a vulgar detail,"
adverting to, with his knack for salacious salesmanship, the unpronounceable
sexual dimensions of white privilege and plantation concubinage.[84]

If one classes these Tom and anti-Tom efforts in their true form, as part of
a series of genre-spanning propaganda exchanges preceding a war, it soon
becomes apparent that rumors of war had grown to a clamor. Already armed
with the double-edged polemics of revolution, the Irish would play a vocal,
sometimes opportunistic part in toning the rhetoric. With their Catholic associations—about which everyone held some opinion—the Irish furnished a suitably protean character upon which the propagandists might dramatize various
visions of assimilation and division, much as politicians now interpret the
"problem" of "Hispanic" immigration. Real-life Irish would soon count the costs
of the saber rattling, leaving a number or remarkable accounts in their wake.[85]

There is an old chestnut about southerners never meeting a war they didn't
like, and the same has been said of the Irish, whose participation in the Ameri-

can Civil War would eventually put them in the first vanguard of its Lost Cause memoirists and candid autobiographers. Consider one son of Irish immigrants, John Lucas Paul Cantwell (1828–1909), of Charleston, South Carolina, who tried the warmaking path to glory. Still in his teens, he likely saw plenty of shot flying in the Battle of Chapultepec, and he might have heard about Robert E. Lee, Pierre Beauregard, and George Pickett, who also were present there. Writing to his uncle on stationery freshly lifted from the "National Palace, City of Mexico," he would confess, "I can tell you what . . . soldiering *aint* what it is cracked up to be, and the singing of Bullets & Grape & Cannister is any thing but comfortable. Glory & all that is nothing but fudge."[86] After serving in the Mexican-American War as a member of the Palmetto Regiment, South Carolina Volunteers, he gave war another chance, moving to Wilmington, North Carolina, where he joined the Thirtieth North Carolina Militia and eventually saw action during the Civil War. Finally imprisoned with the Immortal 600—a group of Confederate prisoners employed as human shields at various potential targets—the everlasting "good" luck he brought to soldiering might have been his mere survival. Throughout it all, his immigrant father, Patrick, would counsel him to keep the faith. He wrote to his son to express his pleasure with his son's progress in business and in learning French, and he was "more than pleased to read your continued desire to make the acquaintance of the R.C. Clergymen & of the Church." "Hold to that my son—," he advised.[87]

Perhaps it is no wonder that southern Irish who embraced the Confederate cause were soon caught up in the possibility of sacralizing it. Consider Florence O'Connor, whose gift to southern literature is a very rare bird indeed: a protagonist who offers a Catholic prayer for the Confederacy "at the feet of the statue of the blessed Virgin which reposed on an altar in [her] room." The heroine/protagonist's prayer reads, in part:

> If my young life would serve as a holocaust on the altar of my country, thou knowest, who readeth all hearts, how gladly I would yield it up an offering to thee and to my own beautiful sunny South and native land! Like the daughter of Jeptha, I would go forth to meet the victorious general and bless the hand that smote me. Thou, blessed Mother, whose arms seem stretched forth to receive me, intercede with thy dear Son in behalf of my country and of me. . . . Jesus, Mary, and Joseph, I retire to dream that I am with you.[88]

One wonders whether Margaret Mitchell ever read the story of this particular heroine. Florence O'Connor's pious heroine is no Scarlett O'Hara, however, but a stock character who bears a much closer resemblance to the too-good-for-life Melanie Hamilton. As late as 1869 O'Connor's book was being reprinted by A. Eyrich of New Orleans, which says much about the bellicose postwar political climate in Louisiana. A bare handful of biographical facts about Florence O'Connor may be gleaned from an entry in *The Living Female Writers of the South:* she was a "a native of Louisiana" and a one-time contributor to the New Orleans *Mirror* whose poems appeared from time to time in the *Sunday Times,* and she purportedly published a collection of poems in Canada in 1869.[89] Thereafter she seems to disappear largely from the written record.[90]

The Heroine of the Confederacy devotes a chapter (19) to describing the movements and stratagems of a Confederate spy revealed, at the chapter's end, to be one "Miss Clayton." O'Connor compares her exploits favorably to those of another celebrated spy, Belle Boyd of Virginia. Whether or not O'Connor considered her, she might have had an excellent real-life model for a southern Irish Catholic spy in Rose O'Neale Greenhow (c. 1817–1864). It is impossible to give Greenhow more than brief treatment here, for her relatively short life was crammed with adventure, travel, and intrigue. "She was a slave owner, a social climber, an elitist, and a snob," writes Ann Blackman, chronicling the accomplishments of a woman who was a close personal friend of James Buchanan and without question a Washington power broker in her time. Greenhow may well have been "the first American-born woman to represent a government (in this case, the Confederacy) on foreign soil," Blackman points out. In the estimation of Stephen R. Mallory, the Irish American Confederate navy secretary, she was above all a remarkably clever woman.[91]

Blackman scarcely needs to add that Greenhow was a confirmed racist. This turns out to be an important fact of her life, not insofar as it is particularly salient but for its relevance to the way she conceived her identity as an Irish southerner. She was born on a modest plantation in Montgomery County, Maryland, near Port Tobacco, a port of call for many indentured Irish. According to Blackman, the redoubtedly Catholic O'Neales may have been in Spain at mid-seventeenth century, suggesting that Rose's ancestors may have taken part in the Flight of the Wild Geese familiar to students of Irish history. Greenhow once described herself as "a Southern woman, born with revolutionary blood in my veins," and one wonders how much of it came by honest way of her family history.[92]

In Maryland, where the family practiced or concealed their faith according to the vicissitudes of state politics, Rose O'Neale's father, John, lived the life of a carousing gentleman who enjoyed squiring his land. He was killed in a murky, alcohol-soaked incident in 1817 that led to the indictment and execution of his favorite slave, as documented in *State of Maryland v. Negro Jacob*. The physician in attendance "discovered an uncommon backwardness on the part of all Oneales negroes to render assistance to him."[93] Rose's father's death left the family in a financially precarious position, with the unintended but (for Rose) beneficial consequence that they arrived at Hill's Boarding House, a popular location for political movers and shakers, especially southern politicians. John C. Calhoun, who once declared, "I have ever taken pride in my Irish descent," was a regular boarder there, and if Blackman is correct, he served as a mentor and perhaps even a father figure to Rose.[94] Greenhow once brought the conversation at her table to a contretemps after Abigail Adams, in the presence of the former president, unadvisedly "launched out into a panegyric on John Brown."[95] Greenhow's set included Chief Justice Roger Brooke Taney, the Catholic proslavery jurist who also was the likely descendant of indentured Irish in Maryland.

Naturally, given her loyalties and degree of political access, she became a spy for the Confederacy, which she would refer to as "the high and holy cause to which I had devoted my life" (63). Her greatest coup in that capacity was passing along the information Jefferson Davis later credited for clinching a Confederate victory at First Manassas, a point that historians are still debating. For her part, Greenhow would deem the battle as "memorable in history as that of Culloden or Waterloo" (17), the former comparison rich in Catholic connotation. Eventually Alan Pinkerton and his agents caught on to her, and she was placed under house arrest on August 23, 1861. She was transferred, along with her daughter, Little Rose, to the Old Capital Prison, where she spent the first five months of 1862. After her release, magnificently unchastened, she put herself at Jefferson Davis's disposal, going as an emissary to Europe.

There she would meet with Lord Palmerston and Napoleon III as she lobbied for Continental recognition of the Confederacy. This was not to be, and when she sensed that the wind was shifting in the other direction, she used her access to channels of Catholic power to once again solicit the pope's support. She would befriend the Anglo-Irish cardinal Nicholas Wiseman and later be confirmed by him on June 29, 1864. When the blockade runner that would return her to the fractured states foundered at the mouth of the Cape Fear River in September 1864, she was drowned, so the story goes, because of the store of gold bullion she carried, the fruit of her fund-raising efforts—but of course this has an element of nationalistic embroidery about it.

Greenhow's singular contribution to literature survives in *My Imprisonment and the First Year of Abolition Rule at Washington* (1863), published, like

The Heroine of the Confederacy, in London during wartime. It documents how "Wild Rose" outmaneuvered and deceived her enemies at every turn. Ironically, her form follows, in many respects, scripture-quoting captivity narratives à la Mary Rowlandson. Sometimes it resembles a slave narrative, beginning in apologetics that explain how a woman might write such an outspokenly political autobiography: "It may be that the language which was sometimes extorted from me in conversation, or some of the remarks now found in my book, are more bitterly vituperative and sarcastic, than in ordinary times, and upon ordinary subjects, would be becoming in the personal narrative of a woman. Those who may think so are only entreated, before they judge, to endeavour to imagine themselves in my position" (7).

As an iron-kneed secessionist with her temper up, Greenhow could give Father Abram Ryan a run for his money. Her red-hot rhetoric blazes across the pages of her book. The Marylander wonders why her Irish ancestors bothered to immigrate: "I did not then foresee that the scourge of Black Republican rule was to come upon us, and sweep from the New World every vestige of civil rights and freedom, as had been often done in the Old" (157). With the steely temper of Scarlett O'Hara, Greenhow reveals that she was at one point prepared to shoot one of her captors, with nerves so steady "I could have balanced a glass of water on my finger without spilling a drop" (61). In studying the "the tactics of my gaolers," Greenhow paid close attention to one of them, a "burly Irishman, with smooth tongue, professing the religion of my ancestors, that of the Holy Catholic faith" (70). Greenhow made light work of him by playing him against her equally adaptive maid, one "Lizzy Fitzgerald, a quick-witted Irish girl, warmly attached to me as a kind mistress, and knowing nothing which the severest scrutiny could elicit to my disadvantage, [who] entered keenly into the sport, and, to use her own expressive words, 'led Pat a dance,' and, under these new auspices, performed some very important missions for me" (71).

Denied access to all visitors, Greenhow experienced something close to solitary confinement in her own house, complaining in her journal, "Even the religious consolation which is accorded to the lowest criminal in the Christian countries of Europe was denied me. Several members of the Holy Catholic clergy applied to see me, and were repulsed with great rudeness at the Provost-Marshal's, as being '*emissaries of Satan and Secesh*'" (113). Her gravestone marked her "a bearer of dispatches to the Confederate Government," and her funeral at Saint Thomas the Apostle Catholic Church (now deconsecrated) in Wilmington, North Carolina, was overseen by the South Carolina–born Rev. James Andrew Corcoran, DD, who offered a eulogy at once "a touching tribute to the heroism and patriotic devotion of the deceased, as well as a solemn warning on the uncertainty of all human projects and ambition, even though of the most laudable character."[96]

It seems altogether likely that had Rose Greenhow survived the war, she would have landed on her feet and reinvented her political career. Such was the case for Anthony M. Keiley (1833–1905), of Virginia, a fiery pro-Confederate and wartime journal writer who, like Greenhow, showed great aptitude as a so-cial climber despite his Irish Catholic status. Keiley is a man in need of a good biography, or perhaps a family biography that would trace the nine remarkable children of immigrant parents John D. Keiley and Margaret Crowley. The fam-ily's American career commenced when in 1825 Anthony's father followed the weaving industry to Patterson, New Jersey, and thence to Petersburg, Virginia, where he would become a school principal.[97] A profoundly troubled man if his journal tells truly, John Keiley would abandon Catholicism and, apparently, his family, but his descendants would play an important role in toning southern Catholicism.[98]

Of the Keiley siblings, Anthony Keiley has the best claims to being a writer. The eldest of the brood, he became the mayor of Richmond and the leading lay proponent of Catholicism there. Like Florence O'Connor, Keiley was swept up in the rhetoric of the Civil War, but whatever regrets he might have had were kept in check by a droll sense of humor and a naturally wicked satiric sensibility. These stood him well through a star-crossed political career and the reverses of war. Following his graduation from Randolph-Macon College, in a pattern that applies to many of the writers in this study, Anthony Keiley edited a series of newspapers. "By 1852," according to Fogarty, "Keiley was a lawyer, editor of the *Southside Democrat,* and, at the age of twenty his family patriarch." Though adamantly a Catholic, Keiley was not uncritical, describing the poor acclimation of Irish priests who arrived to the democratically ori-ented American church as follows: "Accustomed to the most abject reverence at home, treated with a deference which seems to me unmanly, they come to this country and find themselves *men,* and they are treated as they deserve and no better; perhaps not as well."[99]

His newspaper writings abound in wordplay and Latinisms; for example, he describes a bishop who erects a "useless pile near Richmond" as carried away by the throes of *"cacoethes aedificandi."*[100] As a diehard Democrat, Keiley used his press to break with locals in plumping for Douglas and opposing secession. After secession, he took another stand entirely and defended it in a valedic-torian account of his wartime experiences originally titled *Prisoner of War, or*

Five Months Among the Yankees, Being a Narrative of the Crosses, Calamities, and Consolations of a Petersburg Militiaman during an Enforced Summer Residence North (1865). Later reissued with the short title *In Vinculis,* the book is steadfastly unapologetic:[101]

> Never, in reading or in life, has the word [*rebel*] grated on my ears with the harshness of conclusive reproach. The greatest names in history, science, art, letters, are the names of rebels—rebels to established theories of politics, philosophy, or criticism. Rebellion is the name which Stupidity gives to Progress; it is the name which venerable Error gives to speculating Truth; it is the name which the henchmen of the Dead Past give to the warriors of the Living Present; it is the name which satisfied Ignorance gives to thinking Inquiry; it is the name which Superstition gives to Reform; which Tyranny, in all shapes, gives to Freedom in all; it is the name, in fine, whereby the false in life, in literature, in government, in morals, in law, in science, essays to prejudge and prejudice the true. No creature is too contemptible to brandish this weapon. The King of Lilliput had his rebels. No being is so august as to escape the imputation—the Saviour of the world was called seditious.[102]

Indeed Keiley remained a rebel for life. When Federal forces converged on Petersburg, he stood with the ragtag home guard, whose "stout hearts beat beneath gray locks as beneath gray jackets" (19). Wounded at Malvern Hill, he was elected to the General Assembly. At last captured in Petersburg in 1864, he was sent to federal imprisonment at Cape Lookout, where the southern poet John Banister Tabb also served time before converting to Catholicism and becoming a priest in Richmond. Keiley was later imprisoned, in his words, at "Elmira, New York, a sort of fungus of the Erie Railroad" (101). He documented his travails with a mixture of great pathos and humor and smuggled the journal that would become *In Vinculis* to the South by sewing it up, uncomfortably, in his garments.

In Vinculis remains an important source for scholars of Civil War prison narratives, and it is on *In Vinculis* that Keiley must stake his small portion of literary fame. Though Keiley does not make much of his faith in the book, there are some interesting signs of its presence. For example, he opposes Masonry (187), ridicules a Protestant chaplain whom he calls "a freedom shrieker" (166), and associates New England with anti-Catholic attitudes, ultimately sympathizing with Marylanders, "their State controlled by an abhorred race, imported from New England to colonize and *convert* Maryland" (104). "The clerical world in Puritan-dom," complains Keiley, "has not changed altogether from the happy days of Quaker whipping and Papist hanging, whereof the annals of Connecticut orthodoxy are rife" (166).[103]

In like vein Keiley serves as something of an apologist for Irish Americans. "We hear a great deal of the ignorant Irish, the stolid Dutch, etc.," he wrote, "but it is my deliberate conviction that the French Academy, if put on this soup and prison regimen, and deprived of books, papers, etc., for three months, would relapse into Hottentotish heathenism" (160). In 1878 his name would be invoked in an "improving" scheme for Irish: a short-lived and expressly Catholic colony in Charlotte County, Virginia, "to the number of about 120" of "a sober and industrious class of people," was named Keileyville.[104] Called by Fogarty "one of the few postbellum efforts to establish a Catholic colony outside the Midwest," it was part of an enthusiasm for relieving urban Irish poverty by means of resettlement.[105]

A younger Keiley was, for the moment, thoroughly impenitent and unre-constructed. Recently paroled, he witnessed the final days of the Confederacy as one of its malnourished legislators. Following the war, he would be censored and briefly imprisoned for the partisan views he ventilated in his start-up newspaper titled simply *The News*.[106] Confederate credentials would serve him well during his time in the Virginia House of Delegates (1866–67) and then as mayor of Richmond (1871–76), with Keiley's political career blossoming along-side his friend James Dooley's, the legislator and Irish Catholic veteran. "Keiley and Dooley made no secret of their Catholic faith," notes Fogarty, "but they also joined the Conservative Party that had the dual purpose of enfranchis-ing Virginians who had served in the Confederacy and of excluding the newly emancipated Blacks from office."[107] And Keiley was eminently a Reconstruction pragmatist, as he early signaled in an editorial in the *Petersburg Daily News* in June 1865: "The ship has gone upon the breakers, and is going to pieces—let us make a raft—we may save something and float ashore. He who advises that her head be turned going to sea, is an idiot or a traitor."[108]

The Keiley family would play no little part in the salvage work of Recon-struction and southern racial politics. Keiley's brother John gained a repu-tation as "the best quartermaster in the Confederate Army" and afterwards went to work for James MacMaster's *Freeman's Journal*, the epicenter of Irish American racial politics of the most divisive sort.[109] His brother Benjamin (1847–1925), who became the bishop of Savannah, had also fought for Vir-ginia but with the rising of anti-Catholic sentiment in the South found himself blacklisted as a speaker at United Daughters of the Confederacy rallies. He steered a conservative course to suit the racial politics of his diocese, objecting when President Theodore Roosevelt invited Booker T. Washington to the White House and openly criticizing the president in a scathing Confederate Memorial Day address in 1902.[110] Shortly before his death, however, the Confederate veteran turned clergyman issued a remarkable warning:

> I warmly love the South; and her story, her traditions, and her ideals are very dear to me. . . . But I fully recognize the absolute justice of one charge which is made against her, and I look with grave apprehension to the future, for no people that disregards justice can ever have the blessing of God, and we are guilty of great injustice to the Negro. The Negro was brought here against his will; he is here and he will remain here, and he is not treated with justice by us; nay, I will say that he is often not treated with ordinary humanity.[111]

As his brother Anthony would learn, veteran status and the race card could cut both ways, so considerable political dexterity was required of these neo-Confederate politicians and public leaders. Ultimately Anthony alienated many with his outspokenly unreconstructed stance. In 1879, in an early (and thus potentially seditious) Confederate commemoration, he observed to those assembled at Loudon Park Cemetery in Baltimore that "it was a rebellion *failing* that keeps Poland dismembered and Ireland a province." Once again extolling the virtues of rebels everywhere, but departing somewhat from the usual canons of the Lost Cause, Keiley asserted that neither the defense of slavery nor "any abstract theory of government," but rather a love of "State" and "Home," had led Confederates willingly to the grave. In his concluding remarks, he freely mingled his Catholic theology with the Confederate cause. If the "irreversible judgement of concluded war has determined that we who survive shall be and remain one people," it followed that "with sacramental blood and fire that union has been ordained."[112]

Perhaps unsurprisingly, Keiley's habit of sounding off cost him his bid to be the minister to Rome in 1885. In 1871 he had gone on record decrying Victor Emanuel's deposal of Pius IX, comments (specifically, that Victor Emmanuel's triumph had ushered in "socialists and infidels") that came back to haunt him in 1885.[113] Grover Cleveland's election to the presidency put Keiley in line for political favors, but the media made much of the Irish American's earlier position. The *New York Tribune* suggested that Keiley "would cut a sorry figure" if appointed, and other papers argued that Keiley's "medieval" views were inherently un-American.[114] Sympathetic Catholic papers saw the hand of nativism guiding a smear campaign and sided unanimously with the Virginian.

It was not the end of Keiley's political trouble. With utter disregard for convention, he obtained the required dispensation and involved the bishop in his 1865 marriage to Rebecca Davis (1835–1915), a Jewish woman from Petersburg, Virginia. Had the marriage not provided one of the pretexts for his rejection, Keiley might have been ambassador to the Austro-Hungarian Empire.[115] He had not long secured an alternate post as a judge on the International Court in Cairo when Roosevelt's incumbency dictated administrative change, forcing him to move on. Then, as now, this made for indelicacy, and the *New York Times* reported, incorrectly, that he was grieving over the death of the wife, who outlived him by ten years.[116] He died when he was struck by a carriage on the Place de la Concorde in Paris in 1905, abruptly ending the rapid rise of another Irish southerner born for rebellion.[117]

One of Keiley's best friends during his life, James Dooley, had a brother named John Dooley (1842–1868) who quietly walked away from Georgetown University in the company of southern college students determined to make their way to the front lines. John Dooley would leave behind a singularly accessible and honest account of his service as an Irish Catholic in the Confederate ranks. Naturally, the Keileys and the Dooleys moved in the same circles; the parallels between the families are many. Like A. M. Keiley, John Dooley served time as a war prisoner in Union jails and had eight siblings. His diary mentions the extra tour of guard duty that was imposed on him for a junket to "Jack Keily's [*sic*]," referring to the younger John Keiley, one of Anthony's brothers, who was a good friend to John "Jackie" Dooley. John Dooley's aforementioned brother James entered the Virginia General Assembly following the Civil War and worked closely with Anthony Keiley both in politics and in Catholic lay affairs. The Dooley sisters were quite active in Richmond politics as well, and one of them, Sarah ("Sadie"), entered the Visitation Monastery (as did Nora Keiley), eventually becoming superioress in Richmond. The elder John Dooley retained a close friendship with the United Irishman turned Confederate John Mitchel; the younger John Dooley marched into service alongside Mitchel's son James. Joseph T. Durkin, the Jesuit who published an enduring edition of Dooley's diary, placed the Dooleys at the "center of a social group whose importance has never been sufficiently appreciated—the Irish-Americans of the pre-war South."[118]

The Dooleys' integration into Richmond's social center struck later commentators as remarkable, given that they ought to have been outsiders, without name advantage, and excluded by their faith. Indeed, one historian writing in 1959 commented quizzically on the seeming *impossibility* of Anthony Keiley's rapid social climbing and asked whether his case might not merit a reevaluation of southern Irish Americans' "suitability" to the higher social strata.[119] Laissez-faire attitudes among Richmonders and other Virginians toward religious practice might have permitted the ascendancy of families such as the Dooleys and the Keileys. And the Irish of the period ensured their acceptance in part through their visible patriotism: in 1868 Keiley's supporters would take to the pages of the *Richmond Dispatch* to assure the public that "the good citizens of the Old Dominion may confidently rely on the unfaltering support of their Irish fellow citizens, who have never failed to stand by the side of the native children of the soil whenever her rights or interests were attacked."[120] Such reassurances were needful when, in the 1850s, Archbishop Hughes had publicly broadcast the "mission" of the American church as nothing less than "to convert the world—including the inhabitants of the United States—the people of the cities, and the people of the country, the officers of the navy and the marines, commanders of the army, the legislatures, the Senate, the Cabinet, the President, and all!"[121]

As a young southern patriot, John Dooley, ever soberly inclined toward spiritual introspection, availed himself of slack days on the picket to "slip down to Richmond for a day or two and have an opportunity of going to confession" (94). He made a point of going to Mass on Saint Patrick's Day, partaking of "wine and apple brandy in honour of the day" (173). An unswervable if perhaps secretive Catholic, he is shown by his comments to be bemused by Protestant practices. He twits the chaplain of his regiment when he leaves for the Methodist Conference, "where he expects to enter upon a holier and more profitable sphere of duties than he has found in camp" (72). Unimpressed by the "camp meeting" phenomenon and those who sang "through a *sort* of religious feeling of their own," the Irish Catholic southerner saw his Protestant peers as religiously lax (54).

Yet the journal is hardly sanctimonious. In fact, Dooley's account is so good-natured and so funny—full of his age, with accounts of his flirtation with three snuff-dipping sisters from North Carolina, his drinking capers, and newly acquired wisdom—at turns insouciant, sarcastic, and poignant, that it might be easy to forget that there was a war and that he had wandered into it with all the powerful convictions of a nineteen-year-old. He also has a way of making his a very human testament, swiftly bringing the reader back to realities in a fashion reminiscent of Bret Harte's better work. At Gettysburg the thoughtful teenager watches as the men in his regiment "amuse [them]selves by pelting each other with green apples. So frivolous men can be even at the hour of death" (102). He describes combatants "slipping in the blood and brains of their comrades" (23) and at Sharpsburg a "poor soldier" whose "arm had been shot off and was connected with the elbow only by a piece of skin . . . having slung it over his shoulder just as he would his gun" (54), not to mention decapitations, maimings, burnings, and the achingly slow "twenty-two days" required for shreds of clothing from his maggot-infested bullet wound to "go a distance of about two inches" back to the surface (127). He offers a moving account of a man whipped for desertion (83) and is quick to acknowledge his own cowardice in contrast to the enforced bravery of the ranks. He describes, for instance, the awkwardness of a breathless retreat ("Oh, how I ran!") in which he had constantly to "turn half around in running, so as to avoid if possible" the disgrace of being shot in the back (47). "Poor human nature. Ain't you ashamed of yourself?" he asks at one point as he copes with his wounds (128).[122]

Apart from his boundlessly interesting journal, Dooley's few forgettable poetic scribblings, including a memoriam to John Mitchel's son Willie, resemble Father Ryan's. In the hospital Dooley finds himself beside a "coarse bloated looking Irishman" who is "whining and groaning continually" (109). The "Yanko-Irish" soldier from Lowell, Massachusetts, "had been a soldier under John Mitchel in '48 [the year of the Young Ireland rebellion]." He is delighted to find that Dooley knows so much about the Mitchels, but the tables turn when Dooley and his friend Cronin begin a sharp interrogation,

> asking him how was it possible for him who had in '48 fought or intended to fight for the same cause for which we were contending, how could he consistently turn his back on his principles and for the pitiful hire of a few dollars do all in his power to crush a brave people asserting their right of self government; and now that he was engaged in the cause of tyranny, fighting against honesty, Justice and right, and moreover against those very gallant young men he was seeking to hear of, what, we asked, would Mr. Mitchel think of him? (115–16)

If Dooley's account is to be believed, the soldier was suitably abashed and tearful, hastening away after forcing his southern Irish interrogators to accept blankets and a tent. "He said he didn't know how it was at all, but they got him to enlist and if he got back to Lowell he didn't think they'd 'get him again.'" Dooley goes on to suggest that Meagher's famed Irish Brigade was not so called before later spurious histories applied the name and notes bitterly the irony that crops taken from Marye's Hill, the site of the bloody standoff, had contributed to Irish famine relief in earlier years.

Despite this invective, Dooley had, in the words of Joseph Durkin, "a happy faculty for getting the maximum of enjoyment out of life" (xvii). Was this spiritually attuned and thoughtful youth by his wartime ventures miscast into unwonted bravado as a man of war? He himself often seems at a loss for answers. Facing "the temptation to despair" as Confederate defeat appeared imminent, on one occasion he wrote:

> Has not everything that I have set my heart upon turned out contrary to my desires and expectations? What has my religion always taught me but that worldly desires and pleasures bring with them only bitterness and remorse, and if I had followed the inspirations of my College days and entered the Society of Jesus, would I now be exposed to the misery, wretchedness and homeless wanderings from which I now recoil and in vain endeavour to free myself? (199)

Dooley's account of an education in war is crucial to understanding, on a fully human level, the range of motivations that compelled the southern Irish and how they both fomented and participated in the region's baptism in blood. In the postbellum period Irish Catholic writers in the South drew from a common stock of self-reinforcing legend, actively supported by veterans like John Cantwell. It started taking shape during the war, and within its panoply Father Abram Ryan (1838–1886) might be seen as a kind of patron saint (as Donald Beagle and I argue in *Poet of the Lost Cause*), and Margaret Mitchell as the original gospel writer. Father Ryan's stature protected the Tennessee high school named after him at a time when Klan vigilantism menaced southern Catholics; even Protestant veterans contributed to the profusion of Ryan war memorials that sprouted up around the South, some exported to places as far away as Los Angeles. Father Ryan first served as an iconographer of the Lost Cause and was eventually assumed into its pantheon. Ferociously defensive of his Irish and Catholic identities, this son of poor Irish immigrants was nevertheless admitted into the highest ranks of southern society. He consorted for a time with Jefferson Davis, became an honorific "veteran" whose funeral was attended by many a Confederate military politico, and was an early invitee to the clubby inner circle of the Southern Historical Society.

For Margaret Mitchell's family, of Irish Catholic extraction, Ryan's *Poems* (1879) served as a validation of their cultural southernness. It is not by accident that the kindly Father Ryan always drops in when passing through Margaret

Mitchell's Atlanta in *Gone with the Wind* (1936): "He charmed gatherings there with his wit and seldom needed much urging to recite his 'Sword of Lee' or his deathless 'Conquered Banner,' which never failed to make the ladies cry."[123] A folded, handwritten copy of Ryan's "The Conquered Banner" was discovered among Robert E. Lee's papers, with some sources claiming that he kept it on his person until he died. By the 1930s there had been forty-seven editions of Ryan's collected poems.[124] A copy sat alongside Louis D. Rubin's *South: Modern Southern Literature in its Cultural Setting* on a shelf in Flannery O'Connor's famed library.[125] Ryan's often-copied verses from "A Land Without Ruins," a poem prefaced by a kind of Lost Cause creed that turns southern defeat into southern charm, became an exoneration for a generation of southern politicians. It surfaces, for example, in the recollections of Mary Doline O'Connor, whose biography of her father, the South Carolina congressman M. P. O'Connor, bypasses with politic celerity his Confederate military service.[126]

By melding the otherworldly fatalism of Catholicism with Confederate nationalism, Ryan was one of the very first to literally sanctify the Lost Cause through its baptism in blood. His poetry provided a liturgy of mourning for Civil War veterans, reaching an apex with the commemorations of the United Daughters of the Confederacy era. The poem for which he is most remembered, "The Conquered Banner," furnished the marching music of the Lost Cause and was widely publicly recited. Indeed, these rituals are gently lampooned in an O. Henry story featuring Tommy Webster, an office boy who "got his job by having recited Father Ryan's poems, complete, at the commencement exercises of the Toombs City High School."[127] More recently, "The Conquered Banner" was reprised by polemicists, both pro and con, in the Confederate-flag debates of the 1990s. The nature of the adulation changed from one generation to the next: the patriotic plays in the United Daughters of the Confederacy era yielded to a pop-culture Ryan of the mid-twentieth century, when one could buy a vinyl record of his poems, read about him as a comic-book hero with brilliantine hair, or tune in to a radio biography broadcast on WSM, in Nashville, replete with Alan Lomax musical interludes.[128] Yet the basic irascibility of his principles and character remained changeless. Ryan never shied from controversy in his time; one supposes that the pugilistic priest would be happy to play a part in the unresolved business of the Civil War, for he believed that its business was always unfinished.

A composite of the variations of Ryan legends suggests that he had served as an official chaplain in the Army of Northern Virginia (false), that he befriended and influenced high-level Confederate generals and politicos (largely untrue), and that he participated in the cause through some forty battles and skirmishes from Bull Run to Gettysburg (certainly false). In fact, Ryan did come to befriend a few high-level Confederates and even suggested to Jefferson Davis how he might structure his memoirs as a Confederate vindication, but Ryan's presence at the center of incipient Lost Cause ideologies clearly enlarged the scope of his reputed participation in the war effort. His stock increased as the Lost Cause framework of interpretation was sanctioned by presidents, the media, and northerners. "By the end of the century," writes Donald Beagle, "President William McKinley was reciting his favorite Fr. Ryan verses in the White House and Joseph Pulitzer had made a bequest for a Ryan memorial."[129]

After Ryan's death, Father Benjamin Keiley would travel to the Robert E. Lee Camp Confederate Soldiers' Home (a.k.a. Old Soldiers' Home) in Richmond to preside over the dedication of a massive portrait of Abram Ryan. "So far as I am concerned," he would tell the large assembly of veterans representing Richmond's Catholic societies, "there is involved in the evening's proceedings not merely a patriotic motive, but, I confess the existence of a deeply religious sentiment which both combine to justify it, and at the same time, invest it with a species of sacred surroundings."[130]

How in the world did an Irish American priest come to play a founding role in the invention of Lost Cause ideology? Ryan did so partly through his popularity with common soldiers he encountered on the battlefields and partly through his editorship of a newspaper that became their mouthpiece in the immediate wake of the war, the *Banner of the South.* The Catholic newspaper of the Archdiocese of New Orleans, the *Morning Star and Catholic Messenger,* which Ryan edited for some years, recently digitized for the Library of Congress, remains an underutilized regional treasury of Irish American history. His master stroke, however, was combining Lost Cause rhetoric with Christian narratives of loss and redemption almost universally embraced by white southerners, irrespective of sect or class. It is no exaggeration to say that Father Ryan helped to set up the parallelism that the South, like Christ, would rise again.

Indeed, the Dublin edition of Ryan's *Selected Poems,* with a preface by Rev. Francis Boyle, misstates many of Ryan's biographical data, but it gets things exactly right in dubbing him "the poet of Lost *Causes*" (emphasis added).[131] Considering Ryan within a transatlantic and transnational context draws attention to the fact that he was a spectacularly successful ideologue in his own time. In subtle ways he married the Confederate and Irish causes, and in credible ways he lends support to those who argue that conservative southern politics and Catholicism are naturally conjoined systems of belief. By spinning the rhetoric of the Civil War out of a dialogue with nativism and both the American and the Irish revolutionary past, southern Irish writers sculpted an uncompromising

image of the American South. It would fall to the next generation of southern
Irish writers to repair some of the polemical damage by discovering new narratives for framing regional memory and to establish themselves within it.

Strange to say, these exchanges continue to play out in the present time:
today the Confederate flag is unfurled routinely by Cork fans at Gaelic Athletic
Association matches in Ireland—a surreal spectacle for the southern tourist.
Depending on whom one consults, this is because of the team nickname ("The
Rebels") or County Cork's reputation as the Rebel County (cemented by its un-
compromising part in the Irish Civil War), or because Confederate General Pat
Cleburne was born there, or, least convincing, because the flag's red and white
elements match the team colors.

In Belfast, where Palestinian and Israeli flags symbolize, respectively, nationalist and loyalist leanings, interpreting icons and signals is tantamount to
survival. A friend of mine from Tennessee recalled how at a Derry pub he was
asked if he was "for the black man." His answer in the affirmative was, in Irish
translation, a shibboleth for the pro–civil rights rhetoric of Catholic quarters.
It was also the wrong answer in that place, and he wisely betook himself from
there. Along the same lines, in Belfast's Glenbryn Park there is a mural that
today offers a medley of notables from Belfast, including the flutist Sir James
Galway. Until 2009 it offered quite a different panorama: Stuart, Lee, and Jackson, configured in loyalist style as "the Sons of Ulster who led the Confederate
Army during the War of Northern Aggression." Of course, no mention is made
of the Irish Catholics who fought for that same cause.

Meanwhile, the Dubliner Derek Warfield, a founder of the band the Wolfe
Tones (named for the Irish revolutionary leader—recall the tale of Adam Douglass's father), recently recorded an album titled *The Bonnie Blue Flag*. It offers
an Irish setting of southern Civil War ballads, including "The Wearing of the
Gray," an anthem popular among Confederate veterans that was fashioned
after "The Wearing of the Green," a song that in an earlier iteration had been
"The Rising of the Moon," a ballad celebrating the heroes of the failed United
Irishman Rebellion of 1798, and that air was in turn the marching music for
the Fenian Rising of 1867 . . .[132] Some southern neo-Confederates continue to
rally behind Scottish and Irish banners. Then and now, through nationalism,
sectional division, and Irish experiences of revolution, "high and holy cause[s]"
are united, to borrow Rose O'Neale Greenhow's memorable phrase. One might
say truly of the endless permutations of polemics that while the song changes,
the tune remains the same: some sow the wind, and some inherit it.

OLD IRISH, NEW SOUTH
A Bridge to the Moderns

Si quieres aprender á orar, entra en el mar.
—SPANISH PROVERB, quoted in Lafcadio Hearn's *Chita*

No forcing the sea.
—IRISH PROVERB

We must not forget that real literary art is absolutely impartial
and invariably just. None other can endure.
—JOEL CHANDLER HARRIS

This chapter alights toward the end of the long nineteenth century, really, and considers four writers—Joel Chandler Harris, Kate Chopin, William Marion Reedy, and Lafcadio Hearn—who encountered widely variable circumstances. To generalize about them is to flatten. But if there is a common thread, perhaps it is this: from the first, encounters with American conceptions of race defined them.

So we begin with a redheaded bastard named Joel Chandler Harris (1845–1908), who was by some twist of fate slated to play a significant part in transitioning from Civil War hostilities to the uneasy and often compromised peace that ensued. Nearly too young for conscription to the Confederacy, and certainly too scrawny, the intensely shy writer would become the very public face of the southern storyteller—a spokesman for black and white, antebellum and postbellum, critic and apologist. His life story reveals much about the perception of the Irish in the American South following the Civil War.

The biographer Walter Brasch explains that Harris "considered his red hair, more identified with Irish than American Southerners, as a mark of shame; others compounded his alienation by calling him a 'red-headed bastard.' As an adult, he was still shy, still sensitive about his red hair. . . . Even when his hair and mustache turned from red to a sandy blond, he still believed they were 'fiery red.'"[1] "Redheaded bastard" is a curious old southern derogatory that falls somewhere in a class with "dirty egg-sucking dog." Joel Chandler Harris likely heard the taunt hurled at him more than once during his childhood. He might also have heard the phrase "beaten like a redheaded stepchild," perhaps one notch above being "beaten like a rented mule." To say that Joel Chandler Harris's father was "an Irish day-laborer," as his authorized biographer stated it, meant that he issued from the lowest echelons of the social strata.

It is significant that Harris's biographers have repeatedly foregrounded the *painful* immutability of Harris's red hair as confirmation of his Irish patrimony. "He had flaming-red Irish hair and a slight frame that could well have made him the object of schoolyard ridicule," writes Bertram Wyatt-Brown in *Hearts of Darkness*.[2] Paul Cousins, who authored the first scholarly biography of Harris, references his "diminutive size and pronounced red hair and freckled face," which "set him apart from the others."[3] As a cub reporter in Savannah, he carried the baggage, writes Paul Cousins: "He had become highly sensitive about his awkwardness when he was among girls and women, and particularly so on account of the numerous references in the Georgia press to his personal appearance, especially to his red hair."[4] The staff at the *Macon Telegraph* dubbed him "Pink Top from Old Put";[5] his dispatches were elsewhere described as "Hot shots from Red Hair-is," "Harris Sparks," and "Red-Top Flashes."[6] Lucinda MacKethan identifies his red hair as a source of "lifelong embarrassment."[7] Bruce Bickley, Harris's fine biographer, mentions a theory that Harris habitually wore a hat indoors.[8]

Perhaps it is startling to submit that large-freckled, red-headed Joel Chandler Harris was probably not of Irish stock, although he died verily a Catholic. Rather, Joe Harris, as he was known, was branded Irish. His Irishness was widely accepted, although his own family was nonplussed about this strange theory and seemed at a loss to provide reliable genealogical information. The fact that so many of his homefolks would accept the notion is itself revealing. Harris's distance from the southern center was in some respects liberating, as he subversively undermined the Lost Cause edifice in his writing. His Atlanta was home to a small and vivacious Catholic community with its own norms of respectability; Margaret Mitchell was of them, and she drew on their lore when she wrote *Gone with the Wind*. Harris was an irregular churchgoer, and his decision to convert (or to be converted, as Flannery O'Connor would have it) was his last act of apostasy where southern conformity was concerned. It becomes easier to see how the community would accept the Irish story so readily and why Margaret Mitchell, an Irish Catholic from Georgia, would write to the Postmaster of the United States to urge the issuance of "a special postage stamp commemorating the 100th anniversary of Joel Chandler Harris."[9]

Harris did not, however, wear the scarlet *I* of Irishness during his lifetime, so the question lingers, Where did his "Irishness" come from? A number of theories might obtain. The first possibility, which happens to be both the most obvious and the least likely, is that Joel Harris's father was indeed of Irish stock, as his biographers have insisted. Heedful of the full import of Irish paternity for a southern boy, at least one historian hazards that there is something fishy going on here. Kenneth H. Thomas Jr., whose column "Genealogy" has been a staple of the *Atlanta Journal-Constitution* for many years, investigated Harris's paternity extensively and came away convinced that Harris's father was *not* an Irishman. "Is it possible," he asks, "that there is any truth in Fannie Lee Leverette's candidate [for Harris's father], the Irish day-laborer (or ditcher)? In her novel-like story, he was the easiest type of person to be forgotten, one who was not worthy of decent Georgians. Since he was not a member of their community, no one would remember his name anyway."[10] Separately Thomas wrote, "I do not feel the Irish attribution has any real merit," adding that the derogatory register of the word *Irish* was well understood.[11] Harris's immediate descendants and indeed his wife were also in the dark about their progenitors.

So where did the notion of an Irish father originate? The Harris family had chosen Julia Collier Harris (1875–1967), wife of Joe Harris's son Julian L. Harris (1874–1963), as Joe Harris's authorized biographer—a career-making move for Julia Harris, who was a longtime friend of Margaret Mitchell's mother and would maintain correspondence with Margaret too.[12] Julia Harris refers to Joe Harris in the book as "father," not "father-in-law." But when she realized at the outset that the family had no idea who his father was—as Joe Harris's wife Essie put it, "He never bothered himself with kinfolks"—Julia traveled to Georgia for interviews. There she turned to Fannie Lee Leverette (c. 1870–1956), a source trusted by the family.[13] It was Leverette who first supplied the Irish connection.

The story was touched by blarney, or at least an evolving sense of specificity, in the retelling. Julia's *Life and Letters* (1918) first repeated Leverette's claim that Mary Ann Harris had been enamored of an "Irishman, and from him the boy inherited his bright blue eyes and his sense of humor." In the same passage she avers that Harris's father was a day laborer who worked nearby; Julia Harris only went as far as mentioning "a man inferior in education and station."[14] Kenneth Thomas observes that by 1932 "she changed him to be an Irishman (and Catholic by definition) who came to work on Joel's grandfather's plantation and who was served at a second table." Fannie Lee would later specify that the unnamed Irishman worked a "ditcher." Writing to Lucien Harris in 1941, she identified the putative father as "Pat" Barrett. Thomas has identified a number of candidate "shadow-families," but as yet none of them have been linked with certainty to the Harrises.[15]

As Thomas points out, moreover, Leverette's knowledge of Harris's parentage would have come from her deceased parent, and it cannot be reconciled with what is known of the Harrises' arrival in Eatonton. Either "Fannie Lee actually believed that her story was absolutely true, probably because it came through her mother from her great aunt . . . who had been dead for over twenty-five years, or she made it up."[16] Julia Harris came to have her own doubts about the reliability of her source, expressing her concerns to her publisher. Then, perhaps to cover her tracks, she removed the correspondence about which she was uncertain from the Emory archive for a period of years.

Faced with the choice between changing one's mind and proving that there is no need to do so, almost everyone gets busy on the proof. So Julia Harris enlarged on the story, revised it, and published Leverette's comments as quotations, though they are full of paraphrasing and rearrangement. There is not a shred of evidence that the Irish rumor ever surfaced *before* Harris died, and it did not come from within the family, but from a family acquaintance eager to assert her authority. Her story in turn was accepted by a biographer bent on writing *the* authoritative account. Julia Harris's "Irish scoundrel" story, built on the thinnest of evidence, has proven very durable over the years.

Assuming that Harris's Irishness is more invention than fact, how else might one account for the Irish ascription? Another theory suggests that his paternity could have come from a point of semantic confusion: Georgians held the misconception that all Catholics were Irish and so came to call the faithful "Irish." Writing closer to Harris's time in the Jesuits' *America* magazine in 1928, Michael Kenny explained, "The diocesan catechism, published by Bishop Verot in the [eighteen] 'sixties, propounded the question, 'Are the Irish the only members of the Catholic Church?' and returned the evidently unconvincing answer, 'No, the Irish form but a small part,' etc. Augusta's Catholics are still militantly 'Irish,' and, though but a fraction of the population, have exercised a dominant influence."[17] In fact, Harris stayed on friendly terms with Georgia Catholics throughout his life. He married a Catholic, permitted his children a Catholic education, supported the growth of the Catholic Church, and eventually converted.[18] Hence it is conceivable that Harris's Catholicism introduced the Irish confusion, but this is simply unknowable.

Another possible explanation comes from the shadow of racial admixture that hung over the bastard boy. According to this view, Anglo-Saxons did not mingle, but the Irish did. *Irish* in this sense was a term of resort applied to anyone of impure racial origin. No single ancestry cornered the market on poor whites, but Irish, it was understood, were best fitted to James Henry Hammond's "mudsill" (his term for the inevitable drudge class, which in the South denoted African Americans). In this sense, *Irish* is more a class signifier than a racial one. Moreover, Irish ancestry was a plausible choice for a runaway father, and Harris's "unsouthern" ways made it easier for others to associate him with the lowly Irish. One can profitably unravel the chimerical meaning of *Irish,* and its application to a poor boy named Joe Harris, to appreciate the extent of Irish outsiderism in the South. Take, for example, this excerpt from *Out of the Ditch* (1910) by J. Vance Lewis: "It happened that the overseer, who styled himself Jimmie Welch, was born in Ireland. It was no fault of his that he was born an Irishman, but very inconvenient. He had many peculiar characteristics, and the Negroes who have a saying that 'An Irishman is only a Negro turned inside out' disliked him almost to the extent of hatred."[19]

Elsewhere, a variant of the "Negro turned inside out" comes from the Irish-born Anglican bishop and philosopher George Berkeley. In a kind of open letter to Roman Catholics addressing the wretched state of his "countrymen," he says, "The negroes in our Plantations have a saying—'If negro was no negro, Irishman would be negro.'"[20] William Hannibal Thomas, a free black from Ohio whose lineage traced to Virginia, was ostracized as a race traitor after publishing *The American Negro,* which intones, "There are between negro and Irish character many points of resemblance; for example, indirectness in speech, fondness for personal gossip, religious veneration, and social superstitions. Amusing witticism is also a trait common to both races. The negro, however, lacks continuity of endeavor. His temperament is neither heroic nor stable."[21] Variations on this association were endorsed by black writers as well as white southerners. In her wartime journal, Eliza Frances Andrews wrote, "The negro is something like the Irishman in his blundering good nature, his impulsiveness and improvidence, and he is like a child in having always had someone to think and act for him."[22] A widespread attitude in northern states was finding ready acceptance in southern ones too.[23]

As Peter D. O'Neill and David Lloyd write, following Noel Ignatiev's thesis, "The Irish . . . became white in the United States precisely to the extent that both slaves and free Blacks were denied full citizenship, even humanity." And to some extent this holds for the South, as the case of John England, Charleston's Irish-born bishop and slavery apologist, illustrates. Some southern Irish found themselves supporting the regional racial orders, willingly or not. There is an attendant sense of disappointment that the Irish did not always seek solidarity with the oppressed. As O'Neill and Lloyd put it, "All too often, the query is posed within a somewhat sentimental framework, one shaped by a weak ethical desire that the Irish should have identified with another people who were undergoing dispossession, exploitation or racism—or, indeed, shown solidarity with oppressed people in general."[24] This might be termed the Montserrat Problem, in reference to Donald Akenson's *If the Irish Ran the World,* which observes that Irish slaveholders on the small island rivaled any colonial power in cruelty. Even the Irish nationalist hero Wolfe Tone dreamed of an Ireland that might become a colonial power in the Sandwich Islands, and instances where the Irish played the colonial game to their favor, or the ends against the middle, are not counterfactual fancy, but exampled in history. Now many scholars are framing the discussion in terms of movement and contact.

And contact with black southerners was something Harris had in abundance. If blacks and Irish were seen as standing on a comparable social footing, Joel Chandler Harris was already in a peculiar position because his readers *wanted* to see him as black. When Mark Twain finally goaded the shy writer into joining a short-lived lecture circuit (Harris had turned down Thomas Nelson Page's similar offer), he went to New Orleans and joined his friends Clemens and George Washington Cable, both of whom were polished platform speakers. It ended calamitously. A restive crowd of children gathered at Cable's house to meet the man behind Remus and were dismayed to find that Uncle Remus was in fact a white man. The children's protests deeply discomfited Harris, who always sought the good favor of young ones.

Uncle Remus ensured that Harris would remain an outsider—and thereby made him easier to brand as Irish. Walter Hines Page, who had urged Harris to publish his second novel, *Sister Jane* (1896), sketched Harris's literary persona (Joe Harris) as entirely distinct from his personage (Mr. Joel Chandler Harris) —quite appropriately, since Harris himself only half-jokingly referred to his writing persona as the "other fellow," a bifurcation widely commented upon. (The "other fellow" was a habit of Harris's speech, as evidenced in a letter to his daughter: "No doubt Sister Sacred Heart is of the opinion that I have forgotten my promises, but it was the other fellow who did the forgetting.")[25] Uncle Remus's popularity typecast his creator and fated him to be the "other fellow"; as some critics have observed, Harris *was* Remus. He sometimes referred to himself as Uncle Remus, as when he accepted Twain's praise for his work obliquely: "You cannot escape my gratitude for your kindness to Uncle Remus."[26]

But Harris could not be Remus and be taken seriously. How Harris came to be called Irish is perhaps best explained, then, by a third and final theory: by virtue of his southern outsiderism. The extent of Harris's non-southern-ness can be gauged in three different areas. He kept company with a circle of southern writers who had become disaffected with the region. In both fiction and nonfiction he wrote against lynching and advocated for racial reconciliation, views indeed odious if not mutinous to party-line white southerners. His money and his wife's leadership brought about the construction of Saint Anthony of Padua Catholic Church in the West End of Atlanta, which now serves a predominantly black congregation.

A measure of Harris's nonconformity is reflected in the company he kept on the aforementioned failed book tour: George Washington Cable and Mark Twain completed a coterie of writers who were also "failed" southerners. Cable, for one, knew well the exactions of southern conformity. In midcareer as a man of letters, he moved from fairly innocuous local-color writing to full-fledged social criticism in essays and speeches. The more embattled he felt himself, the more severe his repudiation of southern ways, spurred perhaps by, some have suggested, a dour Presbyterian sensibility in freewheeling, meridional Louisiana. (It might have been this tendency that led Cable to break off with Lafcadio Hearn, who freely owned his dalliances in brothels.) But Cable was no prig, as Edmund Wilson points out, and he mitigated his fundamentalism over time.[27] His fall from southern grace marked a fairly severe transformation, especially considering that Cable had served as a Confederate cavalryman, had been a sworn enemy of New Orleans's hated, occupying General Ben Butler, and had been, at first, a supporter of the slavery status quo.

It bears underscoring that the friendship between Harris and Cable flourished because they were politically in agreement and walked the same thematic ground in their writing. Cable developed a literary corpus that moved away from the harmless *Swallow Barn* (1832) sketches for which southern readers showed such appetite. In *The Grandissimes* (1880) Cable's surrogate-narrator, Frowenfeld, serves as an interested northern observer in New Orleans, supplying a convenient mouthpiece for criticizing slavery and southern provincialism—the same kind of narrative device that Harris often employed. *Madame Delphine* (1881) classically follows a tragic octoroon cursed by her "one drop," a motif that Harris picked up in his own work, especially in his stunning, deeply psychological short story "Where's Duncan?"[28] A Cable story with a black hero who was brutally cut down for being "uppity" was regarded as unprintable for its "unmitigatedly distressful effect"; Harris too wrote of black characters held in contempt for demanding respect.[29] Cable also took on prison reform and the South's educational system, two of Harris's favorite editorial hobbyhorses.

In view of Cable's fate, Harris clearly felt himself gagged. He would offer a treatment of southern intolerance, but he would write under one of his fictional guises, in this case the persona of a book reviewer he named Anne Mac-Farland, styled as a wealthy Georgia woman living abroad. In one MacFarland piece he raised the specter of his old friend's scapegoating: "Those who would understand what I mean would do well to recall the hot criticism and social ostracism occasioned by George W. Cable's extraordinary studies of Creole life in New Orleans. Mr. Cable was as sensitive in regards to his art as his critics were with respect to the life he depicted, and he straightaway betook himself to alien skies, bag and baggage."[30] Having run afoul of Cash's savage ideal, Cable found himself permanently shut out, a wounded Confederate veteran left to spend his days in New England. Adumbrating a later generation of writers, he counted himself a southern exile, a designation in which he could take a certain dignified solace but that was also distressful. He still "belonged peculiarly to the South," but, Cable complained, the South could no longer be considered "a free country."[31]

Nor did Harris consider the South a "free country" in that sense. He had Cable as a caution. As a southerner living with his family in the South, Harris walked a fine line. He did not exaggerate when he observed that William Makepeace Thackeray "took liberties with the people of his own blood and time that would have led him hurriedly in the direction of bodily discomfort if he had lived in the South."[32] When Twain was being lambasted for *Adventures of Huckleberry Finn* (1884), Harris flew to his friend's defense:

> I know that some of the professional critics will not agree with me, but there is not in our fictive literature a more wholesome book than *Huckleberry Finn*. It is history, it is romance, it is life. Here we behold human character stripped of all its tiresome details; we see people growing and living; we laugh at their humor, share their griefs; and, in the midst of it all, behold we are taught the lessons of honesty, justice and mercy.[33]

If Harris, like Twain, was a "failed southerner," it might have been easier to think of him as Irish, and if he was aware of Irish ancestry, one might expect a hint of it in his voluminous writing. In fact, Harris does make some passing mention of the Irish. Once asked what "gift of nature" he would most like to have, Harris answered, "the gift of gab." His biography of Henry W. Grady carefully reproduces Grady's speech decrying Irish landlordism.[34] In a letter to his daughter Lillian he describes a Mr. Benson, "one of the most delightful men I ever met. His brogue is as rich as cream, and delicate as a faint whiff of the shamrock bloom."[35]

In "Why the Confederacy Failed," a chapter in *On the Wing of Occasions* (1900), Harris introduces an Irish menial who is also a Confederate sympathizer. The story unfolds in a New York hotel. A southerner who chats with the Irishman is asked to take his regards to James Nagle, in these terms: "The Third Georgia is Colonel Nisbet's ridgment; 'tis in Ranse Wright's brigade. To be sure, I know 'em well, sir. Should ye be goin' to Augusty, an' chance to see James Nagle, kindly tell 'im ye've seen Terence an' he's doin' well. He's me father, sir, an' he thinks I'm in Elmiry prison."[36] Terence garrulously relates the saga of his escape with the help of Father Rafferty, his coconspirator.

More Irish characters carry out an elaborate stratagem to smuggle information about Sherman's movements out of the city. Irish cops are in on the act, and their role is to whisk a spy named Fluornoy from a crowd ("Cheese it an' move on, ivery livin' sowl av ye!"). It is not Harris's best writing, but it shows his ear for dialect and his familiarity with the conventions of stage Irish and the stock Paddy characters of the period. What it does not show is a special affinity for the Irish or a predisposition for depicting them as fully fleshed characters. The self-described "accidental writer" seems to approach the Irish accidentally, not ancestrally.

Before "Why the Confederacy Failed," Harris had created an Irish Union sharpshooter named Private O'Halloran, who stands at the center of "Comedy of War" in *Tales of the Home Folks in Peace and War* (1898). A "big, laughing Irishman [who] liked his pipe, especially when it was full of tobacco," this gentle, rascally giant has "Samson-like arms" and "a large spark of humor glistening in his fine black eyes."[37] He is apparently good-hearted too, having spared a boy Confederate from Union bayonets.

Capers ensue in a scene of doubling: A slave named Tuck encounters the Irishman, who draws a line in the sand. O'Halloran explains to Tuck that he is free on the one side of it but not on the other. Of course, the comedy of the scene is complete only if one sees the Irishman and the slave as equals. The incredulous slave decides to see how freedom "feels" by stepping over and calls back to his young master, who waves him off. In a later scene that links black and Irish, O'Halloran strikes up an unlikely friendship with his one-time enemy, whom he had described earlier as "a red-headed flannel-mouthed Irishman." When he recognizes a Confederate sharpshooter and scout named Jack Kilpatrick on the field, he holds fire, declaring, "Tis the young Johnny, or Oi'm a naygur!" (294). The story presses the conclusion that O'Halloran is indeed, on a symbolic level, a black man, a kind of good-hearted buck Irishman. The tale leaves little doubt that Harris put the Irish on a close footing with slaves in the social hierarchy.

These Irish entries—written during a period when Tom Watson was making trouble for the Irish in Atlanta—were written to suit Samuel McClure, the Irish immigrant whose magazine literally made his name a household world. After running "The Comedy of War," he wrote Harris to ask for more Irish shenanigans stories: "Did not that Irishman, O'Halloran, have any other adventures?" he asked. "It seems to me he is too good to waste on one short story. Cannot you give me four or five short stories like 'The Comedy of War'? If you could have the same character in the heart of the stories, or as a central figure, it would make a capital book, and we could publish it, giving you a good royalty."[38] But Harris obliged him with only one other O'Halloran chapter, "The Ambuscade." Irish characters would be understandably rare on the pages of *Uncle Remus's Magazine,* which held to its motto, "Typical of the South, National in Scope." Perhaps because of its national scope, it atypically picked up a sentimental bit of Irish fluff by Virginia Woodward Cloud titled "The Other Man," the only known piece to run during Harris's editorship that takes an Irish setting and themes.

Ultimately, Harris's ethnic Irish tales demonstrate that he was willing to write what sold. The more profound story, where Harris's "Irishness" is concerned, is in the way the spirits of conformity and rebellion contended within him. Bertram Wyatt-Brown has argued that Harris was himself a trickster who both cottoned to and resented white hierarchy. By making him the son of an Irishman, the last trick was played on him. That we still understand so little of who Harris was and where he came from invites further investigation. One might be tempted by the delicious possibility that "Irish" was a front for racial "impurity" in Harris's lineage. The intrigue is heightened by the weird imagination of the psychically anguished scene in his story "Where's Duncan?" in which a mixed-race bastard boy sets his ancestral house on fire and sees his revenge perfected in his father's murder. A hint of something peculiar in Harris's background surfaces in Mary Fielder's journal entry in which she mentions that he had "not only poverty to contend with, but other things."[39] Harris left the door open to speculation when he wrote cryptically in 1870, "My history is a peculiarly sad and unfortunate one."[40]

But the statements should be considered within the most skeptical contexts. Fielder may simply have been referring, with Victorian delicacy, to the boy's bastardy, or Harris might have been acknowledging the alcoholism that debilitated him in the last years of life. Finally, the notion that Harris came from mixed racial stock remains more grounded in irresponsible speculation than in proof. It is far safer to say that the ascription of Irishness, and the southern public's willingness to accept it, bears witness to the fact that this most canonical of southern writers was a southern outsider during his own lifetime. The conventional narrative of Harris's life is perhaps too staid and inert, and the time is nigh for an exhumation—not of his bones (although the option has been suggested as a means of settling his parentage, genetically, once and for all!) but of his work and his biography. The question of his invented Irishness is most instructive for what it says about the reputation of the Irish in the South. It is appealing to think that Joe Harris's extraordinary empathy, as well as his rare lapses into mean conformity, came from being something less than fully white in the eyes of his society. And that is precisely what I mean to suggest of this southern Irish writer who wasn't.

For exact contemporaries Kate Chopin (1851–1904) and Lafcadio Hearn (1851–1904), racial self-definition would be a defining concern. Their Catholicism supplied a vital connection to a cosmopolitan Catholicism with a Continental critical perspective that was proto-Joycean. Chopin imagined a social order that was largely arbitrary, one that might unwittingly flash signs of its own artifice. She drew attention to the joints in the architecture, the areas where questioners failed to fulfill a social role or met misery by obeying the prevailing social paradigm. In minding these gaps, she had outgrown the omniscient narrator and set about inventing some new devices—coy pauses, arch substitutions, and comment withheld to significant (and sometimes sarcastic) effect. Teresa Gibert rightly observes that Chopin's genius for the implicature—that is, something meant, implied, or suggested as distinct from what is said—permitted her to say much more in writing than might otherwise have been possible in her time.[41]

What she said through indirection endears her to our own time. The welter of critical opinion regarding whether or not she was properly a modernist has subsided, and even those who reject, on principle, that she was an aesthetic modern would probably admit that, on balance, her forward-looking work at the very least foreshadowed the movement. She may not have been a fully credentialed modernist—how could she be, since she did not live to see the Great

War?—but this is largely a matter of terminology. Chopin's influence on the moderns who followed her attests to the broad expanse of her reach.

Her views of religion were also rather modern. In the short short story "The Night Came Slowly" Chopin excoriates a man who teaches "Bible Class," "detestable with his red cheeks and bold eyes and coarse manner and speech. What does he know of Christ?" she demands. "Shall I ask a young fool who was born yesterday and will die tomorrow to tell me things of Christ? I would rather ask the stars: they have seen him."[42] In *The Awakening* (1899) she wrote that Edna Pontellier was "beginning to realize her position in the universe as a human being, and to recognize her relations as an individual to the world within and about her. This may seem like a ponderous weight of wisdom to descend upon the soul of a young woman of twenty-eight—perhaps more wisdom than the Holy Ghost is usually pleased to vouchsafe to any woman." Knowledge is tied to the Trinity, but there is perhaps a sardonic note here, and an implicit criticism of the patriarchal purveyors of certitude. "Lilacs" is Chopin's archetypal Madonna/whore story, rather literally illustrated, and a brilliant study in the connections between Catholic self-denial and self-destruction.[43]

In short, Chopin was what the Catholic writer David Lodge calls himself, an "agnostic Catholic," a term not as oxymoronic as it might seem. Because of that fact, it is easy to undervalue how seriously she took faith, both in her life and in her writing. Indeed, her writing began under Irish Catholic auspices. Sister Mary Philomena O'Meara, a first-generation Irish American, was a fresh-faced young nun with a knack for intuiting her students' talents. Fortunately for literary posterity, she required Kate Chopin (then Kate O'Flaherty) to keep a commonplace book, which now provides the earliest sample of her writings. "As a child," Emily Toth writes, "Mary O'Meara had been much like Katie O'Flaherty: precocious and willful, curious, and imaginative."[44] Kate's "much-loved teacher" coaxed out whatever there was of the serious student in her sixteen-year-old charge, who was not known for applying herself to her studies.

Some of Kate's youthful exposure to racial difference is recorded in the commonplace book. Among the verses she copied one finds a carefully transcribed description of Mrs. Jamison, a character in *Sketches of Art* (1857), by the Irish writer Anna Brownell Jameson: "Her features are regular, and her mouth—, the most expressive of them, has a ripe fullness and freedom of play peculiar to the Irish physiognomy, and expressive of the most unsuspicious good-humor."[45] Kate O'Flaherty's best friend, Kitty Garesché, described her friend as "an Irish beauty" who wore an "arch, sprightly expression" and generally resembled her father.[46] For her multiethnic Saint Louis audience she geared her high-school graduation address to "National Peculiarities," a composition now sadly lost.[47]

Chopin later translated a French piece about phrenology that tendered such observations as the following: "all peoples of Cimbric origin, those inhabiting the borders of the Mediterranean, North-Germans, Swedes and Norwegians are dolicocephalous (having elongated skulls), whilst peoples of Celtic origin, Southern Germans, Austrians, Hungarians, Swiss, Irish and Gaelic are on the contrary, brachycephalous (round-skulled)."[48] Racial taxonomy by craniometry was in the air, and the adolescent girl would have been attentive to descriptions that touched on her family's ethnicities. Around Saint Louis, Kate's Irish-born father, Thomas O'Flaherty, was a well-heeled up-and-comer who gave to the usual Catholic charities and participated in the usual Irish fraternal organizations.[49] He died in a train accident when she was just five years old. The extent of his influence on her during her young years can probably be summed in two formative incidents: first, her enrollment at Sacred Heart Academy, and second, a day on which she accompanied him on his work rounds (with an obligatory first stop at the cathedral).

Following her father's death, Kate was raised by the women of a robustly French Catholic household. In maturity Kate Chopin would write Irish characters who reflected the ambivalence of a girl trained to be a proper Saint Louis Creole. Her great-grandmother Victoria Charleville considered the O'Flaherty surname "an unpronounceable Irish barbarism" and took every measure to ensure that Kate would speak and write impeccable French.[50] Yet even after her father was gone, there was an Irish influence in her household. Following a trend in postwar Saint Louis, Kate's family brought in live-in Irish servants to replace slaves, "three women in their twenties and a thirteen-year-old girl," though "if Kate befriended the youngest Irish servant, who was about her age," writes Toth, "no one recorded anything about that."[51]

One wonders, then, what her Irish inheritance was and whether she had any meaningful sense of Irish ethnic identity. Some of Chopin's early critics attributed her skill as a *seanachie* to her Irish roots. "She was of Celtic blood and spontaneously a storyteller," wrote the critic Fred Lewis Patee in *The Cambridge History of American Literature*.[52] Seen through her fictional opus, though, Kate Chopin's views of the Irish seem fragmentary, incomplete, and thin. Very few of her stories mention Irish characters, and only one of them, "A Vocation and a Voice," offers an Irish protagonist. The tale was written during Chopin's most productive period, 1894–96. Thomas Haddox finds in the *Vocation* story collection Chopin's "portrayal of Catholic decadence" in tales "establishing a fundamental tension between subversive homoerotic pleasure and the unyielding reality of the southern social order, with its codes of honor, gentility, and silence about sex."[53]

Many of the *Vocation* stories were composed during the period when Chopin operated a literary salon from her home that became *the* gathering place for the Saint Louis literati. Indeed, she might have learned something about sexual decadence and eccentricity from the modestly bohemian leanings of her friends, a group that her son Felix would remember as "a liberal, almost pink-red group of intellectuals, people who believed in intellectual freedom and often expressed their independence by wearing eccentric clothing."[54] Among her guests was Billy Reedy, a son of Kerry Patch, the Saint Louis Irish faubourg where "it was still permissible to keep goats and raise cabbage." He would become a friend and, some have suggested, enter Chopin's fiction.[55] Certainly, young and spontaneous Robert Lebrun, who brings back Edna Pontellier's memories of youth and desire, and the troublemaking playboy Alcée Arobin might bear a composite of Reedy's influence in *The Awakening*. After all, Reedy entered Chopin's life in the years before the novella was published, precisely when the widowed writer might be given to wistfulness.

Reedy was an Irish American beginning to make a name for himself in Saint Louis. He reinvented the *St. Louis Mirror* from its days of gossip-column notoriety, transforming it into one of the most influential journals of its kind with a circulation outstripping those of both the *Nation* and the *Atlantic*. In time, Edgar Lee Masters would without exaggeration dub him the "Literary Boss of the Middle West." Reedy's talent for discovering and rediscovering now-canonical writers was legendary. He proclaimed Hawthorne and championed Dickinson in a period when she remained obscure. He was among the first to recognize Chopin's and Dreiser's talent (Dreiser would call Reedy a "Balzac *manqué*"); he would see Edgar Lee Masters's *Spoon River Anthology* (1915) into print; and he brought "Pater, Hardy, Yeats, Shaw, and the French symbolists" to American readers (though he would misjudge Yeats at first).[56]

Twelve years Reedy's senior, Kate Chopin had in certain respects lived a good deal more than he. She had only lately returned to Saint Louis following her husband's death. Now she faced the necessary business of putting her life in order and making a career of writing in her hometown, of seeking like-minded people perhaps in part to simply convince herself that this might be possible. Would she be remembered for more than cadging local-color bylines in domestic journals? What might she have made of the bluntspoken, canny (he had graduated from Saint Louis University at age eighteen), and frequently outrageous Reedy when he arrived on the literary scene as a rakish young man of thirty?

She likely saw him as an Irish boy from the other side of the tracks, the Kerry Patch side, where Kate's contact had been limited to her brief attendance at the Academy of the Visitation. She was groomed for better places. Reedy's parents valued education without having any; his mother supposedly knew no Latin, but "would clench her clay pipe in her teeth and memorize the inflections as the boy recited them, sure to catch him out if he later made a slip." His father was an Irish immigrant who supposedly "toiled on Arkansas levees beside slaves." Later appointed a policeman who became "'night chief' in the headquarters of the bloody third," he could expect the scorn of fellow immigrants on a dangerous beat where "thirty-eight members of the force [were] slain in action." Reedy would recall "a sad man and quiet" whose "affections were treasured almost as secrets." Patrick Reedy's distant and troubled relationship with his son is in keeping with the culture of Irish American fathers, just as his mother's overweening presence is a familiar stereotype: an absentee father who believed in the necessity of physical force for getting by in America and a mother who expected perhaps more than her son or her husband could give. When eulogizing his father, William Reedy would note the hardships his father faced, but he would coldly dismiss the two thousand dollars the man set aside by a lifetime of scraping and frugality as a "small thing to look at as the result of a life of seventy-four years."[57]

Even if he chafed at his father's "rigid devotion to law and property," William inherited many Irish attitudes from his parents.[58] Years later, when he acquired a twenty-seven-acre farm, he would nostalgically call his rural retreat "Clonmel," after the hard-bitten land of his ancestors. Also the town that Father Abram Ryan's family had come from, it was notorious both for land evictions and for its restive inhabitants, whose suspicion of authority was deeply engrained.[59] On returning from the tumult of England after the Great War, Reedy would declare, "More democracy is the cure for the war-madness. There is not enough of it now anywhere." In his politics and in his speech there were always hints of Ireland, as when he instructed an Irish maid to boil his eggs "for [the time it would take to recite] three Hail Marys."[60] Like Lafcadio Hearn, as a cub reporter Reedy attended multiple executions (he claimed as many as twenty) and often sympathized with the condemned. He wrote for the papers that the Saint Louis Irish liked, papers aligned with the values of southern Democrats—papers that had sent Kate Chopin's brother to war. With the usual measure of Irish attention to class difference, he also wrote romantically of the era that predated him, when wealth was human property and the leading ladies of Saint Louis "wore a nigger around every finger"—a sphere more familiar to Kate Chopin.[61]

In contrast to the Reedys, the O'Flahertys had four slaves, plainly signaling the family's social aspirations. Within the ethnic landscape of the city, Saint Louis's Irish community was locked in perpetual competition with pro-Union German immigrants, a rivalry that galvanized young Abram Ryan. The Irish ruefully remembered the Camp Jackson incident in which primarily German troops had fired on pro-secessionist civilians, touching off citywide riots and prompting many Irish to side with the Confederacy. For her part, Kate Chopin became a darling of Saint Louis Confederates when she ripped a Union flag down from the door of her home and refused to say where it had gone. Narrowly escaping charges of sedition, she was nicknamed the "Littlest Rebel."[62] Her family had staked their fortunes on the southern vision of American government, but Chopin would write later of the bitterness of the war and would always regard the loss of her brother as a great stroke.

Spared a Kerry Patch upbringing, Chopin nevertheless remained in a position to empathize with Reedy and to observe the war between spirit and flesh that so many ultimately believed defined him. She saw too his bluster, his generosity, and his constitutional incompatibility with polite society. The Chicago poet Harriet Monroe would later eulogize Reedy by saying, "He could have held his own in the Mermaid Tavern, or across the table from Dr. Johnson, or under the dialectics of Socrates or at the Gargantuan feasts of Rabelais. Indeed, his spirit really belonged to more spacious times."[63] Whatever Chopin saw in outsize Reedy (their mature acquaintance could only have lasted about ten years before her death), they were bound in friendship by their love of literature.

Certainly Toth's summation of Reedy—"a former altar boy . . . [and] a heavy drinker noted for boorish and lecherous conduct"—seems considerably more severe than that of Chopin, whose work Reedy frequently published.[64] He did struggle with alcoholism, becoming a pariah both in the eyes of his church and in Saint Louis generally after a "Vegas wedding" in which, after a drunken tear, he sobered up to the realization that he had gotten married. He could not have been cheered to learn that the marriage had been conducted by a priest he knew and that the bride, Agnes "Addie" Baldwin, was a madam of Saint Louis's White Castle brothel.[65] For too many, this marriage, which took place about the time that his friendship with Kate Chopin was developing, constituted the only significant datum of his life.

Though he would rail against the "social evil" in his columns with unmistakable self-loathing, Reedy could never undo the knot he had tied. He held the former Archbishop Kenrick (who confirmed Kate Chopin and presided when Abram Ryan took holy orders in Saint Louis) in highest regard, but his successor, John Joseph Kain, whom Reedy dubbed "Tittlebat Titmouse Torquemada" in a *Mirror* column, was another story. Reedy simply could not forgive Kain, who took a hard stand against divorce, for refusing to annul the writer's ill-advised marriage. He would air his views in the *Mirror* by denouncing the "unqualified submission to authority" that Catholicism demanded. "There is no use arguing about it," Reedy complained. "If two people love and want to be married, and the Church says 'Nay,' they will marry. Excommunication will not worry them."[66] For good measure, after his second marriage, to a socially respectable woman who predeceased him, Reedy took for his third wife yet another madam.[67] Stinging from his excommunication, he might have found in Kate Chopin someone with similar reservations regarding a church from which she was estranged yet to which she was still attached.

Reedy's war with flesh and his sense of entrapment by the church touched on issues close to Chopin's heart. Indeed, Reedy would mount a spirited defense of Oscar Wilde during his 1895 trial, a signal moment in the history of fin-de-siècle decadence that transpired during the time of Chopin's salon meetings. His confrontational style and his travails might well have provided some grist for Chopin's mill. Among the last of Kate Chopin's collected stories is one that investigates the complexity of Irish Catholic faith, class awareness, and guilt. At first blush, "A Vocation and a Voice" might seem to stretch Chopin's point of view, since her omniscient narrator hovers around a male character from the blue-collar ranks of Saint Louis. But William Reedy certainly furnishes a type, if not the model, for the story's protagonist.

Though the "boy" who emerges from "the noise and grime of 'The [Kerry] Patch'" is never named, Irish names do surface in "A Vocation and a Voice," including Mrs. Donnelly and Father Doran. The "boy" of the story is on the verge of manhood and has a growing sense that he is merely a replaceable part in the social machine—"a vague sense of being unessential which always dwelt with him." The altar boy heeds Father Doran's admonitions to avoid cursing, his eyes like Reedy's, "dark and quiet . . . not alert and seeking mischief, as the eyes of boys usually are." (A New York Times interviewer would one day liken Reedy's gaze to the "concentrated search of a railroad engineer.")[68]

One already has the sense that the boy is somehow a displaced person within his community, or at least in some uneasy relation with it, so it comes as no great surprise when he realizes he has nothing to lose by leaving it. The generic protagonist drifts out of the Patch on a fine autumn day and falls in with a fortune-teller, "Suzima," whose real name is Susan. She travels with one

"Gutro, otherwise the Beast," frequently "drunk and abusive," whose "dialect, when he spoke, was as indescribable as his origin was undiscernable." Suzima's gypsy affectations are simply part of a gypsy persona, but Chopin carefully marks her handler Gutro as the genuine article. One wonders whether Chopin had read Lafcadio Hearn's firsthand account "A Gypsy Camp: A Group of Veritable Bohemians," first published in the *Cincinnati Enquirer* on April 21, 1873: "The contrast between [their] habitations and the fat, sleek horses and stout wagons tells nearly the whole story," wrote Hearn. As in Chopin's story, the gypsies Hearn described survived largely by the "foraging" of the men. "Indeed, the indications were that their thefts are of the most trifling character. It is probable, however, that Chickens would differ from us in this estimate of the honesty of the genuine Bohemian," Hearn added.

Chopin's "unconventional *ménage*" travels to the "South country," where the boy chances upon a priest who is surprised and gratified to learn that the young bohemian is a Catholic. The boy takes on altar duty in town and, the reader learns, rehearses "the service half audibly." After attending a Catholic Mass, the irreligious Susan considers incorporating elements of ecclesiastical hocus-pocus into her fortune-telling routine. Though he admires her powers of invention and the fake Egyptian accent she uses for fortune-telling, the boy rebukes her—"Why, it'd be a sin"—his squeaky-clean Irish Catholic breeding showing through. Suzima sees signs that he is getting a trifle too attached to the village priest, and the reader is invited to *cherchez la femme*: "He had seen indistinctly the shadowy form of Suzima lurking nearby, waiting for him."

Sent on an errand by the increasingly querulous Gutro, the boy from Kerry Patch finds her bathing, naked, in a river: "He saw her as one sees an object in a flash from a dark sky—sharply, vividly. Her image, against the background of tender green, ate into his brain and into his flesh with the fixedness and intensity of white-hot iron." Male desire is quite vividly imagined by Chopin, who understands how intensely visual such an encounter might be. The toothsome girl covers up, but the damage has been done. He cannot escape the *image*.

One cannot say for certain that Chopin modeled Suzima, with her "impulsive tender feeling for helpless and dependent things," on one of Reedy's real-life flames, though if she did, Addie Reedy would furnish the obvious candidate. Susan/Suzima's attraction to the garish trappings of gypsy culture point to a similar desire to escape from the petit-bourgeois sameness of American life, a desire expressed by many of the realist writers Reedy championed, notably Dreiser; Reedy himself protested the "dismal respectability" of Saint Louis.[69] In Chopin's story, respectability is threatened by the sexual mores of another class. Chopin writes, "The boy was not innocent or ignorant," yet it is Suzima who inevitably initiates sexual contact with a touch of her bare foot: "she folded her arms about him," *she* "drew him close," and *she* "held him fast." After tussling with the devilish Gutro and parting ways, the boy wanders directly into a nearby monastery, "the building on the hill surmounted by a gilded cross," where he might invest his energies entirely in religious vocation. Based on his banter with the monks there, it is clear that they are Irish ("You'll not be telling me it's yourself that lifted the stone, Brother Ludovic"). Of a spring day the boy/brother surrenders himself once again to his moonlit vision, and somewhere between dreams and waking he jumps the proverbial wall, which Thomas Haddox interprets as an evasion of homoerotic decadence.[70]

Chopin upends conventional expectation about gender roles. Notwithstanding Freud's declamations, the woman of the story is the force driving the boy *away* from society, rather than forcing his hand to the social contract. Moreover, it is a trope of Catholic hagiography to relate, in frankly erotic terms, the ecstasy of saints; witness Bernini's famous sculpture *The Ecstasy of Saint Therese* and many of Flannery O'Connor's short stories. Saint Therese was struck by a "flame-tipped arrow"; in "A Vocation and a Voice" the boy's flesh "tingled and burned as if pricked with nettles." The question is, who or what does the pricking? Implicitly, Catholicism recognizes the bonds between spiritual and sexual fulfillment, wherein divine creative power is acknowledged in desire. The fundamental good/evil dichotomies of Catholicism are to some degree a matter of the boy's puerile invention, a failed attempt to interpret the good priest's parting words to him: "Forget not your creator in the days of your youth." The boy wars not merely against his sinful nature but against nature's designs for youth. In a Jansenistic framework, *remembering* one's Creator is perhaps not as important as *not forgetting* him, and youthful impulses are to be checked. The story, set in a lush southern landscape, illustrates nicely the deep-seated conflicts of conformity and rebellion so important to Irish Catholic identity.

Similarly, there is a trace of Jansenism, reconfigured, in Edna Pontellier's remembered Presbyterian upbringing in *The Awakening*. A biographical reading of the book suggests an important substitution: when Edna Pontellier recalls a summer day from girlhood in Kentucky when she waded through prairie grass, those who know Chopin's early life will see shades of an earlier Saint Louis perched on the edge of the prairie. That fateful day foreshadows Edna's last journey into the waters, as it is dreamily recollected to Madame Ratignolle: "Likely as not it was Sunday . . . and I was running way from prayers, from the

Presbyterian service, read in a spirit of gloom by my father that chills me yet to think of."[71]

One thinks also of Thomas O'Flaherty taking his young daughter to Mass as Edna continues, "I was a little unthinking child in those days, just following a misleading impulse without a question." She describes a religiosity that wanes after age twelve, yet in her evocation of the sensation of being "aimless" in the meadow, one detects the strong presence of a faith abandoned. In a subtle subversion, Chopin casts a scene in which Mr. Pontellier will discuss his wife's mental health with the family friend and physician Dr. Mandelet. Mr. Pontellier, who describes himself as coming "of that old Creole race," expresses no reservations whatsoever about his wife's piety. As the doctor fishes for a hereditary precedent to Edna's "peculiarity," he points to the solidity of her Presbyterian ancestors: "The gentleman, her father, I have heard, used to atone for his week-day sins with his Sunday devotions."

Once again, Presbyterianism makes a good stand-in for a self-denying, Jansenistic Catholicism remembered from youth. Likewise, the irrepressible sensuality of Mexico—the atmosphere that keeps Arobin traipsing back to that country's tourist kiosks and prayer beads—is contrasted with Edna's buttoned-down spirituality. So, too, the Mediterranean Catholicism of her Creole confidante, Adèle Ratignolle, whose Catholic womanhood—sensually honest and unapologetic—is at odds with a self-abnegating Irish Catholicism. Such fires raged in Chopin's life too; in *The Awakening,* they are dramatized, at times, as veiled allegory.

A few other Chopin stories make limited use of Irish ethnic themes. "A Matter of Prejudice" offers a Creole named Madame Carambeau, "a woman of many prejudices," who may have been modeled in part on Chopin's father-in-law. Dr. Jean Baptiste Chopin hated all things not French and many others besides. As Toth put it, "Kate Chopin did not have an Irish brogue—but she had begun life as an O'Flaherty, which was bad enough in Dr. Chopin's eyes."[72] In any event, the Francophile Mme Carambeau experiences a change of heart after becoming attached to an "American" child whom she takes under her wing. This leads her to some peculiar and unprecedented behavior, including attending Mass at (Chopin's own) Saint Patrick's, where she sits through "a lengthy English sermon, of which she did not understand a word." She declines the help of the child's "red-cheeked Irish nurse-maid" (recall the "detestable," "red-cheeked" Bible instructor) on the "original theory that the Irish voice is distressing to the sick."

Finally, "Nég Créol" offers a more direct look at the Irish, again in contrast to Creole culture. "Purgatory Mary," "a perambulating soul whose office in life was to pray for the shades in purgatory," appears along with an "Irishwoman with rolled sleeves" named Bridget (given "Brigitte" by Mamzelle Aglaé). Both, it can be inferred, are Irish. Purgatory Mary specializes in small-time simony, if Aglaé is to be believed. When the Mamzelle passes away, shrill Purgatory Mary fetches a priest, shrives the body, and starts the vigil; Bridget goes for a doctor. A child who peers in on the proceedings, fascinated, is reprimanded: "Will ye get down on yer knees, man, and say a prayer for the dead!" The child "refused to obey. He approached the bed, and laid a little black paw for a moment on the stiffened body." This prompts Purgatory Mary to mutter, "The black h'athen!"—though she is in the middle of a rite that has many heathen trappings. The tableau of cast-off, lower-class characters once again illustrates the perils of a sin-measuring and prescriptive faith that Flannery O'Connor termed "slide-rule" Catholicism.

Among other New Orleans ethnicities considered in her fiction, the Germans, rivals to the Irish in both New Orleans and Saint Louis, fare little better. "A Shameful Affair" and "Wiser Than a God" both place German characters on a footing with the Irish. Though she was quite capable of writing sympathetically about the underclass, Chopin was endowed with some of the prejudices of her French upbringing, including an awareness of the kind of double standards that permitted Frenchmen to take mistresses. Elizabeth Fox-Genovese offered her own explanation for Chopin's apparent comfort with human estates as they pertained to slavery:

> It's important not to underestimate the influence of her Catholicism which was quite comfortable with the idea—in fact promoted the idea—that every human person could be excellent, valuable in the eyes of God, without occupying the same social situation or standing, without playing the same social role. . . . So I think she was very comfortable with difference in social station, that she did not spend her life feeling that it was an acute injustice that there were social classes, for example.[73]

In short, Chopin's Catholic turn of mind might comfortably reject American egalitarianism while addressing some forms of systemic injustice. Where social classes were concerned, it is clear that Chopin separated herself from the Irish, and given her father's premature death, one might expect as much. It is difficult to determine what sort of regard the family had for that ambitious man, and equally hard to fathom Kate's mother's relationship with a man many years her senior whom she married expressly for money. Some speculate that

Chopin pictured to herself her mother's relief on word of her father's death in "The Story of an Hour." There is additional speculation that Thomas O'Flaherty might have fathered some of the family's mulatto slave children. Regardless, Kate Chopin's education and manners fell to her mother and her relatives, who aspired for the girl to embrace her French ancestry. Embrace it she did, spending most of her life connected to Creole circles, connections subsequently reinforced by her marriage.

Yet she would not find it easy to conform herself to Catholic teachings on marriage and sex. Dogma provided a mainspring of her fictional conflicts too. The documentarians who produced the Louisiana Public Broadcasting program *Kate Chopin: A Re-Awakening* interviewed David Chopin, Kate Chopin's grandson, in 1999. "People knew that Kate had left the church," he told them, and "somebody remembered that they saw her coming down the steps of St. Francis Xavier Church, which is in mid-town St. Louis, and figured that maybe the reason she was in church was to go to confession, and get back into the bosom of the church again. So it's my understanding that on the basis of that little incident that they opened up the gates and allowed her to be buried where she is today in Calvary Cemetery." The parishioners of Saint Francis Xavier were predominantly "the well-to-do Irish," so perhaps it is fitting that Chopin returned to them in death.

William Reedy was interred here too, and under similarly fraught circumstances. With the changing of orders Reedy's friend John Cardinal Glennon had become archbishop and authorized Reedy's funeral at Saint Louis University with subsequent burial in Calvary. In Kerry Patch the story arose that Reedy could only be buried in sanctified ground because he had been given extreme unction, the final sacrament.[74]

Years earlier, when Reedy attended the funeral of his little brother Frank, he had found himself involuntarily overwhelmed by richly sensory memories:

> The odor of incense recalls your own acolyte days! Why, you were once just such a wide-eyed, self-conscious, black-handed, close-cropped arab temporarily turned angel! Those were the days when the priest and the altar boys went to the cemetery [to] a rich bug's funeral and on the way back the priest bought you soda water and sugar crackers and a funeral was a picnic indeed. . . . Those light effects through stained glass and incense are as magically bright as of old—brighter indeed for remembrance, for regrets, for self-pity and self-knowledge, rudely stirred by this return to an elder day, and expressed in tears that burn but do not come.[75]

From innocence to experience, Reedy's tears reflect a church that at times seemed to afford less of voice than of vocation. Max Putzel, who wrote Reedy's engaging biography, notes that Reedy never identified his brother in the article, "and what Reedy omits saying about the Church tells more than what he says. He is revisiting it for the first time since his excommunication."[76] The words from the "Judica me Deus" that Kate Chopin quotes in "A Vocation and a Voice," no doubt by rote, constitute the first prayer of the Mass familiar to her, calling for God's judgment. Altar servers like the protagonist of Chopin's story, and Reedy himself, were required to memorize the responses that followed the *introibo*—the words that famously begin Joyce's *Ulysses*. The complete verse reads, "And I will go in unto the Altar of God: unto God, who giveth joy to my youth," but James Joyce, Lafcadio Hearn, Billy Reedy, and Kate O'Flaherty all found that joy to be evasive.

It is probably no accident that Protestant and Catholic tensions played out in powerfully imaginative ways in Lafcadio Hearn's writing. Ethnicity was a cipher of his family history too. Patricio "Patrick" Lafcadio Tessima Carlos Hearn was an Irishman, a displaced Greek, a citizen of Japan, a vagabond midwesterner, a loyal southerner, a citizen of the Catholic pangaea (sometimes despite himself), a multinational connoisseur of meridional people and places. From this complex of identities emerged a complicated writer, and perhaps it was because of the difficulty of understanding who Hearn was, and Hearn's own quest for self-identity, that he fell for a time into benign neglect.

That is changing, as scholars have come to appreciate Hearn's singular importance as a writer who straddles colonial and postcolonial genres. Indeed, Hearn's work joined the two. Perhaps more than any other writer, Hearn taught southerners and Americans how to *see* New Orleans; the mythos that he created remains the dominant paradigm for approaching a place steeped in Catholic mystery. For that achievement alone, he deserves renewed attention and profound respect. The exquisitely grisly preoccupations of his early journalism reveal the full range of latent tensions between Catholic and Protestant ideologies. His florid and at times prophetic imagination peered well forward into the twentieth century, as will be shown, and the satire and grotesquerie that were second nature to his writing reveal a close kinship to later writers, including Flannery O'Connor, E. P. O'Donnell, and John Kennedy Toole. With mad irreverence, he invented gonzo journalism almost a century before it would be so named—cross-dressing, experimenting with drugs, and racially passing to get his stories.

Crucially, as a tireless promoter of French realist and decadent literature, Hearn brought to American readers such writers as Gerard de Neval, Anatole France, Pierre Loti, Theophile Gautier, Emile Zola, Baudelaire, and Flaubert, in some cases translating them for the first time. Indeed, Hearn's groundbreaking translation in 1910 of Flaubert's 1874 masterpiece, *The Temptation of St. Anthony,* took longer to find its way into print than the thirty years Flaubert required to write it, as Hearn could not persuade American publishers of the "smutty" book's marketability.[77] The book was the apple of Hearn's eye, explains Elizabeth Bisland in the introduction:

> He had brought his unfinished manuscript from Cincinnati to New Orleans, and had continued to work upon it in strange lodgings in gaunt, old half-ruined Creole houses; at the tables of odd little French cafes, or among the queer dishes in obscure Spanish and Chinese restaurants. He had snatched minutes for it amidst the reading and clipping of exchanges in a newspaper office; had toiled drippingly over it in the liquifying heats of tropic nights; had arisen from the "inexpungable langours" of yellow fever to complete its last astounding pages.[78]

Not yet thirty at the time, "the young translator was filled with a sort of astonished despair at his inability to make others see the book as he did," but Hearn did not abandon his mission, and in some ways it repaid him. The French-influenced realism of some of his journalistic sketches places them among the finest ever written about the South.

If American journalists are indebted to Hearn, he has also earned the gratitude of folklorists and anthropologists for writing about the forgotten classes and for his pioneering efforts to document what is now called multiculturalism. His fascination with the exotic compelled him to compile treasuries of the South's little cultures and "little races," supplying a thin record with much-needed, almost voluptuous detail.[79] Hearn left an account of popular black folk songs, for instance, that remains a kind of *ur*-list for folklorists; he also recorded slave narratives, firsthand observations on minstrel shows, drug addiction, roustabout life, and marvels too numerous to enumerate here. Without him, the literary vision of the nineteenth-century South would lose a good deal of color, and the fund of New Orleans lore would be greatly reduced.

Another sign of Hearn's remarkable accomplishment was his prophetic ability to imagine fantastic technologies that would later be realized. Responding to the advent of electrical lighting, he forecast the rapid introduction of the technology by harnessing "hydraulic power."[80] In "Fantastic Possibilities of Invention" he speculated on the use of "electricity as a weapon."[81] Elsewhere he imagined "a microscope powerful enough to enable us to read a brain like a book" and dreamed of "a telescope which would reveal to us the minutest details of life in other planets." He asked, since it is "possible to commingle" the "elements composing human flesh and blood," "why may we not dare to fancy that some future student of the protoplasmic basis of life, might prove a more successful creator than Frankenstein?"[82]

Atomic weapons, aeronautics, magnetic resonance imaging, brain mapping, the Hubble, radio communication, genetic engineering—considered a flake in his own time, Hearn seems to have been something of a technological visionary. Now a man who could not claim a place during his life has been subjected to the réclame of Japanese, Americans, and Irish alike. When Mary Robinson was president of Ireland, she stood before a Japanese audience at Shimane Prefecture that included Hearn's grandson and beamed, "That he was Irish is a great source of pride to me."[83] Hearn scholarship has thrived in Japan, where he is regarded by some as a folk hero whose empathetic double perspective on East and West was unusually clear sighted.

If he was an Irishman, he was in some respects an accidental Irishman; to the Japanese he was "almost" Japanese; and to all who knew him he was a seeker. Though his father was Irish and he spent much of his childhood in Dublin, Hearn wrote little of the Irish. It did not behoove a socially ambitious, new American/southerner to dwell overmuch on his Irish roots. An Irish upbringing certainly influenced Hearn, surfacing in, for example, his love of wordplay, his associations with Irish Americans, his willingness to "consort" with other races, his wanderlust, and finally, his latent Catholicism.

The unsettled circumstances of Lafcadio's birth befitted a life fraught with gothic preoccupations. At age thirty Charles Bush Hearn, an Anglo-Irish surgeon and officer stationed with the British Army Medical Staff on the Ionian Islands, took a liking to a beautiful but reputedly unstable islander named Rosa Cassimati (or Kassimati). She would be confined to mental asylums at various times during her life. Though she bore several of his children, Charles Hearn would treat her as a mistress before marrying and quickly divorcing her. When Rosa went to stay with her in-laws in Dublin, they called her boy Patrick. She called him Lafcadio.

Rosa's mother-in-law was quite convinced that the Greek woman would not do, so she spent most of her time with Charles Hearn's sympathetic sixty-year-old aunt, Sarah Holmes Brenane, who had become the black sheep of the family by marrying a Catholic and becoming a Catholic devout.[84] After Rosa and Charles parted ways, Sarah eventually accepted the boy as her charge. The Hearns became permanently estranged from Rosa, and so by age four Lafcadio would see her no more; his father, perhaps five times; and his brother, as a child, only once.

Still, the most socially advantageous upbringing for young Lafcadio rested with his Anglo-Irish relations. Aunt Sarah gradually despaired of making a priest of Lafcadio, who seemed destined obdurately to become the heathen of the family's fears; she sent him on to the Institution Ecclésiastique at Yvetot, near Rouen. Lafcadio considered the Petit Séminaire, as it was known to its pupils, to be a regular prison. Guy de Maupassant, who entered the school shortly after Hearn left and detested it equally, wrote that it "smelled of prayers the way a fish market smells of fish."[85] Still, the French that Lafcadio mastered there would serve him well as a writer.

After a year he matriculated at Saint Cuthbert's College, Ushaw, in County Durham, England, where his best friend was an Irish boy with the quizzical name Achilles Daunt. There Lafcadio's peers nicknamed him "Paddy." He would find myriad ways to test the religious brothers, asking impertinent questions about the Divine Writ, confessing that he was disappointed when prayers for amorous temptresses went unfulfilled, and scribbling waggish poetry about the Virgin Birth.[86] Already so myopic that he could not read texts unless they were a few inches away from his face, while in England Hearn suffered an injury from rough-housing that blinded him in one eye, an incident not without its influence on the wild and often otherworldly visual descriptions in his writing. Thus Hearn bore all the baggage typically thought to produce a writer: He was abandoned early in life by *both* parents. As a lifelong self-described wanderer he lived on the margins of social acceptability with an outsider's keen insight into cultural norms. He was acutely shy, a swaggerer of the page only. And he bore a visible wound, a sense-limiting physical handicap, for which, as Edmund Wilson might submit, his art attempted to compensate.

His first chance to ply that art was at age eighteen, when his guardians thought it best to send him to Cincinnati. There he honed his mordant streak, holding forth "about his antagonism toward (as he put it) 'hypocrite' priests, 'goblin nuns in black robes,' and 'civilized' folk who considered themselves so superior to the powerless, the 'uncouth,' and the 'savage' types of the world."[87] Certainly he was willing to crawl the underbelly to get his story. Perhaps the most ludicrous illustration of this is a column titled "Feminine Curiosity," in which his deep-cover investigative technique compelled him to dress up as a woman to attend a ladies-only meeting. The subject of the lecture was, in his heading, "A Female Blackguard's Lecture to Prurient Sisters; The 'Escaped Nun's' Matinee at Pike's Hall."[88] Hearn wanted to find out what the hubbub was about, and in so doing he bore witness to the nineteenth-century fascination with so-called convent literature.

The watershed moment in this literary craze was January 1836, when Maria Monk's *Awful Disclosures of the Hotel Dieu Nunnery* was published. The book made for salacious reading in the guise of interested moral defense and, in Mark Massa's memorable turn of phrase, "sold like hotcakes at a communion breakfast."[89] Some three hundred thousand copies flew off the shelves before the Civil War. Maria Monk did for anti-Catholicism what *Uncle Tom's Cabin* did for abolitionism, and indeed, the bestselling fable rivaled Stowe's book for sales volume. It turned out, of course, that Monk's book had been cooked up. For his part, Hearn relished the lecture of Edith O'Gorman, "Escaped Nun," as a salacious farce in which he was a gleeful participant by "judicious use" of wigs, "trails, veils, and brass"—"your smooth-faced reporter did it." His gender bender is a comic vehicle, of course. He trips on his skirts, blushes before the "rude glance" of the ticket vendor, and passes a good deal of comment on finical affectations: "[O'Gorman] told of how good she was, how all the naughty, naughty things other little girls knew she never dreamed of, and then—oh, she made your reporter blush and wish that he had stayed away. The ladies all tittered. Then she got moral and prosy, and one or two virtuous middle-aged ladies left the hall. . . . Everybody began to look bored and disappointed."[90] As Charles Fanning has observed, Irish American writers were most likely to single out convent literature for ridicule.[91] Hearn's supercilious views extended to most subjects, as in this sketch of the Cincinnati courtroom, with its facetious nod to Coleridge:

> It is a sorry place for the student of human nature and in that Courtroom, with its ignorance and sin, and shame, and vice in every shape, and besotted souls, and hang-dog countenances, and low brows, and evil eyes, and lies, and deceit, and treachery one almost doubts over the sweet old lines—
>> For the dear God who loveth us,
>> He made and loveth all.[92]

Some of Hearn's most penetrating Cincinnati reportage concerned the crime and punishment of James Murphy, a nineteen-year-old Irish American tough who might today be dubbed a gang leader. In short, powerful sentences strung together by his beloved semicolons, Hearn related the images surrounding the hanging: "the black gibbet, with its dismal hangings of sable muslin," "Sisters of Charity, in dark robes," and "solemn-faced priests, with snowy Roman collars." The condemned is a double for his priest; he wears "the neat suit of black cloth for which he had been measured a few days before." Murphy survived the first attempt to hang him when the rope broke, an occurrence not altogether uncommon. After a second attempt, it took seventeen minutes for James Murphy to die. Hearn summarized, "But the facts in the case, as they appeared to the writer, were simply that a poor, ignorant passionate boy, with a fair, coarse face"—the disfigured Hearn had an enduring interest in physiognomy—"had in the heat of drunken anger taken away the life of a fellow-being, and paid the penalty of his brief crime, by a hundred days of mental torture, and a hideous death."[93]

The thin veneer on American-style civilization was all too apparent in a city known as the Porkopolis. Attuned to its corruptions and the limited franchise of its supposedly limitless opportunities, Hearn wrote to a friend, "It is time for a fellow to get out of Cincinnati when they begin to call it the Paris of America."[94] Still a young man, he had climbed from cub to star reporter and established a name for himself in America. In Cincinnati he felt himself a stranger in a strange land, but when he betook himself to New Orleans for the first time, his landing was more in the nature of a homecoming. He arrived like some sort of returned pauper king—or perhaps like Paul Newman in *The Long, Hot Summer*—floating down the Mississippi seated atop cotton bales on the bow of the steamer, soaking it up.

Hearn naturally felt at home in New Orleans, "a Latin city," as he called it. For him, North-South divisions were less political than they were romantic and based on the notion of meridional opposites (*meridional* here defined as "along a meridian" or "in the north-south direction" or even in the old astronomical sense, "southward-oriented"). Michael Kreyling maintains that "for Hearn south meant south of the equator; the division between North and South was for him not political but mythic and was rooted in his memory of the opposites brought together in the marriage of his parents."[95] Drawing on the sensitivities of his upbringing, he remarked the culturally Catholic trappings of his new home:

> No Anglo-Saxon, for instance, would ever think of naming a street Goodchildren street, *rue des Bons Enfants,* or Love street, *rue de l'Amour,* Madman's street, Mystery street, Piety street, etc. Old Bernard Marigny christened two thoroughfares in the faubourg Marigny which he laid out, "Craps" and

"Bagatelle" in honor of two games of chance at which he lost a fortune. A curious mistake was that of the first American directory-maker who insisted upon translating Bagatelle into English and described it as Trifle street.[96]

Hearn knew that there were some things that did not translate culturally, all languages being equal. Having spent part of his boyhood in England and part in France, he had an acute appreciation for the differences between freewheeling Mediterranean culture and the staid WASP culture, the Creoles and the *Americains,* the Irish Catholics and the Anglo-Irish. The city's *mañana* ethic suited him well, as it offered some sort of alternative to the relentless, anxiety-producing dollar-driven pace of American life.

As much as he appreciated the laid-back, *savoir-vivre* atmosphere of Catholic territories and their capacity to focus on both this life and the next, he also liked the English rage for order. Hearn's lifelong respect for the English was founded in cautious ambivalence. In "A Conservative," Hearn creates a Japanese samurai-intellectual protagonist who shares many elements of his worldview and experiences. (In an 1878 letter to his friend Henry Krehbiel, Hearn shared his physiognomic theory "that there are such strong similarities between the Mongolian and certain types of the Irish face that one is inclined to suspect a far-distant origin of the Celts in the East.")[97] The samurai-protagonist notes the great economic disparities in London, the supposed epicenter of Western culture, with a veiled reference to the Great Famine: "He studied her wealth, forever growing, and the nightmare of squalor forever multiplying in the shadow of it. He saw the vast ports gorged with the riches of a hundred lands, mostly plunder; and knew the English still like their forefathers, a race of prey; and thought of the fate of her millions if she should find herself for even a single month unable to compel other races to feed them." Hearn's posture, behind the eyes of a Japanese character, might have permitted him to be openly critical, as when "A Conservative" condemns "the conventional hypocrisy that pretends not to see" and with anticlerical feeling indicts "the religion that utters thanks for existing conditions." With Faulknerian certitude the piece concludes, "No: this civilization signified a perpetual wicked struggle between the simple and the cunning, the feeble and the strong; force and craft combining to thrust weakness into a yawning and visible hell."[98]

Separately, in "The Race-Problem in America," Hearn warned that the means of settling racial violence "is a problem of the most serious description. The English press,—reflecting English experience only, and the impulses natural to the most orderly and systematic of all races,—suggests the use of force."[99] Of course, he rejected this particular solution, perhaps mindful of the disastrous consequences of such recourse in Ireland. The South had elements of English order—its peculiar institution, in particular, required it—but New Orleans offered Latin piquancy and deshabille. As he did elsewhere, Hearn immediately set about making himself a person of the place he inhabited. He strove to be a citizen of New Orleans, but it proved difficult because New Orleans is itself a paradox, at once the most and least southern of towns. Hearn knew that "being southern" required extra conformity, but he retained some of his iconoclasm. He thought that dueling, a New Orleans tradition, was barbaric in the extreme. In describing Nathan Bedford Forrest's origins he wrote, with a measure of foreign detachment: "He seemed by nature a typical pioneer, one of those fierce and terrible men, who form in themselves a kind of protecting fringe to the border of white civilization."[100]

"Although the vogue for Southern literature, local color, and the picturesque gave Hearn his chance to be read by a national audience," Kreyling explains, "he was not really a Southern local-color writer."[101] Hearn detested the sentimental southern novel especially, notifying publishers, with Rabelaisian ferocity, "The *Item* will not hereafter notice fourth-rate novels, stupid volumes of poetry, and whatever is generally termed 'Trash' in more than one line, if at all."[102] On the perennial plans to create a great "Southern" magazine to rival Scribner's or Harper's, he editorialized,

> Any tendency toward *Southernism* in the conduct of the magazine would render it ridiculous and finally kill it. It would be absurd to suppose that a literary magazine established in the South, and devoted wholly to "Southern questions," and managed in the interests of Southern people, and having for contributors none but Southern writers, and publishing nothing but articles about purely Southern affairs, could succeed. . . . No real literary success can be purely local; no work of veritable merit can be of merely sectional interest. . . . A Southern magazine must be an American magazine, a United States magazine, an English magazine, if it be worth supporting.[103]

An editor, Hearn explained, must be ruthlessly impartial, a "priest of literature," untouched "by any other principles save those of the Religion of Art."[104] He was simply too well traveled, too expansive, too essentially Continental in his views of culture to embrace an aesthetic based on southern nationalism. He dedicated himself to writing serious literary criticism for the *Daily City Item,* a cultivated habit that stood him well when, years later, he was thrust unexpectedly into teaching English literature at the Imperial University of Tokyo, where Professor Ho-run-san, who had no collegiate education, lectured "twelve hours a week on four different subjects,"[105] leaving staggering mountains of literary criticism in his wake.

If racial orthodoxy was the ultimate shibboleth for admittance to southern society, again Hearn held himself off. While living in New Orleans, he rebuffed the critic Henry Krehbiel, his old friend from Cincinnati, for his bigoted assumptions about art: "I do not see less beauty in what was conceived by the passion and poetry of other races of mankind. This is a cosmopolitan art era: and you must not judge everything which claims art-merit by a Gothic standard."[106] The Raven, the nickname by which he often referred to himself among his old Cincinnati companions, was unfettered by racial exclusivity. He enjoyed attending the quadroon balls, where, in his opinion, the most beautiful women to be found anywhere on earth were presented. But he was not naïve. Observing social divisions in the West Indies and the Code Noir, he wrote, "The greatest error of slavery was that which resulted in the creation of mixed races—the illegitimate union between the white master and the African woman, whose offspring remained slaves by law." This declaration should probably be read narrowly, as it operated within the special constraints of Martinique's brand of slavery: "Everywhere the half-breed race sprang up as an all-powerful element of discord, and finally appeared in the role of an enemy of whites and blacks alike—forcing the parent races apart forever."[107] In other words, he reckoned, correctly, that the mixed-race offspring discomfited both races as a visible reminder of the problem of racial otherness and cruel double standards. He had seen how these slavery principles deformed southern society.

In fact, as a man who courted mixed-race women, Hearn would understand how racial divisions played hell on relationships at every social level. In New Orleans he would never speak of his extralegal marriage to Alethea "Mattie" Foley, his would-be mixed-race bride in Cincinnati. He wrote to Harry Watkin, "You cannot imagine how utterly the news of that thing would ruin me here. . . . The prejudice here is unutterably bitter, and bottomlessly deep." During the more sexually audacious portion of his life, Hearn commented to his friend Henry Krehbiel, "I eat and drink and sleep with members of the races you detest. . . ." As Jonathan Cott revealed, Hearn's early biographer, Elizabeth Bisland, euphemistically changed "sleep" to "converse."[108]

Notwithstanding his attraction to "slums" put off-limits by American bigotry, Hearn's growing stature as a reporter afforded opportunities to ensconce himself within respectable New Orleans. With his impeccable translation skills to gird him, his work would be admired by some of the closed-society, old-country Creoles, including Charles Gayarre and Henri Mercier. Unlike the famous Irish Gallier family of New Orleans (their surname a conveniently Gallicized *Gallagher*), Hearn did not put on Creole airs. After all, he was an anthropologist (or, in his word, an "ethnologist") before the term had come into common use. His was no faddish orientalism. He was genuinely as captivated by the languages and religions of the East—he had native speakers teaching him Spanish and Chinese in New Orleans and studied Arabic on his own—as by the fragments of African speech and culture that studded New Orleans conversation. He is credited with "the earliest documentation of secular African American songs in urban settings" and for preserving nineteenth-century Creole folk tradition.[109] He praised a quality of Whitman's poetry he called "world-beauty" and admired the "inexplicable delight of being."[110] When a Creole musician slighted a roustabout song, Hearn recorded his indignant reply: "Verily, I would rather listen to it, than hear a symphony of Beethoven!"[111]

There was no aspect of what he called "the wind of the vast whirl and striving of the American life" that he was unwilling to engage—a tendency arguably more *American* than southern.[112] Thus he developed a varied coterie of friends who hailed from all walks of life. Like Joel Chandler Harris, he kept company both southern and unsouthern, and not a few of his friends were counted controversial figures, including George Washington Cable, who became a persona non grata in New Orleans after taking his stand against Jim Crow segregation.[113] Hearn was consistently opposed to slavery, and during his New Orleans years he struck up a friendly correspondence with William D. O'Connor, a northern Irish American abolitionist.

Beyond his friendships with New Orleans literati, he kept company with a number of Irish acquaintances. He boarded with an Irish American woman named Margaret Courtney, who was something of a good-natured scold ("Ah! And I pray God every night on my knees to make you a good Catholic, Mr. Hearn; and you an Irishman, too!").[114] He also befriended Mrs. Courtney's "bad, bad" nephew, Denny Corcoran, a well-known character about town. Despite his acquaintance with members of New Orleans's thriving Irish community, Hearn was wont to tell others that his father was English, perhaps in keeping with his Anglo-Irish origins. And as a reporter he sometimes stereotyped the American Irish. Working the courtroom beat in Cincinnati, he sketched an Irishwoman named Ellen Ferris, accused of committing assault and battery on one Mary Buckley, who testified in an Irish accent that she had been "minding" (i.e., mending) blankets for which Mary Buckley failed to pay. When asked what Ellen

Ferris had done, Buckley replied, "Sure, she het me on the head wid a breek."[115]

His drawing of an Irish drunk in New Orleans is even less flattering. The piece was captioned with dialogue including several Irish usages: *spalpeen,* a good-humored term for scamp, and *omadhaun,* more familiarly, a fool. The piece stirred up protest, and the *City Item*'s editor was called in to smooth things over. According to Delia LaBarre, he "defended the piece while heaping praise on the local Irish community."[116] Perhaps Hearn thought he was on safe ground, but he would find that even an Irishman might not safely make fun of Irishmen. More to the point, the ill repute of New Orleans's lower-class Channel Irish might have prompted Hearn to align himself with their lace-curtain cousins. One of his *City Item* articles, "Paying a Dublin Cabby," published on September 21, 1879, explains how the fair city's cabbies, when asked their prices, "invariably 'laves it to your honor;' but when you have paid him, no matter how many times the lawful amount, he is never satisfied." Another entry in this vein of typical light "Irish" humor, on October 4, 1879, reads: "An Irishman who had on a very ragged coat was asked of what stuff it was made. 'Bedad, I don't know; I think the most of it is made of fresh air.'"

Evidently, newspaper articles poking fun at the Irish, so common to newspapers in other major cities, played well to a New Orleans readership too. More commonly, Hearn's humor ran to a lightly satiric vein. One of his earliest productions was a raucous little publication whose title poked fun at the monocle on his good eye. *Ye Giglampz* was "a journal of satire, parodies, and witty debunking of bourgeois pieties," according to Kreyling.[117] Curiously, many pioneering Irish writers brought attention to the play between form and effect and are credited in turn with ushering in postmodern playfulness. Certainly Hearn had this quality and playfulness in spades, as evidenced in his colorful cartoons (both verbal and pictorial), incorrigible punning, affectionate impressionism, and off-the-wall subject matter (his columns ran everything from an ode to cockroaches to roman-numeral games to snatches of pidgin conversation). His jokes often spanned several languages so that only a polyglot readership would get them; in fact, he was very much like the brilliant Irish writer Flann O'Brien in this respect. On the level of plain satire, Hearn's work is in keeping with later southern Irish writers such as Flannery O'Connor, John Kennedy Toole, and Pat Conroy.

His nonsatiric writing also could be breathtaking, even in his period of "gush," as he called it. Take, for example, "The City of Dreams," in which he observed a widely tolerated Big Easy idiosyncrasy: the habit of talking to oneself in public. Such self-talkers, wrote Hearn, tended to be those who "had little hope of favors from the goddess Fortuna"—no doubt Fortuna-fearing Ignatius P. Reilly, of John Kennedy Toole's New Orleans classic, *A Confederacy of Dunces* (1980), would agree. The article's clincher has a poetic meter that is just right: "Seeing and hearing these things, we somehow ceased to marvel that some people dwelling in the city of New Orleans should speak mysteriously and hold audible converse with their own thoughts; forasmuch as we, also, dreaming among the shadows, spoke aloud to our own hearts, until awakened by an echo of unanswered words."[118]

One imagines a writer without a country talking to himself this way. Late in life, Hearn likened Japan to Ireland, reflecting something of his comfort there and attesting also to the circularity of his lifelong flight. Among the globe-spanning tales he recounted for his readership was one of venerable Irish origin. It was a pregnant choice. Saint Brendan (which he gives as "Brandan," most likely because it sounded that way to his ear) "sailed with his twelve chosen brethren in search of the Blessed Island which lies in perpetual calm, bathed in the sunny waves of the Western Sea." Personable and intrepid, Brendan supposedly undertook his seven-year journey in his hoary mid-eighties, with an account of his voyages finally recorded in the *Navigatio Sancti Brendani Abbatis* some five hundred years after his death in the sixth century. It was the beginning of the great age of the wandering Irish *(scotti peregrinni)*, as the island disseminated many Christian missionaries to Europe during the Dark Ages—so many, in fact, that one European bishop was prompted to ask whether any Irish remained in Ireland.

The sources and analogs from ancient literature woven into Brendan's "narrative" are well documented. They must have presented a veritable feast to Hearn, who might have recognized elements from Homer's *Odyssey*. In much the way that the Holy Spirit united the Eastern and Roman Catholic elements of his lineage, Brendan's tale joined Hearn's Greek and Irish ancestry. The writer retells one of the best-known moments from the cycle, Brendan's encounter with Judas Iscariot, who clings to a rock during a brief remission from hell. Saint Brendan, Hearn's kindred spirit in anticlericalism, "had long bemoaned the turbulence and violence of his own land, and"—alluding to Brendan's unusually rigorous asceticism—"the luxury and worldliness of its priests and even its monastics."

It is a story that befits a soul hungry for a homecoming, told by a spiritual wayfarer who sought out his own asceticism by going over the water and whose religious rebellion brought him back to a native conformity, notwithstanding his bohemian propensities. From Irish Catholicism to American liberalism and back again, through Japanese austerity, to conservatism: *Plus ça change, plus c'est la même chose,* as the French say.

Like Hearn, Chopin had the lived experience of "Latin" Catholicism in contrast with a more severe, Jansenist-influenced Irish Catholicism, and to some degree these competing visions of the church fought for the fidelity of her spirit. "This [Irish American] model of Catholicism," writes Haddox, "proved less widespread in the South, and the reputation of New Orleans, St. Louis, and other Catholic cities in the South as centers of vice and hedonism certainly sprang in part from a more tolerant attitude on the part of French Catholicism toward pleasures of various kinds and a less rigorous enforcement of moral strictures—a tolerance that in some places led to conflicts between Irish and French Catholics."[119] In contrast to contemporaries like Mark Twain, who detected in Catholic decadence strong evidence of a moribund and perverse church, Haddox argues, Kate Chopin felt something closer to fascination.[120]

The same might be said of Lafcadio Hearn, another denizen of the decadent Catholic world of the South, whose retreat from Catholicism was backward-looking, incomplete, and ultimately reluctant. Artists are rarely at peace with the circumstances of their birth. For all three New Orleans writers—Reedy, Hearn, and Chopin—Irish Catholicism seemed to leave its greatest imprint in their thinking about conformity and sexuality. Each labored to break from lower-class associations of Irishness, and all were shaped in habits of thought, of reference, and of value by a Catholic inheritance with which they would struggle to be at peace. The personal cost of their rebellion can scarcely be underestimated. All set out to upset certain myths of regional identity: Chopin undermined notions of feminine placidity among southern belles, and Hearn replaced the collective allure of a politically coherent Confederate South with the sacred earth and waters of a culture-expanding transoceanic and meridional South. Joel Chandler Harris, ironically, helped give the lie to the credulous slave. In dispelling these myths, they offered counternarratives of such enduring power that they helped to redefine the southern cultural landscape in the imagination of the twentieth century.

II

HABITS
of
SATIRE
and
INSUBORDINATION

STAGING IRISHNESS

Here they [the New Orleans Irish] subsist on the coarsest fare,
holding life on a tenure as uncertain as does the leader of a forlorn hope. . . .
Such are the labourers I have seen here, and have still found them civil and
courteous, with a ready greeting for the stranger inquiring into their
condition, and a quick jest on their own equipment, which is
frequently, it must be admitted, of a whimsical kind.
—TYRONE POWER, *Impressions of America* (1836)

Some call the Irish a pugnacious people, others call them an improvident
people, and others again a reckless people. Be their general characteristics
what they may, they are certainly a social people, fond of the society of their
fellows, inclined to crack a joke at the expense of others, and always willing to
laugh at a well pointed repartee, even when directed against themselves.
—*New Orleans Picayune,* September 8, 1844

Some day I'll write a novel about a Layman. Can you picture him?
Small, nervous, grayish, timidly knocking at the doors of the
professions, trying samples of things always?
Er—I am a layman.
—E. P. O'DONNELL to Ben Augustin, 1933

How many famous gun-toting western outlaws had the benefit of a
southern cousin in a nunnery who would write regularly and serve
as a moral adviser? In fact, John Henry "Doc" Holliday had one,
and Billy the Kid, likely the son of Irish Famine immigrants, was supposedly
steered from murder by a young Sister of Mercy in Trinidad, Colorado, a tale
recounted in N. Scott Momaday's *Man Made of Words* (1998).[1] Kieran Quinlan
writes of Scarlett O'Hara, an equally rare creature: "There can be few southern belles who have a sister preparing to enter a convent in Charleston to become a nun."[2] Few, indeed, but there was nearly one such: Margaret Mitchell's
mother, a southern belle and child of the plantation, had a second cousin who

in October 1883 entered the Sister of Mercy Order at Saint Vincent's Convent in Savannah.[3]

The same woman connects Doc Holliday and Margaret Mitchell (1900–1949): Martha Ann "Mattie" Holliday, who became Sister Mary Melanie, RSM. With family members like these, Mitchell scarcely needed fiction, but she "purportedly told a nurse tending John Marsh [her husband, then in hospital at Saint Joseph's in Atlanta] that Sister Melanie had been the inspiration for the character Melanie Hamilton in *Gone with the Wind*." In the course of her long career in a religious order Martha Holliday had worked at a hospital, served as a teacher in Savannah, and acted as superior of Sacred Heart Convent in Augusta. Martha was twenty-three years the junior of Mitchell's mother, May Belle Stephens, yet they were "close in the way of southern cousins" and often lived near one another.[4]

Similarly, teenaged Mattie Holliday had befriended her cousin John with a degree of intimacy that was perhaps more typical of this earlier age. Doc Holliday had better prospects as a young man attending the Pennsylvania College of Dental Surgery before taking the rake's path to Texas, gambling, tuberculosis, alcoholism, and laudanum addiction. Until the end of her days Mattie Holliday would maintain that the aspiring dentist she had known in her youth was "a different man"—one can only conclude that an outlaw in trouble should reach for his nun.[5] Whether the relationship between Mattie and Doc was in any way amorous has been the subject of protracted speculation undiminished by those within the Holliday family who have acknowledged the possibility. The Holliday biographer Gary L. Roberts notes that many of Holliday's southern family were happy enough to disown him once he departed Atlanta under the cloud of some kind of scandal. Even so, Roberts points out that the portrait of Melanie in *Gone with the Wind*—hair carefully coiffed, "tiny, frailly built," with a "shy, almost frightened look in her too large brown eyes"—looks very much like Mattie Holliday.[6] In the book it is Carreen O'Hara, "delicate and dreamy" (30), "shy and easily led" (58), and "small for her age" (67), who finally goes to the convent. Mattie's father was a convert to Catholicism, and so, in 1872, was Doc Holliday. The novel plays on family intrigue when Ellen Robillard, Scarlett's mother, falls in love with her cousin Phillipe Robillard, only to receive "a brief letter from a New Orleans priest, announcing his death in a barroom brawl" (75). It is likewise an interesting coincidence that Ellen's father, a Presbyterian, consents to her marriage to Gerald O'Hara only after she threatens to join a convent—could this be Mattie's untold story? Others have seen in Mattie's father the model for *Gone with the Wind*'s Frank Kennedy, since Robert Holliday served as a Confederate commissary.

Or is it all a Rorschach of Mitchell's family memory, re-patterned in her text and by her interpreters? While undeniably intriguing, it makes a gaucherie of the larger legacy of Mattie Holliday's life to dwell overmuch on her association with her lawless cousin, for, like the Melanie of the novel, she lived a principled and earnest life in service to others. Certainly she and relatives like her electrified Mitchell's imagination, and one can see why:

> When we went calling on the older generation of relatives, those who had been active in the sixties, I sat on the bony knees of veterans and the fat slippery laps of great-aunts and heard them talk about the times when Little Alex [Confederate Vice President Stephens] was visiting them and how much fried chicken Father Ryan could put away and how nice thick wrapping paper felt when put between the skin and the corset in the cold days during the blockade when woolen goods were so scarce. And how Granpa Mitchell walked nearly fifty miles after the battle of Sharpsburg with his skull cracked in two places from a bullet. They didn't talk of these happenings as history nor as remarkable events but just as a part of their lives and not especially epic parts. And they gradually became a part of my life.[7]

Mitchell's sense of Irish history ran deep as well. She wrote to Joseph McAvoy, president of the Hibernian Society of Savannah, "Until *Gone with the Wind* was published, I took it for granted that practically everyone who could read or sing knew 'The Harp [That Once Through Tara's Hall]' and knew of Tara's Hill so famous in history as the seat of Irish Kings. . . . But it seems I took too much for granted." She wrote to a fan, Michael MacWhite, of the Irish Legation in Washington, DC, extolling "the part the Irish played in the building up of our Southern section and in the Civil War. . . . Reading the old records as I did, they sometimes sounded like 'The Annals of the Four Masters' because of the many Irish names. . . . When the trouble in the 'sixties began they went out with Confederate troops and did great deeds for their new land." She added that this was true of her family, gesturing toward the patriarch Phillip Fitzgerald, a fugitive of the Irish Rebellion of 1798: "As it was once said of the Fitzgeralds, 'they became more Irish than the Irish themselves,' so our Southern Irish became more Southern than the Southerners."[8] Indeed, her parents had schooled her in a kind of apostolic succession of the southern Irish. She was reverent in her invocation of "General Pat Cleburne, who was Irish born and a good Catholic, God rest his soul, and an officer who would have gone higher had he not been born in another country."[9] She was aware that Father Thomas O'Reilly was credited with saving Atlanta's Immaculate Conception Church from Sherman's torch.[10] "When I went to school and learned to 'recite' on Friday afternoons," she recalled, "my pieces, picked by Father and Mother, were Henry Grady's 'The New South,' 'Little Giffen' and 'The Conquered Banner.'"[11] Both Grady and Ryan were Catholic Irish nationalists and southerners, and in other correspondence Mitchell mentions her familiarity with the nationalistic poetry of James Clarence Mangan, beloved of John Mitchel, James Joyce, and a host of Irish poets.[12]

Mitchell might have taken on other influences from reading in Irish literature as well. Patricia Homer draws thematic parallels between Mitchell's work and Irish Big House literature, tracing biographical and thematic affinities in the works of William Butler Yeats, Maria Edgeworth, Edith Somerville, and Martin Ross.[13] Mitchell's efforts to shore up the southern credentials of Irish parvenus, the privations of the war period that were exampled in family lore, the connections to "Doc" Holliday, and so on—none of this is particularly new; what *is* new is the wealth of scholarship that pays closer attention to the anomaly of an Irish plantation belle who tries to say the rosary faithfully. Because of this new abundance, in this chapter I spend relatively little time with *Gone with the Wind,* pausing instead to place Mitchell in the company where she most belongs: among southern Irish writers with an imagination for satire and pretension-pricking drama. Globally recognized now as a certain type of southern lady, Scarlett's reputation goes before her; one must look to her reception in her own time to appreciate just how punchy she was.

In fact, Margaret Mitchell's book and the journalistic work that preceded it have a sharply satiric edge, all of which would be forgotten as her runaway phenomenon of a character became an institution in her own right. When Scarlett made her screen debut the genie flew from the bottle: three-strip Technicolor and its otherworldly, Orphean panoramas gave the film the unshakable hyperreality of an individually apprehended dream. The enduring image was the thing. That Mitchell had written against that image, that she had, with mythic potency, inadvertently assured the southern Irish contribution to dramatic film for the twentieth century and beyond, are matters of late academic interest.

A flurry of recent scholarship on *Gone with the Wind* takes a renewed interest in Scarlett's ethnicity and the complicated interrelationships between ethnicity and race that characterize Mitchell's novel. Patricia Yaeger and Drew Gilpin Faust have taken up these issues in new criticism,[14] and *Gone with the Wind* receives a thorough treatment, through Irish eyes, in Kieran Quinlan's *Strange*

Kin. Like Kate Chopin, Mitchell believed that Irish features and personalities were racially determined. After the *New Yorker* twitted her for giving Scarlett, oxymoronically, a square jaw and a pointed chin, she claimed from experience that "most women who have jaws that are square in the angle have pointed chins. This seems especially true in girls of Irish descent."[15] Following this trail, ethnicity is pored over in articles such as Eliza Russi Lowen McGraw's "A 'Southern Belle with Her Irish Up': Scarlett O'Hara and Ethnic Identity" and Lauren Cardon's "'Good Breeding': Margaret Mitchell's Multi-Ethnic South." The hierarchy of Irish types by social class (the white-trash Slatterys, the skinflint Scots-Irish MacIntoshes, etc.) are not hard to pick out; class bleeds into race, while Mitchell covertly allays readers' miscegenation anxieties by her assurance that the real Irish, like Gerald O'Hara, *are* white, whatever their peculiarities. Mitchell's interest in contemporaneous debates about eugenics—a stew of social Darwinism and racialism—also has been scrutinized profitably.

Doing some ethnic parsing of her own, Molly Haskell astutely observes in *Frankly, My Dear: "Gone with the Wind" Revisited* that "part of Mitchell's passionate response to *This Side of Paradise* (1920) may have come from identifying with Fitzgerald as an Irish-Catholic outsider among WASPS and a young man with a failure of a father struggling to keep up with the 'in' group of Old Guard rich." Mitchell, Haskell argues, was a little too déclassé for the highest echelons of Atlanta society, notwithstanding the success of her novel and the aspirations of her social-climbing mother. Haskell's work brings Margaret Mitchell into focus as a distinctly *southern* woman of her time and place, her novel at once the "The American Bible" and "a training manual for budding belles."[16] In framing the film as a cultural production of a high order and tracing *Gone with the Wind*'s procession (both gaudy and resplendent) from omnibus novel to omnibus film, Haskell works to rescue it from contemporary interpreters who would as soon pass it by as get dragged into its various isms. As Haskell points out, from political prisoners to black women of the twenty-first century, those who might be expected to oppose the book have very often become its adherents by finding more transcendent points of relation in its mythos. Even the southern Irish Catholic writer Valerie Sayers, who strained mightily to deny any element of soppy Lost Cause southern femininity and to embrace the guilt-wracked consciousness of Catholic propriety, was seduced by "the bonus pleasure that Scarlett is a Catholic Southerner with no spiritual depth whatsoever. No possibility of ambivalence."[17] In like vein, academics who were closet fans—and they have existed ever since the book's debut, as exemplified in Leslie Fiedler's about-face—have been emboldened to take it more seriously.

It also helps to account for new readings of the book's multifaceted portrayal of southern femininity. Eve Kosofsky Sedgwick and Anne Goodwyn Jones have reconsidered Scarlett's skillful navigation of scripted gender roles— the one she must play and the more alluring, forbidden variants.[18] Like her protagonist, Mitchell found "the road to ladyhood hard" in part because of her mother's side of the family, if not because of her mother herself. Indeed, the omnipresence of Mitchell's iron-willed Irish Catholic mother, combined with the stultifying lassitude of the southern *wife,* might go far in explaining why "sex-averse Margaret had an even greater horror of pregnancy and childbirth."[19] As with other good Irish Catholic girls, Scarlett's prophylactically adolescent imagination "carried her just as far as the altar and no further." This is the irony: Mitchell's novel became socially acceptable titillation, though by her own account, her own mother would not have permitted her to read it. Southern women, trained to be sexless, read endlessly of sex in these novels, and, as Haskell demonstrates, for a generation of them *Gone with the Wind* was tied to the advent of sexual awareness. Brought up to be innocent of men, they were educated in the getting and keeping of them.[20]

So transgressive was Scarlett with respect to southern womanhood and religious orthodoxy that Mitchell would be called upon to defend her on moral grounds. Mitchell was consistent in responding to these questions, insisting that Scarlett's many "bad" qualities must be weighed against the good. In a debate that played out on the pages of the Jesuit *America* magazine, Father Raymond J. O'Flaherty objected to the book's use in a high-school classroom, while Thomas F. Meehan suggested that it might be "objectionable in parts." Finally, Monsignor James H. Murphy stepped in to defend the book in general and Ellen O'Hara as Catholic paragon in particular. The latter received Mitchell's thanks, along with her admission that the novel had never been intended for children, "but for mature people who realized the truth of 'as ye sow—.'"[21] Called on the carpet by the ethics police, Mitchell sensed a prosecution by double standard and refused to be abased.

Domestic piety notwithstanding, the deformities of one model of southern womanhood, fully revealed in Scarlett, are countered by Melanie. It should be remembered that Melanie was the original protagonist of the novel, before Scarlett took tenacious hold of Mitchell's imagination, and that Scarlett is based largely on the grandmother whom Mitchell loathed, Annie Elizabeth Fitzgerald Stephens, in family lore "depicted as grasping, possessive, and materialistic."[22] The biographical parallels between Annie Stephens and Scarlett O'Hara, extending to her moment in time, place of birth, family history, and so on, are thoroughly documented in Darden Pyron's biography of Margaret Mitchell. What brought the grandmother and her granddaughter nearly to blows was Peggy Mitchell's divorce and remarriage, leaving the incensed matriarch to storm out of the Mitchell household, where she had been resident for years, and, ultimately, to write Peggy's family out of her will. Of this difficult woman Margaret Mitchell wrote, "She always wanted to splurge and wager and the younger girls . . . got a different education from the older ones. They were sent north to finishing schools where they were taught it was shameful to be the daughters of an Irishman born in the Old Country."[23] Heeding Gerald O'Hara's advice never to forget where she came from, one of Mitchell's strongest indictments of her grandmother was that she had, in effect, gotten above her raising and, worse, betrayed Gerald's triumvirate of "authentic" Irish values: Catholic, nationalist, sentimentalist. This was Mitchell's inheritance too; describing her family's patriarchs (Phillip Fitzgerald and John Stephens) in a letter to Harvey Smith, she wrote, "They were both Irishmen born and proud of it and prouder still of being southerners and would have withered any relative who tried to put on the dog."[24]

Even though her termagant grandmother provided the most immediate model for Scarlett, one hears a bit of Margaret Mitchell's own voice channeled in Scarlett's grandmother when she speaks bluntly about "kick[ing] the folks whose necks we've climbed over." Mitchell's book is nothing short of an *apologia pro vita sua* for the Catholic underdog, a counterhistory that attempts, like Confederate ideologues before her and Tea Party activists today, to burnish such terms as *rebel* and *revolutionary*. Though there is "venom in her [grandmother's] words," her pride in family endurance speaks to the ethnic sensibilities of a Catholic underclass in the less-quoted passage that precedes her declaration on "gumption":

And if we folks have a motto, it's this: "Don't holler—smile and bide your time." We've survived a passel of things that way, smiling and biding our time, and we've gotten to be experts at surviving. We had to be. We've always bet on the wrong horses. Run out of France with the Huguenots, run out of England with the Cavaliers, run out of Scotland with Bonnie Prince Charlie, run out of Haiti by the niggers and now licked by the Yankees. But we always turn up on top in a few years. (1001)

Of course, the narrative resonates in the Irish branch of her family too, where betting on the wrong horses is a matter of course. Never mind that the speech is less than logically consistent; were Haitian slaveholders really in the same class as the hapless tenants conscripted in service of the bonnie prince? Nevertheless, Mitchell unwrites the legends of Norman superiority that led up to the war by offering a counternarrative of Catholic defeat. After all, southern venality was founded on the notion that white southerners were literally a vindicated, superior people, racially and historically. Cavalier ancestors, Huguenot ancestors, John Calvin, the anti-Pretenders Cromwell and James II, the crushers of the Young Pretender, and, in Episcopalian quarters, Henry VIII—these are men whose portraits one expects to see decking the halls of the Anglophilic Old Guard, as any southerner knows (let us not speak of the obligatory fox hunters, since the O'Haras too tally-hoed). Yet in their fervid enthusiasm for the novel, and through Mitchell's ingeniously seductive narrative of "history's losers," southerners seemed able to look past this subversion of their idols, or their replacement by unwashed Catholic come-latelys. One man's rebel is another's freedom fighter; in Mitchell's world, losing is winning, and to the losers goes the mystique, lending them, in Pat Conroy's fine phrase, "the sweet-smelling attar that romance always lends to the cause of a shamed and defeated people."[25] As the book says, "Crackers are short on sparkle" (716).

In this spirit, the "old, knowing parrot" passes on a ruthless lesson about the importance of "gumption" to her granddaughter: "That, my child, is the secret of survival," she says, laughing like a harridan (717). Though Mitchell was brought up to reject such coarse values—money-grubbing was obviously a function of Yankee avarice (besides, "It was ill bred and Yankeefied to hurry" [657])—one cannot help but notice that the bootstrapping of *Gone with the Wind* is consistently informed by the Irish hustler sensibility that Mitchell could not entirely disown. To get past Reconstruction, Mitchell suggests, southerners must get past a reconstruction mentality mired in the anticapitalist legacies of the plantation and slavery, a plantation mind-set that was at once the logical end of capitalism (the absolute sanctity of the chattel) and its undoing. Rhett gives the lie to the Lost Cause by seeing profit in it long before he becomes a true believer. Pyron traces Rhett's oft-quoted "world turned over" speech (which Mitchell revisits a number of times in her correspondence) to the lips of Mitchell's mother, who made a point of showing her daughter how name-proud Confederate dowagers were ruined by their want of useful education, such that the road to Jonesboro became a kind of road to Damascus. Among the authors that Mitchell's mother "bribed" her to read was Darwin; in times of turmoil, social Darwinism becomes the rule. From grandmother to mother to daughter, this line of thinking is called up in Rhett's oft-quoted speech:

This isn't the first time the world's been upside down and it won't be the last. It's happened before and it'll happen again. And when it does happen, everyone loses everything and everyone is equal. And then they all start again at taw, with nothing at all. That is, nothing except the cunning of their brains and strength of their hands. But some people, like Ashley, have neither cunning nor strength or, having them, scruple to use them. And so they go under and they should go under. It's a natural law and the world is better off without them. But there are always a hardy few who come through and given time, they are right back where they were before the world turned over. (772)

Here Mitchell is most demonstrably "un-southern" when she subscribes to the hard-charging "Yankee" values that would soon enough run roughshod over the foolishly fine world that planters had made. Her manual for the southern belle anticipates the fastidiously polite but utterly amoral steel magnolia who inhabits the executive suite in downtown Atlanta (and who will soon enough bring to heel Charlie Croker, the nouveau riche good ole boy of Tom Wolfe's wickedly insightful *A Man in Full* [1998]). All Atlanta has ever had to sell is itself, Mitchell shrewdly surmises, and for developers and war survivors that is just fine. The book that became known for offering a portrait of the soul of the Confederacy is a study in the value of soullessness.

There remains a greater irony of Mitchell's work, and that is the way in which it was overmastered by Hollywood. Through Hollywood the central vision of her book largely escaped her hands, its critical slant utterly blunted, leaving her to watch helplessly as the film overpowered her book in the popular imagination. Resigned to the fact that "everyone would go on believing in the Hollywood version," she sighed in a letter to Virginius Dabney, "Since my novel has been published, I have been embarrassed on many occasions by finding myself included among writers who picture the South as a land of white-columned mansions whose wealthy owners had thousands of slaves and drank thousands of juleps. . . . But people believe what they like to believe and the mythical Old South has too strong a hold on their imaginations to be altered by the mere reading of a 1,037-page book."[26]

The 1,037-page book begins dismantling the Cavalier myth with the First Families of Virginia: Ashley Wilkes is "queer" because the Wilkes's "grandfather came from Virginia." This is because Mitchell was sympathetically attuned to W. J. Cash's vision of the man-of-action southerner, the "stout Irishman" turned plantation squire. So was Mitchell's much-admired Faulkner, who accomplished the same sort of thing with the ruthless, monomaniacal Thomas

Sutpen. When Dabney praised *Gone with the Wind* for dispensing with the mythic Old South, Mitchell confirmed his reading: "I certainly had no intention of writing about cavaliers."[27]

In the film, of course, the opening credits have no sooner finished when these words scroll across the screen to the accompaniment of a heavenly choir humming a quivery "Dixie": "There was a land of Cavaliers and Cotton Fields called the Old South. Here in this pretty world, Gallantry took its last bow." "The sad part," Mitchell complained to Dabney, "is that many Southerners believe this myth even more ardently than Northerners."[28] The book was intended to deliver a searing critique of certain planks of Lost Cause belief, the sort of stuff that Confederate widows in their black muslin, like "old crows," rattled on about: the uniformity of support for the Cause, the nobility of it, southern pretensions to the status of "gods," and so on. As Pyron explains, "In unmasking the plantation South, she debunked her own family" and their planter-class pretensions.[29] Yet the book was cinematically reverse-engineered to become the ultimate valediction of the Lost Cause, with the text enshrined as a supporting Bible of romantic southern orthodoxy.

This bitter irony was rooted in the prior success of *Birth of a Nation,* based on *The Clansman* (1905), by Thomas Dixon Jr., whose tombstone identifies him as a "Lawyer-Minister-Author-Orator-Playwright-Actor / A Native of Cleveland County and Most Distinguished Son of His Generation." Mitchell returned the distinguished son's fan mail for *Gone with the Wind* with a letter of her own, saying: "I was practically raised on your books, and love them very much. For many years I have had you on my conscience, and I suppose I might as well confess it now."[30] How might one account for this mutual admiration, when Mitchell confesses heroism through an Irish Catholic character of the sort spurned by the Klan in Tom Watson's Atlanta?

Though the novel *Gone with the Wind* is hardly uncritical of the Ku Klux Klan, Mitchell's book could meet with Thomas Dixon's approval because it depicts vigilantism as a necessary evil in a time when southerners, and especially southern women, were "defenseless" before their conquerors. Thomas Dixon's incendiary novels had revitalized the Klan and made for salacious reading too, as Dixon was only too ready to supply readers with what resulted when rapacious black males met vulnerable white womanhood. At five years of age Margaret Mitchell would urge her father to take up, literally, the family sword, as she witnessed the Atlanta race riots of 1906 smoldering a mere city block away from their Jackson Hill home. A southern order was precariously close to crumbling, galvanizing the remnants of power into another five decades of iron-fisted rule.

And so to a final irony: Thomas Dixon, the voice of the Klan's rebirth, would have nothing but praise for a novel with a Catholic heroine. Both writers' racial politics were shaped by the outpouring of scholarship in the 1920s and 1930s in the spirit of Claude Bowers's view of Reconstruction in *The Tragic Era,* which became the accepted line of interpretation, explicitly and implicitly imposing the principles of the Lost Cause within the historiography. Mitchell's friend Douglas Southall Freeman stands in this tradition; she regarded his four-volume biography of Robert E. Lee as "unsurpassed and unsurpassable."[31] Ultimately, Dixon and Mitchell's mutually supportive works stem from the complete compatibility of their views of the Klan. "Although [Dixon] condemned the second and subsequent Klans for their lawlessness and for their persecutions of Catholics, Jews, and even innocent blacks," writes Cynthia Lynn Lyerly, "he continued to see the first Klan as righteously heroic, never abandoning his belief that black men lusted after white women and that lynching was a justified response."[32] By 1923 he had turned from the anti-Catholic views he had earlier expressed while on the preacher's circuit. There was nothing in *Gone with the Wind* for him to object to, and in its soothing vindication of southerners' hard choices there was much that would meet his approval.

If Margaret Mitchell spent her energy trying to legitimize her identity as a southern Irish Catholic in print, as the critical consensus now holds, it is telling that she was interred to the graceful English of Episcopalian rites. Such was the fate of Gerald O'Hara too: having borrowed Carreen's Catholic Book of Devotions, when Ashley presides at the funeral, he skips any mention of purgatory, since "half the people present had never heard of Purgatory and those who had would take it as a personal affront, if he insinuated, even in prayer, that so fine a man as Mr. O'Hara had not gone straight to Heaven" (708). Once the Catholic prayers have been exhausted, he turns to rites remembered from the Book of Common Prayer. Tellingly, Scarlett "thought the words comforting and beautiful. Only Melanie and Carreen realized that a devoutly Catholic Irishman was being laid to rest by the Church of England's service" (709). One sees the tensions of her life and family history in this scene, of the need to assimilate and yet to honor the past. Given the way that Mitchell connected her Catholicism with the need to be true to her ancestors (and to reject the falsity of perfidious family members), her awareness that one must do as Romans do is all the more striking. In a late twist in the complicated tale of her relationship to Catholicism, the estate of Joseph Mitchell, one of Margaret Mitchell's two nephews, devised to the Archdiocese of Atlanta "a major gift that includes a 50 percent stake in the trademark and literary rights to the international bestseller *Gone With the Wind* and personal items of its author." However uneasy Mitchell's relationship to her mother's church may have been, it now seems that her work will provide a financial windfall for Catholicism in the South in perpetuity.[33]

Indeed, Mitchell was a maverick to the last, in some respects a modernist writer and in others decidedly antimodernist, and that makes her difficult to account for. The woman in the front seat of Atlanta's flapper scene claimed to have missed the modernist express, giving scholars a recurrent point of debate. There can be little doubt that Mitchell was influenced by the long novels of the nineteenth century—one detects Balzac, Thackeray, and Walter Scott, legacy writers of southern libraries also cited by William Faulkner, for whom she expressed admiration.[34] She followed Faulkner's literary career closely, defended James Branch Cabell, and wrote of Thomas Wolfe, "If ever there was a comet in these Southern skies, he was it."[35] Schooled in the nineteenth-century novel, she devoured Hemingway's *To Have and Have Not* (1937) and explained that "dumb creature that I am, I read it for the story and the characters," missing the "profound social implications, sociological portents et cetera" hailed by critics. "I think I need a practicing left-winger at my elbow to point to me what is what in modern literature."[36] There is perhaps a hint of southern anti-intellectualism in her work and her personal politics, but Mitchell's reading list gives her away. Her intelligence surmounted the feigned parochialism of a "dumb creature" in much the same way as Flannery O'Connor's.

The pity of Mitchell's career is not that she wrote for the popular appetite, nor that she failed to write a sequel to *Gone with the Wind* (a might-have-been that has kept her fans sighing for more than seven decades now), but that she gave her writing efforts over to the exhausting business of the novel's success instead of to other projects, becoming, despite her best intentions, the sort of "professional southerner" she hoped to avoid. In fact, the satirist's gimlet eye in her reportage recalls Lafcadio Hearn and John Kennedy Toole. The titles of her columns bring to mind the sorts of things that Flannery O'Connor liked to write about as a coed: "Atlanta Girl Sees Italian Revolution," "The Cat No Longer Has Pajamas," "Gum Chewed at Both Weddings and Funerals," "Wives Wanted By World's Greatest Freaks," "Shot Three Times and Missed Him—Divorced," "Two New York Girls Out-Walk Death," "Grandma Veal Speaks Her Mind on Her 102nd Birthday."[37] The sheer quirkiness of the pieces is appealing, as in the literal gallows humor of "Gallows Room at Tower Used as Pantry" and the exquisitely droll "Harry Thaw Sees Atlanta's Battlefields," documenting a visit by the notorious aristocrat-turned-murderer. Thaw, well versed in Civil

War history, got a gentle correction from a Veteran who insisted, "The Confederits retook the battery."[38]

Elsewhere Mitchell's humor and skepticism show in her interview with a fortune-teller, Madame Foneda, "Irish by birth." Foneda, "smiling out of her blue eyes," is much like Kate Chopin's Irishy Madame Suzima when she asserts that "gypsies and East Indians are not the only races who have the key to the future in their grasp. A nation that boasts of banshees and leprechauns cannot help but be 'fey.'" The fortune-teller is a consoler of "frantic parents" of lost children, of boys who seek buried treasure, and of wives who want to know whether their husbands are out with "blond women"; she flashes a "genuine Irish smile" at her ability to forecast whether prince charming will "come riding in a Packard or a Ford!"[39]

In the sparkling and disarming wit of Margaret Mitchell's reportage and correspondence one is struck by how much her informal writing resembles Flannery O'Connor's. She invited Virginius Dabney to join her club, "The Association of Southerners Whose Grandpappies Did Not Live in Houses With White Columns": "Its membership would be enormous if all of the eligibles came in," she predicted.[40] Like Flannery O'Connor, she seems to have been claimed, and even teleported, by the Irish, though she never ventured there: "My, how I do travel!" she wrote to Herschel Brickell. "A recent clipping from Dublin, Ireland, reports that I spent Christmas in County Meath and that a number of people met me at a party in a Dublin hotel. Ireland is one country I wouldn't mind seeing. So it was nice of this lady to see it for me."[41] She praised Bell Wiley's *Life of Johnny Reb* (1943) with characteristic wit: "Praise God, the writers are mainly privates, stout yeoman, good Crackers and outspoken po' white trash. No one had ever taught them the proper form of a letter (a disadvantage from which officers suffered) and their letters are the real McCoy."[42]

Fittingly, given Mitchell's family roots and mordant humor, the famously protective heirs of the *Gone with the Wind* estate originally courted Pat Conroy to write a sequel, with the preconditions that "sequel authors must agree not to kill Scarlett, not to include any miscegenation scenes, and not to include any homosexuality."[43] The negotiations foundered on these restrictions, so that Conroy would later joke to an Atlanta audience about the perfect opening line, here given in rough anecdotal form: "The day after Scarlett O'Hara's funeral, Rhett Butler woke up, leaned over the languid form of Ashley Wilkes in bed beside him and said, 'Did I ever tell you that my grandmother was a Negress?'"[44] Like Mitchell before him, as an innately dramatic writer Conroy would devote much of his writing energy to showing what was farcical in staged southernness and then shake his head as readers took his satire as a validation of a southern mystique.

The South could never be staged in the same way after *Gone with the Wind,* but in some quarters it had never been taken altogether seriously in the first place. Of the two twentieth-century New Orleans writers to be treated here in a theatrical context, one was a product of the late emanations of New Orleans theater, and the other, of a New Orleans literary hub with national connections. The second writer, Edwin Phillip "Pat" O'Donnell, would write a novel he dubbed "A Delta Comedy," and his work would eventually reach Broadway.

The first, John Kennedy Toole (1937–1969), was born in a later generation, yet he grew up surrounded by the last petrified vestiges of a dramatic culture that preserved traditions of the Victorian parlor: elocution, recitation, variety, the sort of thing that at mid-twentieth century could perhaps persist only in New Orleans. Attribute it to what you will—a "Mediterranean" flair for broad expression, an "Irish" disposition to mockery, a "Caribbean" taste for subversion, or Carnival itself—New Orleans is a city constitutionally predisposed to savor the inversions of high and low, of drama and melodrama. Thelma Ducoing Toole, John Kennedy Toole's famously melodramatic mother, recalled that her very first memory was of being on a stage—and there, in a sense, the wildly dramatic woman would stay. According to Joel Fletcher, by the time of the Civil War, New Orleans was second only to New York City in the number of its theaters and the quality of its professional performances.[45] Well-known performers called continuously in the city during the years of Thelma's youth, when she haunted the Dauphine Theatre in company with her celebrity-spotting sisters and her aunt. But as S. Frederick Starr submits, by the time Ken Toole came along, those nineteenth-century theatrical traditions "lived on only in her parlor."[46] Fletcher believes that the theatrical scene "played a more important role in educating and forming her than did the Catholic Church." Her brother Arthur attended Mass daily, but Thelma once commented to John Geiser, "Whenever you have to deal with a priest or a nun, you always get a headache!"[47]

Still, the church certainly played some sort of role in her life, though she liked to speak, tongue in cheek, of what she called "pa-roach-al" schools: "I had a good time, but I didn't learn anything from those nuns. They were from Ireland." She remembered Sister Thaddeus as "a tall, Irish beauty. Slightly freckled, very sprightly, and she used to blush a good deal. Beautiful blue eyes. I was frisky in the classroom . . . high-strung. I behaved, yes, but one time I had to write twenty times on my big wide tablet: 'I am a bad girl.' 'Girrrl' Sister Thaddeus used to say. I had an awful crush on her!" In later years she hammed it up by recounting tales of "dem sweet Sisters" in an Irish Channel accent. Though Thelma preferred public schools for her son's education, she taught drama for five years at what she termed the "Convent of the Good Shepherd for Delinquent Girls." If anyone needed the comfort of faith, she would seem a likely candidate: in the course of her life she endured the suicides of her uncle, her former brother-in-law, and, finally, her son. Following Ken Toole's suicide, Thelma Toole returned, accompanied by her husband, to Saint Peter and Saint Paul Church, where they had exchanged vows and where she would look on her son for the last time. The priest at Thelma's funeral Mass, according to Fletcher, was "doddering and had a strong Irish Channel accent: 'In de name ob de fadder, an de son, an de holy spirit.'" The grey-haired priest had "eyebrows still inky black, like two anchovies unrolled on his forehead," and he anointed Thelma "by de earl of Salvation."[48]

Like Kate Chopin, Thelma Ducoing Toole came of mixed Irish-Creole stock. Notwithstanding her pride in her long Creole pedigree, Thelma described her mother and grandmother as "Irish," and whereas her older sister Anna "looked very French," she would describe herself as looking "very Irish." As so often happens, Irish pride trumped, especially where boasting was concerned. Having declared, during a radio interview, that to call her son a "scholarly genius" was "putting it too mildly," she cut the host off and said, "Now listen to me, Tom. I told you when I met you, I'm Irish." Before the host could cut in, she continued, "with great authority": "Someone told me that in Ireland perception extends to the working classes. . . . The Irish *are* perceptive, the most perceptive nation in the world!" Then she added, "Maybe East Indians are. . . . I don't know any East Indians." The radio host wisely cut to commercials.[49]

Yet one trait of the stereotypical Irish mother was conspicuously absent in Thelma: she did not seem much bothered about instilling piety in her son or serving as the transmitter of the doctrines of faith. For his part, her husband had at least one trait stereotypically ascribed to the Irish Catholic father: he seems to have been something of a "bachelor husband." John Dewey Toole Jr.'s family had arrived after the Famine. His grandparents were Irish immigrants who moved into the Channel after consecrating a trans-Catholic, interethnic marriage—Mary Orfila Toole was a second-generation American with a "large Spanish family."[50] A first priority for Thelma Toole, a would-be climber who made much of name cachet but had no wealth, was to move uptown. The book reflects the class tensions endemic to their family life. Her son would pen a ripping yarn with an unregenerate Catholic elitist-yet-proletarian as its hero and then tear the whole thing apart with the satiric exuberance so common to Irish writers.

As W. B. Yeats reminded his readers, Irish satirists were believed to possess powers of supernatural dimensions: "A satire could fill a whole country-side with famine."[51] Satire includes the ability to place a curse on someone, so satirists' words could be fatal; the story of the Pied Piper, for example, might be traceable to the tale of an Irish satirist whose verses sent rats to their death.[52] In fact, Ignatius Reilly enjoys the sounds of "wharf rats" that "played frenetic games among themselves within the walls [of Levy Pants]."[53] The rats of *A Confederacy of Dunces* (1980) come in human varieties too, and Ignatius is their king. Toole proves adept at sending up all aspects of Catholicism, from false piety to hagiography, both of which come together bathetically when Ignatius announces, "I am going to pray to St. Martin de Porres, the patron saint of mulattoes, for our cause in the factory ["The Campaign for Moorish Dignity"]. Because he is also invoked against rats, he will perhaps aid us in the office, too" (110).

The cathedrals in which Ken Toole (as he was known to friends) dwelled were more of the head than of the heart; by creating Ignatius, he might empty himself of all that seemed false and wickedly cerebral in a church from which he had little hope of escape. He was "a Christmas-and-Easter churchgoer," according to his biographers Nevils and Hardy, "but he had a cultural commitment to Roman Catholicism,"[54]—and he certainly had more than a layman's understanding of his faith. During the last year of his life, Toole undertook graduate studies at Tulane, proposing a seminar paper that would focus "on Dreiser's lapsed Catholicism and his relationship with his mother" and perhaps on Dreiser's "anti-Catholic views" as well, both subjects close to Toole's heart. At Hunter College in New York he reportedly conned a line from the writer Peter Viereck in chalking "Anti-Catholicism is the anti-Semitism of the American intellectual" on the board for his students.[55]

Toole's southern manners, his Old World Catholicism and its traditional core—these did not translate into easy acceptance at Hunter. If, as Lord Acton said, "Exile is the nursery of nationality," the anti-Catholic views that greeted Toole during his teaching stint at Hunter activated a sense of southern and Catholic ethnicity that might otherwise have remained latent.[56] There is much of Toole's own experience in Ignatius Reilly's misbegotten attempts to connect with students and radicalized "young people." Writing to his friend Elemore Morgan Jr., back in Lafayette, Toole explained, "The students at Hunter, these aggressive, ill-kempt, pseudo-liberal girls, are extremely interesting and constantly amusing. They are continually off on some new crusade, such as helping southern Negroes, fighting latent Nazism. Where I had to stir up students at SLI [Southwestern Louisiana Institute, now the University of Louisiana at Lafayette], I have to sit on them here. But, for all of their craziness, the girls are likable—almost lovable."[57]

Among the Myrna Minkoffs he was a great distance from home. Ken Toole called himself a "southernist," and at least one friend described him as a "ferocious defender of the South."[58] He kept company with committed liberal activists but was uncomfortable with the confrontational side of the civil rights movement. Like certain other writers in this study—including Flannery O'Connor and Joel Chandler Harris—he was a kind of conservative progressive, the sort of gradualist who believed "the South should handle its own problems."[59] He rejoiced when John F. Kennedy was elected and shared in the elation of Irish Catholics across the country in that signal moment. He was crestfallen in equal measure at the news of Kennedy's death, an event that precipitated a spell of writer's block as he worked on *A Confederacy of Dunces*: "Then I couldn't write anything more. Nothing seemed funny to me. I went into a funk."[60]

In fact, he suggested that Kennedy's death prompted him to finish, if not cut short, *A Confederacy of Dunces,* the book for which he is remembered. The narrative of Toole's life takes on a pleasing tidiness if one treats him as a one-book writer, with *The Neon Bible* (posthumously published in 1989) footnoted as juvenilia. But Toole was not a one-book writer, and *The Neon Bible* should not be discarded; it bears some discussion before turning to *A Confederacy of Dunces. The Neon Bible*'s satiric power reveals a talented artist in the making, and as early works tend to do, it reveals which syllables the author stressed in the larger accents of childhood and puberty. In that sense, the book is revealingly autobiographical in small details, such as this passage worthy of Robert Graves (the poet who penned "The Naked and the Nude"): "No one ever saw me naked but Aunt Mae and Mother and Poppa. . . . I don't know why, but it makes you feel funny to have someone see you naked, it makes you feel nasty, though it shouldn't."[61]

David Hardin makes a case for the novel's closeted subtexts and suggests that scenes showcasing David's nudity point to "a closeted performance of the homoerotic."[62] I would join MacLauchlin and Fletcher in observing that this is not the most obvious construction to put on the text, and I would add that this "performance" must also be interpreted in the light of an Irish Catholicism uncomfortable with the body and anything remotely connected to sex. Nevils and Hardy note that "the open locker room intimidated" the young writer: "He had been raised to be modest and fully clothed in front of other people, and the boys ribbed Ken about his reluctance to undress around them." Shades of Jansenism, once again: an intense (if understandably adolescent) discomfort with sexuality defines the precocious *Neon Bible* and is translated into veiled talk of the sexually irrepressible Aunt Mae, another detail that squares with biography ("Several acquaintances agreed that sexuality in general was a distasteful subject to Ken, and it would remain so throughout his life").[63]

Another defining feature of the text is the unusual way it approaches religion. *The Neon Bible* does something remarkable, all the more so when one considers its sixteen-year-old author: it operates within a religious tradition other than the author's. A number of critics have stumbled over this quality of Flannery O'Connor's work, misidentifying her as a quasi-Protestant writer. It takes a Catholic to know one: like Flannery O'Connor, Toole was offering a veiled critique of the version of Christianity that dominated the southern states. Writing to Robert Gottlieb, his would-be editor for *A Confederacy of Dunces,* in March 1965, Toole explained of his earlier work, "In 1954, when I was sixteen, I wrote a book called *The Neon Bible,* a grim, adolescent sociological attack upon the hatreds spawned by the various Calvinist religions in the South, and the fundamentalist mentality is one of the roots of what has been happening in Alabama, etc. The book, of course, was bad, but I sent it off a couple of times anyway."[64]

Where the book mentions Catholicism, there are satiric undertones and secular tensions: a preacher's ex-wife settles in New Orleans and sends her daughter to a Catholic school; a preacher calls the pope into question; and so on. David (the tale's narrator) has an uncle, away for the duration of the war, who writes to say that "he saw where the Pope lived," leading David to muse, "I had heard about him [the Pope] plenty of times when the preacher was talking over the radio in place of *Amos 'n' Andy,* who I liked" (85). Later he writes of a book-burning deacon who suspects that *Gone with the Wind*'s popularity must be because it is "licentious." Even after he convenes a group of censors "in black masks" at the library, "the sheriff didn't want to do anything about it because he'd get into too much trouble with the people in town, and anyway, the election was next month" (25).

Morality police indeed. School offers no refuge from the tyranny of the majority, for even in *Neon Bible* territory this is a confederacy of dunces. David calls Longfellow's poem "The Day is Done" "the only beautiful thing I ever heard." The class thinks differently: "Everybody learned it because they had to, but thought it was stupid and wanted to sing a song instead. Mr. Farney said we could sing a song too, so that made them feel better. The class voted to sing 'Dixie'" (101). It is this sort of bowed-head, knee-jerk southern conformity that drives Toole up a tree. The quiet delivery of *The Neon Bible* belies its brimming sarcasm, and it shows Toole in progress to the full-throated parody of *A Confederacy of Dunces,* where Ignatius formally indicts "some poor white from Mississippi" who "told the dean that [he] was a propagandist for the pope, which was patently untrue" (45).[65] Consider these examples of how Toole and O'Connor send up the prosaic hymn of the "happy clappy" school:

He said for us to open tonight with "a good rousing chorus" of some song I never heard of.

> "Sinners can be saints if they'll just bear the cross (3X)
> Bear it and reserve your place in heaven.
> Bear, bear that cross, bear, bear that cross
> Bear, bear that cross, bear, bear that cross for Jesus."

. . . It was an easy song to learn, and I sang it with them the second time. It had a good beat *that you could put almost any words to.* (Toole, *Neon Bible* 65, emphasis added)

> Oh, Jesus you be my friend
> Right, oh, yeah, right up til the end.
> . . . .
> I ain't complaining
> Though maybe it's raining
> When I'm with Jesus.
> . . . .
> Oh, Jesus, you give me peace
> When you keeping away them po-lice.
> . . . .
> Oh, Jesus you pay my bail
> When they put me in that old jail.
> Oh, oh, you always giving

A reason for living.

. . . .

I never sinning

I always winning

Now I got Jesus.

. . . .

Oh Jesus, you hearing my woe

And I never, I never, never gonna let you go.

(Toole, *Confederacy of Dunces* 140–41)

[T]he nasal chorus on the radio kept the room from silence:

> *"You go to blank blank*
> *And I'll go to mine*
> *But we'll all blank along*
> *To-geth-ther,*
> *And all along the blank*
> *We'll hep eachother out*
> *Smile-ling in any kind of*
> *Weath-ther!"*

Mrs. Turpin didn't catch every word but she caught enough to agree with the spirit of the song and it turned her thoughts sober. To help anybody out that needed it was her philosophy of life.[66]

Flannery O'Connor's hymn would appear to be set to "The Bonnie Banks of Loch Lomond"—a meaty choice when one considers the reputed Jacobite origins of the old air, a horribly tragic ballad set to trippingly cheerful music. Ironically, the woefully self-deceived and righteously Protestant Mrs. Turpin (Mrs. Turnip, really—you can't get blood from her) believes that by works, even those that originate from an uncharitable spirit, we are saved. O'Connor's real target, then, might be a familiar type of Catholic piety. With similar indirection, David dissembles in his praise for the catchy and entirely made-up "hymn" of *The Neon Bible*. True, Christ required that his followers take up their crosses, but it is a long stride from there to "reserving a place in heaven": merely having a cross to bear does not guarantee passage through the Pearly Gates.

Following the same beat in *A Confederacy of Dunces,* Toole's satiric drive sweeps across targets, with lyrics that go from being simply childish, theologically unsound, and self-contradictory ("I never sinning / I always winning") to an obvious send-up of their interchangeability with vaporous commercial pop music. The "spiritual" takes a nasty potshot at trouble-brewing civil rights assemblies, but an even uglier undertone sounds in the phrase "giving / A reason for living." Even though he understood how religion might provide a refuge for the desperate and the downtrodden, he could not find adequate succor there for himself.

If Toole had a basic grasp of southern old-time religion, his distance from the Protestant center can be detected in the mordant wit of both his books. *The Neon Bible* originated in Toole's experiment in "passing" from Catholic-infused New Orleans to Protestant-dominated areas around it. At age sixteen he joined a best friend from high school, Cary Laird, in visiting Laird's extended family in rural Mississippi. Even the journey to a world so markedly different— through places where roadside signs might admonish, "Drink and Drive and Burn Alive"—was seared into Toole's consciousness. There Toole might try his hand at such decidedly "country" activities as driving a tractor, experiences that he would recall with relish and much fascination and that undoubtedly informed the texture of a life in imagined rural poverty in *The Neon Bible.*

Another formative experience, also documented by Toole's biographer Cory MacLauchlin, is reflected in the novel.[67] About the same time, Toole would go with his mother and Laird to hear the evangelist Billy Graham preach in New Orleans. Young John Toole was no doubt absorbed in a different presentation of religious theatrics, which, to the prejudices of Catholic eyes, might have seemed a crass form of salesmanship. According to Thelma Toole, the widely advertised event, which probably culminated in an altar call, elicited mainly mockery from the teenagers: "We were fascinated—professing for Christ— young minister, very handsome, in a beige suit and a salmon tie showed how wicked social dancing was. I said to my son, 'This is a fine religious meeting.' And they laughed their heads off. I didn't think they were funny. My son gained a great deal from that."[68]

Evidently, Thelma's religious views might have been more latitudinarian and ecumenical than her son's, and there is a measure of wisdom in her response. Even so, some of John Toole's snortling found its way into the pages of *The Neon Bible,* although the novel is tempered by a more serious religiosity throughout. Protestant righteousness is lanced in a *Neon Bible* sermon delivered by a child preacher-prodigy named Bobbie Lee Taylor: "Do you want your son to return home with a foreign wife, maybe even a heathen?" he demands (69). Toole plays the urban against the rural; after all, he came from New Orleans, a city where foreign wives were not uncommon.

Taylor's sermon continues with another cross to bear: "This is the cross you women must bear because you have been asleep to the words of *Jee*-sus. Do you want a Chinese in your house taking care of your grandchildren, nursing them from her breast? The sins of your men may be your burdens in the future." Taylor exhorts the audience to "think of this" and when they write their GIs to include "the glorious words of the Bible, of Matthew, of Genesis" (69). Later David overhears one of the attendees telling his aunt "she didn't want any Chinee grandbabies on her knee with their dangerous-looking mother hanging around the house" (75). When the woman asks why no one from David's family went up to be saved, she says, "We hadn't really made up our minds yet." The woman advises them to do it quickly "because Bobbie Lee [is] going to be here only a few more nights, and you might as well be in God's favor with all they said about Hitler sending a bomb over" (75).

Even at sixteen, Toole knew enough of the Protestant South to "pass" and to poke fun. The satiric voice of the passage is remarkably mature, foreshadowing the brilliance of *A Confederacy of Dunces* and its truculent antihero. On the whole, though, David's voice is achingly earnest in an adolescent way, moderate, modulated, and naïve. Toole delivers David's impressions of the revival in deadpan prose. Perhaps this is why many of those who have commented on *The Neon Bible* have failed to notice the subtle humor of that sharply observant work.

Similarly, Flannery O'Connor would look across the church aisle in a chapter of *The Violent Bear It Away* (1960) devoted to the adolescent Francis Marion Tarwater's visit to a revival featuring a charismatic child preacher. Like Flannery O'Connor, Toole was mature beyond his years in detecting pretension, deceit, and folly. Nevils and Hardy suggest that *The Neon Bible* is a "dark, short novel patterned after the southern Gothic fiction of Flannery O'Connor." The book's gothic villain, however, is more reminiscent of Harry Powell in David Grubb's *Night of the Hunter* (1953) than of anyone in Flannery's *oeuvre,* a charismatic but warped preacher who plots to send David's mother to the insane asylum, leading to the novel's blood-soaked finale, somewhat transparently the device of an immature writer who needed a quick ending for his book. (Again, autobiography intrudes: Thelma's family had sought to have her unstable youngest brother, George, committed, and Thelma's state of mental health was the subject of speculation during her lifetime.)[69] Unlike most gothic fictions, the book offers few distortions and little of supernatural import. If Toole had read O'Connor, he had done so quickly, since *Wise Blood* (1952) had only just been published when he was writing his first book. (Joel Fletcher would recall of his time with Toole in the summer of 1960, "We had some literary tastes in common. We talked about Flannery O'Connor and Evelyn Waugh.")[70]

Precisely like O'Connor, though, Toole discovered one of his first outlets for artistic expression by penning cartoons for his college newspaper, a satiric venue that might fly under the radar of overbearing mothers in those buttoned-down years. The two writers were kindred spirits in multiple ways: "intellectual" Catholics, well-versed in theology and church history, critical of their region yet defenders of it, relentlessly sharp in their caricatures. In a scene worthy of O'Connor's fiction, the adolescent Ken Toole so outrageously heckled a self-styled evangelist who walked St. Charles Avenue that the enraged man swung his cross at him.[71] Based on the contents of Ken's car after he went missing during the last two months of his life, Thelma Toole would later claim that one of Ken's final acts had been to pay a visit to Flannery O'Connor's Andalusia in Milledgeville, Georgia.[72]

Having spent his early years behind Catholic glass, examining the Protestant majority, Toole was equipped to create a splenetic Catholic windmill tilter. A masterwork of the satiric form more usually articulated within southern literature vis-à-vis southwestern humor, *A Confederacy of Dunces* can be placed in a developing chain of tradition. During the Civil War, Anthony Keiley demonstrated a Catholic satiric inclination in *In Vinculis;* Lafcadio Hearn invoked satire wherever he saw injustice; Joel Chandler Harris displayed a genius for submerging his satiric penchant in vernacular allegory; Flannery O'Connor, in some respects his apostle, spoke approvingly of his work. John Kennedy Toole's satiric sensibility resembles O'Connor's insofar as he pokes fun at southern follies, but he shares something in common with Lafcadio Hearn in his love of New Orleans's colorful places and even more colorful personalities.

A Confederacy of Dunces also bears witness to Toole's somewhat bookish appreciation for the intellectual history of the religion. He is able to send up the disapproving spirit of Father Abram Ryan by reincarnating him in Ignatius Reilly, who grumbles, "I do not support the current Pope. He does not at all fit my concept of a good, authoritarian Pope. Actually, I am opposed to the relativism of modern Catholicism quite violently" (51). No doubt Ignatius had in mind Pope John XXIII, perhaps best known for convening the Second Vatican Council, whose election occurred about the time that Toole started work on his book.

Occasionally, elements of Toole's Irish background shine through his one-of-a-kind character too. What Toole thought of moribund Irish hoopla is reflected in his description of the Reilly residence: "Near the dead tree [by the porch] was a slight mound of earth and a leaning Celtic cross cut from plywood" (36). This pitiable talisman of ethnic identity is not the only one. Mrs. Reilly keeps her small savings "in the Hibernia bank" (50) (Flannery O'Connor's grandfather, Edward Francis O'Connor Sr., was a director of the Hibernia Bank in Savannah). Ignatius records in his journal his efforts to show solidarity with the workers he champions by dancing with them: "Having spent countless hours of my life watching those blighted children on television dancing to this sort of music, I knew the physical spasm which it was supposed to elicit, and I attempted my own conservative version of the same on the spot to further pacify the workers. I must admit that my body moved with surprising agility; I am not without an innate sense of rhythm; my ancestors must have been rather outstanding at jigging on the heath" (121).

And always there is Toole's ear for how it is said. "Like his father," write Nevils and Hardy, "Kenny was a natural mimic." From the time he was a child he had been groomed for the stage, playing in local troupes, giving recitations, and even working in radio drama, where he emceed a program called *Telekids* (allusions to radio abound in both of Toole's books). There was more than a touch of bourgeois vaudeville schlock in Toole's childhood; at one point "he had worked up a one-man show of comic impressions titled *Great Lovers of the World*."[73] Until his adolescence his mother reviewed his performances for accent and delivery, and this, in turn, served him well as a writer. Certainly Mrs. Reilly's ritual of going to "make" groceries at Schwegmann's Grocery—a place where "the Irish-Channel accent could be heard loud and sometimes clear," as Joel Fletcher puts it—epitomizes Toole's New Orleans.[74] The dialects of New Orleans are recorded with an exuberance not seen since Lafcadio Hearn.

In terms of satire, Toole harkens back to the Roman masters, as evidenced by Ignatius's concern with overindulgence, purging, and indigestion—fitting, since the tradition is linked to the *satura lanx,* a dish that is best served cold. Ignatius vomits when distressed, as does *The Neon Bible*'s David when he is beaten up for being a "sissy" (12). Satire tends to focus on the body as a place that resists the various means of self- and social control. What galls Ignatius, the classic conservative, more than the unruly, untamable, and disordered body?

Strangely enough, Ignatius seems a dead ringer for the body-conscious protagonist of Anthony Burgess's *Enderby* novels, the first of which, *Inside Mr. Enderby,* was published in 1963. In fact, the novels share so many similarities that one wonders whether Toole indeed read Burgess; if so, he did so in short order, since a letter dated March 23, 1963, gives the first indication that Toole was at work on what would become *A Confederacy of Dunces.* Still, the similarities abound: Francis Xavier Enderby, a fallen-away Catholic, composes on the toilet and suffers from chronic dyspepsia, brought on by upsetting news (compare Ignatius Reilly, who prays to "St. Medericus, the Hermit, who is invoked against intestinal disorders" [240]). Like Ignatius, Enderby is perpetually distressed by the condition of modern culture, especially pop culture and consumerism; he tangles with a feminist foil (Vesta Bainbridge by name), who is at turns inspiring and maddening and who adores him despite his prickly and unapologetic bachelorhood. Enderby too lives a solitary existence in his small quarters, awash in his unpublished scribblings (he uses his bathtub for a filing cabinet, whereas Ignatius is partial to a dresser drawer).

To my knowledge, no one has commented on the overlap between these two satires with their strikingly similar, afflatus-inspired antiheroes. Perhaps great minds think alike, or are shaped alike: both authors came from Irish Catholic families in places that heightened their sense of ethnic identity. Burgess's autobiographical work makes plain the importance of his Irish Catholic roots (he was a cofounder of the Princess Grace Irish Library in Monaco), with some of his stories recalling Irish stylists (and not simply those that emulate Joyce, whom he worshiped). His sense of outsiderism emerges in an interview with Samuel Coale, recorded in 1978.

> Coale: Because you were a Catholic in England to begin with, did that already give you a sense of exile?
>
> Burgess: . . . Throughout the history of my family, such as it is, and throughout my own career, I've always been aware of this inability on my own part—and the part of my own people—to come to terms with the Protestant establishment in England. . . . It was only with the Catholic Emancipation Acts that things began to go right. It's all right if you're a Catholic convert like Graham Greene or Evelyn Waugh. You can have the best of both worlds, but if you're a cradle Catholic with Irish blood, then you're automatically a renegade to the outside.[75]

In the same interview, Burgess comments on the nature of *Irish* Catholicism and "a kind of puritanical element in Catholicism, which you don't get in the South [of England]. You don't get it in Spain. You certainly don't get it in Italy."[76] Though their worlds were in some respects very different, Burgess and Toole faced similar challenges in their respective Protestant establishments. Both learned the value of humor as a means of defense. Of course it is characteristic of Irish parody that the satirist at some point takes aim at himself. Burgess wrote the first *Enderby* novel under the pseudonym Joseph Kell and then had the good fortune to review it for the unwitting *Yorkshire Post,* where he cited literary authority: "Mr. Eliot said recently—and in the *Yorkshire Post,* too—that poetry is a lavatorial or purgative art." The reviewer then concluded of his own work, "It may well make some people sick, and those of my readers with tender stomachs are advised to let it alone. . . . It is a laughing-stock."[77]

A Confederacy of Dunces too is full of an inspired and bittersweet willingness to become the laughingstock, since Toole himself is more often than not the butt of his own joke. For example, when it is discovered that Ignatius has an imaginary girlfriend, "it was sadder than Mr. Levy had thought at first. The poor kook had tried to make his mother think he had a girlfriend" (315). Toole's "good friend and steady date Ruth Kathmann," who attended graduate school at Columbia with him and who may have been a model for Myrna Minkoff, might well have been *his* imaginary girlfriend from a failed relationship that produced "more smoke than flame."[78] Myrna Minkoff reminds Ignatius that "Freud linked paranoia with homosexual tendencies" (79). This is interesting since Toole's sexual orientation and paranoid tendencies have been the subject of much speculation; his latest biographer, Cory MacLauchlin, acknowledges rumors of homosexuality that were put forward as fact in *Ignatius Rising* but thinks it best to acknowledge that the truth of the matter is simply unknowable, while the biographer Joel Fletcher views it as highly unlikely that Toole was a homosexual.[79]

Whatever Toole's sexual preference may have been, he was willing to poke fun at both homophobia and homosexuals in *A Confederacy of Dunces*. His stance on race is similarly cheeky, targeting various races as well as racism, with no quarter for the Irish. There seems a whiff of self-derision when Myrna Minkoff plans to make a film about an interracial marriage and writes to Ignatius about its "sick, reactionary villain," "an Irish landlord who refuses to rent to the couple"—a man after Ignatius's own heart, apparently. "The landlord lives in this little womb-room whose walls are covered with pictures of the Pope and stuff like that. In other words, the audience will have no trouble reading him as soon as they get one glimpse at that room. We have not cast the landlord yet. You, of course, would be fantastic for the part" (80).

Perhaps Toole, as a closeted Catholic, would have been well cast too. It is a testament to his creativity, not to mention his magnificent sense of humor, that he jousted with his Ignatian alter-ego, the crank he seemed likely to become. Bob Byrne and Maurice duQuesnay have both been suggested as real-life forbears for Ignatius, but Professor duQuesnay's caution in a recent interview is particularly apt: "Ignatius is neither Byrne nor Toole: he is a magical amalgamation born of Toole's imagination. . . . Here the warning of T. S. Eliot assumes much relevance: art, for Eliot, is not an expression of personality but an escape from personality."[80] All that Toole abominated about himself—his place and culture, southern, Catholic, stagnant—finds a way into the book. Elemore Morgan Jr. remembered him as "a really brilliant guy, very smart. Ken saw everything as absurd. Life was just a grand folly. He saw the ridiculous easily and quickly. He always gave the impression that he was about to break into an ironic comment or smile."[81] In a lecture delivered at the University of Southwestern Louisiana (now the University of Louisiana at Lafayette) on September 18, 1981, Robert Coles compared Ignatius Reilly to a Roman Catholic Church that "like Ignatius, had to keep trying, keep reaching out to the entire arc of humanity, keep hoping in various ways to become a spiritual instrument in the lives of every possible kind of person, as Ignatius for all his absurdities and tics and postures and excesses manages to be for the characters in *A Confederacy of Dunces*."[82] Such was Toole's ecumenical sense of humor, underpinned by a Catholic way of perceiving the fallen-ness of all.

Viewed with a little distance, Toole's sensibility is a reminder that Irish American literature began in satire, and his contributions to the genre, along with Flannery O'Connor's and E. P. O'Donnell's, marked a needed return to an old tradition. Farcical Irish-themed plays such as Rich Sheridan's *St. Patrick's Day: or the Scheming Lieutenant,* written in 1788, began appearing on the New Orleans marquees as early as the 1830s. *The Irish Ambassador, The Irish Heiress* (an 1857 play by Dion Boucicault), and lesser-known works such *The Irishman in China* drew crowds even in Dixie.[83] "By 1850," writes Earl Niehaus in his treatment of New Orleans's stage Irish, "Paddy was king of the boards," outshining "Negro and Yankee" caricatures in regional variety theater.[84] A farce called *The Irish Tutor* ran for seven seasons spanning 1840–58 and was billed at five different New Orleans theaters.[85] What is Ignatius Reilly if not an Irish laughingstock? In a sense, Toole channeled the theatrical soul of his city truly, and in tribute his work has invited dramatic interpretation. For example, Terence Davies, a gay English writer and director who grew up in a large Irish Catholic family in Liverpool, adapted *The Neon Bible* to the screen in 1995.[86] Affinities of identity might well have brought Davies to the text: As part of the conservative Irish Catholic minority in his native Liverpool, Davies grew up in an environment not unlike Burgess's Irish Manchester. Davies witnessed anti-Catholic bigotry during Orange parades and struggled desperately to reconcile his religious identity with his sexuality, as he documents in his 2008 film *Of Time and the City.*

Tensions over faith and self-identity defined John Kennedy Toole's life as well, and these tensions were covered up by the comedy for which he is remembered. *A Confederacy of Dunces* is an innately theatrical work; it has been

staged in venues ranging from Center House Theatre in Seattle to Balzer Theater in Atlanta.[87] Yet even as *Confederacy* finds it way, slowly, to the stage, it has
cultivated a reputation for being oddly unfilmable. John Belushi, John Candy,
Chris Farley, and Will Farrell were tapped at various times to play Ignatius, to
no avail. In fact, from the early 1980s so many shuttered attempts have been
made to film it that industry insiders widely consider it to be cursed.

Perhaps this is appropriate to a book that savages a number of identifiable
films from the early 1960s, a book that imagines the disapproving visionary
Saint Hroswitha encountering a vacuous teenybopper television show: "The
images of those lasciviously gyrating children would disintegrate into so many
ions and molecules, thereby effecting the catharsis which the tragedy of the
debauching of the innocent necessarily demands" (46). The satiric drive cannot be stifled; mock hagiography meets Toole's sense of self-absurdity via his
adolescent appearances as an emcee on *Telekids.* He was a master of stagecraft
in writing and in life, and his awareness of the "correct" mantles permitted him
to topple those who made bold to wear them, with the joke somehow at his sole
expense.

The belated popular acclaim of *A Confederacy of Dunces* has yet to find Toole's
kindred spirit and predecessor, E. P. (Edwin Phillip "Pat") O'Donnell (March 25,
1895–April 19, 1943). O'Donnell was also from New Orleans, also the author of
two books, and a master of comic dialogue. The scion of "Galway O'Donnells"
and "County Clare O'Briens," according to one biographer,[88] E. P. O'Donnell
grew up in the Irish Channel, writes Eudora Welty, "within close distance of
the shipping wharves and railroad yards." His father was said to be a brake-
man,[89] and this squares with the 1910 census, which lists O'Donnell's Indiana-
born father as a locomotive engineer and his mother, Alice O'Brien, as a native
Louisianan whose parents were born in Ireland.[90] O'Donnell was an omnivo-
rous reader who dropped out of school early; some accounts suggest the fourth
grade, some the seventh. Like another literary man of action, he is said to have
driven an ambulance during his service in World War I. This is harder to cor-
roborate in O'Donnell's case: port records from New Orleans document that
in July 1916, the year before America entered the war, he was employed as an
assistant purser as part of the sizable crew of the United Fruit Company's SS
Coppename, shipping from Belize to New Orleans.[91] O'Donnell's World War I
draft registration card, signed on June 5, 1917, gives his occupation as a clerk

at the Southern Pacific Railway. It notes that the young man is missing three fingers of his left hand.[92]

He would claim to have held thirty-three jobs, including those of paperboy, shoeshine, boxing instructor, factory worker, and, fortuitously, chief publicity writer.[93] A 1927 New Orleans city directory gives his address as 4727 Cleveland Avenue, in a comfortably middle-class district, and indeed lists him as "adv mgr" at Ford Motor Company.[94] After chancing to discover O'Donnell conducting a Ford plant tour at the facility on the outskirts of New Orleans (now closed), Sherwood Anderson was sufficiently impressed by his narrative panache that he advised him to become a writer. (In a letter to Gordon Lewis, Anderson refers to O'Donnell as "The Immortal Pat.")[95]

To the astonishment of everyone, Pat did, selling his first short story at age thirty-six, perhaps in part *because* of his training at Ford: "I learned to write coherently as an advertising man," he explained to Bennett Augustin, "paid to compose sentences with meat in them, and for some years."[96] After placing his first commercial story, "Like a Man!," with *Collier's* in 1931, he followed up with stories in *Scribner's* and in *Harper's,* and he would go on to win a Houghton Mifflin literary fellowship in 1935. According to the jacket of the first edition of *The Great Big Doorstep,* O'Donnell "hiked down the levee from New Orleans to the Delta" and discovered the place with which he fell in love. With his fellowship winnings he bought a "one room shack at Boothville, 90 miles south of New Orleans where he wrote and raised Easter lilies and oranges."[97]

That sounds romantic enough, naturally, but it was a chancy thing for a middle-aged man to do, and the circumstances that prompted the dissolution of O'Donnell's first marriage and his departure from his comfortable New Orleans home are not entirely clear. In any case, Boothville is quite literally at the end of the road, as far as one can travel overland along the banks of the Mississippi before it empties into the Gulf. O'Donnell sketched this land's end in a *Scribner's* article titled "Fragments from Alluvia":

> Unique social and climatic conditions result from the curious arrangement of land and water. The low levee is not a mere barrier, as it is elsewhere. It forms the sole avenue of human movement. There is no other road or path. To go anywhere, you must walk atop the levee, rambling past orange groves fragrant with citrus oils. If you meet any one, you meet him on the levee. It is impossible to go anywhere without being perceived by all.
>
> On one side the levee is the River with its small boats and luggers painted purple, or green, or blue, or yellow; and its peddler packets bring-

ing accurate news of the price of fish and fur; and its great, disdainful ships that never stop, but hurry past, heavy with cargo from every mart on the globe. On the opposite side are the oranges and multicolored truck patchers; beyond these the lush grasses of the marsh, alive with fur-bearing animals; then, still farther out, the Gulf, abundant with fish, shrimp, and oysters.[98]

The setting of Toole's later novel, *The Great Big Doorstep* (1941), is "Grass Margin, Louisiana," and it is redolent of these scenes. The very fact of shared marginality permitted new social orders to arise; O'Donnell's writings make plain that he felt equally at ease among all social castes. When he was not socializing in New Orleans or writing, he worked the shrimp boats, established a small truck farm, and helped growers establish collectives. He was so impecunious, living "close to the bone," in his words, that he resorted to "riding the trucks" between Boothville and New Orleans. (Writing from his Boothville cottage in 1941, O'Donnell would complain about "losing young oranges by the bushel with the drought. It's hurting the lilies too—just when there'll be a shortage of Jap stuff. Son of a bitch.")[99] A man of Hemingwayesque appetites, he could write to his fellow scribbler Bennett Augustin in November 1932, "Three of us caught 125 beautiful trout in a couple of hours. I got drunk on wine and cut my hands opening oysters, but we feasted. It was a real male, elemental feast, strong flavors of garlic and olive oil and plenty of wine and talk of women."[100]

Little surprise that he was resigned to "liv[ing] in the country, where I feel and function best."[101] At this unlikely Walden he penned his first novel, *Green Margins* (1936), the initial title of which had been *Sons of Salt*. O'Donnell's biographical note in the May 1936 issue of *Menagerie* reflects his ambitions: the "poet, novelist, and short story writer" who had placed stories in "Harpers, Colliers, Story, Scribners, etc." expected his "prize-winning novel" to be published that autumn. No doubt partially through the good graces of Sherwood Anderson—whose letters of introduction to Gertrude Stein and others had made Hemingway's literary career possible—O'Donnell was fully launched as 1936 unfolded, gathering favorable reviews, appearing in portrait on the front cover of the *Saturday Review of Literature* (October 3, 1936), and attending the New York Times National Book Fair the next month.[102]

Green Margins is an elegiac book that follows the fortunes of the Slovenian family Kalavich, true to O'Donnell's unfeigned affinity with stragglers at the verdant edges of America's forgotten subcontinent. A letter of May 24, 1936, to Ben Augustin suggests a possible model for the Kalavich family: O'Donnell wrote to seek Augustin's help in securing a post for "Frank Caludrovich."[103] The writer was especially interested in the African American and Creole communities eking out a marginal existence around Boothville, living amid the indifferent detritus of global trade and the occasional windfall from a shipwreck. "Unlike their fellow Negro peasants of the South," he noted, "they own their piece of ground, and are therefore independent of every one save the commission merchant to whom they ship their oranges."[104] In an emblematic scene in *Green Margins* he describes "candles burn[ing] . . . each . . . for a secret intention. The wind had blown two of them out. On the wall was a sign, COLORED NOVENA FRIDAY."[105]

"Pretty John," a piece O'Donnell wrote for the *Menagerie,* is highly reminiscent of the stories of Charles Chesnutt and Kate Chopin. In it, a fair-skinned, mixed-race hunting guide whose handshake is said to bring good luck refuses to clasp the hand of the northern millionaire who has commissioned him. Pretty John has sized his visitor up, and at the end of the story it is revealed that the northerner has "Negro blood" from a "distant ancestor" too.[106]

Unlike Sherwood Anderson, whose unreadable *Dark Laughter* (1925) was more fit for parody than for publication, O'Donnell had an unfeigned understanding of the Louisiana underclass. He skillfully explored the subtle gradations of social standing once again in his second novel, as *The Great Big Doorstep* carefully observes encounters between Cajuns, blacks, and mulattos. In one exchange between Uncle Dewey and Topal, the elder tries to buck her up by saying, "Don't be downhearted, my lil Creole belle," and she fires back, with underdog pride, "Who's Creole? I'm Cajun and proud of it."[107]

Ethnic identity becomes a function of religion. A discussion of ethnic difference in *The Great Big Doorstep* perhaps signals the relationship then unfolding between O'Donnell and the Texan writer who would become his second wife, Mary King, albeit with sex roles reversed. The future husband of the book's protagonist, Evvie, is an outsider named Dave Tobin, who explains, "Texas and Delta people are sure different and hard to agree. We're mostly old Americans in Texas. Most Delta people are Catholics that wear medals and play Bingo. Gambling and drinking ain't much of a sin to them" (60). With O'Donnell's ear for dialect and his interest in "forgotten" races and "Latin" varieties of Catholicism, he seems at times seems to be the very reincarnation of Lafcadio Hearn, who loved to visit the same palustrine fringes.

It was a difficult place, however, for a poor man to find his way into a literary life, but this did not deter O'Donnell from making connections. Even while *Green Margins* was making its way to print, O'Donnell was making other efforts to establish his credibility as a literary figure. He had befriended Gordon Lewis, a lawyer-legislator-litterateur who owned a bookshop near the University of Virginia and liked to cultivate fledgling writers, with Erskine Caldwell among his protégés. Indeed, "Transfusion" (1929), the first piece O'Donnell published, had been in an early number of the Mississippian Charles Henri Ford's celebrated little magazine *Blues: A Magazine of New Rhythms,* whose short run compiled a who's who of modernist luminaries, including Gertrude Stein, William Carlos Williams, Paul Bowles, and Kay Boyle.[108] O'Donnell ran with a similar set of aspiring literati in New Orleans, including Sherwood Anderson and Elma Godchaux, a Jewish literary doyenne who was a very close friend of the O'Donnells. One of them found O'Donnell more garrulous than substantive. Visiting New Orleans in early 1937, Thomas Wolfe met the O'Donnells in the legendary Roosevelt Hotel bar—a place to be seen—and jotted a note: "Pat O'Donnell and wife—young, phony, fast."[109]

Regardless, a circle of his literary-minded friends in New Orleans would contribute to Bennett Augustin's upstart little magazine styled the *Menagerie.* In its way, the *Menagerie* was a sort of delayed response to the success of New Orleans's *Double Dealer* some ten years earlier. O'Donnell made occasional contributions to the magazine and frequent visits to the city for drinking and literary camaraderie. But his timing was off: the enchanting bohemian scene conjured up by Godchaux, Anderson, and Faulkner by that time had effervesced, as John Reed documents in his fascinating *Dixie Bohemia.* Elma Godchaux's death in 1926, arriving on the heels of Anderson's, seemed to announce the end of the experiment and, according to one of his letters, left O'Donnell and his wife feeling "lonely at times."[110] Perhaps inspired by that moment, the homespun *Menagerie* began in 1935 and lasted little more than a year, running poetry, stories, and literary criticism, its mainstay contributors—including Daniel Carroll, John Kingston Fineran, Joseph Kelly, and Clarence Laughlin—hailing from Irish New Orleans. O'Donnell soon conceded that it provided more merriment than money: "The market in magazines is simply shot to hell, Ben," he wrote to Augustin.[111]

A 1940 census-taker found O'Donnell living in his small house in Boothville, listed his marital status with an uncertain "M?," and dutifully listed his profession as part-time fiction writer—from which he recorded no income, or at least none he chose to report. *Green Margins* would sell eighty-eight thousand copies, half the number sold in 1936 by the bestselling novel of that year, *Gone with the Wind,* and quite a respectable showing for a first novel in any case.[112]

Moreover, O'Donnell had a clutch of favorable reviews for *Green Margins,* including three from London papers noting its warmth, vivacity, and energy and one from the *New York Times*'s Stanley Young deeming it a "gorgeous tapestry." Remarkably, Julian Huxley, the biologist and brother to Aldous, pronounced it "powerful, transcending time and space in its depiction of human character."[113] Reviews of *The Great Big Doorstep* were similarly favorable, though some reviewers, such as William Allen White, were mildly scandalized by the book's sexual candor. White described it, along with Faulkner's *Absalom, Absalom!,* as one of the two best of the early-review books of the season but held that O'Donnell's novel was a shade too salacious: "a succession of dirty stories about dirty people, beautifully told."[114] Max Eastman, writing for the *American Mercury,* described O'Donnell as "Sherwood Anderson's young friend and protégé"; the young writer, Eastman concluded, had "succeeded brilliantly" in his follow-up novel, and the critic could not help but mention that O'Donnell "lives largely on oranges and oysters, composes lying down on an army cot with a typewriter canted up on a self-patented contraption in front of him."[115]

O'Donnell seemed always on the cusp of breaking into the national literary scene, and he might have become better known had he not died at about the apex of his gathering notoriety. His correspondence indicates that he intended to write a trilogy comprising *Green Margins, The Great Big Doorstep,* and a third work, with recurring characters in the three books. He also envisioned an autobiographical trilogy from a "New Orleans story . . . beginning when I was a boy and ending with the Ford plant story," having realized that he had "learned how to convey my thoughts clearly and with sufficient subconscious ability to embellish, and that from thence my business was simply to write out of my heart of life as I have seen and imagined it." Sadly, in view of what was soon to come, he wrote in the same letter, "Now my only concern is to keep my health long enough to finish the mass of work I see ahead of me."[116]

Adding to the tragedy of his death a short time later in 1943, O'Donnell had married his second wife, Mary King O'Donnell, also a recipient of the Houghton Mifflin fellowship, just six weeks earlier.[117] Mary King's hardscrabble roots ran to the oil fields of Texas; her biographically tinged *Quincie Bolliver* (1941), still in print through Texas Tech University Press, gives a view of rambling life amid the Gulf Coast rigs.[118] She dedicated her second book, *Those Other People* (1946), to O'Donnell. In any case, when he passed away in 1943, his reputation—a strapping bon vivant with black hair and bright blue eyes, a writer of novels overspilling with life—scarcely seems consistent with the way the *Picayune* eulogized him, as a "quiet and reticent man."[119]

Fortunately, O'Donnell did complete his second novel before his death. *The Great Big Doorstep* garnered an appreciative afterword by Eudora Welty when it was reissued in 1979. It should have been his breakout book, but as Welty points out, the timing of *The Great Big Doorstep* was inauspicious: when it was published in August 1941, war had just been declared, and the nation's attention was "swept . . . away from the appearance of new fiction."[120]

More's the pity, because the book is a verbal work of art, with dialogue that reminds one at once of J. K. Toole. "Everybody in the novel is vocal," explains Eudora Welty, who says that O'Donnell's "supreme gift may be his dialogue." The pages salute the full span of Cajun dialect, bending the patter to his poetic purposes. "What seems extraordinary to me," wrote Welty, "is that O'Donnell has taken a dialect highly distinctive in itself and flamboyant by nature and made it so thoroughly responsive, so echoing, to his needs."[121]

For example, the book's Sister Margaret brings an Irish accent to Grass Margin, where she comes to pick up oranges for her orphans, declaring of her new environs, "Sure a wonderful country." Nothing about the sister is lost to protagonist Evvie Crochet's youthful eye as she contemplates the alternate life the nun leads, material that seems to come straight from O'Donnell's upbringing. When the sister's face is raised, "Evvie saw the whiskers in her nose. Nuns were no different from other women. She stole a glance behind the white fluted bonnet, and saw the nun's hidden hair. It was jet black, thick and live, cut in short locks, not a streak of gray. Nuns hid their hair because nothing lovely was supposed to be seen, and hair was a lovely thing" (271). When the good sister catches a whiff of freshly skinned muskrats, discarded by neighbors, she asks, "And hasn't the trapping season been over a long time?" Of course, the season has long since closed, and Sister Margaret asks incredulously, "Are these people Catholics?" (270).

If there is an aroma of the by now familiar Jansenistic Catholicism, it is dispelled by the power of place. The sister embraces Evvie "against her ample body," whereupon Evvie "heard a long rumble like faint thunder. It was coming from inside the nun's stomach. At first Evvie wanted to laugh, but there was no one to laugh with. She cleared her throat vigorously to cover up the sound. 'Sure I'd fight with me senses in this place,' the nun mused. 'No doubt the body is forever roused from its proper chastisements and meditations and lured sideways to things that flatter the flesh . . .'" (271). "Yes, Sister!" is Evvie's reply; in return, the nun looks at her with twinkling eyes (271). As with Burgess's Enderby and Toole's Ignatius, the body's rebellion against order offers the staple material of satire and, in this case, an insight into the limits of human intentions. The world that O'Donnell has created accurately captures its tropicality. Superabundant in uncontainable life, and life that blossoms early—"The Great Southern Bulb Nursery, Grass Margin, Louisiana," one character dubs it (331)—even the sister must take stock of the fact and appreciate it. Instead of offering the disapproving knuckle rapper of stereotype, O'Donnell gives readers a more complete portrait of a woman homely and beautiful, schoolmarmish and loving.

It is also an infectiously funny book that barely seems to contain its characters, who cackle with a raucous Louisiana accent. *Doorstep*'s half-baked Catholic sensibility, on top of its other graces, comes as a lagniappe. For example, when a Cajun mother defines *peccadillo* for her daughter, in the spirit of Joel Chandler Harris: "Not to God it ain't no sin. . . . You think God's got time to humbug will little ole transgressions like that?" (70). (She also advises, "Never tell people your business. Jesus never tole nobody His business" [70].) Beneath it all is the unmistakable *joie de vivre* that defies the poverty of the place—one chapter is titled "We Got No Troubles A Dollar Won't Cure"—and that endeared the comedy to Eudora Welty. Welty perceptively identified the Catholic dimensions of the characters' marginality, emphasizing in her afterword how Topal and Evvie would kill birds with a slingshot in order to trade them for coffee coupons and a statuette of the Virgin Mary: "It is a strange opening scene, set in a part of the country most of us never saw, had never known was on the map. It is a scene which takes for granted the misuse of everything—birds—young girls—the Virgin—probably even the barter system. It is also true comedy, and is brought about to tell us how desperate life is on Grass Margin."[122]

The alternate economy of Grass Margin, at the mouth of the Mississippi, is tied to a trash culture made of butt ends and discards, all brought into sharp relief by the author's proto-environmentalist attitude toward the place's natural beauty. Nature and religion are so inseparable here that, in an intensely poetic scene, the patriarch of the family, Commodo Crochet, says his rosary in time to the carefully observed mating ritual of a hummingbird (the arc a hummingbird describes might be likened to the movement of the beads). The ditches may be full of trash, but the sights and sounds of nature still prevail— "a waterbird clopping like a man beating a pipe on the palm of his hand," "the slight persistent ticking of a bug near-by trundling a seedpod through the dead leaves" (256), a "tall stern house" surrounded with flowers "colored like fire and ice and milk and flesh," a "waterspout across the river hanging from the clouds, a dark searching tongue swinging about, licking the horizon's jagged crust" (297). These phrases, from the pen of a man with a middle-school education, whisper insistently underneath the boisterous chatter of a deliberately ribald text. As befits a writer who sold Creole Easter lilies for a living, renewal is *The Great Big Doorstep*'s grand motif. Mrs. Crochet declares, "Evvie got to go to church like she tole Father Pennygrass to help those ladies to fix the altar, because tomorrow's Easter and Jesus rose from the dead. Look how pretty this morning outside" (250).

There is pride in this cast-off, flotsam culture, which can still make room for the beauty of the ordinary; grace operates within the most meager of material trappings. The book's title comes from the Crochets' grandiose salvaged doorstep, which awaits a house to match it. In some respects, this brilliant comment on exchange aptly precedes Flannery O'Connor's gimlet-eyed view of falsely paired promises of economic and social progress. O'Donnell might be skeptical about material progress, but he also writes from within the lower class, appreciating how for the poor the purchase of commodities is really about the purchase of dignity. Bartering slain birds and trading coffee coupons for a "blessed mudda" (6), Evvie's icon might be inexpensive. It is not, however, cheap. The artifact of religious culture leads to a scene of deft understatement. When the girls track down Father Pendergrast to have it blessed,

> The girl held it in her arms. She watched the priest. Saying the old Latin words in a sober tone, he lowered his eyes, and with his thin nervous hand drew a cross in the air—two lines, one drawn through the middle of Evvie vertically and the other across her chest. Then he turned and ran whistling inside. Evvie carried off the statue under her arm. She felt the two lines still there, dividing her body into four parts. (7)

Those descriptions, in a book much concerned with the body divided, take on greater significance when the reader learns that the girls in Evvie's family of eight are expected to take care of their younger siblings. It is herself that Evvie glimpses in the figure holding the baby. Such images become more significant again when the reader learns that food is hard to come by and that her hapless twenty-year-old sister Topal "ain't got no tiddies" (26) and can't find a man. In a similarly poignant scene, when the townspeople poison orange-pilfering blackbirds on "nux vomica day" (250), Evvie experiences menarche. Her friend Elna tells her she missed an opportunity to shed her virginity without consequence ("Now you got to fine you a husband" [253]). The loss of sexual innocence is augured by the "curious dim croaking" of a dying blackbird (254). In O'Donnell's earlier novel, *Green Margins,* the protagonist ("Sister") tries to keep her thoughts from veering back to a handsome visitor: "She wanted tonight to keep the exalted mood of the confessional, as a preliminary of her first taste of the body and blood of the Divine Victim, for which she still felt somewhat unworthy."[123]

For a Catholic child, the necessity of innocence cannot be long cherished. The division of the body into split identities—spiritual and sensual, religious and natural—will pose special difficulties in a place of natural lushness, where everything grows up quickly. After Evvie has gotten "the curse," she searches for a lover to renounce so that she can join the Little Sisters of the Poor with appropriate melodrama. No doubt she is driven as well by her mother's warnings against the miseries of family and childbirth. When Evvie flirts with sailors and tells them she is "fourteen going on fifteen," they answer waggishly by way of song:

> I do not know
> It may be so
> But it sounds like crap to meeeee! (32)

In such lines one hears the unmistakable raspberry of Irish satire. The book is strung with bits of song and verse, full of the musicality of language. One of the funniest and most unforgettable scenes comes from Mrs. Crochet's attempt to wean her bottle-rejecting infant, T. J. Crochet. She matter-of-factly "lipped out one of her breasts and rubbed the hot pepper on her nipple, squeezing out as much pepper juice as she could." While hubby Commodo (which means "comfortable") Crochet details his stomach trouble ("Firss, something whistles around my livers like a little bitsy siren blowin. . . . Gas is the curse of my life"), Mrs. Crochet does fair battle with the infant in a repeated cycle: he shrills, is plugged with a bottle, and still fights for the breast (119–20). Mrs. Crochet explains, in spot-on dialect, "The poor lil fella got to learn how to not suck his mama, because pretty soon if we get that property we gunna be better off" (120). Topal leaves the chaos to go to the front room and "massage her bosom" with an oil she hopes will improve it (122). Later, Mr. Crochet relates his own worries:

> I've got some kids myself. I wish they were country-raised. One son dove in shallow water the other day. My youngest daughter smokes cigars and paints pictures in the abattoir. She went to Washington and got locked in the Corcoran Gallery. When they came in the morning, she had to be taken to the hospital in hysterics. We've all got our troubles. (323)

There is no end to these troubles: Mrs. Crochet will attain her dream house to match her doorstep, but for her children, at least, the next big step will be the one leading to the greyhound bus. Delicately balanced on the tensions between the material (in terms of success and the body) and the spiritual (in terms of nature and religion), the novel O'Donnell produces is quintessentially Catholic, ethnically and spiritually.

Of O'Donnell's two novels, *The Great Big Doorstep* has the distinction of enjoying a brief life on the stage, making its Broadway debut on November 26, 1942, and running for twenty-eight shows at the Morosco Theatre before shutting down. Dashiell Hammett was one of its financial backers.[124] *Time* magazine put it in a class with Erskine Caldwell's *Tobacco Road* (1932) and called it of "good quality but very short weight."[125] The novel, in some respects, was made for the stage through its characters, and there is enough dramatic tension and pathos to sustain it. But the market for its Cajun voice, even in late stages of local color, must have been limited, and generally favorable reviews could not save it.

Both John Kennedy Toole's and Pat O'Donnell's books have struggled to the stage, and both have been granted a kind of immortality through appreciative prefaces from masterful writers—Walker Percy, Eudora Welty, Andrei Codrescu. Eudora Welty's imprimatur is all the more significant given that O'Donnell somewhat audaciously centered his comedy around the perspective of a pubescent girl and that by prim southern standards the book is raucous to the point of rudeness. Codrescu was given *Confederacy* by a friend who assured him that it was "*the* New Orleans book," a position that he embraces in arguing for the book's continuing and increasing relevance (regardless of his students' distaste for it). For those familiar with the Cajun prairie beyond New Orleans, *The Great Big Doorstep* might be *the* Louisiana book, at least as far as coastal Louisiana and Cajuns are concerned. In some respects, it surpasses *A Confederacy of Dunces* in demonstrating the thesis that the Mediterranean sea washes, by strange tides, over Louisiana. O'Donnell was too quickly dismissed as a local colorist, when in fact, like a barnstormer just clearing the wires, he flirts with sentimentality and veers away with breathtaking precision. No other work so joyfully captures the contradictions, social complexity, pride, and mixed blessings of people who are passed by, sometimes by choice, and who continue to hold on to the margins of a place besieged by economic, environmental, and natural disasters with an unfailing, if innately dark, sense of good humor. Like the Easter Day that organizes and animates the book, it is a kind of processional, memorably, subtly, "sadly festive" (230).

This chapter about staging Irishness considers the self as a form of performance, and so there is relatively little of the dramatic stage itself. There is a good deal more to that story, which unfolded largely in New Orleans, especially if one considers the American Irish who were performers of various kinds.[126] One of these was R. Emmet Kennedy (1877–1941), a real-life character brought to light in John Reed's *Dixie Bohemia,* who is more likely to be remembered as a figure of cultural interest than for his poems or dialect tales in the mode of the writer Roark Bradford.[127] "Both of his parents were Irish immigrants," writes Reed; "his father was a blacksmith, fiddler, and Confederate veteran. Even as a boy, Emmet was fascinated by the songs and folktales that were all around him in the mostly black neighborhood where his family lived, and he was the first to write down the words and music of many of the spirituals he heard ("Free at Last" was one of them)."[128] With his rooster-comb shock of wild hair, Emmet cut an arresting figure, reminiscent of Tom Waits. Or perhaps it would be accurate to compare him to the performer Malcolm Rebennack Jr., better known by his stage name, Dr. John: like many other New Orleans musicians, Kennedy was repeatedly taken across the color line by his love of music. In another fine instance of Black-Irish affinities, Kennedy popularized many of the songs from his beloved Gretna, making songs from that primarily black district available to white audiences and eventually taking them to the radio.

He was also a sought-after performer of his own "Irish" verses. In keeping with his Irish persona, he published a book of his poems, signed ostensibly under the Irish version of his name, "Robard Emmet Ua Cinneidig." *Runes and Cadences, Being Ancestral Memories of Old Heroic Days* (1926) is steeped in the Irish mythology of the Celtic Revival, and in it Kennedy styles himself Aengus Óg, the poetic hero of the Tuatha Dé Danann cycle. Carl Sandburg reviewed the book favorably and advised readers that it also contained "original musical compositions done in the mood of the ancient Gaelic singers."[129] Evidently, Kennedy's interest in Ireland did not waver. About five years before he died, he made his first visit to Ireland and, as John Reed has documented, "returned to write *Songs of an Alien Spirit* (a second poetic stroll through Irish legends and mythology) and a life of St. Patrick (another fugitive manuscript)."[130]

In a strange coda to Kennedy's tale, he was at most one degree of separation away from Lafcadio Hearn, and it is possible that as a boy Kennedy might indeed have met Hearn before the elder writer decamped for Japan. Moreover,

Kennedy and Hearn shared a mutual friend in Edward Larocque Tinker, an early Lafcadio Hearn biographer who persuaded Kennedy to try out life in New York City. Like Hearn, Kennedy would work as a self-guided folklorist and journalist, freelancing for the *New York Times* and chronicling, as Hearn did before him, a running fascination with Asian literature. The Bohemian culture of New Orleans and the city's stature as a center for American creativity clearly nurtured the writers of its Irish community.

In an earlier generation, writers such as Hearn, Harris, and Chopin had played so carefully to Protestant, Anglo-American readers that the vision of Catholicism they offered was often subdued or linked to "exotic races." Frequently they "pass" as Protestants, only then signaling sympathy with Catholic characters. A perceptible shift occurs with later writers such as Mitchell, Toole, and O'Donnell, who make fewer apologies for Catholic characters and in some cases pass as Catholic voyeurs into Protestant aisles for the sake of parody. Indeed, Flannery O'Connor would perfect this technique and make it the engine of much of her fiction.

Another common denominator among southern Irish writers who dramatized Irishness might be found in their ability to write about race from the perspective of an underclass and thus to satisfy audiences' curiosity about life on the other side of the tracks, where "sins" against the social order might be brought into full satiric view. Had they not been Irish southerners, it is doubtful that they would have been afforded such a fine window—or provided a regional perspective laced with such bittersweet and lacerating humor.

5

FLANNERY O'CONNOR'S
DEAR OLD DIRTY SOUTHLAND

When she was younger, she [the bearded lady Jane Barnell, who was from
North Carolina] often thought of joining the Catholic Church and going into a
nunnery; she had heard of sideshow women who became nuns, although she
had never actually known one. A lack of religious conviction deterred her.
—JOSEPH MITCHELL, "Lady Olga"

My mamma asked me the other day if I knew Shakespeare was an
Irishman. I said no I didn't. She said well it's right there in the Savannah
paper; and sure enough some gent from the University of Chicago had made
a speech somewhere saying Shakespeare was an Irishman. I said well it's just
him that says it, you better not go around saying it and she said listen
SHE didn't care whether he was an Irishman or a Chinaman.
—FLANNERY O'CONNOR

It should be easy enough to tell what sort of creature Flannery O'Connor
was: her family roots traced to Ireland, her accent was pure coastal Georgia,
and she counted meeting the pope a highlight of her European vacation,
if not of her life. Irish, Catholic, southern—more or less the end of the story.

If only it were so simple. She liked to refer facetiously to the "Wah Between the
States" and once wrote Betty Hester, "I never was one to go over the Civil War
in a big way."[1] She likewise dismissed accounts of Saint Patrick's Day parades
in the diocesan newspaper as "the kind of literature I approve of burning" (*HB*
150). She was conflicted about the merits of James Joyce and his unorthodoxy
("Joyce who?" asks a priest in one of her stories) but read him to the extent
of emulation. Remarking the dearth of Catholic intellectual life in America,
she wrote, "The Americans seem just to be producing pamphlets for the back
of the Church (to be avoided at all costs) and installing heating systems" (*HB*
231), while "the Irish sinned constantly but with no great emotion except fear"
(*HB* 304).

A visit to Ireland was precluded by her failing health, but Flannery O'Connor showed little or no desire to go to the land of her ancestors in the first place. Having canceled the Irish leg of her European pilgrimage, she remained in Levanto while her fellow sojourners went to "disport themselves at the Baloney Castle or whatever it is" (*HB* 277). Perhaps the fruit didn't fall far from the tree. Father Hugh Marren came to know Regina O'Connor in her later years, and when she asked him if he had read any of her daughter's work (he hadn't), he tried to change the subject with a blandishment. "That blarney is going to get you nowhere," Regina O'Connor replied.[2]

Her daughter had as wide and deep an Irish pedigree as any native-born southerner yet was loathe to call herself Irish. Flannery O'Connor could be scrupulous about dogma with the seriousness of "a convent-bred high school girl," according to her priest and confidant Father John McCown, yet she was dismissive of Catholicism's "slide rule" mentality in meting out doctrine and measuring sins.[3] Hardly an uncritical defender of the church, she could accept anticlericalism in measure, but not antireligious sentiment. Irish and yet anti-Irish, she was likewise southern and unsouthern, and therein lies the crux of Flannery O'Connor's many contradictions: her Catholicism was the most enduring legacy of her Irish ancestry and mutually insinuated with it. In tracing how O'Connor was both a creation and creator of her southern world, or, more accurately, an Irish Catholic South, one might finally understand her as a reluctant student of Joyce, an astute observer of Protestant Christianity, a woman in flight from the claims of the Savannah Irish society to which she was undoubtedly an heiress, a conservative with underdog sensibilities, a thinker with affinities to Edgar Allan Poe, and an utterly unforgettable writer. And so goes the stream of this chapter.

A fragment from the second sentence of *Finnegans Wake* (1939) references a river in the state of Georgia: "nor had topsawyer's rocks by the stream Oconee exaggerated themselves to Laurens County's gorgios while they went doublin their mumper all the time." Like most of Joyce's famously cryptic book, it requires a little deciphering before it gives up a comment on the progress of the Irish diaspora abroad. Beginning with the famous "riverrun," Joyce launches the novel with patriarchal begetting, invoking "a bland old isaac," panning quickly from Howth Castle to the New World and the whirlpools (gorgios) of gorgeous Laurens County, Georgia. The usual wordplay is here: *ochone,* from the Irish *ochón,* a cry of grief, which in Anglo-Irish usage means "alas." The topsawyer riffs on "Tom Sawyer" and on the man whom Joyce incorrectly identifies as "Peter Sawyer," the legendary founder of Dublin, Georgia (actually Jonathan Sawyer, who purportedly named the place after the mother city of his wife's ancestors).[4]

Ted Spivey, one of Flannery's academic acquaintances, worked out that in this passage Joyce, "by referring to the two Dublins in Europe and America and by using a Creek Indian name for a river, which is also the Gaelic word for alas, announces his theme of the struggle of fathers and sons, mothers and daughters, a necessary struggle in the most significant mythic theme of the *Wake:* life, death, rebirth."[5] Fair enough, but why not interpret Joyce through his proven love of the bathetic and so reach a slightly different interpretation? According to Scott Thompson, "Dublin's boosters claimed their city was 'the only city in Georgia that's doublin' all the time.'"[6] How Joyce got wind of this is unknown, but he must have been well amused by the promiscuous southern undercurrent in Hibernia's seed, for he glossed the passage in a letter in which he annotated some of his allusions: "Dublin, Laurens Co, Georgia, founded by a Dubliner, Peter Sawyer, on r. Oconee. Its motto: Doubling all the time."[7] Given Joyce's interest in the Irish in Georgia, perhaps the selection of the character name Leopold Bloom is not so mysterious, given that Leopold Blome, Patrick Walsh, and Abram Ryan were the editors and publishers, during the 1860s, of Augusta's *Banner of the South.*

Mumper, another bit of bygone slang, means "a genteel beggar," and it runs together mother and father (*mum* and *pa/père*). Playing bathetically on Peter founding his church upon the rock, he paints a grandiose waterscape of the "stream" Oconee (more properly a river). The "rocks" could mean testicles in the way that Molly uses the slang term in *Ulysses* (1922) (Joyce had "sham rocks" in an earlier draft).[8] A strutting Irishman squats, airs his exaggerated genitals to the gorgios of Laurens County, and presto: his orphans mumper around Georgia for quite some time. The Peter of the New World, with his rocks. This, Joyce might well have suggested with churlish delight, is the essence of Irish success in America.

O'Connor's admiration for the Irish American writer J. F. Powers, with whom she corresponded, was vaulting; her esteem for James Joyce, less so. Her fiction and letters reveal her conflicting feelings for the brilliant Irish expatriate whose hometown statue is popularly known to Dubliners as the "Prick with the Stick." In O'Connor's "The Enduring Chill," the protagonist, Asbury—another of O'Connor's purblind and cramped intellectuals—asks the Jesuit who makes a sick call on him what he thinks of Joyce.

"Joyce? Joyce who?" asked the priest.

"James Joyce," Asbury said and laughed.

The priest brushed his huge hand in the air as if he were bothered by gnats. "I haven't met him," he said. "Now. Do you say your morning and night prayers?"

Asbury appeared confused. "Joyce was a great writer," he murmured.[9]

Indeed, O'Connor owned Richard Ellmann's biography of Joyce and marked up her copy of *Dubliners* (1913). In a later letter to Betty Hester, she acknowledged that there was much for a writer to learn from *Dubliners* (*HB* 203). As Brad Gooch notes, she modeled an early story on *Dubliners*'s "Araby": "On Dublin's North Richmond Street . . . 'The other houses of the street . . . gazed at one another with brown imperturbable faces.' On O'Connor's Raphael Street, 'gaunt houses all of somber, grey stone, gaze austerely at each other.'"[10] Not coincidentally, in "The Life You Save May Be Your Own," Mr. Shiftlet takes a line from Joyce's "The Dead" and reminds Lucynell Crater that "The monks of old slept in their coffins!" (*CS* 176). Later, in a literary criticism seminar at the University of Iowa, she would select *Dubliners* and Robert Penn Warren's *Understanding Fiction* for her supplemental texts.[11] In a letter to Father John McCown, SJ, O'Connor makes an astute comment on the work of Hemingway, "where there is apparently a hunger for a Catholic completeness in life, or Joyce who can't get rid of it no matter what he does" (*HB* 130).[12] O'Connor's ambivalence about Joyce surfaces again in a letter of January 11, 1958, in which she reports to Betty Hester that her "opinion of the Irish has gone up" after meeting then U.N. delegate Máire Mhac an tSaoi (Máire MacEntee). Her admiration increased when she determined that the Irish-language writer "seems anticlerical but not particularly anti-religious," a comfort that might be explained by the high degree of anticlerical feeling common to many of Savannah's Irish immigrants. She goes on to relate that most of the "angry young men" in Ireland "go the way of Joyce . . . but it is very painful to them because when they cut themselves off from the religion they cut themselves off from what they have grown up with—as the religion is so bound in with the rest of life" (*HB* 263). In other words, Flannery O'Connor appreciated that in terms of Irish Catholicism, Irishness and Catholicness were merged entities, mutually inseparable.

There is not much evidence of an Irish slant in O'Connor's reading, but the exceptions are interesting. Her family handed down any number of fusty works in hagiography, but the one she marked up was D. P. Conyngham's venerable *Lives of the Irish Saints* (1870).[13] At least three Elizabeth Bowen books were to be found in O'Connor's library, two by Seán O'Fáolain, two by Yeats, and quite a few by Irish Americans, religious and otherwise. She owned *The Stories of Liam O'Flaherty* (1956), and given O'Flaherty's anti-Catholic, anticapitalist stance, it seems clear that she kept on her shelves works of Irish writers with whom she would have dissented.[14]

Her Irishness ran much deeper than her reading. Even where Joyce, with his strongly anti-Catholic slant, disagreed with her, Flannery O'Connor was eminently a product of the ever-doubling Georgia branch. As it happens, it was on the banks of the selfsame Oconee that a patriarch, Flannery's maternal great-grandfather, Hugh Donnelly Treanor, alighted and made his fortune with a grist mill. Flannery would remember that "mass was first said here [in Milledgeville] in my great-grandfather's hotel room, later in his home on the piano" (*HB* 520). His wife's father, Patrick Harty, Flannery O'Connor's first American ancestor, betook himself and his family to Locust Grove in 1824.[15] Johannah Harty Treanor would return to the small Catholic colony at Locust Grove when she was widowed.

In Locust Grove O'Connor's family history becomes entangled with that of another Irish Catholic southerner: the Stephens and McGhan (sometimes rendered "McGhann") families, the latter tracing their roots to County Longford, Ireland.[16] Both branches of Margaret Mitchell's ancestry arrived in the seventeenth century at Calvert's Maryland before marching south to better opportunities and eventually finding their way to Locust Grove.[17] The Georgia enclave within the cotton lands supported its own chapel, the Church of the Purification of the Blessed Virgin Mary, and a well-regarded "classical" school, Locust Grove Academy, where Alexander Stephens, vice president of the Confederate States of America and, as it happens, one of Margaret Mitchell's relatives, was educated. (Stephens was the descendant of Jacobites and would declare for "Catholic emancipation" in an 1866 address to the Georgia legislature.)[18] Initially, the settlement drew from Marylanders displaced when penal laws of the 1790s made the state once again inhospitable to Catholics. In time, French Catholics and Irish Catholics arrived.[19]

But that past is prologue. Within this nexus, Margaret Mitchell and Flannery O'Connor are related in underappreciated ways: they share family histories and indeed bloodlines deeply enmeshed in Georgia's Catholic history. The historian Dennis Clark mentions an early group of "fifty families from Tipperary in Taliaferro County, Georgia, [who] worked their own land successfully without slaves."[20] Their descendants, with various degrees of fidelity to Catholicism, turned up in pockets around Georgia. Two Irish Catholics, both maternal ancestors, married into Margaret Mitchell's family line. Phillip Fitzgerald fled in the wake of the 1798 rebellion and landed in Charleston, moving thence to the Georgia interior. Another of Mitchell's Irish Catholic ancestors, John Stephens, left Ireland in the 1850s to join a brother who kept a shop in Augusta, went west to Tennessee for a time, and returned to Georgia for Confederate service. Following a very similar path, Peter Cline, Flannery O'Connor's grandfather, drifted west on the rails, wound up busted in Louisville, and was briefly imprisoned in Nashville for his Confederate sympathies (as was Father Abram Ryan).[21] A self-made merchant and farmer who did well, he married, successively, two of the Treanor sisters, Kate and Margaret Ida, producing sixteen children in all, including Flannery's mother, Regina.[22]

The family interrelationships of the two writers serve to demonstrate that the Irish Catholic network in Georgia was intimate, highly interrelated by blood, and defined by both accommodation and opposition to the surrounding "cracker" culture (for *cracker* is the word that Irish Catholic Georgians sometimes use, to this day, to distinguish the white, non-Catholic southerner). Margaret Mitchell, staking her ancestral claim to respectability, would place an Irish belle with her temper up at the center of the plantation and later commit the unthinkable in her flirtation with Protestantism. Flannery O'Connor would run in the opposite direction: of respectable Georgia families, she would describe the virtues and foibles of Georgia crackers so drolly precisely because she needed to observe them so closely. She made her southern Catholicism seem so natural that it could be mistaken, at least superficially, for Protestantism.

Still, the clasp of her Irish antecedents may have been a little too tight for her comfort. Ted Spivey sensed as much in conversation with her once:

> Once I told her I had been to Savannah and had tried to find Bonaventure Cemetery . . . had found Savannah's large Irish cemetery, and I walked through it noting the graves of many Flannerys and O'Connors. Then I described to her a Civil War statue I saw in the cemetery, one dedicated to all the Savannah Irish who had died for the South, and I spoke of the strange and sad beauty of the cemetery, a kind of beauty that certain places in Savannah and Charleston sometimes possess. She said nothing but turned her head away from me. On her face was a look of pain.

He concluded from this that "some of O'Connor's [psychic wounds] were possibly connected with her Irish descent."[23]

Or perhaps O'Connor simply desired to get out from under the long shadow of ancestors. Brad Gooch believes O'Connor likely had her mother's family in mind when she wrote, "I don't think [my relatives] have ever been in a world they couldn't cope with because none of them that I know of have left the 19th century," but the statement might apply equally to her father's ancestors.[24] P. J. O'Connor (1859–1908), the patriarch of the O'Connor side of her family, was highly identified with Irish boosterism in Savannah. A nephew of Flannery O'Connor's grandfather, P. J. O'Connor rose to rapid prominence in Irish American circles in his forty-nine years. David Gleeson and Brendan Buttimer deem him a "classic example" of the rising "Irish Catholic assurance" in the southern Irish circles of Savannah and Charleston. P. J. O'Connor's inherited memory typifies the southern Irish of his generation: "American-born in 1859 of Irish parents from County Wexford," he "undoubtedly grew up hearing the lore of 1798."[25] After he graduated from Georgetown, his success at the bar gave him access to new social capital. He made himself visible in building the newly established Sacred Heart parish and affiliated himself with the Jasper Greens, a group of Irish Confederate veterans.[26] P. J. O'Connor's influence spanned social classes as he involved himself in every major Irish "cause" of his time: he established a chapter of the National Land League and arranged for John Howard Parnell, Charles Stewart Parnell's brother, to speak at the Independence Day celebration in 1881. There O'Connor would acclaim the brothers for their "hearty, honest hate of British oppression, and their practical Irish patriotism."[27]

According to Patricia Persse, P. J. O'Connor did everything in his power to "support the Irish in this country," as well as to support Irish independence.[28] Irish allegiances ran deep in the family and spanned sectarian boundaries. P. J. O'Connor refused to host Daniel Tallon, then mayor of Dublin, and the Anglo-Irish parliamentarian John E. Redmond on their 1899 visit to Savannah. Nor would he underwrite their fundraising for a statue of Parnell, insisting instead that a statue to Wolfe Tone and the "heroes of '98" should be first in order.[29] Ultimately, explain Gleeson and Buttimer, "O'Connor had merged his Irishness and southernness into a very successful combination that would propel him into national prominence with the AOH [Ancient Order of Hibernians]."[30] Indeed, he gathered clout on the national stage when he became president of the AOH, a powerful Catholic fraternal organization among Irish Americans.

Brad Gooch writes that "a nagging downside for Regina Cline, in choosing a husband, was Ed O'Connor's background—his family never achieved the social stature of the Clines of Milledgeville, or the Flannerys of Savannah, though they led comfortable middle-class lives," but this simply ignores P. J. O'Connor's considerable stature in his community.[31] The inheritance he passed along to many of his descendants was a powerful sense of the importance of being Irish, a lesson that O'Connor probably chose not to heed.

P. J.'s namesake, another prominent O'Connor man, would say the final words over Flannery's grave. The youngest of the five children of P. J. O'Connor and Winifred Maher and a second cousin to Flannery O'Connor's father, Monsignor Patrick Joseph O'Connor had dropped in on Flannery in 1961.[32] She was delighted to see her "cousin": "I hadn't seen him in thirty years. He was an actor before he became a priest and afterward taught Sacred Oratory at the Catholic University for many years. It was quite a gathering" (*HB* 453).

According to Brad Gooch, "She had been happy to know again this cousin of her father's, with whom she had a rapport, and they had talked enthusiastically of his memories of the family."[33] Patricia Persse enumerated to me some of her uncle Monsignor O'Connor's many achievements. Many of the forty-three priests he recruited during his lifetime had come from Ireland. Persse, a direct descendant of P. J. O'Connor Sr., was Flannery's third cousin and an occasional childhood playmate. She remembered that Irish identity was taken seriously in her family, and she expressed puzzlement over Flannery O'Connor's disinterest in such matters. Persse had never been asked about it before, but she had traveled to Ireland in search of her family's Galway roots.[34]

Not so for Flannery O'Connor. Ashley Brown, a renowned scholar of modernism, recollects in "Flannery O'Connor: A Literary Memoir":

> In July, 1953, I was just about to visit Ireland for the first time. This would be the first stage in a kind of *wanderjahr,* and I was already looking forward to my descent on Coole Park and Joyce's Martello tower and Bowen's Court. It was to be a literary pilgrimage all the way. I was astonished when Flannery brought me up short by saying, "Whatever do you want to go *there* for?" She had in fact a rather developed prejudice against Ireland which I, not Irish at all, could never understand. She was right to make fun of the sham Irishness that takes in so many people, and her caustic remark about Baloney Castle is worthy of Joyce himself. All the same, I thought this was a curious attitude on her part. She gave me the address of one of her favorite writers, J. F. Powers, who was then living in County Wicklow.[35]

In fact, the only Irish landscape O'Connor would visit was contained within the landscape of her mind.

I usually begin by considering various axes of identity and posing basic questions: How southern was this writer? How Catholic? And finally, how Irish? In the case of Flannery O'Connor, the first two questions are much more readily answered than the last. We have already established that O'Connor's ancestors had been in the South for a while, that some of them had fought in the Civil War, and that she wore her southernness plainly on her sleeve. Ever the iconoclast, O'Connor was irritated by those people ("like [Wallace] Stegner") who claimed that southern writers should leave the South and "forget the myth." "I stayed away from the time I was 20 until I was 25 with the notion that the life of my writing depended on my staying away," she wrote to a friend. "I would certainly have persisted in that delusion had I not got very ill and had to come home. The best of my writing has been done here" (*HB* 230). While she was away from home, she laid on the southern part of her identity rather thickly at times, so much so that Paul Engle claimed he thought her mentally retarded on account of her gluey accent.[36]

Privately, Flannery O'Connor wrestled with the usual I-don't-hate-the-South issues and the region's peculiar demands of conformity. She marked a pointed passage in her copy of W. J. Cash's classic study, *The Mind of the South* (1941):

> The final result of conflict and solidification, we have to notice, is that it turned the South toward strait-jacket conformity and made it increasingly intolerant of dissent. . . . We go back to the point that it was the individualism of extremely simple men, shaped by what were basically very simple and homogeneous conditions. The community and uniformity of origins, the nearness in time of the frontier, the failure of immigration and the growth of important towns—all these co-operated to cut men to a single pattern, and, as we have been seeing continuously, the total effect of the plantation world was to bring them to a single focus which was held with peculiar intensity.[37]

O'Connor's marginalia in Cash ("still is," "still are") show that she grokked the essential truth and continuing relevance of his observations; and perhaps, for a cradle Catholic, "strait-jacket conformity" was a phrase that invited a different introspection. She was herself a curious mixture of dissent, primarily in her Catholicism, and a complicated sort of misunderstood conformity, which has led to a certain amount of conflicting commentary on her racial politics. Did O'Connor share in Cash's so-called proto-Dorian bond, which subscribed poor whites to the imperatives of the ruling class? Her shabby-genteel, lower- to bourgeoisie-class characters who affect superiority serve mainly to show that she was aware of its absurdity: Miss Turpin, Tanner, even Mary Maud of "Why Do the Heathen Rage?," whose son, in her mind, is so shiftless that he "could not work, he could not even make niggers work" (*CS* 485).

In the end, O'Connor's Catholicism worked both to liberate her from doctrinaire southern politics and to bring her into sympathy with some of its conservatism. It was this streak of conservatism, aligned with notions of the "timeless" serfdom of the plantation and stratified social orders, not to mention long traditions of authoritarian church rhetoric, that made Catholicism appealing to some southern ideologues. And it was a permutation of the same conservative strand that appealed so deeply to many southern writer-converts of the twentieth century, like the Vanderbilt Agrarians, who were seeking moral absolutism during a skeptical era. Indeed, some saw, in a positive light, the possibility for a working out of racial strife through Catholicism. Even Father Ryan, a master of southern nationalist rhetoric, believed that the church could serve as a powerful force for racial reconciliation. After reviewing Elizabeth Bishop's translation of *The Diary of Helena Morley* (1957), which describes the days of a colonial Brazilian girl, O'Connor wrote to Bishop, "I suppose the two races can live together more agreeably in a Catholic country" (*HB* 265). Certainly in many Catholic-dominated areas, including Louisiana, chattel slavery was mitigated, however partially, by Catholicism's insistence on the full sacramental participation of communicants, thereby bestowing, in some cases, the legal benefits and recognition of personhood incidental to marriage. On the other hand, Catholic doctrine produced a number of slavery apologists among the southern clergy. O'Connor, like the church and the enslaved, had to live with these contradictions.

These were not the only regional impositions. O'Connor's rebellious side showed in her dim view of certain gender conventions. She was a less than enthusiastic participant in such rites of southern womanhood as cocktail-party politesse, and her newspaper cartoons (not to mention certain of her protagonists) take aim at a cult of southern womanhood that produced both beauty pageants ("Miss Gum Spirits of Turpentine has just been elected for the year," she reported in one letter [*HB* 328]) and the dogma that "pretty is as pretty does." But her greatest distance from southern conformity came from the immutable fact of her Catholicism. W. J. Cash argued that the "man at the center" of southern culture—the plantation squire—might be emblematically an Irishman of small means who makes good. It is significant, then, that O'Connor wore her Catholicism plainly, and likewise her southernness—but never her Irishness.

Indeed, Flannery O'Connor's sense of the possible was defined by a Catholicity yoked to her Irishness. Catholicism was the center of the life of a woman for whom taking first communion was as "natural" as "brushing my teeth" (*HB* 164). She succinctly stated her worldview thus: "I see from the standpoint of Christian orthodoxy."[38] As a professedly Catholic devout, O'Connor would also see her potential defined by literary circles, where she was indeed a rare bird. The quizzical attitude of the recent biography *Flannery*, as well as its reviewers, toward this salient fact—when they take stock of it—says much about the continued association of Catholicism with didactic art and anti-intellectualism. Ralph Wood's insightful review of Gooch's *Flannery* begins by noticing a missed opportunity to explore the question that an "eminent author" put to Robert Giroux when O'Connor was posthumously honored with the National Book Award: "Do you really think Flannery O'Connor was a great writer? She's such a Roman Catholic."[39]

She stood at a double remove from the American mainstream, both as a southerner and as a Catholic. But O'Connor's arm's-length Irish ethnic identity may be finally important to understanding her work. In turn, her Catholicism cannot be fully understood without reference to its specifically Irish Catholic contours, and the way she defined herself must be seen partly as a way of claiming some measure of autonomy in a community with strict norms.

Certainly she took pains to dissociate herself from the small world of the Savannah Irish. O'Connor once wrote to Betty Hester, "I was brought up in Savannah where there was a colony of the Over-Irish. They have the biggest St. Patrick's Day parade anywhere around and generally go nutty on the subject."

> If there is a re-run of the program on the Irish in America I'll try to look at it. Between you and Mr. O'Gara it is already pretty vivid to me. I have never been greatly tied emotionally or sentimentally to my own Irish background. The Irish in America are sometimes more Irish than the Irish and I suppose some of my indifference is a reaction against that. . . . On the other hand, all the Irish from Ireland that I have ever seen have been charming. (*HB* 531)

O'Connor went on to explain that the Irish playwright Thomas Kilroy, visiting from Notre Dame, had noted many affinities between the South and Ireland:

"[He] said the South more than any other part of this country reminded him of Ireland" (*HB* 531).

Yet O'Connor was never to go to Ireland. Once, on a visit to Ireland, Patrick Samway noticed signs in the Dublin airport claiming, "with the brash assurance of someone trying to sell a certain bridge linking Brooklyn and Manhattan, that O'Connor regularly visited the film director John Huston at his home in County Galway."[40] Never mind that she never set foot in Ireland; her attitude toward southern Irish is laced with a healthy skepticism, and in this she joins Pat Conroy, a writer of the low country who has long been engaged in a lover's quarrel with Catholicism. Whereas Pat Conroy has enjoyed visiting Ireland, he once shared with me his very low opinion of Irish Americans in general and explained how he nearly wound up in a fight in San Francisco because when asked about his Irish lineage, he made dismissive remarks![41] In all this, perhaps, there is an element of reflexive Irish iconoclasm.

Taking O'Connor's comments in person, in letters, and in fiction at face value, a number of critics have suggested that any vestigial trappings of Irish identity meant very little to her—although she, like Margaret Mitchell, could have "put on the dog" and touted the middle respectability of her Irish ancestors. Of course she protested too much. The way she approached the polyverse of Catholic history, theology, and cultural discourse evolved out of the particularities (and peculiarities) of her upbringing as an *Irish* Catholic in the American South. Her specifically Irish strain of Catholicism was bred in the bone, beginning with seven years of parochial school in Savannah. The culture of St. Vincent's Grammar School for Girls was informed by the Irish immigrant culture of Savannah and the Mercy nuns who taught there, most of whom were Irish women in their late teens, newly arrived, trained in Baltimore, and whisked away to schools down the seaboard. The social world of Irish Catholics in Savannah was old enough to be stratified, both in Protestant and Catholic circles, reflected in the widely held belief that O'Connor's transfer from St. Vincent's (bustling with all comers on Lafayette Square) to the Sacred Heart Academy (more formal, and in another parish) was connected to the shanty/lace-curtain divisions within Savannah's Irish community.[42]

What was the character of that community? No one has done a better job of describing it than Hugh Brown, who was of that community and from whose essay "Flannery O'Connor, The Savannah Years" Brad Gooch borrowed extensively in setting the stage of *Flannery: A Life of Flannery O'Connor.* Brown emphasized that O'Connor "was born and raised in an insular Roman Catholic community within a Southern American city of the twenties and thirties."

First of all, it was *Southern, very Southern.* More years separate us now from the date of O'Connor's birth than separate that date from the end of the Civil War, or, as it was regularly called in the Savannah newspapers of the twenties and thirties, the War Between the States. . . . Second, *the city was not prosperous,* even during the boom of the twenties. The great port of the late 19th century with its shipping agents and cotton factors had fallen off, partly due to the boll weevil, partly due to changing patterns of economic development in the state. . . . Third, *Savannah was a racially segregated city.* Blacks and whites were segregated residentially, educationally, socially, and even religiously. . . . Fourth, and of great importance for O'Connor, Savannah contained *a relatively large Roman Catholic population, most of whom were Irish.* The Catholic community was not simply of shared belief. It was a physical fact, especially in the area where O'Connor's house was (and still is) located.[43]

Hugh Brown's piece is nothing less than required reading for those who would understand O'Connor's childhood, as it captures what it meant to be Catholic in a state where the Convent Inspection Law, generated by anti-Catholic hysteria, stayed on the books until the 1960s. Each of Brown's differentiae is elaborated on below. Additionally, to instantiate his observations in Flannery O'Connor's life, I turn to another portrait of the Savannah Irish community, one that emerges from several unpublished interviews conducted with two men. The first, Monsignor Daniel J. Bourke (1909–1999), described in the Georgia House of Representatives in 1997 as "the beloved clerical leader of the Irish in Savannah and an 87 year old wonder," was born in Birr, Offaly, Ireland, in 1909 and sent to Savannah after his ordination in 1934.[44] The second, Bill Canty (1903–2002) was one of ten children born to John Francis Canty and Elizabeth Fitzgerald, who came to Savannah from Listowel in County Kerry, Ireland.[45] Though Bill Canty never learned to drive a car, he worked for the railroad in Savannah for much of his long life and was highly regarded as a "local personality" within the Irish community. Taken together, Bourke and Canty, widely acknowledged as the institutional memory of twentieth-century Irish Catholicism in Georgia, bring us closer to the heart of the world that made Flannery O'Connor.

Flannery O'Connor's Savannah was, in Hugh Brown's words, "Southern, very Southern." And so were the precincts of rural Georgia just outside Savannah.

O'Connor's world, both rural and urban, was southern to the point of carica-ture. Monsignor Daniel Bourke recalled how "one time in Albany he [Father Tom Brennan] raffled off a mule. The Irish horse traders had given him a mule. And the man who'd won it came to get it. Father should have been in a quandary but it didn't faze him. He said, 'I can't give you the mule.' The man said, 'Why not?' He said, 'The mule is dead.' And the mule was dead! It probably wasn't worth very much, anyway."

Jerry Leath Mills once waggishly proposed that "no good southern fiction is complete without a dead mule," so this would make Flannery's Georgia very southern indeed. Actually, apart from perhaps a distinguishing measure of port-city cosmopolitanism, there is no need to make the case for Savannah as an emblematically southern place. The point to be made here is that if Savan-nah was, as Hugh Brown says, "Southern, very Southern," the Irish community in which Flannery grew up was resolutely southern in most respects (with some important exceptions, to be discussed). Bill Canty was described in the *Savannah Morning News* as speaking "in an accent that was part Irish brogue and part old Savannah."[46] At a Savannah Land League rally in 1888 where P. J. O'Connor presided, the meeting concluded with a band playing "Wearing of the Green," "merging it into 'Dixie' and the applause from the orchestra, galleries and stage almost drowned the music."[47]

White southern attitudes, including a sense of loyalty to Dixie, prevailed among the Savannah Irish. Monsignor Bourke explained simply, "The Catholic population, more or less in social matters, adopted the customs and worries of their neighbors. . . . And I was rather astounded that they were so conservative." (Bourke was not precisely a liberal firebrand, either; he never really embraced many of the Vatican II reforms.) A case in point was Bourke's vivid memories of how parishioners were equally enthralled by FDR and the "Radio Priest," Fa-ther Charles Coughlin, an Irish Canadian priest who famously proclaimed that "The New Deal is Christ's Deal." Father Coughlin eventually veered so far to the right that he aligned himself with fascists, and he is now mostly remembered for editorializing jointly against communists and Jews.[48] He reached the apex of his fame about the time Flannery O'Connor was ten years of age.

O'Connor had a small fascination with radio, along with other modern me-dia that conveyed pop-culture kitsch, an interest, as it happens, in common with Cormac McCarthy, for whom the radio might provide a forbidden telephone to the Protestant world of hillbilly Knoxville. A highlight of her weekly child-hood routine was the *Let's Pretend* program on CBS radio, which she listened to every Saturday morning.[49] When she became a recognized writer, she wrote a piece about "Catlic literature" for a radio program at the behest of Father Harold C. Gardiner, SJ (*HB* 232), and she cheerfully reported on the bad poetry of the "Light Crust Dough Boys" radio segment to Elizabeth and Robert Lowell (*HB* 227). When Regina O'Connor made an appearance on a local radio show, Flannery wrote to Betty Hester, "I am glad you got to hear the rural radio" (*HB* 253).

There is no telling whether O'Connor had Father Coughlin, blistering the rural airwaves, in mind when she created Hoover Shoats (whose stage name was Onnie Jay Holy), the slick evangelist and marketer of *Wise Blood* (1952), who boasts to Hazel Moats about his three years on the radio hosting "Soulsease, a quarter hour of Mood, Melody, and Mentality," "a program that give real religious experiences to the whole family."[50] What O'Connor understood for certain was the points of union in the conservative philosophies of Irish Catholics and fundamentalists. And Bourke saw those conservative tendencies transmitted, unbroken, across the seas. When asked about making the transition from Ireland to becoming a parish priest in Georgia, he replied, "I didn't feel myself a stranger at all. I took to it as a duck to water. . . . I felt quite at home here. I felt just as at home walking down the streets of Savannah, down Broughton Street, as I did walking down O'Connell Street in Dublin, or in the O'Connell Street of my native town. I felt the people of Savannah very similar to the people I'd grown up with. They talked with a different accent—they considered me speaking with a strange accent—but we're thinking the same way, the same background, the same traditions, and everything else." His experience would confirm those whom Flannery had heard compare Savannah to Dublin (*HB* 531).

Bourke added that because of "intense segregation" in the diocese, he was working with whites, mostly of Irish descent. On some "social views"—Bourke likely had in mind labor and the poor—"compared to the people I grew up with in Ireland," southerners were "ultraconservative. There would be a number of reasons for that—the fact that the South had been defeated, and that race entered into that defeat, and their whole philosophy," he mused.

The Irish Catholics were highly southernized in their politics insofar as they tended to support the Democratic Party with near unanimity in the usual Democrat-Catholic-Irish trinity. Monsignor Bourke noted that "all the southern Catholics voted democratic," and he intimated that when he arrived in the 1930s they might well have visited bodily harm on anyone who did not. Flannery's family seems to have largely followed the pattern, and she pointed to the widespread phenomenon of the "White Democratic Primary" in her short story "The Barber" (written after Faulkner's "Dry September," it seems, to rework a tale of a racial dissenter in a barber shop, also echoing a crucial scene in Melville's *Benito Cereno*). Peter J. Cline "was appointed by Gov. Northen [a Democrat] a member of the board of commissioners to the colored school at Savannah" and supported Oscar J. Underwood for the democratic nominee for President in 1912.[51] Kate Flannery Semmes's husband was a well-known Democratic booster. And so on.[52] Flannery O'Connor would take some pleasure in Kennedy's election ("I think King Kong would be better than Nixon" [*HB* 404]) and tell Maryat Lee, "Actually *I* am the conservative in this family. Strictly a Kennedy conservative. I like the way that man is running the country" (*HB* 499). She was not as broken up over the assassination as John Kennedy Toole was, however. On Kennedy's death she would write to Betty Hester, "I am sad about the President. But I like the new one" (*HB* 549).

But there were telling diversions from the party line, too. Bill Canty proclaimed his undying hatred for the Kennedys, who transgressed Catholic values. O'Connor also wrote dryly of Kennedy's election: "Now that we [southerners] have elected him, we can begin to cuss him" (*HB* 418). Flannery's Aunt Katie Cline "worked her entire life at the postal job she secured in the 1920s when elder brother Hugh T. Cline was the Republican-appointee postmaster."[53] (Of course, many Georgians jumped party lines in order *not* to vote for Al Smith, the Irish Catholic Democratic candidate, in 1928, with Hoover capturing an unthinkable 43 percent of the state's votes—giving the name of Flannery's conman Hoover Shoats a hilarious double meaning.) Pat Persse recalls that her father, who "liked to go against the crowd," was a strong supporter of the Republican Thomas Dewey in the 1944 election.[54] Though Flannery O'Connor's mother would defect on integrationist fears (in common with many Georgians) and cast her vote for Eisenhower in 1952, Flannery supported Adlai Stevenson.[55] Bill Sessions has documented other instances in which O'Connor's kin and kith may have moved toward the Republican column and suggested to me that some of the Clines were disaffected with the way blacks were treated under Democratic administrations.[56] One hesitates to make too much of it, except to note that the Irish community was not a political monolith and that Flannery's people, like her, were not afraid to break from the pack.

How were they un-southern? First and most obviously, they were Catholics (more on which later) in a state that had responded viscerally to Governor Tom Watson's anti-Irish, anti-Catholic campaigning. Second, the charitable work they directed toward African Americans, especially in the field of education, stood out in a place where most religious institutions did not challenge the status quo. (Father Bourke had his own suspicions about adamantine segregation, noting that "most of the crackers had the suspicion somehow that they were about half-negro.") Third, their complicated history with "rum and Romanism" set them apart from many Protestants, who generally treated alcohol as a vice to be concealed. Catholic temperance movements had flourished in nineteenth-century Georgia, and Bourke recalled how Father Matthew (Theobald Matthew), the famed temperance speaker, had made the rounds in Georgia. But by the time of Flannery O'Connor, Irish Catholics were more likely to see drink as something to gladden the heart, and Bourke recalled how a Catholic cop in Prohibition-era Savannah had grumbled about a nosey informer who made trouble by reporting speakeasies. Bill Canty suggested that alcoholism was a problem among priests, recalling his mother's ire when a drunken priest muddled the Stations of the Cross. Once, when a visiting priest pressed his mother for a drink, she supposedly "took up a can of lye and said she'd drink that first." There is a whiff of this in "The Comforts of Home," in which "the little slut" Sarah Ham prompts an outraged call from a boardinghouse chatelaine: "Drunk! Drunk in my parlor and I won't have it! . . . My house is respectable!" (*CS* 393–94).

Finally, in Savannah as in other parts of the country, Irish Americans had played a significant role in organized labor movements. Indeed, the proximity of Irish and black laborers in Savannah, especially on the wharves, led them to a close working relationship and shared stakes in labor unions. Of course, many southern Irish opposed the unions. Monsignor Bourke was bemused by the tendency among many of his parishioners to see any attempt at organized labor as smacking of communism. Flannery O'Connor too was conflicted on the subject. When the foundress of the Catholic Worker Movement visited the Monastery of the Holy Spirit at Conyers, O'Connor admitted to Betty Hester in a single breath, "All my thoughts on this subject are ugly and uncharitable—such as: that's a mighty long way to come to get shot at, etc. I admire [Dorothy Day] very much" (*HB* 218). With southern independence of mind she would later mention to Hester, "D.D. wrote up her trip to Koinonia [Clarence Jordan's interracial commune] in the *CW* [*Catholic Worker*], which I duly enclose. It would have been all right if she hadn't had to stick in her plug for Their Way of Life for Everybody" (*HB* 220). Flannery O'Connor's art may have been visionary, but the conservative undertone of her politics was much in keeping with that of the Irish Catholic community that produced her.

Hugh Brown contended that the Savannah familiar to Flannery O'Connor "was not prosperous," but perhaps this was in the eye of the beholder. For his part, Bourke arrived about the time of the Depression and felt that it could only be a "depression" by American standards, because, from his perspective, the standard of living was still relatively high. Along the same lines, Bill Canty identified a second cousin who had rejected American prosperity altogether and returned to Ireland, declaring, "I'd rather be poor in Ireland than rich in America." All in all, Bourke felt that there were relatively few at the extreme ends of the economic spectrum; most of his parishioners were middle class, "hard-working people" by his account.

But Bourke also worked with the poorest of the poor as he rode the rural circuit. He conceded that their poverty was, if anything, worse, in some respects, than what he had seen in Ireland. "Their houses were terrible little things— I never saw such poverty." He described Catholic sharecroppers as "very very poor people and ill educated. Most of them we were dealing with had Irish names and they'd gone out there for the building of the railroads and all. Some of them settled down and some of them acquired farms. Some of them made good, like around Valdosta and Lakeland."

Both men affirmed that in their time, for the majority of Savannahians, a high-school diploma had been adequate for obtaining decent employment. In an earlier generation, as Bourke acknowledged, a primary-school education might have sufficed. And Savannahians would never consider themselves recovered from Reconstruction. For Irish immigrants, jobs in railroads, on the wharves, and in heavy industries were the norm; the O'Connor brothers/patriarchs were wheelwrights and blacksmiths. According to Bill Canty, himself the son of a blacksmith who later became a city alderman, "Girls of the red light district would come up and put money in Mama's hands. My aunt said, 'I don't see how you could stop on the street and talk to a woman of ill fame.' Mama said, 'If I didn't meet the train and give you a home, maybe you'd've been a woman of ill fame.'"

Elizabeth Fitzgerald Canty's empathetic attitude is typically Irish American insofar as it acknowledges the mutability of human estates and demonstrates a deeply engrained compassion for the poor and desperate. Elizabeth Canty extracted a promise from her son that he would take care of the graves of the poor and forgotten, and he carried out the work throughout his life. Bill Canty virtually *lived* in that graveyard—"the only place where people didn't talk back to me," as he was fond of quipping—a human testament to the importance of ancestry and kin-keeping in Flannery O'Connor's Irish community.

Canty especially esteemed the woman for whom Flannery O'Connor was named, in part because she helped put up the funds to maintain the cemetery. "You heard about Ms. Katie Flannery Semmes?" he asked his interviewers.

"Oh, she was an angel—if there's a heaven and earth that woman is in heaven." Though his mother was an immigrant and his family obviously came from modest means (the Canty house had once been a brothel), Bill Canty insisted that "we were what they call the lace curtain Irish and Mama always had lace curtains up on the windows, too." Flannery O'Connor joked to Richard Gilman that she could hardly publish under the name Mary O'Connor: "Who was likely to buy the stories of an Irish washerwoman?"[57]

Savannah's Irish Catholics, then, occupied a broad lower to middle class in which social distinctions could be parsed fine according to one's ancestry (for example, by "Old Catholic" associations) and contributions to the community. Bill Canty claimed that the Yamacraw Irish "didn't associate" with the Old Fort Irish in Savannah, but this was probably an overstatement, for the Savannah Irish community in general "displayed a remarkable ethnic cohesiveness that seemed to transcend class and religious differences."[58] Flannery O'Connor's readers will notice that her very often petit- and haute-bourgeois characters tend to be acutely class conscious and obsessed with appearance, like the Grandmother of "A Good Man is Hard to Find," and that the characters who express these views sometimes seem to channel the voice of the woman Flannery O'Connor sometimes called "Maw" and sometimes "the Mother."

Like Margaret Mitchell, Flannery O'Connor's emphasized the importance of keeping the land—both in her life and in her fiction, for example, in the character of Mary Fortune in "A View of the Woods"—an emphasis that may reflect the premium the Irish diaspora placed on owning land long after memories of land-lordism had faded into family lore. Moreover, her stories strongly associate leisure with the upper class in the old southern belief that the ruling class should not be seen to labor. As Mrs. May reminds Mr. Greenleaf in "Greenleaf," if his boys had "any pride . . . there are many things that they would not *allow* their mother to do" (*CS* 313). Whether an Irish Catholic fear, a southern worry, or middle-class insecurity, in O'Connor's fiction marriage tends to produce class anxiety because it is far easier to lose status than to keep or enhance it. Mrs. May expresses this attitude when she whispers to herself, "I work and slave, I struggle and sweat to keep this place for them and soon as I'm dead, they'll marry trash and bring it in here and ruin everything. They'll marry trash and ruin everything I've done" (*CS* 315). Attendant to this principle is the idea that Continental refinement and emphasis on manners can breed social status:

> They could not be told from other people's children. You could tell, of
> course, when [the Greenleaf boys] opened their mouths but they did that

seldom. The smartest thing they had done was to get sent overseas and there
to marry French wives. They hadn't married French trash, either. They had
married nice girls who naturally couldn't understand that they murdered
the king's English or that the Greenleafs were who they were.

. . . [Their children] on account of their mothers' background, would be
sent to the convent school and brought up with manners. "And in twenty
years," Mrs. May asked Scofield and Wesley, "do you know what those people
will be?"

"*Society*," she said blackly. (*CS* 318)

Emphasis on "blackly." The final piece of the class puzzle in Flannery
O'Connor's world was of course race. Mrs. May's son boasts that he is "the best
nigger-insurance salesman in the county," enflaming her fears: "What nice
girl wants to marry a nigger-insurance man?" (*CS* 315). Geography determined
both destiny and anxiety. Walter Fraser lays out the racial and economic matrix
of Savannah's storied Yamacraw neighborhood thus: "The canal basin abutted
the black and Irish neighborhoods of Yamacraw in Oglethorpe Ward on the
western edge of the city, the freight yards of the Central of Georgia Railroad,
and the nearby Savannah River Wharfs."[59] The industries surrounding Yamacraw demanded proximity between black and Irish communities. But for white
Georgians of the time, to be seen consorting with blacks, unless one was man-
aging their labor, was potentially to be adjudged in the lower class.

O'Connor sends up this sensibility in "Revelation" when Claude Turpin suggests that blacks want to "marry white folks" to "improve their color" but that
the only thing that can come of it is "white-faced niggers" (*CS* 496). The joke, of
course, is on him. O'Connor wrote to Maryat Lee in November 1962 about her
visit to Greenville, Texas, a place with an infamous town motto only slightly
misquoted in O'Connor's letter: "'Home of the Blackest Dirt and the Whitest
People.' Their 'white' means 'fair & square,' not Caucasian. In Greenville they
say, 'Our niggers are white, too'" (*HB* 499).[60] And so the blacks of the story are
most white when they try to soothe Mrs. Turpin after her close encounter
with Human Development. Mrs. Turpin frames her own dilemma: "What if
Jesus had said, 'All right, you can be white-trash or a nigger or ugly'!" (*CS*
492). Which of the "evils" would she pick? She later permits herself to imagine being fat, ugly, and poor, but not black, and it is worth remembering that
for the southern Irish, as for whites generally in the South, the mere fact of
being white conferred at least one measure of human superiority. As to the
"white-trash": "Help them you must," thinks Mrs. Turpin, "but help them you

couldn't" (*CS* 497). Schooled in the importance of good works, O'Connor persistently points to how noblesse oblige can operate as a form of false charity. Of the farm at Andalusia she wrote to the Fitzgeralds, "Noblesse obleege with a vengeance as my mama runs it but very peaceful" (*HB* 232).

"When the Catholic Irish rose to prominence in Hibernian societies later in the nineteenth century, they maintained this theme of charity as self-help, a very American value," Gleeson and Buttimer point out.[61] Yet O'Connor never embraced the very American values of bootstrapping (which was rooted, after all, in a middle-class sense of Waspish economy), offering instead a Catholic counterpoint. She revealed the emptiness of self-reliance, with its strong ties to individualism, in characters such as the Misfit, who rejects the Grandmother's prayers and declares, "I don't want no hep . . . I'm doing all right by myself" (*CS* 130). As Robert Brinkmeyer explains, the notion of genuine Christian charity "is an integral component of O'Connor's Catholic vision."[62] If self-help runs to individualism, Flannery O'Connor's exploration of social class insists that most of us are spiritually impoverished. Christian charity turns attention to the perceived Other, and thence to God. Her values looked to the evolving nineteenth-century magisterium that complicated Catholicism's uneasy relationship to capitalism and wealth.

Yet O'Connor seemed to relish living in a place that could only be reached "by bus or buzzard" and frequently made light of the shabby-genteel lifestyle she had elected, as well as her forced participation in upper-crust family rituals. Ultimately, the sense that in poverty Georgians were all "in it together" appealed to her, much as she was glad to participate in a church that could not be identified with any one social class and that aspired to put aside class differences. At the Yaddo colony in New York, according to Brad Gooch, Flannery "kept a close watch . . . on the staff of mostly Irish maids, a type she was familiar with—'all well over forty, large grim and granit-jawed or shriveled and shrunk.'"[63] She befriended the Irish caretaker and cook, Jim and Nellie Shannon, who lived in an outbuilding on the property. Jim Shannon "had been a ragpicker on the docks" before moving upstate.[64] Every Sunday she hopped in to the family's crowded old station wagon to attend Mass with them.[65] She had already decided that "the help was morally superior to the guests" (*HB* 364). This was no mere "slumming," for, as she explained in "The Teaching of Literature," "The poor love formality, I believe, even better than the wealthy, but their manners and forms are always being interrupted by necessity. The mystery of existence is always showing through the texture of their ordinary lives, and I'm afraid that this makes them irresistible to the novelist" (*MM* 132–33).

❧

Hugh Brown acknowledges that Flannery's Savannah "was a racially segregated city," a fact not without formative influence in her worldview. Yet Catholicism had a peculiar role to play in how the lines of segregation were drawn. Bill Canty noted that the religious sisters played a large part in taking in "colored orphans," and according to him, his mother was personally responsible for the Roman Catholic conversion of a black woman during his lifetime. Monsignor Bourke regarded the signal success of the church in social matters to be the free Catholic schools that served the black population. There, in his words, "they got the best possible education in Savannah that they could not get in public schools." Blacks who acquired an education in Catholic schools often sought employment in other parts of the country. (The best-known Savannah graduate in this regard is the Supreme Court justice Clarence Thomas.) At the same time, the parishes remained segregated. When John Howard Griffin staged his *Black Like Me* (1961) experiment in autumn 1959, passing as black in the South, he was "deeply shocked to be driven away from churches that would have welcomed me any time as a white man."[66] Approximately one year later, on 28 October 1960, O'Connor wrote to Father McCown: "If John Howard Griffin gets to Georgia again, we would be delighted to see him; but not in blackface." She went on to explain that Griffin must have been "a pretty horrible-looking object" (*HB* 414). "Everything That Rises Must Converge" was one of the last stories O'Connor would complete, and her awareness of Griffin's *Black Like Me* project raises the intriguing possibility that O'Connor's story was written partly in response to Griffin's book. A culminating scene in *Black Like Me* finds Griffin in a racial catch-22 when he prepares to give up a bus seat to a white passenger; viewed as a race traitor by other blacks on the bus, he nevertheless draws the woman's scorn. In O'Connor's story, a white woman's saccharine charity meets with neither her liberal son's approval nor that of the black mother she would patronize. But it is ultimately the white liberal who plays the part of the fool.

If, as Hugh Brown remarked, Flannery O'Connor "would have seen few blacks who were not in menial roles, mostly servants"—including the black workers who stayed on at Andalusia—one might see this as a direct consequence of segregation policy: itinerancy and brain drain for blacks who left, resignation and frustrated lives spent behind the mask for those who remained. "He can hear what he hears and he can hear two times that much. He can hear what you don't say as well as what you do," the white barber says of

George, his "boy" in "The Barber" (*CS* 24). O'Connor appreciated a piece in the *Southern Vanguard* ("It possibly takes a Canadian to throw a sharper light on things here") and marked the observation that in the South "formality becomes a condition of survival" (*HB* 70). Yet in story after story O'Connor removed the mask of faux subservience by holding up a mocking and corrupted reflection, a grotesque and crippled likeness of the whites who strove to perpetuate the grotesquerie of the racial status quo. Hard-line segregation became the perfect metaphor for unseeing pride in stories such as "The Artificial Nigger," "Everything That Rises Must Converge," and indeed O'Connor's last story, "Judgment Day." Thus she might in the same letter observe, "The formality that is left in the South now is quite dead and done for of course," perhaps a veiled comment not just on the decline of manners, elsewhere observed in "The Fiction Writer & His Country" (*MM* 29), but on passing racial orders.

The very notion that there were orders, that they endured, and that one belonged to them constituted the bedrock of southern political thought and would engender a good deal of personal conflict in Flannery O'Connor's life. Her library contained a copy of *Ideas Have Consequences* (1948), the unsmiling study of the latter-day Agrarian acolyte and rhetor Richard Weaver, whose work perfectly realizes the unflinchingly conservative and generally monolithic southern conformity, the "savage ideal" that W. J. Cash railed against. As Cash recognizes the apparent contradictions of southern individualism, no one could accuse O'Connor of a cheerful consistency when comparing some of her off-the-record statements with the high-minded investigations of her art.

Flannery O'Connor's difficulty accepting those she saw as interloping crusaders—like Dorothy Day and John Howard Griffin (with whom she might have gotten on famously as a Catholic convert of Irish descent and an extensive correspondent of Maritain and Merton)—led her to comment, "I hope that to be of two minds about some things is not to be neutral" (*HB* 218). The comment might aptly be applied to O'Connor's thinking on race, as mixed signals from family, from church, and from the southern Irish community reached her from earliest childhood. It seems that her work benefited from a heart troubled by the options closest to hand: complicity, indifference, inaction. And mere self-righteousness was perhaps worse than inaction, as Julian, schooled in correctness, reminds us in "Everything That Rises Must Converge."

Scholars and writers have been much exercised over some of O'Connor's off-the-record statements. *Flannery* talks up both sides of the latter point and diplomatically leaves it to an anonymous Trappist monk to call the writer a "cultural racist."[67] Joy Williams, in a review of Brad Gooch's *Flannery*, concludes by citing O'Connor's objection to "someone turning one of my colored idiots into a hero" for a proposed staging of a story. This quotation is never mentioned in Gooch's book, and the reader is left to wonder whether Williams found this comment delectably impolitic, scandalously revealing, or both. Elsewhere she writes, in a risible generalization, that "the civil rights movement interested [Flannery O'Connor] not at all."[68] True, Flannery O'Connor was not interested in clambering onto the mule train, but her long-standing engagement with the movement is revealed in her letters and her stories.

An aroma of this prejudice suffuses Joyce Carol Oates's review of *Flannery*. With the backhanded observation that "O'Connor managed a brave public persona, when addressing mostly Southern college audiences by way of 'talks' about fiction writing," Oates writes,

> She was unapologetic in her allegiance to her place of birth and her parochial upbringing: "I'm pleased to be a member of my particular family and to live in Baldwin County in the sovereign State of Georgia, and to see what I can see from here." (As Brad Gooch notes, at this time in the early 1950s Georgia was ranked highest in the nation "in the rate of lynchings and other murders.")[69]

The quotation attributed to Flannery O'Connor that Oates insinuates here is taken out of context. It comes from Rosemary Magee's *Conversations with Flannery O'Connor,* and the question that was originally put to her went thus: "You live in a region where family roots lie deep. This surely gives you a sense of stability, lacking in many fellow Americans. Has it had any meaning for you as a writer?"[70] With its knowing air, Oates's juxtaposition, to paraphrase Melville's "Bartleby the Scrivener," purchases a morsel of delicious self-approval by implying that O'Connor was an unrepentant, hard-shell racist.

This rendition of Flannery O'Connor—acerbic and politically incorrect— has become something of an ascendant standard critical line. The reality is considerably more complicated. O'Connor's mother never adjusted to a civil rights mentality, and Flannery knew that "Everything That Rises Must Converge" might disagree with her: "I guess my mama likes it all right. . . . She's accepting all the changes in her stride. The Church makes itself felt along those lines. I take several Catlic papers which are always yapping about racial justice" (*HB* 499). The church "made itself felt," but how did Flannery O'Connor, with her awareness of sins of omission, make herself felt? For some southern Irish Catholics in the South, differentiation from blacks was hard fought and not easily surrendered. For others, common cause was the thing. And for still others, the awareness of southern ethnicity writ large, with the race-blind frustrations of limited opportunities and poverty fanning a sense of all-in-it-together grievance, dictated mean charity (as with the patronizing grandmother of "A Good Man is Hard to Find") or its opposite, expansive charity (as with the paternalistic but paradoxically genuine mother of "Everything That Rises Must Converge").

This is not to praise O'Connor for being something less than a hard racist but to show just how she might be of two minds. Were her racial epithets that fell hard on the ears of other students at the University of Iowa calculated to shock or indicative of a serpent in the bosom?[71] How should they be reconciled with her friendship with a black graduate student, over her mother's protests? The "colored idiots" passage that Williams cites comes from a letter to Cecil Dawkins in which O'Connor admitted that she would only be interested in whatever money might come from the stage adaptation of her work. "It's nice to have something you can be completely crass about," she explained. "The only thing I would positively object to would be somebody turning one of my colored idiots into a hero. Don't let any fool director work that on you. I wouldn't trust any of that bunch farther than I could hurl them. I guess I wouldn't want a Yankee doing this, money or no money" (*HB* 547).

Idiots are idiots, black or white, O'Connor might insist; don't sentimentalize my work or patronize me. If anything reveals a heart in conflict with itself, it is the last line, which implies a familiar tactic, that the "Negro problem" is a southern problem, utterly inscrutable to outsiders. O'Connor never offered a formal southern racial-conversion narrative of the sort common to twentieth-century southern literature, brilliantly described by Fred Hobson in his book, *But Now I See*. The process of conversion to the truth of the ugly racial stalemate was, rather, the work of her fiction. The consistency of latent awakening in her stories hints at the turbulence within her, and so do some of her personal remarks. Hearing a bus driver order "stove pipe blondes" to the back of the bus marked the "moment I became an integrationist" (*HB* 253). Such idiocy could hardly pass muster with the likes of O'Connor, who recognized how such "innocent" meanness put a millstone around the neck. For Flannery O'Connor's two minds, ironically, gave her fine insight into how day-to-day racism might be naturalized within a community, as well as the discredit it brought to those who propagated it among the truly innocent. Betty Hester called her friend "in some odd ways truly strangely innocent," but on the issue of race, at least, O'Connor was neither innocent nor comfortable.[72]

Hugh Brown asserted that Savannah harbored "a relatively large Roman Catholic population, most of whom were Irish, and the character of that population, as Flannery O'Connor knew and experienced it, is the final theme to be examined in the contexts of her young life. If Lafcadio Hearn told W. B. Yeats of a nanny from Connaught who shaped him, a militant church was to be O'Connor's tutor. "Catholicity in our day was strong," Bill Canty declared simply. Catholicism in Savannah, dominated by the Irish, was a muscular affair, both in terms of its public face and in terms of old-fashioned American violence. Both Canty and Bourke were within living memory of the period when Catholic armed watchmen patrolled convents and churches to secure them against anti-Catholic vandals. Bourke described what he called "a sort of fierce Irish spirit" that dominated Catholicism in Savannah. The Catholic Laymen's Association, founded in 1916, adopted a conciliatory strategy during a period when signs on Georgia trains warned against associating with Catholics. Others would attempt to stand down anti-Catholic feeling more directly. Bill Canty would say with some pride, "Bishop [Benjamin Joseph] Keiley was a man who took nothing off of no Protestant minister. He answered 'em."[73] Canty also recalled how Irish Catholic railroad coworkers taunted the Masons who removed their lapel pins when a Catholic became their new boss.

Canty consigned Katie Semmes to heaven, but separately he would say of Tom Watson, "If there is a hell he's in it—he's responsible for all the hatred in Georgia toward the Catholics." Bourke also condemned Watson for *knowingly* inciting the people to bigotry, when, as one of the most learned men in the state of Georgia, "he had not the excuse of ignorance." At times, a siege mentality controlled, and an atmosphere of insularity prevailed. Hugh Brown aptly refers to the "circumscribed world" of the Savannah Catholic populace. "Catholics in Savannah were aware that they were different," he explains. "In the city, they numbered perhaps 5,000 in a population of 75,000; in the state they totaled 18,000 in a population of 2 million. In a way, they lived in their own little world, a world in which the word Catholic was exclusive and the term non-Catholic categorized the rest of the population."[74]

Despite that insularity, or perhaps because of it, Canty claimed that he was more likely to befriend Jews than Protestants. Bourke, however, maintained that he encountered little visible anti-Catholic feeling in all his years as a priest in Georgia, and said, "I have never been mistreated by a Georgia cracker." Commissioned to take a census of Catholics, he asked the hotel clerk in the little town where he was overnighting if there were any Catholics living there. "No, we wouldn't allow any Catholics to live in this town," came the reply. The collarless Bourke responded dryly, "Well, you never know." The fierce independence and theological turn of mind that characterized Georgia Protestants became a staple of O'Connor's fiction, and some of Bourke's startling experiences have the texture of one of her stories. On one occasion the priest got a lift from a man who noticed he was wearing his collar. Were the Catholics established by Christ? the man asked. "I said yes. That didn't seem to worry him too much because he said, 'Well, where should I establish my own church?'"

Bourke also expressed a certain kind of admiration for ordinary Georgians. "Most of the Baptist ministers could just read and write. They were holy sort of men, often sharecroppers themselves. They wouldn't know too much about the church but they were good natured enough, and they'd a great reverence for spiritual things." These were indeed the "Protestant saints" that Flannery wrote about, like Mason Tarwater of *The Violent Bear It Away*. Though some of her ancestors arrived after the devotional revolution that revitalized Irish Catholicism in the mid-nineteenth century, some of the Irish who arrived in Georgia assuredly came from a culture whose traditions of language and religion were endangered by mutually entwined colonization and poverty.

Both Canty and Bourke referred to "mixed marriages"—by which they meant not racially mixed but unions between a Catholic and a Protestant—as something of a taboo, even if they were commonplace in Georgia's small Catholic world. Canty's mother said she would "rather be going to bury" one of his brothers than see him marry a Lutheran.[75] She conditioned her son to attend Mass several times a week, to regularly observe the Stations of the Cross, and to say the Rosary with his family. Public participation in Catholicism marked a "good" family in those watchful circles, and keeping up appearances was important.

As Flannery O'Connor wrote in "The Regional Writer," "You get . . . manners from the texture of existence that surrounds you. The great advantage of being a Southern writer is that we don't have to go anywhere to look for manners; bad or good, we've got them in abundance" (*MM* 103). Flannery O'Connor learned these lessons early, as her mother carefully vetted her friends and exerted a hovering influence over her social life that lasted well into her daughter's maturity. O'Connor would revisit the darker side of the fishbowl effect with characters who premised their sense of superiority on appearances—the grandmother of "A Good Man is Hard to Find" and the procession of pious mothers and older women like Miss Turpin, who mistakenly come to believe that the social order might reflect the divine order. Rituals emphasizing hospitality, reciprocity, and good breeding carried from Ireland into the homes of Irish American southerners. Time and again, O'Connor demonstrates how these rituals can be perverted in stories where "good country people" are revealed to be monstrously selfish.

Even if O'Connor disavowed her ethnicity, she bore something of the imprint of its institutional memory. For example, when she wrote to Betty Hester that "the only thing for apostate priests to do is to be violently anti-Catholic and write books against the Church or go on the sawdust trail with 'I was a Catholic priest but I was saved by the Bible,' etc." (*HB* 431), she might well have had in mind family lore about Joseph Slattery, formerly a priest in Ireland, who was apparently laicized for alcoholism before becoming a Baptist and taking to the U.S. lecture circuit. Inflammatory leaflets circulated before his 1895 visit to the Masonic Temple in Savannah sparked a riot that was suppressed only by military action. Accusations flew that the whole event had been orchestrated by the American Protective Association, a group that Bill Canty remembered bitterly. The anti-Catholic association enrolled many Irish Protestants with ties to the Orange Order, but it never had any real traction in Savannah.

Caught in the middle, the Jewish mayor, Herman Myers (with whom Bill Canty's father served as an alderman), had to call up an armed escort. Jerome Caminada, son of an Irish father and an Italian mother and celebrated detective superintendent of Manchester, England, was evidently brought in as a freelance investigator and would later record that it had the "ingredients of a Belfast riot."[76] A "spokesman" for the Ancient Order of Hibernians told a reporter that Slattery was "unworthy of their attention," though the organization in fact kept a dossier on the ex-priest.[77] The incident revealed unflattering class divisions among clergy, priests, and Old Fort Catholics.[78] Since P. J. O'Connor was a higher-up in the Ancient Order of Hibernians, one of the main parties to the fracas, the tale of the nationally reported Slattery riot might well have been handed down to Flannery O'Connor.

If the Irish had a special role to play in the defense of Catholicism in Savannah, it is equally clear that O'Connor was fascinated by the world that lay beyond the reach of Irish insularity and conformity. Disenchanted believers, apostates, and the fallen away are the movers of Flannery O'Connor's fiction, and what is Hazel Motes if not an ex-priest of a kind and a saint in the making? Flannery O'Connor loved to flirt with the heretic within by putting herself in Protestant shoes, and this led to the often mistaken impression that she was masquerading as a "fundamentalist." For example, Joy Williams recently reported that in her "avid reading" O'Connor "found Protestant theologians superior to Catholic ones, though she was pleased to discover Teilhard de Chardin."[79]

Of course, this is not quite true. Among *living and working* theological writers, she preferred the Protestant ones, mainly to the extent that they provided a model for a Catholic literary renaissance; she deemed the crisis theologians "more alert and creative than their Catholic counterparts."[80] "Let me assure you," O'Connor once wrote Ben Griffith, "that no one but a Catholic could have written *Wise Blood* even though it is a book about a kind of Protestant saint. It reduces Protestantism to the twin ultimate absurdities of The Church Without Christ or The Holy Church of Christ Without Christ, which no pious Protestant would do" (*HB* 69).

To be clear, O'Connor did not choose Protestants to caricature them for the sake of bigotry, and she did not choose them to illustrate fallen Christians because of presumed heterodoxy. Rather, she made them characters because of their everyday contention with the Christ-haunted South and their literal-minded encounter with the language and imminence of faith in a defeated place. She once wrote to Maryat Lee, "I am glad you find me a good Protestant. That is indeed a compliment. All good Catholics have the best Protestant qualities about them, and a good deal more besides; my good deal more besides I try to keep from view lest it offend your delicate sensibilities" (*HB* 418). When she wrote to explain the title of *The Violent Bear It Away* to her friend Thomas Stritch, a Nashville-born Notre Dame professor and church historian who was the nephew of a bishop and a cardinal, she cited the Bible directly: "Matthew 11:12 as the Protestants say" (*HB* 325). The point is that notwithstanding Flannery, most of the Catholics she grew up with did not reflexively quote chapter and verse. Certainly their emphasis on biblical literacy—and Catholics' distance from it—drove her to become more conversant with the Bible.

O'Connor knew the dominant culture inside and out, and some of her stories show her looking across the Protestant threshold. She devotes chapter 5 of *The Violent Bear It Away* to the adolescent Francis Marion Tarwater's revival visit. There, Lucette Carmody, a brooding child missionary of "dark gaze" who has "been to India and China" and "spoken to all the rulers of the world," delivers a testimonial much like the one in John Kennedy Toole's *Neon Bible*. The preacher introduces the savant by saying that "because He knew that it would be the little children that would call others to Him, maybe He knew, friends, maybe He hadda hunch."[81] The episode might seem parodic at first: the girl's mother, decked out in "a long dramatic cape" with a red lining that could evoke Hester Prynne, Fulton Sheen, or both, refers to the family's travels in Rome, "where minds are still chained in priestly darkness" (128). Mr. and Mrs. Carmody may have been something of an inside joke for Flannery O'Connor. Martin H. Carmody served as the seventh Supreme Knight of the Knights of Columbus from 1927 until 1939, and since the Knights of Columbus enjoyed the hearty support of Savannah's Irish Catholics, it seems altogether likely that she may have come across this particular Irish name.

In any case, in typical form O'Connor avoids the straight parody, for little Lucette Carmody does seem to be a vessel of grace for Rayber in *The Violent Bear It Away*. Moreover, O'Connor repeatedly fixes on Lucette's eyes in the space of her testimonial: "dark gaze. . . . Her eyes remained on his face for a moment. . . . Her eyes moved directly to Rayber's face in the window and he knew they sought it. . . . held there before the judgment seat of her eyes. . . . a lowering concentration in her gaze. Her eyes still fixed on him. . . . Her eyes were large and dark and fierce" (131–34). She might be alluding to little Saint Lucy, who suffered torture and in familiar iconic representation carries her eyes on a plate ("There was St. Lucy, whose eyes had been put out during her martyrdom," recalls Anne Rice of the saints who fired her childhood imagination).[82] Gabrielle Rolin, a French novelist who visited O'Connor in Paris, was captivated by Flannery's eyes: "But her eyes . . . perhaps she owed this interior light to her faith, this look so sharp and blue. 'I owe it to my Irish origins,' she said. But there was something more."[83]

Perhaps O'Connor was enlivened in faith and in fiction as she peered across the Protestant threshold. Given the surge of anti-Catholic feeling in Georgia, which did not begin to drop off until the 1920s and which was epitomized in the Slattery riot, O'Connor's position is all the more remarkable, for she never simply took to the trenches, but retained a wry humor about the battle cries of the "Christian soldiers" on both sides. Of course, when it came to fighting sectarian battles, *men* had a way of taking to the front lines. And among Irish Catholic men in Savannah anticlerical attitudes predominated. The reasons for this are as complicated as the strategic acting that pitted the interests of Rome, the Protestant state, and the laity in an ever-shifting order. The American Irish remembered certain perceived betrayals: the clergy's condemnation of the Fenians, their demands for civil order during the famine, and the shaming of Parnell (indeed, the Savannah chapter of the Land League was named the "Parnell Branch"). On the other hand, they remembered that clergy had frequently been powerful advocates for the interests of the laity. The memory was ever selective, a diverse set of opinions arose in accordance, and many Irish became adept at compartmentalizing their loyalties.

O'Connor understood that one could be "anti-clerical but not particularly anti-religious," as she said of the Irish U.N. delegate. While men waged their rhetorical battles in various associations and jockeyed for Irish legitimacy within the social order, the women often carried out the unheralded work of religious instruction, charity, and, in Bourke's words, simply "keeping the faith." Bill Canty was never schooled by nuns but took pride in imbibing his religious instruction at "my mother's knee." His father refused to keep up their house, but his mother had a hard time doing anything about it "because everything was in his name." Once in his absence she refurnished the house, and when he demanded, "Who the hell gave you permission?" she responded, "Nobody gave me permission. It [the house] needed it." In their somewhat fraught marriage, it was Canty's mother who seemed to bear the greater burden, and when he asked her how she managed to get along with his difficult father, she said simply, "I made up my mind I was gonna get along with him." Similarly, Bourke observed how women in sodalities carried forward the intellectual work of Catholicism, and he recognized the work of the Sisters of Mercy in Savannah—a story too long to be related here.

For purposes of this discussion, what bears underscoring is the important gender dimension to O'Connor's relationship to the Irish. In a church that permitted women to receive only six of its seven sacraments, women were often the driving force behind filling the pews and thoughtfully carrying out the aspirations of the faith. O'Connor's distance from the Savannah Irish may have stemmed in part from the simple fact that at the highest levels the Irish community's public and religious face was male-dominated, sentimental, and at times "phony" and that it devoted much of its palaver to upholding an exalted position for the Irish, ironically reducing Irish identity to little more than a fetish within American culture. The tenders of the flame had limited use for women in their social organizations in Flannery's time. (It should be mentioned, however, that when Savannah's chapter of the Ancient Order of Hibernians all but sputtered out in the mid-twentieth century, the women's auxiliary kept it alive.)

Less cynically, Irish American pride in Savannah had the character that O'Connor imputed to her father's very masculine American League speeches— another world closed off to her, but of which she was quite proud. "Last year I read over some of the speeches he made and I was touched to see a kind of patriotism that most people would just laugh at now, something childlike, that was a good deal too good and innocent for the Legion. But the Legion was the only thing provided by the country to absorb it" (*HB* 166).[84] Ed O'Connor was following in P. J. O'Connor's footsteps with his Legion boosterism, yet his daughter could never get "tied emotionally or sentimentally" to any form of Irish nationalism. Indeed, she seems to have been skeptical of all schemes of nationalism. Although she was adamantly a southerner and some of her ancestors were Confederates, she had scant patience for Lost Cause–variety nationalism, a fact plainly evident in the naked satire of "A Late Encounter with the Enemy," where the last fetid breath of an insufferable oldest living veteran cannot compete with the allure of a Coca-Cola machine.

O'Connor's fealty was tied instead to a faith that was bigger than, if much influenced by, the Irish Catholics who shaped it. She was not so much a cathedral Catholic as a no-nonsense communion seeker, independent minded but never particularly anticlerical, nurturing close friendships with many Catholic religious in the course of her life. Patrick Samway points out that the "simple, Congregationalist-looking brick structure" of Sacred Heart Church in Milledgeville is emblematic of her Catholicism: "Inside you would have been struck by the rather confined, unpretentious liturgical space, which allowed for close, almost intimate, contact between the congregation and the sanctuary. To the left, behind the altar rail, stood a baptismal font, and to the right a free-standing ambo—thus visually reminding the congregation of the importance both of baptism and the proclamation of the Word of God, both of which are of major significance in O'Connor's fiction"—and not coincidentally, the pillars of many Protestant denominations as well.[85]

If all this seems too speculative, it bears mention that O'Connor herself validated the importance of her formative (i.e., Savannah) years when she wrote, "I think you probably collect most of your experience as a child—when you really had nothing else to do—and then transfer it to other situations when you write" (*HB* 204). Separately she wrote, "The weight of centuries lies on children, I'm sure of it" (*HB* 136–37). Surely, some of the "weight" came from the inherited duties and what might be termed the blood weight of bloodlines.

By now the interplay of Flannery O'Connor's Georgia upbringing and her Irish Catholic roots should be more tangible. But how did she express that influence? O'Connor wrote only one story that explicitly engages an Irish Catholic upbringing, so it makes sense to turn to it next.

If campaigners have famously rallied to "Keep Austin [TX] Weird," it might be said that Flannery O'Connor has done much to keep the South weird in the eyes of the nation, in part because she was such an unusual person. She came from an unusual world and became a creator of unusual worlds. Even so, O'Connor's gothic South arose from roots quite different from those of William Faulkner's or Erskine Caldwell's South. From the start it was premised in a religious worldview that came from a distinctive southern subculture. It has been suggested that O'Connor's fiction is too allegorical and bizarre to be biographical, but if this is the rule, then "A Temple of the Holy Ghost" is the exception. It is perhaps the most Irish Catholic offering in Flannery O'Connor's *oeuvre,* and it brims with traces of experiences collected from childhood: the singing of "Tantum ergo Sacramentum" (the same hymn that Anne Rice says "rocked" her childhood chapel),[86] "brown convent uniforms" from "Mount St. Scholastica," and one Sister Consolata, who advises girls that they can shut down an overheated suitor by simply saying, "Stop sir! I am a Temple of the Holy Ghost" (*CS* 238). The tale's allusion to Thomas Aquinas as "the big dumb ox" leads Ralph Wood to point out that

> Thomas's *sed contra* method of answering his opponents also provided O'Connor a means for dealing with her sometimes domineering mother, Regina Cline O'Connor. If she insisted that her daughter turn off the light because the night was growing late, Flannery imagined her ideal response: "I with lifted finger and broad bland beatific expression, would reply, 'On the contrary, I answer that the light, being eternal and limitless, cannot be turned off. Shut your eyes,' or some such thing."[87]

Along the same lines, Anne Rice would note that her mother

> did something which now seems to me intensely and distinctively Catholic. She addressed a multitude of questions which had never come up. For example, I remember her explaining to me almost casually why there was no conflict between theories of evolution and the words of the Bible. Genesis tells us God created the world in six days, she would say, but Genesis doesn't tell us how long a day was for God, in God's time. End of conflict.[88]

The *sed contra* method makes sense when one considers self-definition in terms of what one is not: a Catholic girl hard against a sea of southern Protestants. Minds trained in catechistic response and legalisms might perform well in point-counterpoint debates, and there was always recourse to the mysteries of *via negativa.* In one of her letters Flannery O'Connor attempts to explain the Miraculous Assumption of Mary to Cecil Dawkins, but sensing that this is perhaps something of a hard sell, the self-described "repressed schoolteacher" (*HB* 84) declares magisterially, "Dogma is the guardian of mystery" (*HB* 365). She lobbied for a literary organ that would publish like-minded Catholic writers, and with remarkable aplomb she navigated the Vatican's notorious *Index Librorum Prohibitorum* (which was not put aside until the Second Vatican Council) while remaining true to the letter of her faith, even when it was become strained and formalistic. For example, she consulted Father James McCown after inadvertently eating meat, in the form of southern vegetables cooked with meat, fretting over the distinction between drippings and stock. He concluded that the "problems in her spiritual life" were "of the scope and seriousness found in a convent-bred high school girl." She had already concluded independently that she would not suffer hell "over a plate of butter beans."[89]

To be a mackerel snapper was to her a source of pride. James Joyce writes of a childhood in which Protestant and Catholic mockery between boys was a fact of daily life. As an Irish Catholic in the South, O'Connor was no doubt used to being put in a class along with "Jews and non-Christians," and she was probably familiar with another common prejudice, the notion that Catholics are easily given over to corporeal temptations. This accusation is one that the girls of "A Temple of the Holy Ghost" do little to refute. In the end, though, the story is concerned largely with the methods by which spiritual innocence is lost well before sexual innocence is lost, a point that O'Connor makes after the visiting twins relate the experience of seeing a hermaphrodite at the fair.

The hermaphrodite unsettles the confident theology of natural law. If male and female he created them, what does one do with someone who is both? Of course, O'Connor thought that freaks were mostly, in essence, the distorted version of ourselves that we become, which is to say, the version that must appear before God, and that the good frequently appeared freakish to human eyes.[90] But there might be a more prosaic source for the hermaphrodite of the story, who says, "God made me thisaway and I don't dispute hit. . . . God done this to me and I praise him" (*CS* 246). Joseph Mitchell's well-known *New Yorker* piece "Lady Olga," about a bearded lady from North Carolina who appeared in the Metro-Goldwyn-Mayer film *Freaks* (1932), might have given Flannery O'Connor a good name for Hulga (who changed her name from Joy) in "Good Country People." Barnell considered joining a convent to find solace, but she did not object to the term *freak,* explaining her resignation: "No matter how nice a name was put on me, I would still have a beard."[91] Although the scholar Sarah Gordon acknowledges that she cannot prove that O'Connor read Mitchell, she argues that "O'Connor's impulse to present portraits of the unlovely and the eccentric was encouraged and sometimes directly influenced by Mitchell's work."[92] The North Carolinian Mitchell, whose favorite writer was James Joyce, had a southerner's eye for freaks too.[93]

As for the "fearful" freakish lessons of "A Temple of the Holy Ghost," after reading a book about the demise of the Irish by Seán O'Fáolain, O'Connor wrote, "Apparently someone had suggested that there wasn't enough sin in Ireland to supply the need. O'Faillon [*sic*] said no, the Irish sinned constantly but with no great emotion except fear. Jansenism doesn't seem to breed so much a love of God as a love of asceticism" (*HB* 304). The fear and guilt that pervade the consciousness of the child of the story are unmistakably Irish Catholic in character.

O'Connor understood the finer points of their origin. She clucked at the Irish when they permitted moralism to trump faith and action, and she was quick to detect the humorless Jansenistic influence of "being taught by the Sisters to measure your sins with a slide rule," driving "some folks nuts and some folks to the Baptists" (*HB* 263). She also wrote, "I like Pascal but I don't think the Jansenist influence is healthy in the Church. The Irish are notably infected with it because all the Jansenist priests were chased out of France at the time of the Revolution and ended up in Ireland. It was a bad day if you ask me" (*HB* 304). O'Connor very clearly responded to Jansenism in her thinking about faith. For example, in *Wise Blood* Hazel Motes, in his salad days, makes a mistake in common with the child of "A Temple of the Holy Ghost": "There was already a deep black wordless conviction in him that the way to avoid Jesus was to avoid sin" (16). The fallacy points to Jansenism's overarching concern with fallen mankind, which shares much in common with Calvinism. (Bill Canty would claim, "We never knew what sex was—I was fourteen years old before I knew where a child came from.") Of course, O'Connor recognized a slide-rule mentality that set up a faith based on the mere avoidance of sin is little more than a hollow shell belying an immature view of the fullness of faith.

It might have been this recognition that prompted her statement to Ted Spivey: "She made several Nietzschean statements that still stand out in my mind because of their vehemence," writes Spivey. "One was that 99 percent of people in the world had lost the ability to believe in God at all, and the other was that what was wrong with the Catholic Church was the Irish and that she could say this because she was Irish."[94] Spivey veers away from interpreting the statement, though he eventually suggests:

> The deepest element in O'Connor, except for her religion and her love of literary art, was her Irish heritage. And that heritage is connected with re-

ligion and literature because the Irish, whom the English so long had sought to disinherit, always had Ireland, Catholicism, and their own native folklore. O'Connor had felt it all in Joyce, including his flight, which is finally a failure, from Catholicism. And the Irish heritage gave O'Connor another arrow in her literary quiver, that of social critic in the Blakean sense. She carried in her mind that holocaust of nineteenth-century potato famines (thus her admiration for Hannah Arendt) and the awareness that the American Irish were despised foreigners, even though they often became quickly involved in Southern society, some even becoming "aristocrats" who furnished soldiers for the Confederacy. But one wonders if the whole Irish-Southern aristocrat's life was not a kind of pose, hiding the powerful, never to be fully repressed, Irish suffering of centuries.[95]

Spivey concludes that O'Connor never came to terms with "problems of her Irish past because two other matters were sometimes fanatically, but most often not, at the center of her thinking: religion and literature." Spivey's speculation on repressed ethnic "traumas," as he elsewhere puts it, seems a bit fanciful, but his observations on the Redemptorist revival are very useful. "Theological interpreters of O'Connor's work have often seen *Wise Blood* as an attack on the ferocity of certain aspects of Southern fundamentalism," he writes, "but O'Connor as a Catholic and a literary follower of Joyce was aware that Catholics also had been affected in the twentieth century by too great an emphasis on hell in the previous century."[96]

Accordingly, Joyce drew from a reissued Redemptorist favorite, *Hell Opened to Christians* (1889), in the hellfire-and-brimstone sermon of *Portrait of the Artist as a Young Man.* The hellfire sermons of southern street preachers would not have been altogether alien to Flannery O'Connor, for if the Jansenists had chastened the body, the Redemptorists had helped to consign it to the flames. The Redemptorists were famed for their charismatic and fiery sermonics. Father Ryan had studied their tactics as he shaped himself into a dynamic and self-described "Southern" homilist, and a hint of their flair survived in the likes of Fulton Sheen.

For her part, Flannery O'Connor might acknowledge her own Redemptorist streak. She told Louise Abbot, "I believe in a good deal of hell's fire on this earth," and few of her readers would dispute that she liked the scourging kind.[97] But she was turned off by shows of piety and declared herself "a long standing avoider of May processions and such like doings" (*HB* 286), demonstrating an instinctive aversion to showy Irish forms of piety. May processions, which bridged pre-Christian May Day celebrations (and in Ireland, the bonfires of Bealtaine) with the veneration of Mary, had enjoyed a resurgence of popularity beginning in the Victorian era. Under the leadership of Irish American clergy like Father Abram Ryan, who promoted Marian sodalities and published a devotional on the subject, *A Crown for Our Queen* (1882), May processions flourished well into the twentieth century, providing, as they did, an appealing way to enact feminine ideals. Accounts of the processions, which were widespread among Catholics in the British Isles and in Ireland, are something of a fixture in accounts of American Catholic childhood at mid-twentieth century. Hugh Brown explains:

> In May there was always a special May Day procession. All the girls took part. They lined up, 350 or so of them, on the sidewalk by the Cathedral, each wearing a white dress, each carrying a small bouquet, and then marched into the Cathedral for special ceremonies honoring Mary as Queen of May. Once inside, they played a part, singing the somewhat sentimental Marian hymns (Oh Mary we crown thee with flowers today / Queen of the angels, queen of the May), and joining surely in the recitation of the rosary.[98]

Perhaps Flannery was worn out by the annual ritual, with its staging of pretty feminine virtue and chastity, but this too became the stuff of imagination. She wrote to Sally Fitzgerald that she especially liked the part of Hemingway's *Old Man and the Sea* (1952) "where the fish's eye was like a saint in a procession; it sounded to me like he was discovering something new maybe for him" (*HB* 56).

Beyond her historical awareness of the peculiarities of Irish Catholicism, Flannery O'Connor's Irish roots may have shown plainly in the tonic of her self-criticism. For example, when writing to a friend that she did not care to "wash" in Lourdes on account of lack of privacy, she added automatically, "This is neither right nor holy of me but it is what it is" (*HB* 258). Ever the writer, she prayed there "for the novel I was working on, not for my bones" (*HB* 509).

With Jansenism, the mortification of the body, and so on, Flannery O'Connor reveals something of the Irish Catholic tenor of her religious instruction. Her Catholic worldview raises interesting connections with other southern writers who bear similar influences, including one named Edgar Allan Poe, whose sympathies with Catholics and immigrant Irish betray the complexities of a curious kinship. Beyond O'Connor's fiction, the Irish receive passing mention in some of her correspondence. She told Father James H. McCown about a priest in Milledgeville who "orders green carnations for the altar" on Saint Patrick's Day and decorates the altar with a statue of Saint Patrick statue and whose favorite interjection was "as the Irishman said."[99] The same priest also "objected to Roman Catholic girls at GSCW [Georgia State College for Women] attending the baccalaureate sermon at the college."[100] McCown, an Irish American whom Cash describes as O'Connor's "personal priest," could have provided the model for the mercurial, catechism-reciting, and singularly literal priest of "The Enduring Chill." In that story, the Irish Catholic priest Father Finn— "Faththter Finn—from Purrgatory," as he says it in Irish accent—shares his name with the legendary Irish hero.[101] He is as unshakable and wise as a serpent, like the priest of "The Displaced Person," who "spoke in a foreign way himself, English but as if he had a throatful of hay," drawing out his *r*'s in the style of Irish eye dialect.

And where are O'Connor's southern Irish today? Where she left them, apparently. A recent sociological survey of Savannah's Irish community concluded that "most of the members of Savannah's Irish organizations state that their ethnic identity is more important than their regional or southern identity" —which would seem to be the opposite of Flannery O'Connor's stance. Of 239 Catholic respondents (almost three-quarters of whom attended Mass at least once a week), 205 considered themselves southerners. "Twenty-eight percent of them said that their identity as a southerner is much more important than their other identities. The vast majority of respondents are native Savannahians and their families have resided in Georgia for several or more generations. They do not feel unwelcomed nor are they new to the region."[102]

This may simply be a sign of the Irish community's confidence in its southern identity. When Monsignor Bourke explained that he had always been certain of his vocation, he added with a laugh, "So many people are getting a crisis of identity now that I'm beginning to think there's something wrong with me." Flannery O'Connor never doubted her identity either; the question for her was how to shape it in the long shadow of the cathedral and in full view of ancestral ghosts. By largely disavowing Irish ethnicity, O'Connor was free to locate the main of her identity in its Catholic remnant and in a qualified kind of southernness. And occasionally—rarely—she permitted herself to be at ease in an Irish Catholic skin. John Sullivan, one of the few to date her during college, hailed from a large Irish Catholic family in Ohio.[103] Midwesterner or Yankee though he may have been, he was at the same time an Irish Catholic who was contemplating the priesthood—one of the few who might vault splendidly over the high bar of her mother's values test.

Whatever her misgivings, Flannery O'Connor knew that to be Irish Catholic was to be part of a larger culture, for better and for worse. In fact, on at least one occasion she explicitly identified herself as an Irish Catholic: "On bidding [Roslyn Barnes] goodbye, the Msgr. said, 'Don't try to be an Irish Catholic, but you'd better read some more theology.' Roslyn was greatly puzzled by this and asked me what an Irish Catholic was. 'You are in the presence of one,' says I, bowing" (*HB* 497).

As Margaret Mitchell's work makes clear, these southern Irish Catholics made good characters in stories because so many of them were characters in real life. In that respect, Flannery was both creator and creation. In sum, even if Flannery O'Connor kept her Irishness at arm's length, it shimmers in the subtexts of her work. She signed one of her letters to Maryat Lee with "love from the dear old dirty Southland," an apt substitution for the usual "dear old dirty Dublin" (*HB* 266). A fine sentiment for a woman sprung wholesale, like Athena, from the banks of Joyce's Oconee River.

III

LEGACIES
of
FLIGHT
and
RETURN

6

CORMAC MCCARTHY, AN IRISH SOUTHERNER AMONG THE HERESIARCHS

But the Irish are wonderful, God bless em. If I say it myself.
—CORMAC MCCARTHY

God made everything out of nothing. But the nothingness shows through.
—PAUL VALÉRY

"He," saith the Buddhist text, "who discerns that nothingness
is law—such a one hath wisdom."
—LAFCADIO HEARN

Actually, you've lower-cased all such designations. The Greek, the Nigger are
capped, but they're used as names. As I see it, only Sunday, Christ, God,
Pope, Mass, Christmas; Daddy (and a couple others) are capped.
—BERT KRANTZ, copyeditor, to Cormac McCarthy

A t 4:00 p.m. on June 5, 2007, Cormac McCarthy set the literary world on its ear.

He rapped with Oprah.

While everyone was debating what this meant—whether it was the proper thing for a writer of his stature to do—McCarthy's reputation for monklike inscrutability was finally thawing out. True, he remains a purist who once told an interviewer that "teaching writing is a hustle."[1] He could boast to the collector Howard Woolmer, "I've been a fulltime professional writer for 23 years and I've never received a royalty check. *That,* I'll betcha, is a record."[2]

Or at least a record for such a good writer, especially if he was not receiving advances; even Melville got paid. Contrary to rumor, and notwithstanding his confirmation in the Oprah Winfrey interview that "money has never really interested me," McCarthy (b. 1933) has never been entirely indifferent to money.[3] His correspondence reveals a writer who, like most, *must* worry about means of survival. "As far as applying to a foundation for a grant, let me say that I am absolutely willing to receive any amount of money from any source. My finances have reached some sort of nadir or sub-nadir even," he wrote to Robert Coles about 1980, "and I am all but out of business." After explaining how he had failed to secure "development" money for a film project, he added, "I suppose asking writers about their finances is a bit like asking a hypochondriac how he feels."[4] The luxury of indifference arrived only after the outrageous fortunes of bestselling novels, a MacArthur grant, and a place to hang his hat at the Santa Fe Institute.

Another persistent misconception: though he keeps his own counsel and is vigilant about his family's privacy, it should be pointed out that McCarthy's "man alone" mystique has been largely the invention of admirers only too eager to separate him from his privacy. One can see why in the rifling of *Cormac's Trash,* a short documentary in which a filmmaker and her husband did indeed pick through McCarthy's trash can in, as they put it, "a quest to understand the reclusive novelist" and "to explore the meaning of privacy."[5] Never mind that admirers picking through one's rubbish would drive *anyone* into seclusion. Meanwhile, someone started a Facebook group called "I want Cormac McCarthy to be my Grandpa."[6]

Other admirers have taken an entirely different tack: as with the unapproachable cheerleader at the dance, to burn for McCarthy is to leave him alone. A member of this camp wrote in a punky alternative magazine, "Critical comment on Cormac McCarthy is the usual academic pap and journalistic jabber. Ignore it. It's itch weed. McCarthy has said that anything you need to know about his work is in his books."[7] *Ecce homo.*

In a way, the wonder of it is that McCarthy, under double threat from the cant of his hangers-on and popular adulation, has been so generous. Contrary to the "cult of the recluse" image attached to him, he has, from the beginning, been aware of the critical escapades of academics, as when he wrote to Woolmer on September 6, 1989, "It never occurred to me that folks would pronounce Suttree to rhyme with shoe tree but they do, and if enough of them do, that, of course, is what it will be. Is this deconstruction?"[8] He keeps abreast of his critics, consistently engaging those who have made a principled investigation of his work and selectively encouraging them in their efforts.[9] His greatest gift to them is his most recent, the breadcrumbs strewn across the ninety-six boxes of his personal papers in the archives of the Wittliff Collections at Texas State University–San Marcos. Among the holdings are extensive notes selectively documenting *some* of his sources. That selectivity might itself be revealing:

within those boxes his notes for individual texts are most often typed, giving the impression that he has vetted precisely which clues would find their way into scholars' sweaty palms.

In the case of *Blood Meridian* (1985), many of them had already been scooped by John Sepich in his intrepid *Notes on "Blood Meridian,"* a labor of love that met with McCarthy's approval. Already there are documented gaps in the archived material. Did the writer transcribe the originals to protect the innocent? to vouchsafe his legacy to the curiosity of future admirers? Was there method in it, or did he simply hand over what was on hand? Did he do the most generous thing of all, that is, protect the mystery of his work for its own sake? These questions are not the focus of this chapter, but if they could be answered, they would likely speak to McCarthy's consistently heartfelt sense of obligation to his readers, succinctly stated in one of his letters to Robert Coles: "The only love the writer can legitimately show the reader is a desire to communicate to him the truth, and this is not the same thing as confession or candor."[10]

One of the most tantalizing things about the newly available papers is that through careful scrutiny one can see how McCarthy takes pains to efface his influences. For example, his notes on *Blood Meridian* include a quotation from Heraclitus followed by a note to himself: "See *other* translation. Let the judge quote this in part without crediting the source." "The ugly fact is books are made out of books," McCarthy offered in an interview. "The novel depends for its life on the novels that have been written."[11] But that does not mean he is going to be obvious about it. Consider this example, from *Suttree* (1979), of an allusion in the making. Let us begin with the possible source text in Yeats's "Crazy Jane Talks with the Bishop":

> A woman can be proud and stiff
> When on love intent;
> But Love has pitched his mansion in
> The place of excrement;
> *For nothing can be sole or whole*
> *That has not been rent.*[12]

McCarthy's reworking of the material in his journalia and notes reads as follows:

> As I grow old will not my *spirit mend by rending*? And my eyes gather a visionary's light all dusty with loveliness like the sun by morning? Until my heart is an ash charred by charity . . . [torn page].[13]

The muted allusion in the final text of *Suttree* reads:

> Were he therefore to come to himself in this obscure wood he'd be *neither mended nor made whole* but rather set mindless to dodder drooling with his ghosty clone from sun to sun across a hostile hemisphere forever. (287)[14]

In each reworking McCarthy interrogates the notion of being made whole by rending from Yeats's poem. An extra reference tucked away here reveals McCarthy's familiarity with Dante's work in *la lingua originale:* "obscure wood" = the *selva oscura* in which the great poet finds himself. *Suttree* will take the skeptic on a tour of hell with Harrogate. Virgil is conventionally depicted in red garb as he explores hell; Harrogate's stolen red road lantern makes him resemble a "cherrycolored troll or demon cartographer in the hellish light charting the progress of souls in the darkness below" (260). Harrogate's part is to harrow those gates of hell that cannot prevail upon Christ's church. Dante's work, vis-à-vis the "obscure wood," informs the Catholic concerns and subtexts of descents and slumming in *Suttree* (e.g., the excremental Harrogate, covered in Knoxville sewage, who resembles Dante's flatterers/advertisers, sunk in filth), much as the *Inferno* informs the structure of *Dubliners*'s "Grace," with its "filth and ooze"–covered Mr. Kernan.[15] Like those saved by the reproving Christ who knocks in Revelations ("But you do not realize that you are wretched, pitiful, poor, blind and naked"), Harrogate the "bloodcolored troglodyte" (259) is blind (from plasmosis), wretched, and naked after seeing the "people down here" in hell (276).

One allusion leads to others, and McCarthy's polyglot reading only thickens the broth, with his notes revealing a self-deflating awareness of his own shenanigans. He acknowledges Joyce's long shadow in a bit of doggerel he struck from an earlier draft of the novel's notorious "moonlight melonmounter" episode: "Je crois c'est trop Joycean" (I think it's too Joycean).[16] "Calypso," the fourth chapter of *Ulysses* (1922), where Bloom has his kidney breakfast and brings Molly's to the bed, is often thought of as the food chapter, though the Linati schema for Joyce's novel gives the vagina as its organizing symbol. In *Suttree,* Cornelius will have a morning-after scene with a whore—named Joyce—who brings him something to drink. As in Dusty Springfield's song "Breakfast in Bed," he won't have to say he loves her.

If this is catch as catch can, McCarthy cannot take strong issue with the gamesmanship of his pursuers. This is the paradox of tracking McCarthy: we murder to dissect. One might strive to reveal the genius of his designs and in the process cheapen them by raking over the parts to the detriment of the whole. Can it be done without dumpster diving?

Perhaps the issue is better framed as a Joycean riddle: how do we distinguish between self-effacement and artist effacement, between artist and artificer? When Max Eastman pressed Joyce on why he had made *Finnegans Wake* so difficult, he famously replied, "To keep the critics busy for three hundred years." The Wittliff Collections contain a McCarthy self-portrait, a sketch showing him having fun at the typewriter with a wicked glower on his face. McCarthy's reluctance to comment on his own work, a form of self-insurance, may well keep academics out of breadlines for millennia.

His sense of caution served him well in the Oprah interview. He had started by channeling Hemingway, pointing out that interviews were not good for a writer's "head," since writers should spend more time writing than thinking about the act of writing. For all her charisma, he did not take the bait when Oprah asked whether he was "passionate" about writing ("Passionate sounds like a pretty fancy word"). Looking for an opening to McCarthy's personal life, Oprah asked him whether *The Road* (2006) was "a love story" to his son John Francis, a question he found "embarrassing." Changing tactics, Oprah would appeal to ethos, mentioning in passing that she had interviewed "many, many writers over the years" and was forced to conclude that McCarthy was "a different kind of man" and "a different kind of writer." Her attempts to get McCarthy to talk about "the God thing" did not get very far, but in a separate *Wall Street Journal* interview the writer would suggest that being raised Irish Catholic "wasn't a big issue."[17]

Much of this chapter is devoted to giving the lie to this last statement by following the tracks—through the texts, the archives, and the patchwork biography of a purportedly lone wolf (who is in fact quite social). To be clear, I am not calling McCarthy a liar, which, in any case, he could do for himself; writers are and should be fictionalists. He might very well have meant that being Catholic wasn't a big deal in the same way that Flannery O'Connor meant it when she said that taking first communion was as "natural" as "brushing my teeth" (*HB* 164). But if we trust the tale instead of the teller, a strikingly more complete portrait of the man emerges, an image more reliant on the testament of his work than on the shrinking glare of studio lights or the tractor beams of Oprah's charm. As James Olney wrote in *Metaphors of Self,* "A theology, a philosophy, a physics or a metaphysics—properly seen, these are all autobiography recorded in other characters and other symbols,"[18] and McCarthy himself affirmed to Oprah the importance of the subconscious in the writing process. Here is a southerner much influenced by Irish writers and culture, a man gripped by the need to make sense of the pottage of faith and ancestry. A man who uses the lightning rod of heresy to stalk an authentic theology. Trust him, he knows what he is doing: let the gainsayer be gainsaid.

Like the names of other writers with Irish roots, real and purported—the Reverend Abram Ryan, Joel Chandler Harris, and Flannery O'Connor—McCarthy's Irish name invites some romantic attributions. Richard Woodward notes that McCarthy, "clean-cut and handsome as he grays . . . has a Celtic's blue-green eyes set deep into a high-domed forehead. 'He gives an impression of strength and vitality and poetry,' says [Saul] Bellow, who describes him as 'crammed into his own person.'"[19] An early reviewer of McCarthy's work remarked the writer's "Irish singing voice imbued with Southern Biblical intonations. The result is an antiphony of speech and verse played against a landscape of penance."[20]

In this vein, some reviewers have been more eager to embrace McCarthy as an Irish American than as a southerner. Gary Goodman, described as a long-time friend and rival of McCarthy's, is supposed to have said that *Suttree* was "a copy-cat of the Faulkner, Southern Gothic thing. . . . And he's really a Yankee carpetbagger. Must we eat all the egg to know it's rotten?"[21] Strictly speaking, even as a Knoxvillian at the tender age of four he *was* a northern transplant. John Grammer argues insightfully that McCarthy writes in an antipastoral tradition that is narrowly characteristic of southern literature. Others have claimed that McCarthy deliberately eschews the usual southern preoccupations.[22] If *Suttree* has been seen as an unwriting of southern moonlight-and-magnolias mythology, we can think of it, on the one hand, as an antimythological novel, one that sings, in Michael Kreyling's phrase, the South that wasn't there. But if we peel back the surface of this critical anti-mythos, we soon see, on the other hand, that McCarthy's novel is deeply engaged in mythogenesis. McCarthy's effort to invest Knoxville with the mythic stature of Joyce's Dublin creates a novel both steeped in place and highly critical of it. As a Catholic outsider looking into Knoxville's storied streets and resident folklore, McCarthy created an anti-myth to Knoxville's own pastoral idyll, with the ironic result that he secured Knoxville's mythic dimensions—from the Goat Man to its Dantean underworld—to the literary imagination. Either way one looks at it, this much is clear: McCarthy has been fully occupied with telling about the South.

So this study, at least, will assume, *arguendo,* that McCarthy may be southern in complicated ways but that he is ultimately a southern writer, whatever the term means. Woodward noticed that McCarthy spoke with a "soft Tennessee accent" and would describe him as "a quiet 72-year-old southern conservative." More tellingly, McCarthy hinted at the essential importance of his southern upbringing in an interview with David Kushner: "You grow up in the South, you're going to see violence. . . . And violence is pretty ugly."[23]

In light of this, McCarthy's sense of the South helped to sharpen his perception of a region from which he had a measure of familial distance. So if McCarthy is southern in the landscape of the mind, what is Irish about him? It is difficult to delve into his family history on his father's side, especially without speaking to his family. Somewhat less common names on his mother's side make the tracing easier. The parents of his mother, Gladys Christina McCarthy, were William Henry (b. 1876) and Helena "Ellen" McGrail (b. 1875), who resided at 28 Eames Street in Providence, Rhode Island, from 1914 until 1947.[24] According to census records, William McGrail was born in Rhode Island, but both of his parents were born in Ireland. In 1922 Helena McGrail applied for a passport, giving her name as Ellen, perhaps because she had a daughter who also was named Helena.[25] She intended to call out of Boston on a trip to Ireland to visit her relatives. Forty-seven years of age, she was five feet three inches tall with "hazel" eyes, a "straight" nose, and "dark brown" hair, her place of birth given as Queenstown (now Cobh), Ireland.[26] In sum, McCarthy had an Irish-born grandmother and Irish great-grandparents on his mother's side. Though this is impossible to verify without confirmation from the McCarthy family, it appears that Cormac's paternal great-grandparents and great-great-grandparents were born in Ireland as well. Tantalizing for readers of *Suttree,* a Cornelius McCarthy (b. c. 1837) is listed by profession in the 1880 Providence, Rhode Island, census as a "stone & brickmason." According to the 1880 census, both Cornelius and his wife Mary were born in Ireland, and their six children, then ranging in age from six to fifteen, were born stateside. Could this Cornelius have been a McCarthy patriarch? Or does life imitate art?[27]

For now we will not know, but it is possible to demonstrate McCarthy's long-standing interest in Ireland. In an undated letter to Robert Coles (c. 1980) he wrote, "I envy you and your trip to Ireland. I spent a month or so there back about ten years ago and have always wanted to go again. I still have cousins there on my mother's side of the family."[28] He would regularly return to Providence to visit his Irish American aunties, one of whom was a retired Wellesley professor. Echoes of their voices can be heard in *Suttree.*[29] Apparently it was they who brought "Cormac" into the family: "The Gaelic equivalent of Charles, [Cormac] was an old family nickname bestowed on his father by Irish aunts."[30] According to the Cormac McCarthy Society's website, McCarthy was "originally named Charles (after his father)," but "he renamed himself Cormac after the Irish King." Cormac Mac Airt (*Cormac McCarthy* is a variant spelling) was the "good king" of Tara, according to James Potts, and, writes Farrell O'Gorman, an early "patron of the Church."[31] In addition, "another source . . . says that McCarthy's family was responsible for legally changing his name to the Gaelic equivalent of 'son of Charles.'"[32] Either way, McCarthy started life as his father's namesake in a large Irish American family, "the oldest son of an eminent lawyer, formerly with the Tennessee Valley Authority, [Cormac] McCarthy is Charles Jr., with five brothers and sisters."[33] The Knoxville native Robert Gentry, born within a few years of Cormac McCarthy, recalls, "The McCarthy, Sr. I often saw praying at Immaculate Conception Church with his large family was at least in outward appearance a devout man."[34]

The arrival in Tennessee of his Irish American family, transplanted by way of Rhode Island, was not without precedent. Father Abram Ryan had presided over a small Irish Catholic community in Knoxville during the Civil War period, and by the 1880s the town would elect Martin J. Condon its first Irish-Catholic mayor. The Irish community's legacy endured in the established parochial schools, where the McCarthy children performed well. (Cormac McCarthy remains "a traditionalist" who "worries how well reading and writing are taught in [Santa Fe, the] easygoing New Age enclave" to which he has inured himself.)[35] The Catholic community in Knoxville remained a small enclave; in Bob Gentry's 1954 graduating class, three years after McCarthy's, twenty-nine students were graduated from Knoxville Catholic High School.[36] Following his student days, Charles Jr. eventually betook himself to Ireland in apparent pursuit of his Irish roots. In 1965, with a traveling fellowship from the American Academy of Arts and Letters, he embarked on the liner *Sylvania,* "intending to visit the home of his Irish ancestors (a King Cormac McCarthy built Blarney Castle)."[37] En route he fell in with Anne DeLisle, "a young English singer/dancer working on the ship."[38] His 1966 marriage in England likely deepened and shaded his perception of the Irish.

Drawn to the Isles by birth, marriage, and literature, as recently as the summer of 2004 McCarthy spent six weeks writing in Ireland by himself.[39] Writing to his longtime correspondent Howard Woolmer on December 13, 2005, he confirmed this: "I was in Ireland most of last summer and got quite a bit done. The place has changed a lot. Money will do that."[40] In January 2006, apparently in response to an invitation to visit, Woolmer wrote to McCarthy, "I'll have to give Ireland a pass on this trip I'm afraid. I'd be interested to hear where you go in Ireland."[41] Among the undated fragments of *No Country for*

Old Men (2005) are three pages that McCarthy evidently typed on the verso of a printout for Dublin properties from an Irish real-estate consultancy.[42]

McCarthy's travels may indicate an enduring pattern of interest in Ireland, but he is far from the oblivious Yank in green plaid. To Robert Coles he wrote about 1980, "Did you get to Ireland? I've never been to Northern Ireland but I can understand your interest in it. I'm afraid they are in for a protracted siege of ills. What is surprising to me is that war & revolution & other major upheavals are not more disruptive to the body social in fact. 'The only horror is that there's no horror.'"[43] In "Whales and Men" (c. 1985), McCarthy's unpublished screenplay, John Western, an American who has been visiting Ireland, asks his girlfriend, "Do you think you could live here?" She replies, "I don't know. Is that a loaded question?" He answers, "This place is a powder keg"—and certainly trouble was on the horizon when McCarthy made his first visit to Ireland.[44] In lines excised from later drafts of the screenplay, he demonstrates his awareness of the complexities of Irish history and loyalties: "Unusual for an Irishman to marry at his [father's] age. It was the war and all. Bloody loyalists. Loyalist Catholics at that, to compound the offense." In an appended fact-checking note he asks, "Could there have been writs of attainder issued against rebel peers in 1916?"[45] His interest in the Easter Rising, reinforced perhaps by his love of Yeats, extends to small details.

Like the fiction of Flannery O'Connor, whom McCarthy has quoted when asked why he is a writer, his fiction hints at a complicated relationship with his lineage of "distaff Celt's blood in some back chamber of his brain," the stuff that moves Suttree to "to discourse with the birches, the oaks" (286). In an earlier draft of *Blood Meridian,* McCarthy described the lineage of the Kid (his protagonist) and his links to Ireland.[46] He removed the material in the final draft. The amendments are revealing: in the oft-quoted final version the Kid "can neither read nor write and in him broods already a taste for mindless violence," but in the earlier draft this "taste" was something of a racially inherited predilection, attributed to "Black Irish. Enough Saxon and Spanish blood to augment a simple Celtic truculence into a taste for mindless rapacity." But this is typical of the shifting narrative voice. "Can you see it in him?" asks—who? the father? the author? the omniscient voice? The reader is meant to be implicated in the answer, as "race" will hardly answer for the mystery of violence. On the other hand, McCarthy pushes against the assumption that the Irish must be mere "hewers of wood," a phrase from Joshua 9:23, applied to slaves and then to Irish Catholics.

The opening passages of the earlier draft read:

See the child. He is pale and thin, he wears a thin and ragged linen shirt, he strokes the scullery fire. Outside lie dark turned fields with rags of snow and darker wood beyond that yet keep wolves. His folk are known for hewers of wood and drawers of water but in truth the father is a schoolteacher. No. We dont need one. We might could use a onehanded paperhanger but we dont need no Irish schoolteacher.

He has a sister in this world somewhere that he will not see again. She has been sent to live with a relative in North Carolina since the mother died. The father lies deep in drink. In his cups he quotes haltingly from classic poets. Or talks of old dead times.

Night of your birth in thirty three the skies were fairly drained of stars, ah god how they did fall. All night long by handfuls. I looked for blackness, holes in the constellations. The dipper stove, shape of the heavens changed forever. But all was as before. You were a grand child, your mother fine, fineboned.

Black Irish. Enough Saxon and Spanish blood to augment a simple Celtic truculence into a taste for mindless rapacity. Can you see it in him? He kicks the door shut behind him, bearing a tottery armload of firewood like a man going to an altar. The cold plumes about him. All history present in his visage. The child the father of the man.

In the final, Vintage edition, the text reads:

See the child. He is pale and thin, he wears a thin and ragged linen shirt. He stokes the scullery fire. Outside lie dark turned fields with rags of snow and darker wood beyond that harbor yet a few last wolves. His folk are known for hewers of wood and drawers of water but in truth the father has been a schoolmaster. He lies in drink, he quotes from poets whose names are now lost. The boy crouches by the fire and watches him.

Night of your birth. Thirty-three. The Leonids they were called. God how the stars did fall. I looked for blackness, holes in the heavens. The Dipper stove.

The mother dead these fourteen years did incubate in her own bosom the creature who would carry her off. The father never speaks her name, the child does not know it. He has a sister in this world that he will not see again. He watches, pale and unwashed. He can neither read nor write and in him broods already a taste for mindless violence. All history present in that visage, the child the father of the man. (4)

Instead of "rare old times," we have "old dead times." McCarthy's earlier draft examines the faux genealogies of racial mysticism (and McCarthy himself has "typical" "black Irish" features: dark hair, light eyes).[47] A common folk explanation for Irish people with "dark" features (and especially hair) is that they are descendants of the wrecked Spanish armada at Galway, though this claim has been widely discredited. In American usage, the term *Black Irish,* like *Black Dutch,* sometimes became a term of last resort for mixed-race Irish who faced census takers in the wake of Indian removals and other racist campaigns. In any case, the father's Irish accent comes into the story when the child is described as "grand," and McCarthy is revealed to be a poet-quoter himself: both versions retain "the child is the father of the man," from Wordsworth's "My Heart Leaps Up."

The question whether children have any sort of inborn moral bearings has played heavily on McCarthy's mind, to judge by his correspondence with the psychologist Robert Coles, who takes up the issue in his own work. McCarthy wrote to Coles,

> There are a few people investigating the notion as to whether there is such a thing as innate morality (in other words, such a thing as morality at all) but to most people I think even the question must appear odd. Kant's admiration of the "starry sky above me and the moral law within me" must appear a quaint and uninformed confusion of realities attributable to the times. Sort of like alchemy.
>
> The kicker of course is that if people are really just discrete and somewhat freakish biological entities rather than expressions of some spiritual order of the universe then we are obliged to allocate them only those rights and that status and that degree of humanity which is convenient to us to acknowledge. How children are going to continue to survive this I don't know.[48]

This is the matter McCarthy will investigate in *Blood Meridian* and dramatize so chillingly in *The Road.* The child we see in *Blood Meridian,* like young Immanuel Kant, must look to the skies to discern that creation *is* self-organization. In his *Critique of Pure Reason* (1781) Kant would maintain that morality indeed required a wise God as a ruler, or else moral laws would be little more than "idle dreams."[49] McCarthy's letter would seem to suggest that he rejects a secular basis for ethics, insisting that if morality is to hold at all, it must be referential and inborn—profoundly Catholic notions at their core, even if, on the face of it, *Blood Meridian* would seem to rebuff any possibility of "some spiritual order of the universe."

Yet the Kid's days are to be bound together not so much by "natural piety" (though in maturity he will become an illiterate Bible toter) but by primal violence.[50] The earlier draft plays on other Irish stereotypes: the Irish need not apply to the hostile workplaces of the United States of Anglo-America; the Irish inclination to drink, to recite, to pursue little education (and perhaps, on page 9, to become cops, with the *shellalegh* as lawgiver); and so on. While many characters have the *ye* of rural vernacular (and in *Suttree* Reese has the distinctive *ye'ens* of southern Appalachian dialect), the Expriest's speech, carefully developed in McCarthy's revision, marks him as Irish.[51] The Ivy League–educated Expriest apparently followed two common Irish American vocations—soldiering and the priesthood—and he speaks with such Irish locutions as "Dont be a fool lad. What other bait has he?" (290). In both the earlier and later drafts McCarthy's intuition for the deeper themes and movements of diasporic history rings true to life. His imagination draws the Kid to pathways realistic for an Irish southerner: from Memphis he follows work to Saint Louis, thence to New Orleans and the West, familiar circuits for some of the writers in this study, including, in broad contour, Abram Ryan, Kate Chopin, and Lafcadio Hearn. Nor was this the only time that McCarthy imagined an Irish family in southern migration: *The Gardener's Son* (1976), a piece adapted for television, features a nineteenth-century Irish Catholic family that has come to a South Carolina mill town for work. It could be seen as McCarthy's reimagination of his family history, grafted to a different region.

No writer shows a better ear for Irish trappings of southern speech than Cormac McCarthy, a talent that scattered commentators have appreciated.[52] McCarthy's interest in language and dialect helped, and his Irish American relatives may have advantaged him in providing him the chance to *hear* the Irishness in the voices of the generations-deep mountain folk who surrounded him in his youth. When Suttree visits his Aunt Martha, she remembers a dog named "John L Sullivan cause it was the fightinest little thing you ever seen," bringing an appropriately proud accent to her reference to the renowned Irish American boxer (128). Irish speechways underlying Appalachian dialect are brought to a high plane in *The Orchard Keeper* (1965) and *Outer Dark* (1968) and in the southwestern vernacular of the Border Trilogy. The "spalpeens" of *Suttree* (457) follow in the same tradition, delighting in the deliberate archaisms of the Knoxville tongue.[53] *Suttree* mentions "Clooty's [the devil's] brood" (105), drawing on a Bobbie Burns idiom that derives from the same root as

claw/cloven. Outer Dark gives the reader the colorful "shitepoke" (173), a word
that the Irish poet Paul Muldoon employs and that endures in Appalachian
vernacular. Among the novel's characters is the unnamed "tinker" who drives
a cart laden with tinware (186). Giving voice to the rootlessness of his people,
the tinker complains in Irish syntax, "I give a lifetime wanderin in a country
where I was despised." *Tinker* is a pejorative term for an Irish Traveler, "an
itinerant tradesman or craftsman, without even the status of gypsy."[54]

McCarthy's ear for the Irish influence in American speech is simply one
element of his powers of observation, partly literary and partly experiential.
Both his friend Leslie Garrett and his former wife Annie DeLisle deem him a
"chameleon": "On the one hand he was sophisticated," DeLisle said. "He loved
the niceties of life, but he would live on the levels that people would understand. He would sit by the old pot-bellied stove, spit and chew tobacco. That's
how he lived."[55] His understanding of the mountains clearly derives both from
his personal experience and from the studied perspective of books (recipes
for gunpowder in *Foxfire* were handy in his writing of *Blood Meridian,* for
instance).[56] He knew enough of dogs and bear hunting to request *Forty-Four
Years of the Life of a Hunter* (1883), an obscure nineteenth-century volume by
Meschach Browning, from J. Howard Woolmer for a "bearhunting friend." "Tell
you about bearhunting (with hounds) some time if you're interested," he prom-
ised.[57] The trapping licenses mentioned in *The Orchard Keeper* are something
that McCarthy might have known about, since his wide-ranging adolescent
hobbies included taxidermy and trapping. "Cormac ran all these forests and
hills," Annie DeLisle once explained. "He used to put his traps out here; he
trapped muskrats and things."[58]

In sum, McCarthy was Irish partly by way of the mountains. He could understand what it meant to be an Irish American through the received history of
his family, through his personal exploration of Ireland, and through its refrac-
tion in the mountain culture of which he was both a participant and a student.
One might thus expect to find the influence of Irish culture and literature on
McCarthy's writing. And this is indeed the case.

Sifting through the elements of mountain culture in McCarthy's work, some
have traced "Irish" concerns in the traditions from which he draws. For example, Barbara Brickman turns to Irish Ulster mythology to explain the thorough-
going "Celtic" pedigree of *The Orchard Keeper,* which she sees as offering its

own group of heroes, based on the Red Branch Cycle of Irish mythology, with Cú Chulainn at the head of its pantheon (the community in the novel is called Red Branch).[59] Observant of the excesses of king and city, she claims, "Mc-Carthy carefully aligns a number of laws with oppression of the Red Branch community," including such measures as property taxes, taxes on whiskey, and license plates. Brickman moves beyond Irish mythology to find remnants of what she calls "the Irish way of life" reflected in the Appalachian folkways and especially in the clannishness and ritualized rites of passage of the people.

This is the least sturdy part of Brickman's argument. Grady McWhiney also suggested in *Cracker Culture,* at his peril, that this sort of mistrust of central authority was a defining characteristic of "Celtic" peoples and an Irish way of life. McCarthy probably did observe these attitudes firsthand in the people around him, Scots, Irish, and otherwise. So it is easier to accept that McCarthy should be influenced by the Red Branch Cycle, whose mythic hero (Cormac) might have caught his ear. Arguing along the same lines, James Potts suggests that indeed Cormac McCarthy was well aware of the Irish high king who shares his name when he wrote *Suttree,* and he explains that McCarthy "borrows structural devices from Irish tales of the high kings [and specifically Mac Airt] to give shape and meaning to Buddy Suttree's wanderings." Of course, the mere presence of elements similar to the Mac Airt cycle does not prove that McCarthy intended to "use" them. When Potts writes that "it is probably more than coincidental that Suttree is haunted to the last by imaginary hounds"— like the Irish hounds of legend—he presumably has in mind the closing scene of the novel.[60] In that much remarked scene, as Cornelius Suttree departs, an "enormous lank hound" approaches him. "Somewhere in the gray wood by the river is the huntsman," whose "hounds tire not"; they are "slaverous and wild and their eyes crazed with ravening for souls in this world" (471). Douglas Canfield suggests that "the hunter and the hounds are thus demoniac, and they can represent some Manichaean prince of darkness."[61]

The puzzling scene has prompted a host of theories, offering a case study in the allusive complexity of McCarthy's work. The disappearing waterboy might reference Mark 14:13 (or Luke 22:10), where Jesus sends two disciples to the city, where they will meet "a *man bearing a pitcher of water:* follow him." From there they are conducted to the Last Supper, supporting the Suttree-as-Christ-figure reading of the story. In keeping with McCarthy's interest in gnosticism, he might be following the tradition that marks the end of the Age of Pisces (with the death of Christ/old Suttree) and the ushering in of the Age of Aquarius. It is equally possible that he alludes to Alexander Pope's translation of the *Odyssey* (1726):

> There huge Orion, of portentous size,
> Swift through the gloom a giant-hunter flies:
> A ponderous mace of brass with direful sway
> Aloft he whirls, to crush the savage prey!
> Stern beasts in trains that by his truncheon fell,
> Now grisly forms, shoot o'er the lawns of hell.[62]

In *Suttree*, Aquarius (the waterboy) has yielded to Orion, apparently in company with his hounds (Canis Major and Canis Minor). Together they drive the shades of his slain quarry over the fields of asphodel in Hades. In the concluding sentence of the novel, McCarthy dispels them all with two words: "Fly them." If Suttree shares the exact vision of Ulysses in hell—now tied to the underworld of Knoxville and the encroaching man-made hell—McCarthy might be giving Joyce's *Ulysses* a final nod and wink as he moves to greener pastures.

In any case, the book's close offers a good example of how McCarthy's imagination, so acquisitive and syncretic, is heir to Joyce's. Both *Ulysses* and *Suttree* were many years in the writing: Joyce claimed to have spent ten years working at *Ulysses,* while McCarthy hammered on *Suttree* intermittently for twenty years. Critics will have their work cut out for them if they want to discern the carefully planned framework of Christian and pre-Christian mythologies underpinning *Suttree.* (Joyce, at least, revealed his design and confessed that he might have "oversystematized.")[63] Like Joyce, McCarthy concocts a complicated symbology to create the sense of chronological order within the book, as evidenced in its use of moon phases, sums of money and debts discharged, the zodiac with attendant deities, epochs of ancient civilizations, encounters with mythic creatures, newspaper dates, and other motifs. To illustrate one of these categories, one might turn to the newspaper reports, often appalling, that provide important subtexts in *Suttree* (235, 403, 416), as they often do in *Ulysses.* Harrogate's detonation, leading to the quizzical newspaper headline "Earthquake?," is like the line of "bitched type" that makes Leopold Bloom into "L. Boom," the god of thunder, in *Ulysses.* Suttree too will puzzle over an undated newspaper and its "rash of incomprehensible events" (292). He yearns for "some stray scrap of news from beyond the pale" (66), an expression that harkens back to the fence palings that surrounded and protected "civilized" Dublin.

Or one might look to the novel's enmeshment with astrology. As McCarthy's friend of long standing, Guy Davenport, observes, "Bloom's breakfast kidney is a correspondence to the zodiacal position of the sun on the 16th of June; because he burns it, it is a sacrifice to his former god Jehovah."[64] *Suttree,* and, for that matter, other texts, such as *Blood Meridian,* abounds in McCarthy's fascination with tarot symbols and astrology. Events come to pass because of zodiacal alignments. Suttree's Uncle Milo, a merchant seaman ("What family has no mariner in its tree?" Suttree thinks, in Ulyssean terms), is "lost under Capricorn" off the coast of Chile, where even the stars are "foreign": "A whole new astronomy Mensa, Musca, the Chameleon." Hearing "sounds of fish surging in the sinking skiff," Suttree thinks of "the sign of faith" and leaps to Renaissance astrology obscurantism: "Twelfth house of the heavens. Ushering in the western church" (12). The twelfth house is linked to Pisces in Renaissance astrology, making Saint Peter indeed the "patron of fishmongers"—those, like Suttree, who gather under the sign of the fish. Suttree frequently consults the stars and is relieved, on an overcast night, when "there were no stars to plague him with their mysteries of space and time" (332).

McCarthy knew of Joyce's Linati schema, and he devised a similarly baroque plan of his own in order to make Knoxville a fit companion to Joyce's Dublin, as the careful sequencing of key events in his typed précis of the novel would indicate.[65] Some of the critical perplexity surrounding *Suttree* stems from the fact that the story is, in essence, utterly dependent on *Ulysses,* a book McCarthy includes with *The Brothers Karamazov, The Sound and the Fury,* and *Moby-Dick* on his "great list" of novels.[66]

That McCarthy read and studied Joyce punctiliously admits of no doubt: the writer would remind Oprah Winfrey that "James Joyce is a good model for punctuation; he keeps it to an absolute minimum."[67] His archival marginalia include many notes that bear on Joyce, some of them just single words, including, for instance, such likely *Ulysses*-derived jots as "Mulligan," "propinquity," and "usurper." Others are more carefully concealed. For example, Bloom kicks open "the crazy door of the jakes," enters the reeking tomb, and thinks, "better be careful not to get his trousers dirty for the funeral." The first man who tries to kill the Kid staggers out from "the jakes" in *Blood Meridian,* and the book concludes by bringing the Kid's funeral directly to the jakes. Leopold Bloom hopes his activities will not "bring on piles again"; Suttree, found "bleedin out of his ass," will cause one of his rescuers to remark, "Maybe he's got piles" (451). The first chapter of *Ulysses* has two men searching for a waterlogged corpse: Suttree the fisherman "made to go," whereas the sailboat of *Ulysses* is "making for Bullock harbor" (line 671). But both stories will begin with a drowned man: the "Here I am" that bobs up in Joyce's and the "I am, I am," "cast up" in McCarthy's (129).[68]

Some might see these similarities as passing or superficial, but there is a fundamental resonance between the texts in *Suttree*'s playfully Joycean voice.

The whore who becomes Suttree's companion is named, naturally, Joyce. Her morning-after encounter with Suttree recalls the domestic scene at the start of the Calypso chapter: Molly has her first word there ("Mn"), where McCarthy's Joyce has one the night before ("Mmm"), and Suttree has his ("Mggh") when she offers to bring her "lover" "liquids" (388–89). The pages where Joyce appears are full of cross-dressing episodes and might serve as a send-up of Bloom's unusual habits—or an arch comment on McCarthy's ambiguous love relationship with his wanton muse.[69]

McCarthy's love of run-together coinages speaks for itself, as does his interest in Irish Knoxville. We learn of Cornelius Suttree that some spirit of Irish genius operates within him: "Old distaff Celt's blood in some back chamber of his brain moved him to discourse with the birches, the oaks" (286). Even the names of Suttree—Billy Ray "Red" Callahan, McCulley, Judge Kelly, Dr. Neal, Tarzan Quinn, the brothers Clancy, and Irish Long—might lure one into believing that he has one foot in Knoxville and another in Dublin. Wesley Morgan has documented many of these real-life characters: Judge (John Moore) Kelly was a respected judge who attended Immaculate Conception with the McCarthy family. The brothers (John and Thomas) Clancy were high-school classmates of McCarthy's. David J. "Irish" Long's father was born in Ireland; Long's mother, in Virginia, to Irish-born parents. As described in the novel, Long refused to let his grocery store customers go hungry even during the leanest years of the Great Depression. The first to greet Suttree at the Huddle in his vision of the afterlife is Red Callahan, "a beardless Celt with spattled skin and rebate teeth. Three eyes in his head he has and he is covered over all with orange hair like unto a Cathay ape" (456). Elsewhere Callahan is described as a mythic Irish brawler, "one eye blue shiny, smiling, his teeth in a gout of blood. His busy freckled fist ferrying folks to sleep" (186). The real-life Billy Ray "Red" Callahan took his long rap sheet to the grave after being shot in a local club.[70]

If McCarthy accustoms the reader's eye to the poetic dimensions of his writing, they should not be lost on the *ear*. Jay Ellis captures McCarthy's love of language in an essay titled "McCarthy Music," and of course this *literal* musicality, wrapped in prose that is just this side of poetry, is something he shares with Joyce.[71] The technique permeates the page, but this example is as good as any: if one lets the accents fall in "His busy freckled fist ferrying folks to sleep" (186), it becomes clear that this sentence is a flurry of blows made by the fricative *f*, imitating the gasps of a fistfight, pulsing with the energy of the melee before coming to rest—like the poor pummeled victim—with the final drop of "sleep." The epic alliteration is a nice touch too.

Beyond dialogue, both *Suttree* and *Ulysses* engage readers with a narrative voice that is hard to pin down. *Suttree* offers a floating second-person *you* that is close kin to what Joyce called the "initial voice" of *Ulysses*.[72] Eventually, the *you* unobtrusively extends McCarthy's canvas into the territory of the reader's soul. The composition notes for *Suttree* contain a handwritten note—"Miller 'gnomic aorist' 1st person histor[y?]"—apparently referring to the Henry Miller–Lawrence Durrell correspondence, where Durrell explains, "In order to destroy time I use the historic present a great deal—not to mention the gnomic aorist."[73] The gnomic aorist is used in Greek to present timeless, general facts, and one sees it in *Suttree* with a shift from past action to present tense timeless, for example, "Lights from the house limn them and their sorry tableau" (35), "Somewhere in the gray wood by the river is the huntsman" (471). The *I*s that creep into the narrative unannounced begin to blend with the *you*s. As with Joyce, the reader is pacified by repetition, so that this strange and truly unreliable narrative voice—which might be called "fourth person" for want of a better term—eventually seems natural. Moreover, the shifting voice often offers a lens for ethical revelation, as Lydia Cooper argues in *No More Heroes*.

This is not the least of Joycean influence on McCarthy's work. "From James Joyce's *Ulysses*," explains Rick Wallach, "the masterpiece of Cormac McCarthy's Appalachian canon derives its very motor power: the intersecting peregrinations through Knoxville and environs of its two principal figures, Buddy Suttree and his hapless would-be protégé Gene Harrogate, inflect the wanderings of Leopold Bloom and Steven Dedalus through Dublin, another city one could navigate successfully with its most illustrious book in hand."[74] Indeed, both books attempt to "preserve" cities by testament. Knoxville is McCarthy's Eternal City, brimming with the minute details of actual places equivalent to what Joyce called "Dublin street furniture." Like Joyce's Dublin, McCarthy's Knoxville trundles along in scatological bathos, replete with its own "Cloaca Maxima" (13), the sewer being a gateway to the underworld and the very first order of civilization. What H. G. Wells termed *cloacal obsession* in Joyce is simply his familiar territory; Joyce's Liffey floats the morning toast just as surely as McCarthy's filthy Tennessee River. Dianne Wynne, producer of the documentary *Joyce to the World* (2007), once observed that "the paradox [of *Ulysses*] is that the book is a giant fart joke," and the same might be said of sections of McCarthy's excremental *Suttree,* as when Harrogate accidentally blasts himself out of Knoxville's bowels.[75] William C. Spencer suggests that Suttree's half-moon birthmark might recall the familiar outhouse vent. The Joycean satiric drive in McCarthy's work is alive and well, fittingly all-encompassing, musical, and relentless. Scarcely a page of *Suttree* goes without wordplay. Some of it can be crude, as when a priest delivers last rites and unction to Suttree: "He lay aneled. Like a rapevictim" (460). It meanders through various phases, toying with the conventions of drunken banter, epic catalog, and jurisprudence. The mock trial that plays out in the fevered imagination of Suttree's typhoid hallucinations should have a familiar Joycean ring to it, as Rick Wallach establishes beyond doubt: Suttree's trial quite clearly connects to the inquisition of Leopold Bloom in the Circe chapter of *Ulysses,* right down to his excuse for his behavior ("I was drunk").[76]

If the singers and barflies of the Sirens chapter of *Ulysses* offer Bloom a version of heaven, Suttree's rough companions offer a song of their own and toast the hero, who is descending unto death, warbling "When the moon shines down upon my Wabash then you'll recognize your Indiana home." According to high-school newspapers, Cormac McCarthy loved "hillbilly songs, his favorite being 'Valley of the Shenandoah Eve'"—as far as I know, not a real song but either a misquote or some strung-together hybrid title.[77] The *Suttree* lyrics come from a risqué parody of "Indiana" called "The Tattooed Lady"; "Wabash" substitutes for female anatomy. "The whores at the oval table raise their steins" to this double entendre (456). The prostitutes and brothels of *Suttree* are pure *Ulysses.*

The books also share a mutual and sometimes scatological interest in the many-splendored varieties of human sexual interest, for they too are part of the systolic energy of life. In comparing the high style of McCarthy's *Blood Meridian* with that of Thomas Pynchon's *The Crying of Lot 49* (1966), Harold Bloom explains that with Pynchon at least, "we can never be sure that [the passages] are not parodistic."[78] Surely this holds for *Suttree* too. As Rick Wallach writes, "McCarthy's pilferage from both [James] Agee and Joyce, and the spirit in which he revises his stolen material, are quintessentially parodical."[79] Harrogate's adventures in the melon patch—vegaphilia or vegiality?—recall Jewel's mysterious nighttime visits to the pasture in *As I Lay Dying* (1930), or perhaps Ike Snopes's special affection for his cow in *The Hamlet* (1940). Harrogate's subsequent legal defense, involving the definition of bestiality, provides the hee-haw punch line. This, McCarthy suggests, is one gothic view of southern "civilization": madmen and perverts in the woods, the discarded fighting poor of various racial hinds, and the destruction of any shred of the noble in the preceding culture. Like a Snopes, Harrogate cannot be extinguished; the sort of scrappy, shady, hickish/ Huckish character he represents will resurface in other McCarthy works, notably in the stripling Blevins in *All the Pretty Horses* (1992). On the other hand,

if McCarthy's humor has a touch of the Quixotic about it—literally in the case
of the Border Trilogy—Richard Eder concludes that "McCarthy's spirit is closer
to the fabulous prophetics of the Celtic legend than to the melancholy comedy
of the Spanish satire."[80]

As for the doomed necropolis of Knoxville, McCarthy is mindful that it was
built on the shoulders of giants, while he remains skeptical of its ability to produce such like again. Some of this ambivalence seems to come from his admiration for, and repudiation of, "respectable" men such as his father, editor of the
Yale Law Review and chief counsel for the Tennessee Valley Authority. If one
considers the elder McCarthy's profession, *Suttree* is at times a breathtakingly
defiant book. In an article celebrating the accomplishments of the TVA in the
years since he had arrived from the North, Charles McCarthy would proclaim
that "the hungry-looking mule is being replaced by modern machinery. The
look of poverty has left the land."[81] By contrast, this sort of socially engineered
industrial progress is precisely the enemy in his son's novel. Even as the elder
McCarthy credited the TVA with bringing an end to the "scourge of malaria,"
his son was exploring the finer points of rabies and typhoid fever in the pages
of his book. *Suttree* exposes every sort of human poverty—material, moral,
intellectual, and cultural—and the novel questions the worth of jurisprudence
as it goes.

This is not to say that Cormac completely repudiates the law in *Suttree*
but rather that he points to its human fragility, notwithstanding pillars of the
community such as his father. For instance, the "old tattered barrister" Suttree encounters, "who'd been chief counsel for Scopes, a friend of Darrow and
Mencken and a lifelong friend of doomed defendants, causes lost, alone and
friendless in a hundred courts," has entered his dotage, and to use the Yeatsian
phrase, strikes Suttree as little more than a tattered coat on a stick. In real life,
this was John Randolph Neal, an eccentric onetime University of Tennessee law
professor, TVA booster, and Scopes defender who indeed cut an increasingly
shabby figure about town. Suttree runs into him as he searches for the old train
station—trains are doomed juggernauts in McCarthy's landscapes—with its
"fireplaces and the inscriptions from Burns on the mantels" (367). This culture
proves as fleet as the trains, which only symbolically remember with "romantic
stencils" such place names as Lackawanna, Lehigh Valley, Baltimore and Ohio,
and the Route of the Chiefs, to say nothing of the chiefs that preceded them.

If Joyce offers a holistic critique of Dublin, McCarthy does the same for
Knoxville. As Rick Wallach points out, "The policemen who beat Suttree's
friend Ab Jones to death are variations upon the British soldiers who dominate

Dublin's nighttown."[82] Though Knoxvillians will tell you that self-deprecation is something of a local obsession, McCarthy did not have to look far for material. One gets a sense of a police state where bedlam is barely contained in an eyewitness account he sent to Howard Woolmer in 1981:

> Went downtown yesterday & suddenly found myself surrounded by fleeing felons firing off revolvers, police running up the street returning the fire, several detectives dragging another man from an alley & fastening hand- cuffs & leg irons to him, etc. A newsboy rushed up to me with a microphone & a tape recorder & asked me what was going on. I told him I had no idea, but it certainly seemed like the good old days for a few minutes.[83]

More appalling than the city's cultural disconnection with the past are the uses to which it puts its besotted populace. McCarthy's Knoxville, likened already to the "ruins of many an older city" (179), consumes its poor as if they were consumer products. He draws attention to this fact by repeatedly sketching the stratified debris of the city, including the many bodies among the forgotten rubbish. Even the dead may be repossessed by the operations of capitalism, as Leonard learns when his mother fails to make payments on his father's cemetery plot. The cultural paralysis of McCarthy's Knoxville, made of equal parts failed agrarianism and unfettered capitalism, comes of slightly different roots than Joyce's Dublin. What monument can possibly withstand American rapaciousness and love of the new?

McCarthy sees *Suttree* as a memento mori to endure long after Knoxville's old Cumberland Hotel was torn down, much as Joyce saw *Ulysses* as his monument to Dublin. When Suttree discovers that road construction is obliterating parts of the old McAnally neighborhood, he shuts his eyes: "He knew another McAnally, good to last a thousand years. There'd be no new roads there" (463). Here McCarthy alludes to the close of Allen Ginsberg's *Howl* ("good to eat a thousand years") and its transition to the juggernaut of Moloch, now descended upon Knoxville. Having butchered the life out of himself in *Suttree,* McCarthy places his faith in *ars longa* and the hope that the book will be "good to last a thousand years." (In another echo, the iron hardware of the derelict ship in *The Road* is "good to last three hundred years against the sea" [288].) Yet McCarthy seems to recognize the futility of Cornelius Suttree's attempt to sort through the bric-a-brac of a ruined American civilization and shore its fragments against ruin. Exorcism and embrace—of family, of faith, of personal demons, of unruly life itself—are the keys to *Suttree* and its dark vision, and these elements help to explain the oft-repeated comment that "*Suttree* is Mc-Carthy's *Ulysses*." Joyce and McCarthy erect two different cities in their work, faced with distinct but related dilemmas, and in the process they build up, as Yeats puts it in "Sailing to Byzantium," "monuments of unageing intellect."

Like Joyce, McCarthy insists that stories are made of stories, but his love of poetry shows plainly too, with Yeats well represented.[84] How much Irish Tuatha Dé Danann lore McCarthy incorporates into *Suttree*'s large menagerie of folkloric critters is not certain, but among McCarthy's composition notes for the text is *sheehogue*, glossed thus in Yeats's *Fairy and Folk Tales of the Irish Peasantry* (1888): "The Irish word for fairy is *sheehogue* [*sidheóg*], a diminutive of 'shee' in banshee." Yeats's "Easter, 1916" enters *Suttree*'s hallucination about the birth of a new world, which "does not come slowly. It rises in one massive mutation and all is changed utterly and forever" (459). The passage is also evocative of "The Second Coming," except that this rough beast does not slouch, but arrives suddenly. The "strange beauty" that the father sees in his lean child in *The Road* (87) also echoes the poem. Farrell O'Gorman suggests that "Suttree as druid-priest would seem to owe more to Yeats than to Joyce," and one might wonder why McCarthy draws from a poem about the Irish Easter uprising here.[85] Since *Suttree* broods over the rise and fall of social orders, one interpretation might be that it again draws attention to the suddenness of social change (Knoxville turned concrete jungle) when, to riff on Yeats's "Easter, 1916," "a terrible beauty is born."

Many of the examples of Yeatsian influence are glancing and hard to work out: a single page of *A Vision* (1925) contains a description of the Fool, the Hunchback, and "The Child of God," all characters of import in McCarthy's work but conceived differently in Yeats's writing, where the Fool, for example, is linked to the carefree Fool on the Hill.[86] The "judge . . . standing on the rise in silhouette against the evening sun like some great balden archimandrite" (273), according to Rick Wallach, "mordantly suggests William Butler Yeats' 'sages standing in God's holy fire' from 'Sailing to Byzantium.'"[87] As John Grammer points out, Arthur's version of the pastoral ideal in *The Orchard Keeper*, replete with log cabin (i.e., a wattle house) and honey, is clearly taken from Yeats's "The Lake Isle of Innisfree."[88] Yeats is not the only Irish poet of influence; "Whales and Men" refers to the poetry of Douglas Hyde. McCarthy's marginalia in early drafts also show that he considered using Joyce's "A Flower Given to My Daughter" as well.[89] In *The Road,* the references to "the mummified dead everywhere" (20)—e.g., "the black skin stretched upon the bones and their faces split and shrunken on their skulls" (161)—might well be tied to the explicit reference to "latterday bogfolk" (20), perhaps an allusion to Seamus Heaney's bog poems, for the victims, some with topknots, some caught in tar, resemble the peat-brown Tollund Man. The Tollund Man's "last gruel of winter seeds" recalls the seeds gathered in the hayloft (100). *The Road*'s horrific scenes of pastoral slaughter are certainly reminiscent of "The scattered, ambushed / Flesh of labourers, / Stockinged corpses / Laid out in the farmyards" in Heaney's "The Tollund Man." McCarthy's victims too are always "discalced" (21) (as are certain Catholic religious orders, one might add).[90]

McCarthy's Irish influences go well beyond Joyce and the poets. But only one McCarthy work, his unpublished screenplay "Whales and Men," goes so far as to borrow an Irish literary form, albeit incompletely. In the screenplay, a group of American beautiful people—young, brilliant, affluent, and fancy-free—detour from their wanderings to Ireland. In its concern for the class contrasts within Irish society and its painfully accurate view of the American abroad, "Whales and Men" contains elements of the novel of manners—an ironical circumstance in light of the fact that McCarthy has professed not to understand or value the work of writers such as Proust and Henry James. Crucially, beyond its investigation of manners, the screenplay owes its form in part to the Big House tradition in the Irish novel.

One likely avenue of influence, where the Irish Big House is concerned, is John Banville's Big House novel *Birchwood* (1973). It is not clear whether McCarthy knows Banville personally, but McCarthy did receive notice, via Woolmer, that Banville and Roddy Doyle had named him in a *London Times* poll as one of "the greatest living novelists writing in English." John Banville was among fourteen recipients designated to receive a complimentary copy of *All the Pretty Horses* (the list also included "Mrs C J McCarthy" [his mother] and Shelby Foote).[91]

Why should it matter that McCarthy borrows an Irish form in "Whales and Men," a largely unknown piece? For one thing, it makes clearer the extent of McCarthy's interest in Irish culture and literature outside of the American canon. He does not strictly adhere to the conventions of the Anglo-Irish Big House tradition—the Irish family in his Big House, the Gregorys, appear to have been so-called Castle Catholics (Irish sympathizers for British occupation). Even so, he is certainly familiar with the form as a gateway to the inner chambers of Irish identity. In the elegiac poetry readings that follow the dinner, Peter "intones" the "last lines of *Fern Hill* much in the manner of Thomas himself," according to McCarthy's instruction, singing in his chains by the sea. The Welsh poet's work apparently made quite an impression on McCarthy, who alludes to the poem also in *Child of God* (1973), according to Edwin T. Arnold.[92]

Peter goes on to explain that his father, a spitfire pilot in the Great War and later an MP, had been a racecar driver as well, competing "with the greatest drivers of all time in their own vehicles." This Irish airman seemed to foresee his death in the cockpit of a racecar, however, and was killed in practice at Reims in late 1957. As he holds forth on racing, Peter recalls Mille Miglia, Stirling Moss, Ascari, and others, noting that Portago's mother was Irish and that Fangio's wife was an Irishwoman. McCarthy's passion for sports cars and racing finds an outlet in these pages. True to form, he prefers the Continental and occasionally aristocratic golden years of Formula One at the mid-twentieth century to the NASCAR era. There does not appear to be an exact analog for Peter's father in Formula One annals, but given the associations between plantations and racing, there could be quite a few candidates. For example, the revised edition of Elizabeth Bowen's account of her family's estate, *Bowen's Court* (1964), reprints a photograph of a delighted Carson McCullers seated in a vintage racing car borrowed from one of Bowen's cousins.

In all of this there is a pleasing ring of authenticity, since motor sports have a storied history in Ireland. In fact, the earliest Irish Motor Tour took place in 1900, and the first major motor race to be held in Ireland, the Gordon Bennett Cup, took place in 1903 in County Kildare, as "hostility to the automobile had prevented the race being held in England, and a strong Irish lobby led to a special act of Parliament that enabled the race to be held [there]."[93] The racecar as a popular-culture phenomenon surfaces in "After the Race," one of the stories in *Dubliners*. In Joyce's story the race brings an air of short-lived excitement to Ireland, where "sightseers had gathered in clumps to watch the cars careering homeward and through this channel of poverty and inaction the Continent sped its wealth and industry."[94] For centuries, racing, from horse racing to car racing, has been a part of Irish life, precisely as Peter explains in the screenplay. This is not the only moment in McCarthy's *oeuvre* to make connections between racing and passing orders. In *Suttree,* Cornelius's grandfather believes the mysterious beauty of a horse race to be imperishable: "that they had witnessed a thing against which time would not prevail" (136). Young Cornelius suspects otherwise: "The clock has run, the horse has run, and which has measured which?" (136). Without admitting an afterlife, the Reaper dispenses with all intimations of immortality. Thus McCarthy's answer to Yeats's epitaph: these horsemen will *not* pass by.

The section of "Whales and Men" that is set in Ireland also mingles racing with family traditions. As it unfolds, it raises the second convention of the Big House novel enumerated by Vera Kreilkamp, as it offers "an account of a decaying family line."[95] Peter enters the story as a rake. Surveying the "lovely things" in a nightclub, he meets a woman who calls him English. "Irish actually," he corrects her, and asks, "You're not an heiress by an odd chance are you?" In essence, though, Peter faces a real problem. Kreilkamp observes that children of the Big House are often sexually dysfunctional (yes in "Whales and Men") and have "powerful mothers" (yes again): "Ascendancy families fail to produce heirs and legitimate lines of succession are threatened."[96] When Guy comments that the grounds are "very beautiful," Peter replies, "Beautiful as it is and much as I love it I have not always been able to exclude ennui from its precincts." When Guy asks if this is a quotation, Peter invokes a celebrated source: "Yes. What can't be improved upon must be quoted. It's George Moore on Moore Hall."

As an Anglo-Irish writer who wore his aristocratic origins on his sleeve and criticized them openly, George Moore would certainly resonate with Peter. Unlike many Big House stories, however, there is no Catholic usurper here, for the Catholics have already arrived. As Peter watches his friends depart, his voiceover is from a sixteenth-century Irish poem that has been rendered by many Irish poets, including Thomas Kinsella.

> I shall not die for thee
> Oh woman of body like a swan
> I was nurtured by a cunning man
> O thin palm, O white bosom,
>
> PETER: I shall not die for thee.[97]

In a later sequence, Kelly will recite Yeats's "Cradle Song" to the children she has had with Peter: "The angels are stooping / Above your bed; / They weary of trooping / With the whimpering dead." The tone is hopeful and bittersweet, like Yeats's uncharacteristically light verse. Peter takes a magnificent stand in the House of Lords on behalf of whales as a sort of "nation" that, bearing no arms, was put to the sword. In sum, this is the rare Big House story that ends well. It evinces McCarthy's understanding of fading orders in an international context and shows that he appreciates the complexities of Irish identity and politics. Knowing what he appropriates, McCarthy can hold his own with Continental sophisticates. And he is no more innocent of tradition than his beloved Joyce or Yeats.

By now, much has been said of McCarthy's Irish connections. What about the Catholic side of his Irish Catholic roots? Farrell O'Gorman, himself an Irish American southern writer, brings penetrating insight to *Suttree* in a way that sheds light on McCarthy's sense of artistic purpose. Without arguing that "McCarthy's novel is derivative of Joyce's in any reductive sense," O'Gorman considers "McCarthy's own quasi-Joycean identity as an apparently 'defrocked' Catholic of Irish-American background." O'Gorman observes that McCarthy's younger brother William "Bill" C. McCarthy apparently "entered a Jesuit seminary in Louisiana in the late 1950s—i.e., at about the time that McCarthy began working on Suttree."[98] Records from the Jesuits of the New Orleans Province confirm that Bill McCarthy entered the Society in August 1958 and left in December 1968—not long enough to become a priest, but perhaps long enough to begin teaching.[99] Patrick Samway spoke with Cormac McCarthy at length on one occasion and recalled that McCarthy "knew things that only a Jesuit would know";[100] his brother's time with the Jesuits explains how he might have known them. Thus the vocational calling came close to home for McCarthy. The affinities between the lot of the priest and that of the artist are joined at the spine in ways that need little explanation. As McCarthy scribbled in an early draft of "Whales and Men," "ART is failed religion."[101]

O'Gorman focuses on Stephen Dedalus's description of himself as a "priest of eternal imagination, transmuting the daily bread of experience into the radiant body of everliving life." As he explains, "Suttree himself is—problematically but insistently—a sort of stand-in for Christ in the novel. The son of a woman named Grace, he prefers the company of poor fishermen, criminals, and prostitutes to that of the apparently righteous."[102] O'Gorman's hunch finds new validation in sections of *Suttree* later excised by McCarthy that now are visible in the Wittliff Collections. Moreover, through the frequent mirrored images of Suttree/Othersuttree (McCarthy's term) and priests, and in the repeated intimation that he "might have been a fisher of men in another time" (14), O'Gorman carefully makes a strong case for Suttree's transformation from a failed priest to an acolyte in the artistic priesthood of the imagination. When asked if he considers himself a Catholic, Suttree replies, "I've been defrocked" (191); his priestly garb has been taken away, just as O'Gorman's reading suggests. Read thus, Suttree's artistic maturation, reflecting Joyce's and McCarthy's development, comes at the cost of the religion of his youth. The section that follows goes further along this track in exploring the complicated interrelationships between McCarthy, Joyce, and Catholicism.[103]

A search of the MLA bibliography for McCarthy and Catholicism turns up just two items: one article and one dissertation.[104] McCarthy did not make the task any easier in a recent interview with the *Wall Street Journal:*

WSJ: You grew up Irish Catholic.

CM: I did, a bit. It wasn't a big issue. We went to church on Sunday. I don't even remember religion ever even being discussed.

WSJ: Is the God that you grew up with in church every Sunday the same God that the man in "The Road" questions and curses?

CM: It may be. I have a great sympathy for the spiritual view of life, and I think that it's meaningful. But am I a spiritual person? I would like to be. Not that I am thinking about some afterlife that I want to go to, but just in terms of being a better person. I have friends at the Institute. They're just really bright guys who do really difficult work solving difficult problems, who say, "It's really more important to be good than it is to be smart." And I agree it is more important to be good than it is to be smart. That is all I can offer you.[105]

Trust the tale, not the teller? Apart from his fiction, some of McCarthy's own correspondence demonstrates how he values the work of other Catholic writers. His debts to Flannery O'Connor, by his own account, are significant. Writing to a student of Robert Coles who completed a paper on McCarthy's work, McCarthy frames "intellectuals" in the same unflattering terms as Flannery O'Connor. He writes: "An intellectual is a person who feels that his learning—and it may be pitifully little—entitles him to status. . . . People who really do *know* are inevitably returned to the common ground of man. I think too that O'Connor is a better writer than [Ignazio] Silone or [Georges] Bernanos for the simple reason that she is able to dramatize love and grace strikingly in their absence."[106] Separately, McCarthy's correspondence with J. Howard Woolmer shows how closely he followed O'Connor's legacies. In a letter dated April 1, 1980, he writes that "*Wise Blood* has not appeared here [in Lexington, KY] yet" and relates the details of its production: "Some friends of Flannery's getting together and deciding to do it and asking Huston if he would direct."[107] McCarthy and Coles corresponded on the work of the staunchly Roman Catholic French novelist Georges Bernanos as well.[108] In March 1993 Robert Coles would write to McCarthy to thank him for sending a copy of Jesuit-educated Ron Hansen's *Mariette in Ecstasy* (1992). The book's young protagonist enters a convent about the turn of the century and there experiences the stigmata and other possible theophanies. A novel delicately balanced between devotion and doubt, it is grounded in Catholic mysticism.

Elsewhere, in correspondence with Robert Cumbow, the author of *Once Upon a Time: The Films of Sergio Leone,* McCarthy noted that he "was particularly stuck by the section on the 'Catholic filmmaker' and your roundup of images and scenes. Some of his films I think are very good. He really is a *filmmaker.*"[109] The roundup McCarthy refers to shows how Leone's films are visually informed, at every level, by a "specifically Roman Catholic" mythos—much like McCarthy's stories, one might add. To an attentive reader McCarthy's Catholicism can be discerned in its varied liturgical, cultural, Irish, and even Joycean registers. Taken together, the plain significance is that McCarthy, so often deemed anti-Catholic, has an unshakably Catholic worldview.

It can be easier to see the anti-Catholic, though. The deflating impulse Suttree directs at the church is unrelenting, so that in the early pages Suttree thinks of "St Peter patron of fishmongers"—the founder of the Roman Catholic Church, first among equals—in the same breath as "St Fiacre that of piles," a patron to whom Leonard, who has "gonorrhea of the colon" and is "otherwise covered with carbuncles," would be well advised to pray. Suttree's hand-carved billiken (a bizarre Buddha-with-topknot talisman, faddishly popular in the early twentieth century, that became the mascot of the Jesuit Saint Louis University), recovered from the ruins of his Catholic school, implies a wryly sacrilegious, interchangeable Christ totem. Elsewhere the epitome of coldness is crudely described as "a nun's cunt . . . on good Friday" (175).

Is this mere bathos, a tearing down of the novel's pietà motif? The nuns of *Suttree* tend to be beldams, more than saintly visionaries, and false piety is the norm. McCarthy revisits the miseries of a suffocating Catholicism in flashbacks when Suttree, drunk, enters Immaculate Conception Church in Knoxville, of which Abram Ryan was a founder. There is still an aroma of Father Ryan's severe and self-denying Catholicism in precincts that almost certainly derive from McCarthy's childhood, including a detailed description of a "sad chapel" where "a thousand hours or more he's spent" as a "spurious acolyte, dreamer impenitent. Before this tabernacle where the wise high God himself lies sleeping in his golden cup" (253). The golden communion chalice and the sleeping God recall Yeats's "Sailing to Byzantium":

> But such a form as Grecian goldsmiths make
> Of hammered gold and gold enamelling

> To keep a drowsy Emperor awake.
> Or set upon a golden bough to sing
> To lords and ladies of Byzantium
> Of what is past, or passing, or to come.[110]

Suttree's calling will be to awaken his drowsing God through his art. The church recollected in *Suttree* is epitomized by the experience of confession:

> This kingdom of fear and ashes. Like the child that sat in these selfsame bones so many black Fridays in terror of his sins. Viceridden child, heart rotten with fear. Listening to the slide shoot back in the confessional, waiting his turn. (253)[111]

Moreover, one hears echoes of Joyce's *Portrait of the Artist as a Young Man* (1916) in the clergy "grim and tireless in their orthopedic moralizing. Filled with tales of sin and unrepentant deaths and vision of hell and stories of levitation and possession and dogmas of semitic damnation for the tacking up of the paraclete. After eight years a few of their charges could read and write in primitive fashion and that was all" (254).[112] McCarthy's remembered Catholicism, bristling with iconography and statuary, is a cheerless detention center for children. Helpless kids pass out in May processions; summer afternoons are spent in the clammy "smell of old varnish" while "the distant cries of children in a playground" remind them what they are missing.

It persists into adulthood: while an old woman dusts the altar rails, a priest reminds besotted, filthy Suttree that he is in "God's house." Like Yeats's Crazy Jane, Cornelius Suttree too has been admonished to "Live in a heavenly mansion, / Not in some foul sty" (121).[113] Suttree-as-artist rejects this sterile and cramped vision of what God's house might be. With his fish-stained shoes, he once again evokes a fisher of men—or a slumbering Fisher King. "The priest gave a little smile, lightly touched with censure, remonstrance gentled" (255), McCarthy writes, using words charged with Catholic connotation. Ecclesiastical censure, per canon law, is imposed on a "baptized, delinquent, and contumacious person," the Catholic equivalent of contempt of court.[114] And "remonstrance," given the "monstrance" that holds the consecrated host for adoration, intimates a re-apparition. If the priest fails to see that Christ has knocked on his door, the exchange with Suttree—"Do I know you? . . . No, you don't know me" (255)—reminds the reader of the various times in scripture where Christ was not recognized (e.g., Jesus to Phillip, John 14:9; the narrow door of Luke

13:22–28; and, of course, Peter's denial). *Suttree* indeed insists that love pitches its tent in the place of excrement. The problem is that the bedlam of Suttree's Knoxville also seems very much a part of God's house, the "crapgame" that the ragpicker "couldn't put any part of . . . together" (258). Once again, McCarthy points to the problem of belief in a world where the rococo splendors of Catholic theology crash against Hamlet's unweeded garden. As Vereen Bell puts it, Suttree is "like Stephen Dedalus, an imperfectly lapsed Catholic, left impaled upon the wrong end of a coherent theological dogma in which the world can only be a place of death and suffering."[115]

In the usual way, it is a church that he left but that never left him; one must see through the object to the objection. Suttree's unyielding criticism of the church and its "Christian witchcraft" taught at a "school for lechers" (304) extends so far as to label the priest who administers last rites to him a "praetor to a pederastic deity" (460). In a universe where God buggers his own—or permits something as monstrous as the gang rape of "a female simpleton" for sport (416)—Suttree seems to have a very slim margin for belief.

Significantly, when Suttree sojourns in the wilderness, stalking his "doublegoer, some othersuttree" (287), what brings him back to lucidity is Eucharistic snow: "a delicate host expired upon his filthy cuff" (289). (The image is reprised in *The Road* when a snowflake melts on the father's hand "like the last host of christendom" [13].)[116] In Catholic theology, the body of Christ does indeed take away the sins of the world; thus in the penitential Asperges of the Tridentine rite is the antiphon "Lavabis me, et super nivem dealbabor" (Thou shalt wash me, and I shall be made whiter than snow).[117] In a later passage there is perhaps another symbolic reference to these fallen wafers, traveling "innocently and unburnt" to cover grimy Knoxville. The cleansing snow, suspended in a "livid phosphorous tunnel" of light from a train's headlamp, evokes the preternatural ambience of death and final journey. The Eucharistic significance invites another comparison to Joyce but in this case links *Suttree* even more clearly to *Dubliners*.[118] The final lines of *Dubliners*'s "The Dead" read:

> A few light taps upon the pane made him turn to the window. It had begun to snow again. He watched sleepily the flakes, silver and dark, falling obliquely against the lamplight. The time had come for him to set out on his journey westward. Yes, the newspapers were right: snow was general all over Ireland. It was falling on every part of the dark central plain, on the treeless hills, falling softly upon the Bog of Allen and, farther westward, softly falling into the dark mutinous Shannon waves. It was falling, too,

upon every part of the lonely churchyard on the hill where Michael Furey lay buried. It lay thickly drifted on the crooked crosses and headstones, on the spears of the little gate, on the barren thorns. His soul swooned slowly as he heard the snow falling faintly through the universe and faintly falling, like the descent of their last end, upon all the living and the dead.

Page 403 of *Suttree* reads:

It snowed that night. Flakes softly blown in the cold blue lamplight. Snow lay in pale boas along the black treelimbs down Forest Avenue and the snow in the street bore bands of branch and twig, dark fissures that would not snow full. . . . The snowflakes came dodging out of the blackness beyond the lamps to settle on his lashes. Snow falling on Knoxville, sifting down over McAnally, hiding the rents in the roofing, draping the sashwork, frosting the coalpiles in the crabbed dooryards. It has covered up the blood and dirt and claggy sleech in gutterways and laid white lattice on the sewer grates.[119] And snow has made cool bowers in the blackened honeysuckle and it has hid the packingcrates in the hobo jungles and wrought enormous pastry rings of trucktires there. Where the creek addles along gorged with offal. Upon whose surface the flakes impinge softly and are gone. Suttree turning up his collar. In the yards a switchengine is working and the white light of the headlamp bores down the rows of iron gray warehouses in a livid phosphorous tunnel through which the snow falls innocently and unburnt.

While not exactly congruent, the paratactic passages reveal some important similarities, not least of which is a culmination in Eucharist. Gary Wallace remembered a conversation in which McCarthy said he "thinks the mystical experience is a direct apprehension of reality, unmediated by symbol, and he ended with the thought that our inability to see spiritual truth is the greater mystery."[120] Thus the unmediated encounter with the Eucharist, free of the human embroidery of ritual symbolism, becomes a spiritual desideratum in McCarthy's world.

The last line of "The Dead" has a particularly Catholic register, with the familiar intonation from the Nicene Creed—"He will come again in glory to judge the living and the dead"—imparting a liturgical conclusion to a collection of stories brimming with paralysis and spiritual stagnation. McCarthy too has a liturgical imagination, returning to phrases from the Mass. For example, the phrase from the Nicene Creed concerning Christ's coming to judge "the living and the dead" is echoed in both *Blood Meridian* ("passing their blades about the skulls of *the living and the dead* alike" [54, emphasis added]) and *Suttree* ("through conjugations of space and matter to that still center where *the living and the dead* are one" [447, emphasis added]). Also from the Nicene Creed, in *The Crossing* (1994): "He saw pass as a slow tapestry unrolled images of things *seen and unseen*" [325–26, emphasis added]). The tormented life of the heretic of *The Crossing* reads like a bitter refutation of the Catholic doxology ("Glory to the Father, and to the Son, and to the Holy Spirit: *as it was in the beginning, is now, and will be for ever*" [emphasis added]): "There in the ruins of that church out of whose dust and rubble he had been raised up seventy years before and sent forth to live his life. *Such as it was. Such as it had become. Such as it would be*" (150, emphasis added).

Significantly, when John Grady Cole rides off more into the twilight than into the sunset in the final pages of McCarthy's *All the Pretty Horses,* the reader learns that the world seems to hold "Nothing for the living or the dead" (301). The last line of *All the Pretty Horses* is, "Passed and paled into the darkening land, the world to come" (302). Some readers of the Border Trilogy may find it easy to accept a dark interpretation: the losses of life can only be gathered against the world to come. Perhaps this is Yeatsian ("Of what is past, or passing, or to come") or even a reference to the Jewish hereafter (*Olam Haba* in Hebrew, literally the "world to come"), but there is a crystal-clear suggestion of one of the most important refrains in Catholic belief: "We look for the resurrection of the dead, and the life of *the world to come*."

The echo continues, as these examples demonstrate, in a liturgical rhythm that runs through his books. In *Cities of the Plains* we find:

The world to come must be composed of what is past. (286)
The world past, the world to come. Their common transiencies. (71)
Carrying the blind man's words concerning his prospects as if they were a contract with the world to come. (82)

In *The Crossing:*

He sat in the sun and looked out over the country to the east. . . . All of it waiting like a dream for the world to come to be, world to pass. (135)
He crouched in the sedge by the lake and he knew he feared the world to come for in it were already written certainties no man would wish for. (325)

And in *The Road:*

> He'd not have thought the value of the smallest thing predicated on a world
> to come. (158)[121]

Thus McCarthy suggests, across novels, that if you wish for the life of the world to come within the temporal order, you had better be careful what you ask for, for something wicked may this way come. One could take this beyond McCarthy's altered, emptied-out profession of faith in order to discern his Kyrie, his Gloria, and his penitential rites. J. Cameron Moore, for instance, notes that Sherriff Bell in *No Country for Old Men* reflexively "undertakes three of the seven corporal works of mercy" (87) and draws on the Mass's Confiteor: "Knowing that Chigurh is coming for him and that death is very close, at this moment he thinks to himself, 'What have you done. What have you failed to do'" (85).[122] Even though his prose is liturgically informed and driven, McCarthy stays on the razor's edge between salvation and despair.

One might very well ask, Isn't this the liturgy of a "dead" church reduced to ghostly presence? Possibly, but even in despair McCarthy resorts to the order of liturgy. Despair is not merely a sin against hope; it is the "hallmark of that obverse Catholicism known as Jansenism," much endemic to Irish Catholics, that in "Catholic context . . . takes the extreme form of feeling irredeemably unworthy," explains Robert Cumbow. McCarthy responded appreciatively to Cumbow's writing on the films of Sergio Leone, where Cumbow argued that Leone answers a Jansenist insistence on the necessity of the church for salvation by creating "a world in which there is no established order, and in which—not coincidentally—there are no churches. *Empty* churches, *ruins* of churches, belltowers *without* churches, yes—all are reminders of the absence of moral order."[123] One thinks immediately of the ruined church in *The Crossing* and the abandoned church of *Blood Meridian;* as in Leone's films, churches can become a place of slaughter. These orders too pass away. As the blind man of *The Crossing* frames it in Eucharistic terms, "The world which he imagines to be the ciborium of all godlike things will come to naught but dust before him" (293).

Even in absence, impairment, and collapse, Catholicism runs through *Suttree* like a subterranean stream under a mountain. Suttree's imagination operates by Catholic iconography, so that Mary becomes something of a leitmotif, for example. Whereas *Blood Meridian* opens with "See the child" (which seems almost a response to the opening passage of Faulkner's *The Sound and the*

Fury), *Suttree* tells the reader, "See the mother sorrowing" (61), as Suttree sees his own mother in terms of the pietà. Elsewhere a mourning mother recalls the *Stabat Mater Dolorosa* (153), and a weeping mother is transformed into "an image of baroque pieta" (362). Significantly, McCarthy glosses the Mary statue in Immaculate Conception with terms that point to her pre-Christian analogs: "Mater alchimia in skyblue robes" (253). In Carl Jung's analysis of alchemy, a persistent point of interest for McCarthy, Mater Alchimia is linked to the Virgin Diana, the First Mother and the First Matter, "the vessel and the matter of good and evil."[124]

A story fragment that McCarthy seems to have based on a clipping about a suicide in Black River Falls, Wisconsin, on December 18, 1973, describes a hunter encountering a young woman's body, which he initially misapprehends as "a still hunter in a treeblind":

> The eyes that looked down at him had frozen in the cold and in their wild eclectic blue they bore a false and frozen light carried to his heart. He stood his rifle against a tree and knelt in the snow and made the sign of the cross. As if he'd come across the Madonna herself deep in the woods. And some part of the hunter understood that beauty was no more. That beauty hanged herself by a rope from a tree in the wood in the snow and that beauty was dead and it would come no more.[125]

Below the draft, McCarthy handwrites "ora pro nobis pecatoribus" (pray for us sinners), familiar from the Hail Mary, clearly intending this to be a Marian apparition in a doubtful register. McCarthy's symbolic universe is shot through with such startling encounters and legions of inadvertent members of holy orders, from Indians swinging turtles like censers in *Suttree* to the discalced dead of *The Road*. He has a southerner's awareness of Catholicism's potential distancing effect, similar to that seen in encounters between Protestants and Catholics in Joyce's work. When Leonard asks Suttree to say a prayer over his deceased father, Suttree replies, "The only words I know are the Catholic ones," to which Leonard responds with reflexive blasphemy, "Hell fire. He sure wasn't no Catholic" (251), demonstrating that Suttree's Catholicism sets him apart from other Knoxvillians. Some of these divisions are treated with an air of bemusement. For example, J. Bazzell Mull, a Protestant radio evangelist well known to Knoxvillians, receives a mention in *Suttree*; the dialogue references the show's opening schtick, with Mull's wife (Mrs. Mull) chiming in:

> I like to hear old J. Basil [*sic*]. He's all the time sayin: Aint that right Mrs Mull.
> Old deep voice. And she'll say: That's right Mr Mull. You like to hear him?
>   He's all right, Suttree said. (134)

Suttree's equivocal response probably goes unnoticed by the driver who has offered him a lift. For McCarthy, the radio might place a discreet stethoscope to the Protestant walls of hillbilly Knoxville.

There is no mistaking the sectarian tensions in an earlier scene where Suttree narrowly avoids a "proper" baptism by full immersion, but not before twitting his would-be savior by asking him for a drink. The preacher has only contempt for "sprinklers":

> You been baptized?
> Just on the head.
> Just on the head, he says.
> That aint no good. That old sprinkling business wont get it, buddy boy. (122)

The dunker urges Suttree to attend a camp meeting with Billy Byington and the Sunrise Singers. Wes Morgan confirms that McCarthy had a local preacher, "Brother Bob Bevington," in mind. Bevington, a vocal critic of Catholicism, pastored the Knoxville Baptist Tabernacle, a short walk from Knoxville Catholic High School.[126] Clearly, McCarthy was aware of Protestant-Catholic clashes in Knoxville, and the passage does seem a tongue-in-cheek response to those who would not recognize the legitimacy of a Catholic baptism. Suttree "knew the river well already and he turned his back to these malingerers" (125):

> You aint fixin to leave are ye? the old man asked.
> I sure as hell am, said Suttree. (124)

As the work of Flannery O'Connor and Cormac McCarthy demonstrates, few Roman Catholics raised in the South escaped encounters with evangelists, well-meaning and otherwise. Perhaps there were other encounters. *Suttree* has cameos from a Greek restaurateur named Ulysses, who, in a passing Bloomish moment, admires Suttree's clothing with a Jewish patois, saying, "Oy. . . . Iss qvality" (301). The anomalous Catholicism of McCarthy's Cornelius Suttree, irrespective of Knoxville's small but long-standing Catholic community, is no stranger than the Jewishness of Joyce's Leopold Bloom. It is simply another case in which the outsider gazes in, and in which Catholicism is most present in its absence.

If Catholicism is so important to McCarthy, one might ask, why does he not profess it? His acquaintances have commented on his disillusionment with Catholicism. Bill Kidwell, a friend of McCarthy's from Knoxville, explained to an interviewer, "I think it [Catholicism] embittered him. Because of that, he was never fully at peace with his parents. That's directly reflected in *Suttree,* the same story, essentially an autobiography." Annie DeLisle adds that he may have "felt guilty he couldn't encompass [his family's beliefs] in his work."[127]

If McCarthy experienced a loss of faith, what precipitated it? It would seem that the problem of evil poses the greatest bar to his belief. To bring some order to the disordered worlds in McCarthy's fiction, critics have labored to find the right interpretive framework. Among the most intriguing of these, expounded by Leo Daugherty and Rick Wallach, is the notion that McCarthy's knowledge of gnosticism informs some of his writing, particularly in *Blood Meridian.*[128] By this view, creation is actually hell, and the chillingly evil Judge is a gnostic archon, or demonic demigod, the evil demiurge of heretical Manichaean belief. The theory helps to account for McCarthy's repeated suggestion that the world is somehow off its track and that we are trapped in a second-rate reality that we but dimly perceive.[129] As scholarship surrounding the gnostic gospels has reached a fevered pitch lately, it is worth remembering that these "gospels" at core attempted to explain the coexistence of evil and divine power. They were also very quickly declared heretical by the early church. When McCarthy writes about gnosticism in *Blood Meridian,* then, one should be mindful that the Ex-priest sees the Judge as an "old hoodwinker" (252). It seems more likely that McCarthy sees gnosticism as one of many doubtful answers to the mystery of suffering. If Genesis 18:25 asks, "Shall not the Judge of all the earth do right?," McCarthy's Judge seems to return a supercilious answer.

Gnawing agnosticism, waning gnosticism, nihilism, and the apparently anti-Catholic tenor of McCarthy's writing—all these things have made it easy to write him off as anything but a Catholic writer. But perhaps McCarthy is most Catholic in this respect: his work confronts the fear that Catholicism's cosmology offers an inadequate response to the mystery of evil and to a world where belief itself seems a kind of travesty when an interventionist God seems far too remote a possibility. In *Child of God,* the grisly catacombs of Ballard's creation contain "pallets of stone where dead people lay like saints" (135). In one of the few articles to consider McCarthy's Catholicism, William Deresiewicz writes thoughtfully, "Call it Catholicism minus revelation."[130]

Consequently, Cormac McCarthy has repeatedly committed in print what for an Irish Catholic may be the greatest, perhaps even satanic, rebellion: the principled examination of agnosticism. It is no accident that Mark Twain's Forty-Four, the satanic character of *The Mysterious Stranger* (1916), is in some respects a ringer for McCarthy's Judge in *Blood Meridian*. McCarthy's fascination with satanic rebellion, his sympathy for the devil, might well be tied to a difficult faith. Satan, he points out in earlier drafts of "Whales and Men," was a latecomer to church canons.

Of course, there is no rebellion without realizing the substance of order. In his notes for *Suttree* McCarthy observes, "Revolutions follow decadence." In his "southern" subject matter, McCarthy demonstrates a keen awareness of the decrees of his native culture seen in other southern Irish writers—the nuances, the accents, and the eccentricities. *Child of God* shows in almost allegorical terms how easily a questioner becomes a pariah. The terror of McCarthy's violent universe is that the orthodox presumptions predicating it might be terribly mistaken. As James Wood shrewdly suggests, "Like most writers committed to pessimism, McCarthy is never very far from theodicy."[131] What if we inhabit a world truly gone out of order, where we cannot connect with a savior and where, as the Judge suggests, "the mystery is that there is no mystery" (252)?

Only the most pat understanding of the "Catholic novelist" would eject McCarthy from the canon of Catholic writers for framing these questions. In "The Catholic Novelist in the South," Flannery O'Connor peered into the future of southern writing:

> The American Catholic trusts the fictional imagination about as little as he trusts anything. Before it's well on its feet, he's busy looking for heresy in it. The Catholic press is constantly broken out in a rash of articles on the failure of the Catholic novelist. *The Catholic novelist is failing to reflect the virtue of hope,* failing to show the Church's interest in social justice, failing to show life as a positive good, failing to portray our beliefs in a light that will make them desirable to others. *He occasionally writes well, but he always writes wrong. Now if in the next twenty years we find ourselves with a batch of wild Southern Catholic writers who fail in all these things and, in addition, have certain positive obnoxious qualities—such as a penchant for violence*

and grotesquery and religious enthusiasm—we are doubtless going to wonder
how these strange birds got hatched in our nest.[132]

If McCarthy is essentially and inescapably a Catholic, how could he "write
wrong" and fail to reflect the virtue of hope? It appears that he is the strange
hatchling prophesied by O'Connor. "If I wrote about violence in an exaggerated
way, it was looking at a future that I imagined would be a lot more violent," Mc-
Carthy explained in a recent interview. "And it is. Can you remember, 20 years
ago, having beheadings on TV? I can't."[133] The "penchant for violence" seems
more prophetic than gratuitous in McCarthy's case. After all, he was writing
about the moral no-man's-land on the border between Mexico and Texas in
the 1980s, with *No Country for Old Men* well under way, but most Americans
would take little notice until horrific cross-border drug wars almost twenty-
five years later (and still less attention to American complicity in the evils of
that moral "hinterland").

McCarthy's church is so far divorced from social justice that it seems powerless to prevail against the gates of hell. The ruined churches in his work
neither receive nor dispense justice; John Grady's intended shrine in *Cities of
the Plains* offers no quarter. When John Grady Cole and Lacey Rawlins emerge
from the jail just barely intact, the scene is described thus: "A few drops of rain
had begun to fall in the street. They dropped on the roof of the bus solitary as a
bell. Down the street he could see the arched buttresses of the cathedral dome
and the minaret of the belltower beyond" (208). In one of many apparently in-
effectual purifications, rain, which ought to be cleansing, serves mainly to remind of a drought of compassion. In theory, the bell tower is a bulwark against
savagery; in practice, the jail is the best symbol of social organization, "so like
some site of siege in an older time, in an older country, where the enemies
were all from without" (208). At the outset of the cowboys' travels, in more
innocent times, as they cross the darkening prairie, "they heard somewhere in
that tenantless night a bell that tolled and ceased where no bell was" (30), like
one of Sergio Leone's bell towers without churches.[134] In McCarthy's work we
cannot ask for whom the bell tolls; it seems that even the bell, like the church,
has gone missing.

But inculcation in Catholicism, and particularly a Catholic upbringing,
shapes one's cosmology and moral bearings in distinctive ways. McCarthy's
readers should be attentive to what might be termed the "deep Catholicism"
of his writing, which works on both an ordinary cultural and a moral level.
Critics have taken scattered notice of his marked tendency to see the world in

terms of Catholic rite and language. For example, Susan Gunn points out that the judge of *All the Pretty Horses* (not *Blood Meridian*) performs the exact office of a priest when John Grady Cole seeks absolution, a point that may seem obvious enough in retrospect but might well escape a first reading.[135] Elsewhere, McCarthy's inconspicuously Catholic imagination likens Mexican songs emanating from a radio to "an agony"; the description of the agony in Cole's heart is similarly depicted as "like a stake" (256). *Agony* has a special Catholic register, and so does McCarthy's imagery.

Add to these Catholic flourishes Farrell O'Gorman's argument that McCarthy's concern with the last things (and especially, as the author himself has acknowledged, with death) comes from a Catholic worldview.[136] If Flannery O'Connor allowed that "I see from the standpoint of Christian orthodoxy,"[137] Black insists in McCarthy's *The Sunset Limited* (2006) that "the first thing you got to understand is that I aint got a original thought in my head. If it aint got the lingerin scent of divinity to it then I aint interested" (13). Traditionally, the "last things" of Catholic eschatology were death, judgment, heaven, and hell— the terrifying brimstone poured out by Father Arnall in the third chapter of *Portrait of the Artist as a Young Man.* McCarthy's list "of those whom he calls the 'good writers'—Melville, Dostoyevsky, Faulkner—precludes anyone who doesn't 'deal with issues of life and death.'"[138] Years later, the writer elaborated a little: "Most people don't ever see anyone die. It used to be if you grew up in a family you saw everybody die. They died in their bed at home with everyone gathered around. Death is the major issue in the world. For you, for me, for all of us. It just is. To not be able to talk about it is very odd."[139]

Beyond last things, McCarthy's deep Catholicism can turn up in places where it is least expected, for example, in his treatment of necrophilia (sometimes linked to Catholic decadence, in the specialized sense of the phrase) and in the moral absolutism of which critics accuse him. As to the objection that McCarthy is simply too bleak in his outlook to be a "Catholic writer," however one defines that phrase, it should be pointed out that the triumph of evil in the temporal order is not unnatural to Catholic thought. In fact, evil is the order of the day, just as it is in most of McCarthy's work. The problem of evil in a God-created universe can be surpassingly more interesting than prescriptive morality or the "orthopedic moralizing" (254) of Catholicism, as he terms it in *Suttree.* In short, McCarthy's fascination with evil is inextricable from his Catholicism. It is equally inseparable from the "atavism" and "nihilism" that Matthew Guinn and Vereen Bell, respectively, ascribe to McCarthy.[140] For McCarthy, the problem of evil is the scaffolding upon which all moral questions must hang, but, paradoxically, it is least likely to be acknowledged, because a property of evil is that it always requires external attribution. The satanic Judge tells the Expriest Tobin, "Your heart's desire is to be told some mystery. The mystery is that there is no mystery." Tobin, who elsewhere refers to the Judge's "blasphemous tongue" (250), either thinks or says in response, "Aye. . . . As if he were no mystery himself, the bloody old hoodwinker" (252).[141]

This is because the Judge represents the mystery of evil, and McCarthy's fictional universe confirms Flannery O'Connor's observation that "evil is not a problem to be solved but a mystery to be endured."[142] Indeed, in some respects, this view accords more neatly with Catholic belief than with mainline American culture and values. McCarthy rewrites O'Connor's observation as a kind of parable in *All the Pretty Horses,* when Perez explains to John Grady that "superstitious" Anglos, unlike Mexicans, do not understand where "good and evil have their home." Evil is not rooted in material circumstance and cannot be destroyed, he goes on to explain. Rather, "evil is a true thing in Mexico. It goes about on its own legs" (195). And so, as O'Connor says, the mystery of it must be endured.

McCarthy's entire philosophy in literature can be seen as searching to find the right mystery to counter the mystery of evil. In part of *The Road* that has the ring of parable about it, McCarthy shows the gropingly inadequate human response to evil in its true dimensions as a group of men, finding a nest of vipers ("a great bolus of serpents") underground, burn them:

> Like the bowels of some great beast exposed to day. The men poured gaso-
> line on them and burned them alive, having no remedy for evil but only for
> the image of it as they conceived it to be. The burning snakes twisted hor-
> ribly and some crawled burning across the floor of the grotto to illuminate
> its darker recesses. As they were mute there were no screams of pain and
> the men watched them burn and writhe and blacken in just such silence
> themselves and they disbanded in silence in the winter dusk each with his
> own thoughts to go home to their suppers. (159)

The word *grotto,* with its Catholic connotations, makes an interesting choice, for it would seem that these men attempt to illuminate the sanctum sanctorum through a primitive and inadequate response to the problem of evil—and indeed, through actions that, if better understood, might be seen truly as evil in their own right. This helps to explain, allegorically, how the good intentions of religious systems have a way of running to the evils they deny. In *Blood Merid-*

ian, the celebration of the Resurrection with a mock crucifixion of Judas demonstrates the naïve approach to the problem of evil. Like his beloved Melville in "Bartleby the Scrivener," McCarthy retells the betrayal of Christ in *All the Pretty Horses.* But in McCarthy fashion the story is inverted: it is Blevins, betrayed, in a sense, by Rawlins and John Grady's failure of courage, who slips "silver" (a wad of dirty and crumpled peso notes) to his betrayers as his captors haul him away. This last gesture later buys the shiv that saves John Grady's life.[143]

As significant as betrayals in McCarthy's work are silences of the kind that answer *The Road*'s serpent burners. In "Whales and Men," McCarthy muses that even torture might be a means by which men grope for the presence of God—call it the Ahab impulse—since it would seem that he might make himself known by his very refutation and destruction. In *The Crossing,* the caretaker of the ruined church, a former Mormon, expresses this test by refutation when he tells Billy Parham, "I thought there might be evidence of something suitably unspeakable such that He might be goaded into raising his hand against it" (142). Paradoxically, God might also be revealed by acts of destruction, as the caretaker earlier explained: "I was seeking evidence for the hand of God in the world. I had come to believe that hand a wrathful one and I thought that men had not inquired sufficiently into miracles of destruction" (142). The same concern is wrapped around the sinister and engulfing horrors of cruelty in *Blood Meridian,* where, as the epigraphs suggest, evil acts are as "irresistible" as the killing of the whale—a primitive means of sounding the universe for some kind of theophany; or worse, to see if they are in accord with the universal plan.

Until the Border Trilogy, most of McCarthy's books contained some element of implicit or explicit necrophilia, which has produced a certain amount of snickering literary criticism. Some have interpreted it as proof positive that McCarthy's universe is so depraved as to lack any meaningful communion with the divine. Certainly *Child of God* would seem to make this case, and from its protagonist comes the a fortiori case that all God's children are capable of monstrously *rational* action. The necrophilia also connects, in strange ways, to McCarthy's literally subterranean Catholicism. What is necrophilia? An extreme love of death, the ultimate bride? Loving attention focused on the last things of life? In Flannery O'Connor's "A Good Man is Hard to Find," Mr. Shiftlet (conning Joyce's "The Dead") sternly reminds Lucynell Crater that "the monks of old slept in their coffins!" (176). In a good deal of southern gothic fiction, beginning notably in Poe and continuing through Faulkner's "A Rose for Emily" and McCarthy's *oeuvre,* necrophilia and incest are antifertile behaviors entwined with a sense of cultural collapse. Thomas Haddox connects necrophilia and incest to fin-de-siècle decadence. This, in turn, he links to Lewis Simpson's southern "culture of failure" and Catholic associations with aesthetic decadence. Completing the triangle, he writes, "If failure is indeed beautiful to a decadent, then the ruined, faux-aristocratic South becomes a splendid back-drop for all manner of aesthetic and erotic practice."[144] If one accepts Haddox's theory, McCarthy's interest in necrophilia, however distracting it has been to commentators, gestures more obliquely to his simultaneously Catholic and southern sensibilities.

McCarthy's interest in extravagantly cardinal sins, all common enough to the course of human history—necrophilia, cannibalism, incest, the dismem-bering of children—points to the great question of McCarthy's work: What is evil, and where does it come from? Even if no evil is unthinkable, how can what is utterly revolting to me ever be enacted by another? Sherriff Bell explains that the complete absence of a soul is what sets off the "boy" he sent to the "gas-chamber." The story borrows much from Flannery O'Connor's "A Good Man is Hard to Find." Like the Misfit, the killer knows that he is hellbound, if there is a hell, since if one rejects the divinity of Christ, nothing but "meanness" remains. And yet, like the Misfit, McCarthy's killer admits that there is no pleasure, or at least no passion, in evil acts: "The papers said it was a crime of passion and he told me there wasnt no passion to it" (3).[145]

Child of God, which ends with the dissection of its sickly fallen protago-nist, signals that evil is no mere matter of physiology, but something far more elusive—a retort to scientific materialism. In some ways, Ballard does indeed present an Antichrist. Since hell is simply self-chosen distance from God—an idea that finds plenty of support in Catholic theology—Lester's descent be-comes both morally and logically "natural." A hint at how McCarthy might rec-oncile this human perversion with divine order is to be found in an interview with his second wife, Annie DeLisle, who "suggests . . . that her former hus-band's singularly authentic literary bent has more to do with a centuries-old theological construct, with the notion that God, in His grace, can justly bestow life, and therefore adoration, on even the most imperfect creatures."[146] And why would a God-created soul be placed in a monstrous pervert, a "wormbent tabernacle" (*Suttree* 130), or, as in *The Road,* chained to a dying animal? In "Whales and Men," John Western writes to his former girlfriend about meeting a card counter (McCarthy apparently befriended J. Doyne Farmer, a physicist fascinated by gambling, and Betty Carey, a renowned poker player) who "spoke to him about evil and the power of evil and the last thing he said was that ultimately there would be nothing to worry about. Because everyone who is greater than us will love us."

Perhaps McCarthy was cribbing Saint Anselm in this dialogue. His papers show that he removed from an earlier draft the line, "Like Anselm's god, love could not be so small that things could exist outside of it."[147] Careful readers can be certain that McCarthy has explored the fine points of Catholic intellectual traditions, including various theodicies and proofs, a point confirmed in the marginalia of archival material. In the papers of the Wittliff Collections one finds phrases beloved of Jesuit logicians, such as "tertium non datur," Latinisms like "quinquagesima Sunday" (the last before Lent) and a snatch of the Athanasian Creed (box 35, folder 6), a note about Medawar's criticisms of Teilhard (box 97, folder 2), and lines from Flaubert's *Temptation of St. Anthony* (1874) in both French and English (box 19, folder 14).[148]

This last may be particularly important because of the way it triangulates James Joyce, Cormac McCarthy, and their respective mythic canvasses. *The Temptation of St. Anthony* can be read as a reworking of Circe (as mentioned earlier, important both in *Suttree* and in the critical chapter of *Ulysses*), and so, too can the Walpurgisnacht episode of Goethe's *Faust* (crucial to *Blood Meridian*). "The Circe chapter," explains Guy Davenport, "is Joyce's *Temptation*, the work's great fantasia of themes, its Descent of Orpheus into Hades, its Faust among the witches."[149] Likewise, the witches, hogs, and underworld of Knoxville swirl around *Suttree*'s fantasia. Davenport offers a wonderful treatment of Flaubert's too often bypassed *Temptation* in *The Geography of Imagination* (1997), a polymathic volume McCarthy read with great admiration and that he deemed a "marvelous book."[150] There Davenport explains that in some respects Flaubert's masterwork is the real subtext of *Ulysses,* especially the Circe chapter, pointing out that Bloom's name is kin to Anthony (the Greek word for *bloom* is *anthos*) and suggesting that "of all Bloom's guises, that of St. Anthony—Flaubert's St. Antonie—would seem to be the one that has most poignantly intensified in the fifty years of the book's existence." "The reality before Anthony was the empty desert," writes Davenport, "solitude and the adoration of God fulfilled his being. But he never saw this reality, for the devil veiled it with monsters, philosophers, professors, and the flesh. What reality there is before Bloom is harder to see, for Joyce hides it like a Heraclitean principle." What Davenport observes of Bloom is equally applicable to unstrung Cornelius Suttree: "his education has melted, the wealth of knowledge he has learned from books and newspapers is in disarray, sex is underwear, he is a Jewish Catholic Protestant Agnostic."[151]

As Davenport explains, Saint Anthony is the patron of stubborn faith and Orpheus is the patron of "art over the death of spirit."[152] Both have their part to play in McCarthy's opus. Indeed, McCarthy's notes cite *The Temptation of*

St. Anthony repeatedly, and almost all of the anathemas put forward by the devil in chapter 6 have been reworked into McCarthy's fiction, especially the teleological argument. The gnostic gospels of Eve, Judas, and Thomas assail Anthony's faith, bolstering the argument that the Judge is a gnostic archon. The fact that Glanton's party is so frequently described in religious terms—as anchorites, tonsured victims, and so on—might owe something to *The Temptation* as well. For at one point Saint Anthony does indulge in the evil thoughts of the Judge's ultimate art and finds himself "at the head of a wild army of monks slaughtering the heretics and the pagans, without mercy for age or sex."[153] Indeed, as they swarm Alexandria, they come in "whirlwinds of dust," "roaring a canticle of battle and of faith" (34). With pikes and cudgels, they "rush into one . . . mass of men," in which "the men with the long hair always reappear" (35). In his bloodlust, Anthony "disembowels—he severs throats—he fells as in a slaughter house—he hales old men by the beard, crushes children, smites the wounded," with blood "streaming from the trunks of decapitated corpses" and forming huge pools (36). The scene might recall any number of bloodlettings in McCarthy's novel, most especially the Comanche attack of chapter 4 in *Blood Meridian,* with the long-haired "legion of horribles" (54) carrying out their slaughter with "men lanced and caught up by the hair and scalped standing" (56), the Comanches disemboweling and decapitating their victims, and merging with their enemies amid the unreality of the dust.

Following the slaughter, Anthony has a vision of "a new city," overhung by a "cypress wood," where the "line of the sea is greener, the air colder" (37). McCarthy's notes quote, in French, this last verse, and there is some resemblance to the Kid's entry into San Diego after camping out in a frosty juniper wood above the sea. The devil's lectures on "physics and scientific naturalism," as Guy Davenport summarizes them,[154] of a piece with the Judge's disquisitions, terrify Saint Anthony. Here McCarthy's papers record a line from *The Temptation* that he slipped casually into *Blood Meridian:* "Those who travel in desert places do indeed meet with creatures surpassing all description" (282). Hilarion is described, in Lafcadio Hearn's translation of *The Temptation,* in terms that bear some resemblance to the Judge's fool:

> This child is small like a dwarf, and nevertheless squat of build, like one of the Cabiri; deformed withal, and wretched of aspect. His prodigiously large head is covered with white hair; and he shivers under a shabby tunic, all the while clutching a roll of papyrus. The light of the moon passing through, a cloud falls upon him. (60)

The Judge rescues the fool, who resembles a "balden groundsloth," on a night when "a fishcolored moon rose over the desert east and set their shadows by their sides in the barren light" (258). *The Temptation of St. Anthony* is valuable not just for understanding McCarthy's desert landscapes but also for comprehending McCarthy's homegrown heresiarchs (especially the Judge and Chigurh) and assorted doubt sowers, who, like Anthony's perverted Hilarion, turn to the consolations of science. Quoth the writer, it is more important to be good than it is to be smart.[155]

Cormac McCarthy may not be a closet evangelical, as some have claimed, but if he were merely didactic, his work would fade away soon enough for want of discussion. What McCarthy offers is something slightly different, a literature of warning that draws on ancient metanarratives. *No Country for Old Men* cautions of an incipient age in which life holds scant value; *The Road* complicates ethical certainties in a world where euthanasia seems very nearly a moral imperative and the ability to resist it becomes a test of faith. McCarthy succeeds at something that only the most daring writers, like Melville, can do: he recasts a biblical story, in this case of Abraham and Isaac, in a startling way that complicates the allegory and makes it newly relevant.

If McCarthy finds sympathy for the devil, a strong rebellious streak in his own character seems to have taken him away from the church and at times from his own family. Woodward writes with sensitive understatement that "the psychic cost of such an independent life, to himself and others, is tough to gauge."[156] Annie DeLisle explained that McCarthy "didn't carry insurance. He was such a rebel that he didn't live the same kind of life anybody else on earth lived."[157] Reference to "Easter, 1916" in *Suttree* brings to mind Yeats's warning about the power of ideologies: "Too long a sacrifice / Can make a stone of the heart."[158] Is McCarthy, like Sheriff Bell, become a man oddly out of time, as critics accuse him of? Even his trusted interviewer intimates that "only in his disdain for contemporary architecture, or for the modern world in general, can he sound off-key and crankish."[159] If McCarthy is indeed a truly Catholic writer and thus bears some of the same bred-in-the-bone ideological conservatism as Lafcadio Hearn and Flannery O'Connor, why should we expect him to be any more in step with modern predilections than the Roman Catholic Church itself?

In the final assessment, then, it is doubtful that McCarthy is *not* at least ethnically Catholic, and equally doubtful that he is anti-Catholic, an argument that comes not through biographical fallacy but by a careful reading of his work. If he is agnostic, judging from his texts, his outlook would seem to resemble that of Guy Schuler, who says,

> I don't believe in God but I think whales force you into these theological metaphors. Mother Theresa was interviewed a while back by a *Time* correspondent and he asked her if she didn't get discouraged with her work. I mean all she does is deal with hopeless poverty and terminal disease. And she seemed puzzled by the question. And then she said: He didn't call upon me to be successful. He just called upon me to be faithful.[160]

McCarthy's heroes, who so rarely "win," strive to keep courage and to hold open the possibility of a logos scripting their ends. In this cosmos, dignity is the only answer to death; faith is the paradoxically logical response to cosmic uncertainty; courage is love's sole defender. The origins of McCarthy's cowboys are in the born rebels, losers, and seekers of American mythology. Perhaps, without acknowledging it even to himself, he was drawn to the Southwest for its Catholic south, where he might freely explore, as John Sepich put it, "a set of conflicts he may well first have encountered growing up Catholic in Knoxville, Tennessee."[161] His fiction speaks to how the faith in which he was raised may be tied to his brooding vision and offers glimpses of his attempts to come to terms with it. As a southern Irish Catholic, he was born with only such countries as he should elect. Far-ranging, searching, and rebellious, yes; yet God-fearing and obstinately his own individual, constantly testing belief against hard experience. Perhaps a cowboy Catholic for that.

AFTER MARY FLANNERY,
MORE STRANGE HATCHLINGS

> Now if in the next twenty years we find ourselves with a batch of wild
> Southern Catholic writers who . . . have certain positive obnoxious
> qualities—such as a penchant for violence and grotesquery and
> religious enthusiasm—we are doubtless going to wonder
> how these strange birds got hatched in our nest.
>
> —FLANNERY O'CONNOR

> Catholicity has given me my perspective on the South
> and probably gives you yours.
>
> —FLANNERY O'CONNOR

> My Catholic upbringing caused me to focus on ritual and metaphor,
> both things which play an important part in my writing.
>
> —MARGARET SKINNER

Some rather colorful candidates for inclusion in this study specifically declined its terms of identification. Before his death, I wrote to William F. Buckley Jr. His mother was a debutante from (German) New Orleans, a significant part of his childhood had been spent in Texas and Mexico, and his writings admitted no doubt that he identified strongly with his father's Irish Catholic ancestry. Could he, then, be counted among southern Irish Catholic writers, notwithstanding his immaculate New England mannerisms? Buckley answered my letter, as he was famously wont to do, responding politely, in essence, that this was too faint a possibility: "I'd like to help, and there is no questioning my parents' affiliation with the South. But I am really a New Englander, so I don't think I'd qualify for your valuable study."[1]

When I put a similar question to Pat Conroy (b. 1945) after I chanced to meet him at the University of South Carolina, his good-natured response was considerably more forceful than Buckley's. Voluble, winsome, and plainspoken, he was fully in raconteur mode when he told me, in no uncertain terms, that "he couldn't stand Ireland."[2] There are reasons to take this with a grain of salt: Conroy devotes an entire chapter of *My Reading Life* (2010) to the importance of *Gone with the Wind* (1936) and explains, "I became a novelist because of *Gone with the Wind,* or more precisely, my mother raised me to be a 'Southern' novelist . . . because *Gone with the Wind* set my mother's imagination ablaze when she was a young girl in Atlanta."[3] His introduction for a new edition of Margaret Mitchell's novel comments extensively on his mother's adulation of Scarlett and her nearly religious devotion to *Gone with the Wind.* "My mother saw in *Gone with the Wind* the text of liberating herself," he told a CNN reporter. "She took [it] as the central book in her life, and made it the central book in her family."[4] Conroy went on to explain that his mother was a climber who steadfastly refused to remain in poverty. In his preface to the sixtieth-anniversary edition of *Gone with the Wind* he wrote, "It was this same Scarlett who gave Southern women like my mother new insights into the secrecies and potentials of womanhood itself, not always apparent in that region of the country where the progress of women moves most slowly."[5] In addition to the feminist solidarity that became part of Peggy Conroy's own narrative, there were ethnic and religious affinities: "Together, we visited the grave of Margaret Mitchell at Oakland Cemetery and my mother would say a decade of the rosary over her tombstone, then remark proudly that the novelist had been a Roman Catholic of Irish descent."[6] Conroy's mother did more than encourage him to pursue writing; she gave him a role model from his birth city who shared his ethnicity.

If Mitchell cited Father Ryan, Henry Grady, and Joel Chandler Harris among her literary heroes, southern Irish Catholic writers who followed her could cite the recognition of her work as a sanction for their own efforts. Some, like Pat Conroy, would face Mitchell's dilemmas of popularity. "I've always felt a bit like cheap cologne because the movies usually do buy my books," Conroy wrote to Louis Rubin in 1982. "There are always boys and centerfielders in my books and it's kind of an embarrassment to me because there are no centerfielders in Hollywood."[7] Perhaps signaling an awareness of his status as a bestselling southern writer whose work critics have sometimes treated dismissively, Conroy writes in his introduction to *Gone with the Wind,* "I have come across legions of critics that deplored my mother's taste in fiction, but this was my mother and I was heir to that taste, for better or worse."[8] He was also heir to his father's standard-flavor Irish American pride, of a piece with Gerald O'Hara's— sentimental, Catholic, and nationalist.

Or rather, he *might* have been heir to it, had not he rejected it viscerally. He is wonderfully dry in describing Scarlett when she "swears to God after rooting around for that radish in the undone garden of Tara that she will never go hungry again."[9] The "Garden of Tara" is what the old country must remain in the aspic imagination of men like Donald Conroy (Pat Conroy's father) and Gerald O'Hara. By contrast, both Mitchell's grandmother and her mother unsentimentally yielded to the demands of American success, in which looking back might indicate weakness. Like Flannery O'Connor, Conroy would come to reject any association with sham Irishness even as he wrestled with the tortured, if unshakable, Catholicism that accompanies it.

Unlike Flannery O'Connor, however, he would not allow himself to be called an Irish Catholic. Donald Patrick Conroy would explain to me that "St. Patrick's Day was like Kristallnacht at my house," when the drunken beatings his father administered, so wrenchingly recalled in *My Losing Season* (2006), reached a high frenzy. He also mentioned that his mother, a convert, made a much better Catholic than his father. During a trip to the West Coast, he rankled members of the Irish American community there, whose attitude toward him was, as he put it, "Who the f—— are you?"[10] In *South of Broad* (2010), when the protagonist Leo Bloom runs into the sister of a classmate, Conroy has a chance to confront the heart of Irish American life, where "family is a contact sport"[11] in a few lines of dialogue:

> "Mary Ellen Driscoll wore pigtails," I say. "You were a Catholic family and I always wondered why you didn't go to Bishop Ireland."
>
> "No money," Catherine explains. "Dad was a bum, Mom an angel. Same old story. The Irish psycho play."
>
> "I know it well," I say. (507)

Like the nonexistent Yamacraw Island of *The Water is Wide* (1972), named after the old Irish neighborhood in Savannah, Conroy has some fun in alluding to Charleston's Catholic high school, named for Bishop John England, who was, confusingly, most certainly from Ireland (Mary Boykin Chesnut admired his "richest of brogues"). And what he terms the Irish "psycho play," a familiar part of his childhood, is a topic that he seems bound to return to, though he is wary of all the attendant clichés. Conroy's mother "always won the award for most books checked out of the library" and presented him with a copy of Joyce's *Ulysses* when he was in the ninth grade:

> "I'm sure she never read it, and I had no idea what it was about. She told me, 'It's based on *The Odyssey*.'"
>
> "'The hell it is,' I told her."

Only as an adult, Conroy says, did he learn to appreciate Joyce, even visiting Ireland to follow in the original Bloom's footsteps in and out of pubs, "becoming a cliché of my time."[12]

Thus the writer who could not stand Ireland nevertheless made a literary pilgrimage there. Never afraid to go his own way, Conroy told me about a stunning repudiation of the Catholic portion of his Irish Catholic identity, saying that he was visited by a monsignor who asked him to autograph books for John Paul II. The monsignor explained that Conroy was the pope's "favorite American writer." Poking fun at the grandiose titles of the prelates, Conroy gleefully told me that he declined a papal audience. His father was flabbergasted.

The invitation came when Pope John Paul II visited Columbia and the University of South Carolina campus on September 11, 1987. According to an article in the *New York Times,* then bishop Ernest L. Unterkoefler, of Charleston, South Carolina, had visited the Vatican in 1984, where he was "asked a curious question by Pope John Paul II. 'How is it to live with 98 percent non-Catholic people?'" "It's a great challenge," was his laconic response. The *Times* article goes on to point out, South Carolina could then claim "the smallest percentage of Catholics of any state; 2.1 percent of the state's 3.35 million residents, just over 70,000, are Catholic." The percentage had remained virtually unchanged since 1850, when perhaps 1.3 percent of South Carolinians, some 6,030 souls, were Catholics.[13] Conroy's upbringing as a military brat in places like Beaufort, South Carolina, posed its own challenges of assimilation, and his wicked satiric sensibility might well have been honed by his lifelong perception of himself as something of a misfit in the WASP's nest inviolate.

If he has declared utter disaffection from the church in the past, Conroy's memoirs and fiction paint a considerably more complicated picture and hint at a lover's quarrel. Ironic for a man who became alienated from Roman Catholicism, it was a Catholic subculture that may have come closest to giving him a fleeting sense of belonging. *My Losing Season* and *South of Broad,* taken together, offer readers an intimate map of the small Catholic world of Conroy's South, from Bishop England High School to the Sacred Heart Convent of the Mercy Sisters in Belmont, North Carolina. In *My Losing Season* Conroy vividly describes the atmosphere of Catholicism during his youth and explains how basketball brought him into the crosscurrents of Catholic schools and a world beyond the South. Conroy recalls that before an away game in New Orleans when he played for the Citadel, "the five Catholics on the team rose early for mass at St. Louis Cathedral. Conroy, DeBrosse, Bornhorst, Connor, and Kennedy—

you can hear the shuffle of immigrants' feet from Ireland, Germany, and France in that muster of fresh American names" (189). His relatively pleasant memories of parochial education at Blessed Sacrament in Alexandria, Virginia (grades six through eight) and Sacred Heart Academy in Belmont, North Carolina (ninth grade), where "even the nuns were pretty . . . as well as being the kindest women wearing habits and rosary beads who ever taught me," might be set against his time at the all-male Jesuit Gonzaga High School in Washington, DC, where "the whole school smelled like eau de Catholic boy, cheap pipe tobacco, and stiff drinks on the rocks. Gonzaga was the kind of place you'd not even think about loving until you'd left it for a couple of years" (60).

When he finally arrived at Beaufort High School, old habits died hard: "My Catholic education had brainwashed me to such an extent that I had never sat down in any classroom without saying a prayer, then having a nun or priest grant permission for me to sit" (75). *My Losing Season* also documents his loss of faith during his college years, when he "was receiving the Eucharist every day of my life and fighting this war with faithlessness with every cell of my body," but "could feel the withdrawal taking place without my consent" (275)—a scene reprised, in some respects, in *South of Broad,* when Leo King's depression is not palliated by valium or bourbon: "Even receiving Communion every day cannot daunt its repellant powers" (503).

Early aspirations to enter the priesthood and a Catholic secondary education left quite a stamp on Conroy's character: "I was so prudish as a young man, so Catholic-shaped and South-haunted and goody-two-shoes, that my roommates used to tease me that I never looked at the pictures of girls in *Playboy* magazine" (255). In parallel to Flannery O'Connor's phrase, "the Christ-haunted South," Conroy describes himself as "South-haunted," perhaps aware that southern claims on manners and conformity are in competition for his conscience, as they are for that of *South of Broad*'s Leo Bloom King, who suffers "the Southern boy's disease of needing to be liked by everyone I met" (69). Conroy's awareness of southern religious traditions and rhetoric made his experience of pre-Vatican II Catholicism seem more stultifying, as lines like these in *South of Broad* suggest:

In the Catholic world, the priest's sermon at Sunday Mass was the only part of the service rendered in English. But it might as well have been spoken in Sanskrit for all the spiritual nourishment it provided. When it came to their homilies, there was nothing living that a Catholic priest could not put to sleep. (85)

He also recalls roving nuns whose rosary beads sounded a warning of approach "like eastern diamondbacks"—Flannery O'Connor would surely approve —and one sister who, whenever she heard sirens, led his class "in the recitation of the Lord's Prayer that it was not a Catholic home on fire" (27). His understanding of the Catholic mind is profound, for example, when he writes that Leo might "pray to Steve [his dead brother] and not the God who had stolen [him]" (103).

Incisive though his understanding of this Catholic world might be, Conroy complains, with some justification, that he has been passed over by the canons of academic taste, fated to be marginalized by his sheer popularity. Certainly he can write in the more overtly "literary" vein that academic critics favor, and there are moments in *South of Broad* when he does precisely that. Even so, *South of Broad,* in its obvious deference to the screen, remains defiantly indifferent to "academic" endearments, even though it is perhaps the most allusive Conroy work to date, with Conroy plainly signaling that he would have the book be his *Ulysses* for the city of Charleston. Calling Charleston by its sobriquet, the Holy City, plays at double meanings, both satiric and, in protagonist Leopold Bloom King's case, purposefully Catholic. This is a city where "the sun light[s] up the harbor with a deep shade of gold that makes it look like a Communion cup" (510). Monsignor Max, who plays a large part in Leo's religious development, utters "I will go to the altar of God," words delivered "in his operatic voice," which "washed over me like a clean stream from my boyhood, the delicate latticework of memory and language" (21). Of course, the words from the *Introibo* at the start of the Mass also begin *Ulysses.* Leo's love is ecumenical in character, beginning with "the touch of God on my tongue, His taste in my palate, His bloodstream mingling in my own" and the knowledge that "the Church was patient and would always be waiting for me to return" (20). Unlike Joyce, he holds to this hope despite having every reason to reject the church. The lifeblood of *South of Broad* has a Catholic character: Conroy's Liffey is the Ashley, a "saltwater river" that permits one to "return to first things," in Conroy's Catholic language, "as pretty a river as ever a god could make" (17).

There is a Joycean playfulness in Conroy's love of reference too. When he mentions holes in a football team's offensive line "that you could drag a dead mule through" (337), he makes a writer's in-joke, drawing once again on Jerry Mills's widely circulated observation that the presence of a dead mule in a story is the true litmus test of the southern writer. Joyce's Stephen Dedalus, for whom Leo King's lost brother is named, famously set out in *Portrait of the Artist as a Young Man* "to forge in the smithy of my soul the uncreated conscience of my race."[14] In Conroy's text, a boy in puberty first discovers the Joycean furnace within, "that his body has become a firestorm and undiscovered volcano where lava is made in the furnace of his loins" (343). And a girl's first experience of menstruation connects her, like Joyce's archetypal Anna Livia Plurabelle, to "the sacred stream of life . . . the world's thunderous answer to decay and death" (343).

The lifeblood of *South of Broad* has both a Catholic and a Joycean character. There are other effluvia in *South of Broad* too. Writing for the *Washington Post,* Chris Bohjalian dubbed Pat Conroy "the Prince of Tears," explaining that he "began to feel that the characters were crying a lot, which wouldn't have bothered me if the characters were children. They're not." Bohjalian recorded dozens of times when characters "cry, sob, tear, weep, wail and well up," but it seems at least possible that Conroy had other, less maudlin aims in these tiny tears.[15] They are made of the same saltwater that trickles through the major incidents of the book, among them Leo King's coming of age, his first romance, and the destructive rescripting of Charleston via Hurricane Hugo. "'Riverrun,' Leo," are the words Sheba Poe's psychotic father uses to menace the teenager, "taunting" him "with the first word in Joyce's silly-assed novel *Finnegans Wake*" (105). But later, "standing in front of [a] fire," he will redeem the word by teaching children "the most important lesson" they will ever learn: how to write a story. He begins by borrowing from Joyce with the word *Riverrun:* "As the river runs beneath us, I dive deeply into the sweet-water fathoms of story itself" (476). Elsewhere Conroy writes pointedly, "You can bury all the streams and creeks you want to, but salt waterways remember where they came from" (470)—an answer to *Finnegans Wake*'s diasporic longing for wholeness, represented in the Anna Livia Plurabelle sections. The novel undertakes one *Ulysses*-like genre experiment too, when Conroy reconfigures the entire story in mythic terms as a children's tale, told by Leo, in chapter 28.

Bloomsday marks the last day of the novel, and Joyce is honored with the last word of the novel too, which echoes Molly Bloom's life-affirming "Yes." It also marks the day that Leo's mother was taken to the convent she would later leave so that the "date acquired a magical significance" (89), and it becomes significant again in bringing together a lifelong circle of friends who first met on Bloomsday in the summer of 1969 with the tagline, "Anything can happen during a Bloomsday Summer" (511). Leo has little love for the novel that is his namesake, but demonstrates a Joycean turn of mind in his expatriate sensibilities and the pleasure he takes in satire. He is at once a southerner abroad and a southerner not fully at home in his Catholic outsiderism (reflected in his self-deprecating "Papist" perspective [456]). Conroy seems to appreciate how dangerous Joyce's religious defections were in the eyes of his society. Though Leopold Bloom King is named for the protagonist of his mother's favorite book, Monsignor Max prefers G. K. Chesterton to Joyce, "a flagrant anti-Catholic" (20). The "convent romance" of Leo's religiously devout parents has the makings of melodrama, replete with a censorious nun who reads the thwarted lovers' letters yet ultimately approves of the courtship. It nevertheless makes a larger point about how faith can change the course of life for the young, who are especially open to its exactions.

Ultimately, the book details Leo King's difficult return to a faith that "rejected the corpse of my brother" who committed suicide (20), partly through the kindness of one Monsignor Maxwell Sadler. The reversion to faith is hardly facile, though; it turns out that Sadler was in fact Leo's brother's rapist. Pat Conroy was prostrated by the suicide of his youngest brother, Tom, in August 1994. Tom Conroy suffered from paranoid schizophrenia, an illness reputedly all too common to the Irish, and Pat pledged to write about it in "the fullness of time."[16] Facing a series of personal disasters, he would be a long time in the writing, briefly mentioning Tom Conroy's suicide in *My Losing Season* but not grappling with the incident in fiction until *South of Broad* some fifteen years later. There are many elements of autobiography in *South of Broad,* though Conroy deliberately mixes them up. Harrington Canon, for example, is reminiscent of Conroy's meeting, as a teenager, with South Carolina's then poet laureate.[17] Other biographical material is distanced from the real incidents of Conroy's frangible marriages and stormy family relationships. As far from the east as the west—that is how far the father of *The Great Santini* (1976) is from the father of *South of Broad,* a novel that imagines the perfect pap personified in Jasper King (though an incestuous, murderous dad stalks *South of Broad* too). Tellingly, a brother's suicide is laid at the feet of the church in the novel. Conroy's narrative modus operandi, picking through psychological wreckage to give a forensic account of disaster, seems somehow to quail before suicide, which by its nature effaces meaning. And yet his work criticizes humanely, as one of various Catholic double standards, the kind of double damnation reserved for suicides.

But it is a concern with sexual sin, not to mention sexual abuse, that perhaps most reveals Conroy's Catholic cast of mind. Arguably, Lindsay King most embodies a realized Catholicism as she "yields to [the Eucharist's] mysteries with a submission that permitted no contention or rivalry" (85). By contrast, Starla King represents the incarnation of the anti-Catholic when she delivers her "soul-killing tirade" and announces to her husband Leo, a childless "uncle" to many, that she aborted their child. Leo ruminates over this heart of darkness: "I think of my own son, the one whose arms and legs were counted by an unnamed nurse—'one two, three, four: all accounted for, Doctor'—and think of playing catch with him or taking him fishing in the Ashley River where my father fished with me" (419).

Conroy's engagement with Catholicism in *South of Broad* is complicated but persistent, acknowledging a church that at its worst is the sum of human hypocrisies and at its best an unlikely avenue to godhead. It both vindicates and dismisses Joyce's genius. And so, in spite of itself, it says much about an Irish Catholic writer who loathes that label.

Among writers at work today, Valerie Sayers (b. 1952), who grew up in Beaufort, South Carolina, not much more than thirty miles (as the crow flies) from Flannery O'Connor's Savannah, writes most expressly about the experience of being Irish Catholic in the South. To read Sayers is to enter directly into the worldview of a southern Irish Catholic; in this respect, any of her novels will offer a representative vision. The middle of seven children born to transplants Paul and Janet Hogan Sayers, Valerie Sayers would self-consciously choose to identify with southern culture despite self-professed "cultural ignorance."[18] By her own account, her childhood in Beaufort profoundly shaped her worldview. As it happened, her life path was such that she would not go home again, or at least she would do so only infrequently. After leaving for college, she spent several decades largely in New York, until her appointment in 1993 to the English faculty at the University of Notre Dame, where she directed the creative writing program and now chairs the English department. Asked in 2010 how southerners have received her work, she replied, "Oh, the only people who read my work in the South are my family and some generous reviewers and other Southern writers, and people who read my kind of books are generally the most tolerant of folks. Some friends from high school have been kind enough to read one or two. Being a non-best-selling writer (well, *that* was a gentle way to put it to myself) means a writer can fly *way* beneath the radar."[19]

With her ear for southern dialect and her eye for regional peculiarities, Sayers's writing is often infused with the *terroir* of her Catholic South. Though distinctly in the region's religious minority during her childhood, she did not feel herself precisely embattled:

Along the coast Catholics were plentiful enough to thrive. Though we were officially designated a mission parish, we had three nuns imported from New York and three priests—a pastor and two curates—all witty and sophisticated enough to leave me with the mistaken impression that Catholics were by definition intellectuals. We were a jolly, social bunch: Catholics drank and smoked and danced, and my Baptist friends were scandalized by our raucous ways. In the summer we bunked at Camp Saint Mary's, on the Okatee River, where we recited the Magnificat at picnic tables and met Catholic kids from upstate who told us they tried to keep their religion quiet, on account of the Klan. My mother insisted on the opposite: We must let people know we were Catholic, and if we accidentally wore a bit of orange on Saint Patrick's Day, back we went for greener clothing.[20]

Sayers grew up with an awareness of the importance of being Irish. When asked to define the "authentic Irishman," she riffed on James Joyce's *Portrait of the Artist as a Young Man* (1916): "The one living in silence, exile, and cunning?"[21] Within the nexus of the small Catholic world of coastal South Carolina and Georgia, Valerie Sayers and Pat Conroy, one generation removed from Flannery O'Connor, were likely to meet, and indeed they did cross paths. Graduated from Beaufort High School in 1963, Pat Conroy returned from the Citadel as a rosy-cheeked teacher in the autumn of 1967, enthralling students, including Sayers, who took his psychology class. (Sayers's father, a civilian psychologist who vetted Parris Island recruits, liked to cross-examine her about the course.) The Beaufort the two writers knew was an unassuming military beach town of "some 7,500 souls" that "held rich and poor at a short arm's length from one another." The prevailing atmosphere of beach town insouciance, military functionalism, and older South brought together shotgun shacks and the shabby genteel of old cottages. "If I was acutely aware of wealth and poverty, I was also pretty sure my family's identity wasn't based on economics but on religion. We were Catholics in the Protestant South."[22]

Sayers graduated from Beaufort High School to attend Fordham University in 1969—and like Conroy, she returned to teach for a year in Beaufort, in her case, "at a brand-new technical college, where my classes were almost evenly black and white and full of frank, angry, forgiving talk about race. It was a hopeful time to be living in the South, possibility crackling everywhere."[23] Both Sayers and Conroy were protégés of John Eugene "Gene" Norris and Millen Ellis, legendary English teachers and proto-integrationists at Beaufort High School.[24] Sayers remembers her teachers this way:

[Pat Conroy was] a dead-serious teacher: great joking performer, but extremely rigorous and a gifted lecturer. He gave us a college-level intro psychology class. Gene Norris was a wonderful soul, gentle and sardonic in equal measure; he offered us long lists of American literature to read and then sent us off to read—devour—it. Millen Ellis was a wonderfully quirky teacher: he had us write one of our exams in Faulknerian style, which more than any single act I was asked to do in any class anywhere made me think I might actually *be* a writer. When we did a big poetry project he assigned us each one poem to examine in depth and raised his eyebrows when he gave me "Ode to the Confederate Dead." He knew just how much it would provoke me. They *liked* gawky ill-formed teen-agers—they delighted in us—which I think is the only insight you really need about teaching: if you like your students, you enjoy them and you expect the world of them.[25]

Sayers's novel *Who Do You Love?* (1991) speaks to the charged days of integration turmoil in Beaufort. In the context of the novel, the title lyric, borrowed from Bo Diddley, has the texture of the Song of Songs, where Christ is the pursuing lover: "I'm a old woman's wish and a young woman's dream." The novel also reflects the whose-side-are-you-on stakes that raged within her family and the community at large:

My father was very liberal, my mother unpredictable. She went to confession over the Gulf of Tonkin resolution: she didn't think we should be carrying out that war (the priest told her not to worry). She boycotted Nestle over their distribution of infant formula throughout Africa. She is also extremely conservative about many issues and has to put up with her children lecturing her over her Republican voting habits.[26]

Growing up in a military town also shaped the way that Sayers viewed human conflict and the politics of conscience:

My father had been in the navy and disliked the macho culture of the marines, though he liked many individual marines well enough. A terrible moment between us: I was a snot-nosed college freshman, seventeen years old, when I asked him whether working for the marines didn't make him feel guilty during the Vietnam War. The marines, of course, were paying my tuition. He said yes: just that, just yes. What a good man he was. I learned later that he had started a memoir about his journey toward an antiwar stance he hadn't yet fully defined, but he died before he got more than a chapter or two in. That encounter of course fueled my own interest in pacifism.[27]

The necessity of taking a stand, so much a part of the zeitgeist, became a motif in Sayers's writing on race. One sees why in her recollections:

> I was still in junior high when Beaufort High was integrated—the first student, Rowland Washington, was by all accounts a paragon of dignity. I went to high school with his younger brother Craig, now a musician, and a friendly, funny guy when we were in high school. Jefferson Davis [a black student and first-wave school integrator in *Who Do You Love?*] is imagined but certainly suggested by multiple BHSers [Beaufort High Schoolers], male and female, who performed an intricate dance: the black students who integrated that school were restrained, warm, demanding of respect, patient, impatient. I don't mean to suggest that all the black kids I knew were saints . . . but the first students had to choose to be there, and they were all most definitely brave.
>
> The Church didn't have much to say on the subject of racial integration in Beaufort: a shame, in all senses. Teachers had mixed reactions and it was hard to know what most of them were thinking: no stirring inspirational speeches for us. But I'll say one thing for integration in the South—it changed people's minds so fast you could get whiplash watching them work it through. I was just appalled when I got to New York City and discovered the racism there, because I had spent a childhood inventing an enlightened New York in my imagination.[28]

Sayers describes the childhood atmosphere of Jim Crow in terms strikingly similar to those used by Andre Dubus, who, like her, came from a family with Irish ancestors, was connected to the military, and was raised as a Roman Catholic in a southern port town. Both authors experienced the latent guilt of white privilege in the surreal racial codes at the movie theater, still ground zero for the mingling of classes and races in public space. She recalls her local theater, the Breeze, in fiction and in essay, while Dubus remembers film escapism ruined in "Sorrowful Mysteries" (1983), a coming-of-age story.[29] Both writers recount how their sense of outrage was toned by a social gospel imperfectly received at church. Sayers writes movingly about the halting steps and mutual awkwardness of conciliation, for example, in *The Distance Between Us* (1994), when a documentarian turns his lens to "the help" of his youth, only to find himself mired in the complexities of unresolved history, compensation, and double-edged good intentions.

In addition to writing about the moral fragility that perpetuates racial stalemate, Sayers investigates the tensions endemic to the Irish Catholic experience of the South, the relationship between politics and religion, the ensuing inner and outer conflicts of conformity and rebellion, and the divine sense in the madness of faith and family. Her exploration of Irish Catholic identity in the South, in America, and over the Atlantic is unusually balanced, sensitive to the interfering Yank on Irish soil and at the same time to the dilemma of American rootlessness. *The Distance Between Us* in particular offers a searching exploration of many varieties of Irish identity. Sayers's work is open to the great human intelligence of the Irish people, while unapologetically showing their warts. And it takes on "phony" Irish boosterism of the kind that Flannery O'Connor disliked and yet is open to the possibility that to be Irish is to stage Irishness. In short, Sayers's relationship with both Irishness and Catholicism— terms she does not shy away from—complicates any facile identification.

Indeed, *Brain Fever* (1996) remains one of her favorite projects, precisely because it was "the most daunting." "I was frightened to write in a man's voice," she explained, "frightened to contemplate madness from the inside out, frightened to confine the action to the space of a liturgical forty days. As I tell my students, if it scares you, it must be what you're meant to write."[30] Because she is a *rara avis*—a southern Irish Catholic writer whose stories have an ethnic flavor to them—Sayers, like Flannery O'Connor, has occasionally dumbfounded critics. Whereas O'Connor admitted to mixed feeling about Dorothy Day's activism, Sayers's writing bespeaks a life of bold convictions in the mold of the Catholic Worker Movement. Sometimes her daring is in the craft of her fiction: she drops a screenplay *in media res* into her novel *The Distance Between Us,* and in *Brain Fever* she imagines a male protagonist who is sliding into what is conventionally called insanity. Critics who took issue with the latter failed to credit her—as women rarely are credited—for writing a male protagonist, and those who took issue with the former failed to notice that Sayers's screenplay is the knot that must be untied to resolve the novel.[31]

On the whole, critical praise for Sayers's work has been uniformly positive— perhaps a little too blandly positive, since this verges on a form of patronization. She has been seen as an heir apparent to Flannery O'Connor's spiritual universe as well as Walker Percy's troubled, sensual southern Catholicism. One senses a real kinship there, certainly, with Sayers, like Percy, taking the trouble to understand the semantic wrinkles of Søren Kierkegaard's work, but she has not always been given her due for besting Percy in important regards. Unlike Percy, she was not raised to be a southern conservative with the burden of family history, apropos to which she writes, "If I chafed against the ongoing lessons in How to Be a Great Lady (lesson one: bat those eyelashes) and railed against the Small-Mindedness of the South, I suppose I secretly rejoiced that my little rebellions looked outsize in Beaufort. It didn't appear that I was doomed to be a Southern belle anytime soon."[32]

Whereas Percy was given to scourging the temple with the zeal of the convert, resounding his dissatisfaction with modernity and his fixation with sexual sin in novels such as *Lancelot* (1977), Sayers's work insists that the mere fact of human fallenness is no reason to abandon hope or to expect the world to come unstrung. Rather, this is something to be worked out in both the human and the divine order of things and in the fashion common to Irish and Irish American writers, to be talked through even where silence prevails. Reflecting on didacticism and writing, Sayers says she likes what the writer Susan Sontag says "about art's need to disturb, to provoke, to unsettle."[33] Consequently, her novels brim with the real messiness and moral missteps that characterize ordinary human life. Although they abound in an awareness of Catholic intellectual traditions, they are too exuberant, too wryly bemused to tumble into gloomy caverns of ethical abstraction. Sayers's protagonists confront the humiliations of naïveté and the wounds of experience, recognizing somehow, in the midst of it all, the possibility of triumph.

One gets a sense of the making of a unique voice, of vocation revealed, in her responses in interviews conducted via e-mail in August 2010 and January 2012.[34]

What was the spirit of Catholicism in the Sayers household? How was being Irish American honored?

Both were givens . . . intrinsically a part of daily life. We said the rosary every night at 9:15 and we children moaned that 9:15 always came smack-dab in the middle of a TV show. My mother went to daily mass when that was possible, and one of us—the one currently in a fervent phase—might go along. I loved mass; I loved all the sacraments, especially confession; I loved Good Friday most of all. Does this suggest I have something in common with Mel Gibson? Hope not. I do think imagining the Crucifixion helped me struggle with all that terrified me: Anne Frank, the bloody car wrecks and shark attacks around the Sea Islands, iron lungs and childhood cancer and insanity. I was decidedly into the suffering end of things, the "giving up," the pat on my own back. My father was also very much a part of the parish, but mocked showy piety and put a good brake on my sanctimonious tendencies. (He was not part of that daily rosary.)

As for being Irish, I thought that meant liking puns, being witty and musical and on the right team. Though one grandmother emigrated (from Killorglin, Co. Kerry), the other side of the family had been here much longer, and whatever sense we had of being Irish was pretty standard: toora-loora-loora stuff. We sang *She died of the fayver and no one could save her* and worked our sad selves up. I did not learn much Irish history or literature or tradition for that matter, till college . . . but we followed The Troubles closely. My dad was keen on Bernadette Devlin. And if anyone asked me who I was, that might have been the first tag I trotted out.

Your work touches on some of the ways that southern Catholics feel set apart from other southerners. What did it mean to you to grow up Catholic in the middle of a WASP's nest? What differences were most salient?

Like the protagonist of [Flannery O'Connor's] "A Temple of the Holy Ghost," I thought Catholics were vastly superior to Protestants: we were intelligent, good-humored, broad-minded, well-read, decent. I had no evidence for this whatsoever. Certainly the parish of St. Peter's did absolutely nothing to promote civil rights, though there were role models for me there. My father spoke of civil rights as the moral imperative of our time, and there was a wonderful woman named Mae Clements who was, I believe, some kind of activist—she spoke as if she were, in any case, and that made a big impression on me. I sensed that Catholics were more liberal, but really I think I just wanted them to be.

Culturally, however, there was no question: WASPs were uptight, "polite," separated by caste. Catholics were noisy and a little crass, but by God they had fun. Or perhaps that was just the identity I wanted us to have.

How did your parents approach Protestant/Catholic tensions in Irish history?

They made sure we knew what the right side was. I was stunned to learn, in adulthood, how many Protestants were involved in Republican movements. I was raised with two biases: against the English (this was mainly implicit rather than explicit and never applied to the particular) and (this one was more good-humored) against Protestants.

The Irish Catholic mothers in your novels are at once omnipresent censors and paradoxically faintly present, willed, as it were, to a place over the shoulder. To what extent are these dreadnaught mothers specifically Irish Catholic? Irish? Catholic? Do you see their relationships with their daughters as more than usually fraught? Beyond the scope of your fiction, is there anything you would say to characterize the Irish Catholic mother?

Unusually fraught? No. Not among women of my generation, anyway.

Some of my best friends are mothers. . . . Come to think of it, I am one myself. My ninety-two-year-old mother is quite an amazing combination of charm and warmth. She has always been so generous that I think of my siblings' generosity as a natural extension of her own. She's also ingenious: I am forever grateful that she got me to New York by calling up everyone she'd known twenty years before and tracking down leads till she found me a place and a way to live while I was going through college (I was what's now known as an au pair but then just a live-in babysitter).

So I don't think of any of my mothers as *terrifying*. Terrified, maybe. When I was growing up, mothers were under such perfection-pressure that they put on amazing plasti-faces for their children's visitors—but I'd learn later how many of them were alcoholic or prone to nervous breakdowns or just downright miserable.

The sex stuff is very much a product of its time, though I do suspect Irish Catholics were more adept at repression than many, maybe most, ethnic groups (easy enough to see how they got in the habit: delayed reproduction means fewer mouths to feed in a struggling culture, but that historical understanding isn't much help to a sexually confused adult, much less a teenager).

I like all of my fictional mothers at least a little bit and some of them (Doris especially, but also Norah Burke and Lola Morehouse, and certainly Mary Faith Rapple) a lot. I'm glad Doris *survives* having all those children and I like the way you can't shut her up (I realize this is not what most readers think of as an endearing trait). Some of my readers have assumed that Dolores Rooney is some kind of portrait of my own mother, but she could not be more different.

Most of these women don't have a particular gift for motherhood, but I'm not convinced that a lot of women in contemporary culture do (Franny does enjoy her children: bonus points). And yes, their Irish Catholicism envelops most of them: like Maura with her communion veil, they grew up longing for sainthood, but were diverted by high heels and mascara and Barbie, diverted by their own desires. I am a daughter of feminism, and interested in exploring the legacy of the burden these women carry: the expectation that they be saints and pure and perfect mothers and also endlessly desirable. *That* old story, amplified in the South. I'm on their side before I get rolling, but I do feel obliged to be . . . frank about their foibles. And sometimes I am (not too cheaply I hope) looking for a laugh. I maybe have abused Doris in that regard, which is maybe why I'm so fond of her. Mary Faith Rapple was my first attempt to embody all those pressures, so I have a deep and abiding affection for her, and regard that first novel as the closest to allegory.

Did you learn anything from Flannery O'Connor? How did she influence your work? How is her work meaningful to writers now? To you?

In March 2012, I'm delivering a short paper at Fordham University—the Curran Center's celebration of sixty years of *Wise Blood*—with the title "The View from O'Connor's Shadow." You have already pointed out my geographical, religious, and cultural proximity to O'Connor's legacy, and her shadow seemed quite large and dark when I was starting out—talk about the anxiety of influence. As one of only three or four women writers I studied as an undergraduate, she also held a special place of hope for me (here we are deep in romanticized literary hierarchical territory). I was a devotee of her fierce humor, her insistence on the primacy of religious belief as her subject, and her very sentences: my students now often find those sentences a tough slog and I find myself losing patience. O'Connor? A slog? That language is music I want to hum.

But from the very beginning, I knew I didn't have her gifts. She is not just a rare bird, she's the only one of her species, so why try to copy? Harold Bloom and I may not agree about much, but I do like his idea that the great writers are strange, and FO'C strangeness wasn't something I could have absorbed or wanted to duplicate: I had to find my own strangeness. For complicated reasons, I'm not nearly as fierce a moral judge as she was or as merciless a satirist. (I will admit to hiding behind her, however. I like to read her most withering comments on beginning writers to my fiction students. They never laugh quite as hard as I do.)

My own fiction seeks to hold psychological and emotional depth in balance with conceptual and intellectual depth; O'Connor often tips the scale in favor of the conceptual, of the moral point. Her work leans toward the allegorical, which appeals to me and shows up in my work, but I am more attracted to complication, ambiguity, layer upon layer of possibility in both the narrative and the moral sense. (I will also admit here that today, as a more experienced reader, I find her more ambiguous and open-ended than I once believed her to be.) Finally, the formal classical structure of her fiction (of her stories particularly, which all follow the same arc) appeals to me as reader of a different era's work, but not as writer exploring narrative possibility in 2012: and that is as it should be.

There's so much to say about this subject that I'm about to write a paper about it. I will simply end by saying that the stab of jealousy I feel when I read FO'C is still, and ever will be, acute.

Who Do You Love? is set on the eve before and day of the Kennedy assassination. *I've talked to Irish Catholic families in Savannah who viewed JFK as an embarrassment to Catholics and others who revered him. How did he figure in your household? In your life? Did you idolize him in the way of Kate Rooney?*

Revered in our household. I was Kate Rooney's age, almost, when he was killed: one of the first great sorrows of my life. I don't think I idolized him quite the way she does; she sees him almost as a lover-figure, a movie star crush, and I believe I perceived him as fatherly: like my own father, in fact. I saw JFK as kindly and firm, and after he sent the troops to Alabama, I thought of him as the civil rights president (I love Taylor Branch's history of the King years, and the way he traces our misperceptions of Kennedy's attitude toward civil rights). I was consumed with civil rights by the time I was eleven or so. It was a minority position, and that was my favorite position. I was a deeply contrary child, so the South was made for me: I could be contrary to most everything in the culture.

Søren Kierkegaard enjoys a large presence in your work, as does Dorothy Day. Aquinas, Augustine, and company are there, too. What other religious figures and thinkers do you find compelling?

Thomas Merton, St. Francis of Assisi, St. Teresa of Avila. Bill Moyers, Jimmy Carter, Sr. Helen Préjean, Thich Nhat Hanh. Desmond Tutu I mentioned earlier. In the broadest terms, most of the religious thinkers I admire are activists in one way or another . . . and perhaps this is the case among secular philosophers who've influenced me, too: [Hannah] Arendt, [Susan] Sontag, [Albert] Camus (*The Plague* is worth scores of "religious" novels). I am greatly influenced by feminism, but not a great reader of theoretical texts: Tillie Olsen's odd collage *Silences* is one of my favorites because of its subversive, writerly form and because of the way it links the female writer's dilemma to the strug-

gling male's. I am, as FO'C says, no inerrleckshual, or however she spelled it.
. . . Indeed, I'm a dilettante in the world of philo, where the prose is so often
like wet concrete. Even my man Søren can be a trial. I find much of my phi-
losophy disguised in or as fiction—George Eliot, Tolstoy (even if he did lose it
there at the end), Faulkner, [Heinrich] Böll, [Walker] Percy, [Muriel] Spark,
[J. F.] Powers. A few Catholics in there—and among contemporary novelists,
I do find myself attracted to once-a-Catholic writers like Robert Stone, Louise
Erdrich, Toni Morrison, George Saunders. Hilary Mantel: top of the pops. But
I will stop with the list-making already: many writers of all stripes to admire,
and I believe the question had to do with religious thinkers.

*How does being a southerner of Irish descent inform your thinking about "win-
ners and losers" in history? Do notions of loss inform your religious worldview?*

I've never identified with the Confederacy—it's always the other South that
calls up my affections—so the question's especially tricky (and it's doubly tricky
because the South may have lost, but the Irish eventually won). This idea of
loss *does* inform my religious worldview, in the sense that the story of Christ's
suffering transcends any traditional understanding of winning and losing.

*Your fiction observes how the cult of southern womanhood can be stifling—and
perhaps southern manhood, too. Was there a moment in your life when you realized that growing up in the South had shaped your sense of gender roles?*

I probably had a *physical* awareness in the labor room, as I was born.

Is there some sort of heightened awareness there?

Oh, brother, is there a heightened awareness. When I teach Southern fiction,
I like my students to ponder the "Key-Ice" ceremony at the University of Alabama that W. J. Cash describes in *The Mind of the South;* it's a wonderfully
creepy commingling of the concepts of purity and frigidity. I also like to show
them the pictures of the Mississippi State Capitol statue dedicated to the Ladies
of the Confederacy: two of them are shown cradling a Confederate soldier. The
four sides are inscribed to mothers, daughters, sisters, and wives, as if to say,
Ladies, all this slaughter was to save your virtue.

I grew up learning how to simper and primp and generally be just as false
as I could possibly be. I loved it. I was an arrogant little kid who thought I was

utterly above it. I thought I could *define* myself against this absurd standard of "the Lady." I was a tomboy (in an uncoordinated, unathletic kind of way) and crazy for boys always: and I never thought I'd succumb to that southern belle stuff. Then I turned eleven. Things got rough in the presence of desire: Southern women—women in general, but in the South the lessons can be extreme—are taught to be the objects of desire, and so desire itself arrives as an alien visitor, possibly knocking on the wrong door. I imagine the rigid gender roles made things rough, maybe rougher, for boys. Like the mothers of my childhood, my boyfriends were always cracking up or breaking down or generally having a tough time.

Where are you aware of an Irish influence in your writing?

I wish it were everywhere, but when I read Irish writers I am reading a different English, a far cagier and stylized English, an English adapted for the purposes of subterfuge and subversion. If I am influenced, it is only in those impulses—but not in the execution of those impulses. Wit is far more refined and relentless in the Irish of Ireland than it is in Irish-Americans. Among contemporary Irish writers, I am especially drawn to the poets Paul Muldoon and Medbh McGuckian (Seamus Heaney too, so obvious I practically forgot him), and they often make me want to go back to poetry. I don't, too much. Once a year I break down and start a poem, and sometimes I finish it.

You've obviously read Irish writers extensively—Yeats, Behan, Joyce, to name a few. Have you brought them to the classroom? Which do you see as most important in your work?

I have taught *Dubliners* and a few contemporary Irish writers (Roddy Doyle at his best, Mary Morrissy) in short story and fiction-writing classes—but we've had so many world-class Joyce scholars at Notre Dame that I generally leave the biggies to the experts. The Irish literature I responded to most strongly in my own youth was drama—I was quite taken with Synge and Shaw and Beckett and O'Casey (a whole lot of different aesthetics packed in there).

In Due East *you wrote, "symmetry, and worry, were what marriage was all about." Infidelity[35] and adultery function as something of a motif in your writing. How does it speak to your views of the so-called institution of marriage? The difficulty of faith?*

I've always found fidelity in matters of marriage and faith good correlatives for one another: for most of us, both are chosen freely, difficult to maintain, mysterious. Fidelity can lead to peace and blessings or stultification and blind obedience. That story of mine you mentioned, "The Age of Infidelity," suggests that fidelity is not just difficult within the confines of marriage: it's hard to be faithful to anyone suffering, anyone difficult.

What's the best thing about being a writer?

Having written.

Anne Rice (b. 1941) might have been easily written off as a long shot for inclusion when this project started years ago. After all, she was yet another southern Irish writer who disavowed her Irishness. She had renounced her Catholicism and made her name in vampire stories; the body of literary criticism bearing on her work was scanty. Who could have foreseen her passionate return to Catholicism or her equally passionate exit?

If one pays careful attention, however, the Irish Catholic dimensions of her work were there all along. In her overview of Anne Rice's work, Charmaine Mosby notes "the combined influences of Southern rhetorical syntax and Irish cadence" in Rice's voice, as well as the author's insider/outsider viewpoint in New Orleans, straddling "New Orleans' Irish Channel where she grew up and the physically near but spiritually remote Garden District where young Anne O'Brien wandered as an outsider."[36] As if in answer, Anne Rice, born Howard Allen O'Brien, declares in *Called Out of Darkness: A Spiritual Confession* (2008), "I didn't grow up in the Garden District. I didn't grow up in the Irish Channel. I grew up on the margins of the world that included both." Though demonstrably Irish Catholic and southern in her family affiliations and outlook, Rice avers, "I don't belong anywhere. I don't come from any particular milieu."[37] Moreover, she associates the streets of the Irish Channel with hard-nosed capitalism in a world that one of her *Blackwood Farm* (2003) characters calls "as narrow as the gutter":[38] "The noisy and narrow streets of the Irish Channel were the map of the world that I feared—the world without art, the world without timeless beauty, the world of necessity and raw experience, and random suffering, into which anyone at any time might suddenly drop, the world in which someone by circumstance might be completely trapped" (*CO* 159).

No wonder she sought distance from those streets: like Margaret Mitchell, she wrestled with Irish and Catholic claims on her soul, becoming one of the bestselling authors of the twentieth century. There could be little doubt that her family's Irishness was entwined with its Catholicism. As Rice notes in the foreword to *Christ the Lord: Out of Egypt,* she grew up "in an Irish American parish that would now be called a Catholic ghetto, where we attended daily Mass and Communion in an enormous and magnificently decorated church which had been built by our forefathers, some with their own hands."[39] In a familiar story, the severest test of Irish ethnicity occurred when "an entire branch of our family had been lost to us in the 1950s because they became Protestants" (*CO* 153). Rice would "lose" as well "the whole Irish Catholic clan—all the New Orleans family—by living for 30 years in California."[40] Yet with an Irish hunger for family, and notwithstanding her awareness of its power to suffocate, Rice would recall that her father's final gift was reconnecting her with her Irish relatives in New Orleans, including "his surviving brothers and sisters, and aunt and uncles, and all the cousins he so cherished and loved" (*CO* 153). *Pandora* (1998), a book that quotes W. B. Yeats's epitaph in the same breath as Poe's "To Helen," is dedicated to Rice's husband and children and "To the Irish Of New Orleans, who, in the 1850s, built on Constance Street the Great Church of St. Alphonsus, while passing on to us through faith, architecture, and art, a splendid monument 'to the glory that was Greece and the Grandeur that was Rome.'" Rice clearly appreciates the centrality of the Irish sons of empire in her meridional South; St. Alphonsus has been preserved in large part through her efforts.[41]

It is not a large leap from vampirism to Irish Catholic ancestor worship or, for that matter, Rice's position in New Orleans when she explains the appeal of the vampire figure in her work: "The vampire is a perfect metaphor for people who drain us dry, for our fear of the dead coming back, *for the outsider who is in the midst of everything and yet feels monstrous and completely cut off.* And I think most people feel that way at heart."[42] Such might well be the isolation of the Irish Catholic in the American South. After her "reversion" to Catholicism, Rice would frame the vampire metaphor in tellingly revised terms for the interviewer Cindy Crosby: "For me, the vampire was a metaphor for a sentient human struggling to find redemption—a creature condemned to darkness, though he or she longed for the light."[43] Patricia Snow links Rice's "secular books" to the writer's sense of spiritual alienation and quotes Rice's own estimation of them: "These books transparently reflect a journey through atheism and back to God. It is impossible not to see this" (*CO* 245). Vampirism, Snow concludes, has to do with Rice's sense that faith and disbelief are intimately transmissible: "One can propose that the whole edifice of Rice's vampire fiction had its origin in a terrifying anxiety: that the author herself was a kind of vampire, who had infected her daughter with atheism."[44] Asked to reply to this notion, Rice said, "I do not feel any guilt whatsoever for 'infecting' my daughter with atheism. My daughter was by the way a baptized Catholic. Even during those years after I returned to the Catholic Church (1998 to 2010), I have to confess I was profoundly thankful that I had never infected my gay son, Christopher, born 1978, with Roman Catholicism."[45]

Whatever the merits of religious vampirism, Rice's secular work manifests a range of Catholic anxieties in some sense not terribly different from Cormac McCarthy's blood-soaked musings. Recent years have provided very good reasons for considering Rice's work here. She has published one of the most evocative portraits of a southern Irish Catholic upbringing available to contemporary readers, which offers a new framework for understanding her work to date. Perhaps more important, she has brought out the first two of four proposed *Christ the Lord* novels, reimagining the life of Christ. Each of these merits consideration, especially Rice's account of how she returned to the fold, *Called Out of Darkness*. But one might begin with a by-now familiar trope: the New Orleans Irish from which she distanced herself offered fertile ground for Rice's novels. In *The Feast of All Saints* (1980), Marcel, a free person of color,

> wandered astonished along the levee the day that the H.M.S. *Catherine* docked, her load of starving Irish the scandal of the summer. Wraiths too weak to walk, they were carted to the Charity Hospital and some of them right to the Bayou Cemetery, where Marcel stood watching the burials, and all this when he must have seen it so many times in the past with yellow fever coming on every summer and the stench from the cemeteries so thick in the steaming streets that it became the breath of life. Death was everywhere in New Orleans, what of it? Why go stare at it?[46]

In point of regeneration, one might compare Lafcadio Hearn, who also liked to quote Poe, on the tombs of New Orleans: "Under our Southern sun, the vegetation of cemeteries seems to spring into being spontaneously—to leap all suddenly into luxuriant life! . . . All that rich life of graves summoned up fancies of Resurrection, Nature's resurrection-work—wondrous transformations of flesh, marvelous transmigration of souls!"[47]

Here is a place so subtropically fecund that death itself becomes indistinguishable from the lush overabundance of life. Or perhaps the cycles are simply so accelerated that they must be more apparent. Rice's account is laced with the melancholy backdrop of Irish immigrant history but also hints at "Nature's resurrection-work." In the same text Rice will consider, as Hearn does in his *Daily City Item* sketches, the city's ethnic tensions: "The Irishmen were raging at the bar, and the black laborers kept apart. But he had trouble understanding what the Irish raged against, and no trouble whatsoever shutting them out" (*FAS* 28).

The most Irish American of Rice's fictional works, however, are the Mayfair Witches novels, published during the first half of the 1990s. Rice mines the Irish vein in her family history to generate a witches' dynasty, male and female, in *The Witching Hour* (1991): "In spite of the huge family gatherings which included French-speaking cousins by the hundreds—the core family was an Irish-American Catholic family."[48] Some of the details of the uber-Irish protagonist Michael Curry's life are clearly lifted from the stock of family lore. Like Rice's father, Howard O'Brien, Michael's father, a product of the Irish Channel, is called away to military service and woos his mother with love letters from abroad. There is home-turf pride when Rice mentions the Redemptorist School, "which had always been the poorest white school in the city of New Orleans": "The underdogs had won [the City Championship], the kids from the other side of Magazine, the kids who spoke that funny way so that everyone knew they were from the Irish Channel" (*WH* 52).

Rice was herself a Redemptorist student, walking to school through the Garden District, where her mother's mother had worked as a domestic.[49] The gallery of characters in *The Witching Hour* spans the gamut of Irish (stereo)types: drunks, schizophrenics, religious fanatics, xenophobes (who violently intercede to keep an aunt from getting romantically involved with an Italian "dago"), and teachers, including Sister Bridget Marie, who "told them tales about the Irish Ghost of Petticoat Loose, and witches—witches, can you believe it!—in the Garden District" (*WH* 61). She also gives Curry an appreciation of Irish folklore: "Like in the old days when people would be lured by the Little People. You know, they'd go off and spend one day with the Little People, but when they came back to their villages they discovered they'd been gone for fifty years" (*WH* 203).

Incidental details of the novel, such as the local landmark Parasol's Bar, give it New Orleans street credibility, and some of the most interesting flourishes are in the minutiae, for example, when Rice writes about the accent beloved by John Kennedy Toole:

> Like many New Orleanians, they had no discernible French or southern American accent. But they tended to call people they knew by both names,

as in "Well, how are you now, Ellie Mayfair?" and to speak with a certain lilt and certain deliberate repetition which struck the listeners as Irish. A typical example would be this fragment picked up at a Mayfair funeral in 1945: "Now don't you tell me that story, now, Gloria Mayfair, you know I won't believe such a thing and shame on you for telling it! And poor Nancy with all she has on her mind, why, she's a living saint and you know she is, if ever there was one!" (*WH* 463)[50]

Ultimately, per Rice, the Irish character of Rice's New Orleans endures in its churches more than in its accents:

> Back home, he had left a city of bigots perhaps, but it was also a city of characters. He could hear the old Irish Channel storytellers in his head, his grandfather telling about how he'd snuck in to the Germans' church once when he was a boy just to hear what German Latin sounded like. And how in the days of Grandma Gelfand Curry—the one German ancestor in the entire tribe—they'd baptized the babies in St. Mary's to make her happy and then snuck them over to St. Alphonsus to be baptized again and right and proper in the Irish church, the same priest presiding patiently at both ceremonies. (*WH* 60–61)

But what happens once those churches are shuttered? Some of Rice's appeal, in terms of contemporary literature, derives from an appetite for nostalgia that becomes self-perpetuating. Ever since Lafcadio Hearn sketched it, New Orleans has been a city in recession: paradoxically receding from the living yet vibrant in its celebration of the dead, receding from the work ethic, receding from modernity while becoming a national center for hedonism, and so on. By its very nature, this "authentic" New Orleans has always been in retreat—a theme that is both reinforced and taken apart in the HBO series *Treme*—and it is in retreat Rice's fiction too. When Michael Curry returns to the Crescent City after thirty years away in San Francisco, he finds the Irish Channel of his youth unrecognizable, much as Rice must have found it after years in California:

> He chose Philip Street for the walk out to the Irish Channel. . . . At last he crossed Magazine, wary of the speeding traffic, and moved on into the Irish Channel. The houses seemed to shrink; columns gave way to posts; the oaks were no more; even the giant hackberry trees didn't go beyond the corner of Constance Street. But that was all right, that was just fine. This was his part of town. Or at least it had been. (*WH* 739)

Litter-strewn Annunciation Street "broke his heart," the reader learns; in a neighborhood now predominantly black, "all the people he might have known around here were long gone" (739). The one fixture of the neighborhood that remains is Rice's beloved church: "Only the churches of St. Mary's and St. Alphonsus stood proud and seemingly indestructible. But their doors were locked" (739).

And this was before Hurricane Katrina. Even Rice might acknowledge that her devotion to St. Alphonsus is partly nostalgic, like *Called Out of Darkness,* her book documenting her return to those doors. The writer and Catholic convert Patricia Snow observes that Rice came of age during "the Golden Age of American Catholicism, when seminaries were full and Fulton Sheen was a household word, and [she] takes pains to demonstrate that religion in this world of her childhood *included the world.* Whether she is describing the inquiring intellectualism of her bohemian Catholic parents, the confident professionalism of the nuns in her Catholic school, the night parades of Mardi Gras, or the movies of Cecil B. DeMille, she is describing a world that, in rich and effective ways, extended the sacred space of the Church."[51] Unsurprisingly, Rice's writing about the "unbroken" fabric of this world is charged with her sense of enchantment. Like Savannah's Bill Canty, who described his mother's part in his religious education, Anne Rice absorbed her "concept of God . . . through the spoken words of my mother, and also the intensely beautiful experiences I had in church" (*CO* 6).

Those memories included the School Sisters of Notre Dame as well as the Sisters of Mercy, who figured prominently in New Orleans, as they did in Savannah. The name of Rice's aunt, Sister Mary Immaculate, "shines bright" in her memory. A great aunt, Sister Mary Liguori, "the last of thirteen children," served as an educator in the order as well. Of the nuns that taught her, Rice writes, "There are great stories to be written about [them]" and about "how these orders often fought with the male hierarchy of the church to gain the freedom to minister directly to the people, at times when the hierarchy wanted to put these sisters in cloisters and keep them out of the active world" (*CO* 49). Like the nuns who educated Flannery O'Connor, the School Sisters of Notre Dame were "younger women, highly educated, and extremely refined. They were from the North" (*CO* 48).[52] Following a path similar to that of Father Abram Ryan, Rice's father had studied at the Redemptorist Seminary at Kirkwood, Missouri, but decided not to become a priest. She nevertheless credits his education as the guiding force in his life and thus a large one in hers. As in the O'Connor household, the popular media brought Catholicism to the O'Brien home, making Fulton Sheen "a household word" (*CO* 107). Rice's grandmother listened to

Mass on the radio, and Rice herself recalls "passionate anti-Communist words spoken from the pulpit" (*CO* 52). It was not a church of half-measures, so during her period of rapprochement Rice was shocked to be embraced by her "extended Catholic family": "The Catholics of my time had been bound to shun people who left the faith. Indeed one reason I stayed clear of all Catholics for three decades was that I expected to be rejected and shunned" (*CO* 153).

There could be other reasons for her worry. Curiously, or perhaps faithfully, in her earlier fiction Rice eroticized many elements of her Catholic upbringing. For example, in *Belinda* (2000), May processions provide the stock for schoolgirl fetish. After dressing sixteen-year-old Belinda in a white nightgown, forty-four-year-old Jeremy is transported by memories of the Catholic May processions of his youth, "The little girls in white lace and linen up in the cloister outside ready to go in."[53] Likewise, memories of May processions also inform the reverie of Cormac McCarthy's *Suttree:* a boy's hair catches fire in the procession of "small Christians in little white fitted frocks . . . The boys laughing. The girls in white veils, white patentleather shoes with little straps. Snickering into the roses they hold in their prayerclasped hands. Small specters of fraudulent piety" (253–54). "Fraudulent" purity might be the expected result of a religion that fetishizes innocence, as Rice's work suggests. At the same time, Catholicism has a tradition of eroticizing the ecstasy of faith.

Writing in a different mode, Rice devotes three pages in *Called Out of Darkness* to vivid recollections of the May processions of her youth (100–102). She gives considerably less ink to the pedophilia scandals after her own investigations into the lives of recent popes led her to conclude that "things were good at the top"; ergo, "the church would reform itself" (*CO* 203). Moreover, she has tidily reconciled the legacies of her writing with her Catholicism, writing that it "confuses" her to be called a "prodigal daughter": "I feel no guilt whatsoever for anything I ever wrote. The sincerity of my writings removes them completely from what I hold to be sin" (*CO* 232).

Even if she is not a prodigal daughter, Rice has clearly reflected extensively on where her place might be and how she might reconcile where she has arrived in life with a childhood that indeed seems to belong to a separate world, time, and place. The portrait of Rice's family that emerges from her account of "spiritual confession" shares strong themes in common with O'Connor's family in New Orleans's sister city Savannah, including a complicated matrix of ethnicity, social class, and status. Rice's education started at St. Alphonsus, a relic of the competition between German and Irish immigrants to New Orleans. Like Flannery O'Connor, she was aware of her movement between "the treeless sun-baked streets of the working-class neighborhood where some of my ancestors had been born" and the comfort to which her family now aspired: lace-curtain versus working-class, the social hierarchies of parochial schools, and so forth. As Michael Curry confesses in *The Witching Hour,* "I haven't been around lace curtain Irish very much. I guess they're as crazy as all the others" (894).

Both Rice and Flannery O'Connor knew that they were at best invitees to the Anglo-southern world of high society. Rice had a view to both the Irish Channel and the Garden District, a position in many ways analogous to Flannery O'Connor's place in Savannah, though Rice's family instilled that she was both of and apart from the Irish children at the Cathedral School. She writes of going to birthday parties in the Irish Channel where she "really didn't know these people, but they all knew each other. They were part of something. I wasn't part of it" (*CO* 102).

Like O'Connor, Rice grew up in a household where precocity was not only tolerated but nurtured. Literature, from mythology to the devotional, was in every sense acceptable. When Howard O'Brien returned from his military service after World War II, he "needed to reintroduce himself to two little girls who had been just babies when he left home" and so composed a children's novel titled *The Impulsive Imp* (2009). Anne's sister Alice went on to become a fantasy writer too.[54] As is the case with the Cajun and Irish family of Andre Dubus (including Andre III, James Lee Burke, and others), there are signs of a writer's dynasty in the making, as Anne Rice's openly gay son Christopher has embarked on his own writing career.

Rice wondered aloud in one interview before leaving the church, "'How can I go back to a church that says my son will go to hell?' But in the end, I left it all in God's hands. . . . I went back for the man at the top, Jesus Christ. I go to my local church weekly, I pray daily, but I stay away from the politics."[55] By her own admission, staying away from politics has not been easy, a point she confronted head-on in a *First Things* interview with Father Dwight Longenecker, who asked, "Some conservative Catholics are worried that you are a dissenter in the area of abortion, homosexuality and women's ordination. How do you answer them?" Rice replied,

> Some very conservative Christians have voiced concerns about me personally because I am a prolife Democrat. But there are many other prolife Democrats. I am an old-guard Social Justice Roman Catholic and must vote for the party that I believe will do the most good on earth. And we have only two parties—just two.[56]

Certainly "old-guard Social Justice" has a venerable history of association with "Irish Catholic." Rice also made clear, in *Called Out of Darkness,* that she was aware of Catholics in her childhood precincts who had broken away from the faith of the mothers in her family: "And these Catholics were not having thirteen children like my great-grandmother Josephine Becker Curry, nor were they having nine children like my grandmother Bertha Curry O'Brien" (173). In the aftermath of her announcement on July 28, 2010, that she had "quit being a Christian,"[57] it was not surprising that she cited the Catholic Church's aggressive opposition to gay marriage.

Remarkably, reviewers of the two *Christ the Lord* novels published to date have generally paid less attention to Rice's orthodoxy than to her skill as a storyteller; she has drawn strong reviews from Catholic journals, evangelists, and to some extent, the literary establishment. The first of the series, *Out of Egypt* (2006), drew generally positive reviews, but there were some loud dissenters. One such was the *Guardian (UK)* reviewer who sniped, "All that's missing are muddy-coloured illustrations of darkish people with tea towels on their heads, and we'd be right back in the subtle and complex world of the Ladybird Books."[58] The National Public Radio reviewer Alan Cheuse deemed the book "an earnest mess of pottage, ill-conceived, ill-wrought and—worst sin of all—quite boring."[59] Some were not prepared to permit Rice or perhaps anyone else the narrative voice of the son of God: "A return to faith should never be belittled," wrote Cynthia Grenier in a *First Things* review that drew letters of protest from readers, including a priest who came to Rice's defense. "But to celebrate her return by undertaking what is planned as a trilogy from the manger to the Cross as narrated by Him surely bespeaks a certain arrogance."[60] How many were discomfited that a writer of witches and vampires might so deftly imagine the life of Christ?

Yet Janet Maslin might declare, by the time of the publication of the second novel, that Rice had "silenced doubting Thomases," a claim supported by an NPR review of *The Road to Cana* (2008) declaring it "a masterful book written by an extraordinary writer at the height of her powers."[61] Some sources have simply avoided getting drawn into any discussion of the legitimacy of Rice's project—or into sanctioning what might not be orthodox—by declining to review it. It is interesting that the *New York Review of Books* has reviewed neither of these novels and that no review that I could find makes mention of a tableau early in *The Road to Cana* when a crowd stones two young men accused of homosexuality, a bold and inventive stroke on Rice's part. If the text had been published under Ron Hansen's name, would it have been differently noticed?

On the other hand, those who have been paying attention and who might be disposed to doubt Rice's powers routinely have good things to say about her. Sizing up the scope of her project, an interviewer in the Jesuit *America* magazine observed, accurately, "There's probably no other character or person in history that you could write something about as difficult as Jesus."[62] Books that take on "The Greatest Story" naturally court controversy, and reviewers noted some humbling predecessors, including Nikos Kazantzakis's *Last Temptation of Christ* and Shusaku Endo's *Life of Jesus* (and one might add the Anglo-Irish writer George Moore's unorthodox *Brook Kerith*). Patricia Snow probably comes closest to the truth when she attributes the books' winsomeness to Rice's "consistent and elegant solution . . . to the thorny problem of *kenosis*—What powers does the human Jesus have, and what does he know?"[63] The drama works on the external level, through Jesus's family, and on the internal level, for example, when Jesus must control his desire for Avigail. "We know that he is sinless," Rice explained in her *America* interview, "this is what we believe. That was the challenge: can you write a realistic novel about a vital character who is God and man, and be absolutely true to the creeds and to the Bible?"[64]

While some have quibbled with Rice's use of the gnostic gospels (principally the Infancy Gospel of Thomas) and apocryphal sources, her scrupulously Jewish Jesus has generally met with the favor of the scholars on whose work she draws extensively. Rice cites a long list of biblical and theological writers, including N. T. Wright, John A. T. Robinson, Walter Kasper, Craig Keener, Donald Carson, Raymond Brown, John Meier, Karl Rahner, *ad aspera*. In short, Rice studied her way into a period of Catholic reconciliation, a rediscovery that was informed by wide reading. Borrowing from Flannery O'Connor in *Called Out of Darkness,* she writes of her period of atheism, "I was Christ haunted" (177).

One can draw strong comparisons, in terms of Rice's Catholic mode and quirkily cosmopolitan upbringing, to Flannery O'Connor, and in her difficult years of atheism and early literary fame, to the dashingly obstreperous Pat Conroy. Yet the figure in this study to which she might best be compared is Kate O'Flaherty Chopin, and not merely because of the New Orleans connection. She is similarly fascinated by *gens de couleur libres* and the Caribbean rim, by the inadequacy of the term *local color,* and by her sense that the world of art must necessarily lie outside the confines of Irish Channel conformity. She shares with Chopin a willingness to push boundaries and to quarrel with a church that offers a necessary, if unsuitable, spiritual home.

As with the other writers considered in this chapter, the story of Rice's relationship with Catholicism and the stories that come out of it are still being written. Marked as outsiders in the southern mainstream, these writers have played a large part in reclaiming a Catholicism that regional literature had often disguised, ignored, or rejected. For if there is a common theme among the writers of this chapter, apart from their ability to write bestselling fiction, it is that the right to dissent is fundamental to self-discovery and self-definition. They tend to question American narratives of success and social order. And the questions they ask of a church-cum-ethnicity have a much broader bearing on the future status of American Catholicism and immigration. How are the old stories—the narratives that *used* to be so important to identity, didactically illustrated by the lives of saints in an earlier era—made new? How are they relevant to contemporary culture (held to be postcolonial, postmodern, post-southern, post-Christian)?[65]

While these writers have been conditioned to be skeptical of unfettered romantic individualism, their imaginations seek a spiritual rest point, where individual dignity might be reconciled to totalizing ideologies of nationalism and belief. Even when American identity is rendered apathetic, atomized, re-agglomerated, and pure-T blandified by the engines of Facebook and Youtube, these writers tell transcendent stories precisely by failing to be at peace with place, ethnicity, and religion. In a so-called postnational age, to be of two hearts is the unfinished and yet cherished story of the immigrant in imagined exile. As Joseph Campbell might say, the hero's journey is a familiarly human one.

8

CODA

The Irish . . . are the damnedest race.
They put so much emphasis on so many wrong things.
—RHETT BUTLER

It was the kind of talk he'd heard all his life at home,
however, the endless Irish dramatizing of the morbid, the lusty
tribute to the tragic. Truth was, it wore him out.
—FATHER MATTINGLY, in Anne Rice's *The Witching Hour*

The twists and turns of Anne Rice's writing career and the drama of her journey in faith perhaps serve to illustrate why it is impossible to speculate about what the future holds and why it is irresistible to do so: can a church that goes against the current of modern opinion at every turn retain its numbers, even in the conservative South? As the demographic center of the American Catholic population floats from the Northeast to the Southwest, more than one in eight southerners are now Roman Catholic.[1] Looking ahead, Catholic writers in the South are likely to seem far less unusual in coming years.

On the other hand, Americans in all regions are becoming less Christian, and, "as demonstrated by comparatively low attendance at church and by a propensity of many to leave Catholicism, many Southern Catholics may have only a tenuous relationship with the Church."[2] Nor does the influx of Latinos to the American South guarantee a revival in southern Catholicism, as many assume, according to the findings of the American Religious Identification Survey: "Whereas Latino immigrants are contributing significantly to the stability of American Catholicism, the younger generation and the U.S.-born population are tending to polarize between those moving away from religion and those moving towards conservative Christian traditions."[3] More broadly, a church that has alienated many of its bedrock adherents through sexual abuse has, by definition, entered an age of uncertainty.

Meanwhile, census data show a fairly dramatic surge in the number who claim Irish ancestry over recent decades—a pronounced trend in the South, where respondents have been defecting from the "Scotch-Irish" column and migrating to the generically "Irish."[4] Combine these facts with the rapidly changing ethnic landscape of modern immigration, and southern Irish writers appear quaintly anachronistic, virtually relics from a bygone time. In 2007 just 13.1 percent of the foreign-born population of the United States was of European origin, compared with 26.8 percent for Asia and 53.6 percent for Latin America.[5] In 2005 there were 148,000 foreign-born Irish living in America; in 2003, just 1,010 Irish would be granted permanent residence in the United States.[6] Now that the emerald tiger rampant is once again a kitten recumbent, those numbers are likely to change again. Asked what might be applied "to our current immigrant situation from what we know about the history of Irish American immigrants," Timothy Meagher replied, "In a broad sense, think of a people practicing a religion that is anathema to all your ideals, a religion that seems the epitome of anti-democratic thinking, a people poor, disorganized, rowdy and raucous, filling up your jails and poorhouses, mucking up your politics, and apparently incorrigible."[7]

You know the rest of the story: not only were those same Famine Irish immigrants assimilated, but they became the exalted Americans of a new century. Significant European immigration to the South was relatively unknown in the first part of the twentieth century, but Americans generally tend to think of each new immigrant group in negative terms, and over time they come to regard them (without irony) in increasingly positive terms—again, witness the Irish example. If there is a lesson in all this, Meagher has the clincher: "Immigrants today may not be perfect, but then none ever were. Be patient, and recognize that immigration and the American faith in the common man and woman may be the best thing this country has going for it."[8] As the channels of Irish immigration have dried up and the South becomes more Asian, more Hispanic, more African and Middle Eastern, one might anticipate new hybrids of southern identity as a similarly keen-eyed class of writers emerges and begin anew the work of reinterpreting the South.

That is a glance forward. Looking back, it bears reiteration that this study cannot claim to be comprehensive. Space constraints have left more than one hundred pages of this manuscript on the cutting-room floor, pages documenting the perception of the Irish in southern racial hierarchies, the Irish on the early southern stage, and the work of Irish journalists who toured the American South. Nor is there space for many minor candidates from the southern fringes, occasional writers like Charles J. O'Malley, Thomas Walsh, and James Hilary Mulligan—oddly enough, all nineteenth-century lawyers and poets from Kentucky. Irish American history, language, and characters feature importantly in the writings of contemporary African American writers, among them Toni Morrison *(Sula)* and Edward P. Jones *(The Known World).* The Mississippian and poet laureate Natasha Trethewey has acknowledged a familial interest in the Irish, as well as her great esteem for Irish poets, including Seamus Heaney. One might look to Ralph Ellison's lectures comparing Irish and black writers, the "backward" Tennesseans "still speaking Gaelic" in Ernest Gaines's *Autobiography of Miss Jane Pittman,* and so on. A study needs to be made of recent black writers who attend carefully to the Irish roots of southerners, black and white, but it cannot be made here, alas.

In addition to these omissions, there are other major candidates overlooked, including Andre Dubus, whose non-Creole ancestry traces to Irish immigrants to Louisiana. Were there space enough and time, not to mention more readily available biographical material, the tensions of Mediterranean and Irish Catholicism in Dubus's family would make a fascinating study. Margaret Skinner, who grew up in the Irish district of Memphis, has written two fine novels, *Old Jim Canaan* (1990) and *Molly Flanagan and the Holy Ghost* (1995), a mid-1950s southern coming-of-age story full of the ordinary moral and theological perplexities of a Catholic adolescent. Then there are emerging candidates such as the South Carolinian critic, essayist, and fiction writer Farrell O'Gorman. Or the Kentuckian John Jeremiah Sullivan, whose Irish Catholic roots go to the North through his father's family. As southern demographics change, there will be more like him.

And what does all this mean for understanding how Irish Americans have participated in southern literature? Looking ahead, the reevaluation of their role will entail a closer inspection of familiar biographies and a willingness to engage with belief and family culture, which is so often a hive of individual complexity. Those writers who are identified primarily as Scots-Irish might be trued against a deeper past. Consider, for example, how a complete study of the Catholic Other (as a critical term of art) in Mark Twain's work would enrich our understanding of his writing. Thomas Haddox begins this work in *Fears and Fascinations,* but he does not consider how Clemens's potentially "impure" Scots-Irish roots, not to mention his growing up in an area of heavy Irish Catholic in-migration, compelled him to love what he loathed, leading a writer who often castigated Catholic conformity to his quizzically beloved *Joan of Arc* and the strange possessiveness of the *Mysterious Stranger.* Tracy

Fessenden rightly observes that race can be a cover for a subterranean Catholicism in American literature and pursues these notions into her "Mark Twain and the Ambivalent Refuge of Unbelief" (chapter 6 of *Culture and Redemption*). Though she pays little attention to Fitzgerald's unmarked southernness, her eighth chapter opens wide the door of "F. Scott Fitzgerald's Catholic Closet," providing an exemplary study of the subtle reevaluation of disavowed Irish and Catholic origins.

Edgar Allan Poe is another figure of potential interest in this vein. Many traces of Catholic influence can be discerned in the work of the *Raven* writer, who penned one of his stories entirely in Irish dialect. The fact that some of Poe's Scots-Irish ancestors lived in Ireland undeniably complicates his relationship to what he terms "a forgotten church" in "Fall of the House of Usher." Poe's friendship with Jesuits at Fordham and his solidarity with a branch of the Irish Repeal movement in Philadelphia hint at a kind of kinship that may be rooted in the complexities of family history. The Irish-born Father William A. Tobin, a Catholic priest who pastored tiny St. Anthony's Parish in Florence, South Carolina, had no doubt about it: in a pamphlet titled *The Irish in South Carolina* he declared: "Poe was Irish . . . on both sides of the house."[9]

Some years ago Michael Burduck wrote a provocative article titled "Usher's 'Forgotten Church'? Edgar Allan Poe and Nineteenth-Century American Catholicism." While acknowledging that there is no smoking gun that would definitively connect Poe to the Catholic faith, the article goes on to trace many instances of Catholic influence in Poe's stories and among his associates. There is not space enough to recapitulate his evidence here, but it should be apparent to even casual readers of Poe that a Catholic Other pervades many of his texts.[10] What Burduck argues, convincingly if in leading terms, is that Poe had a "more than passing interest in Catholicism."[11] One interesting support comes from Poe's review of James Fennimore Cooper's *Wayandotté, or the Hutted Knoll,* in which he took the author to task for "Jamie Allen, with his prate about Catholicism," whom Poe deemed "insufferable."[12] Poe objected to the sort of obnoxious litany found in chapter 21 of the novel, where, in Burduck's phrase, the "good Scottish Protestant Mason" indulges in an anti-Catholic rant, saying, "Ye'll no deny that the creator' o' Rome wears a mask, and that Catholicity is, at the best, but a wicked feature to enter into the worship of God. . . . All Protestants . . . agree in condemning the very word catholic, which is a sign and a symbol o' the foul woman o' Babylon."[13]

Flannery O'Connor sends up the same attitudes through the character of "The Displaced Person"'s Mr. Shortly, who declares, "I ain't going to have the

Pope of Rome tell me how to run no dairy."[14] Another of her characters, Hazel Motes, asserts that "no priest taking orders from no pope was going to tamper with his soul."[15] (In one of her letters describing a furor over church and state separation, she observed, "You'd think the Pope was about to annex the Sovereign State of Georgia.")[16] What is remarkable is the way in which both authors are so sensitive to the presumptions of both Catholic and Protestant sectors of their societies. Jenny Franchot finds in Poe's "The Pit and the Pendulum" an allegorical critique of religious bigotries, both Catholic and Protestant.[17] (And one might consider Jesuitical and Masonic secretiveness in stories such as "The Cask of Amontillado" too.) Poe's attraction to arcane and "secretive" elements of Catholicism pertaining to death is not hard to explain, for he delighted in all things occult. Hence his inside joke referring to an obscure tome in Roger Usher's library, a Roman Catholic book of prayers for the dead, *Vigilae Mortuorum secundum Chorum Ecclesiae Maguntinae* (c. 1490), which he calls "the manual of a forgotten church."[18]

Forgotten, perhaps, but not gone. Poe's family history includes ancestors who moved to Cromwellian plantations in Ireland. His great-great-grandfather David Poe "was a Protestant tenant-farmer amidst the endless bog and stony fields of Dring, Co. Cavan, Ireland, about seventy-five miles northwest of Dublin," according to Poe's biographer Jeffrey Myers.[19] Poe's paternal grandfather, a later David Poe, may have been born in Ireland, according to the Poe Museum of Richmond's genealogy.[20] David Poe's wife, Elizabeth Cairnes, bore a name of common distribution and many variants among both Protestant and Catholic Irish and Scots. In his youth, Poe resided for a time in London. As a young man, he retained friends in Irish societies,[21] and his humorous stories would include a number of Irish caper pieces (e.g., "Why the Little Frenchman Wears His Hand in a Sling"). In short, Poe's perspective on the Irish might well have been grounded in the circumstances of personal history. Perhaps his broadminded stance toward Roman Catholicism offers another avenue to appreciate what Kieran Quinlan would call his strange kinship with Flannery O'Connor.

Arguing against Poe's possible "Irishness," Quinlan admits that the writer "has on at least one occasion found himself confined within the strange and eerie precincts of an anthology of Anglo-Irish literature," but he sides with Thomas MacDonagh, "a college lecturer in English until executed for his part in the 1916 Easter Rising," who "quite rightly considered Poe's association with Ireland to be far too 'slender' to merit such inclusion."[22] The early Poe biographer William Gill, in a chapter entitled "Founding of the Race in Ireland," arrived at an Italian lineage for the Poes, who he believes went to Ireland after the Norman invasion. Given the long Irish traditions in poetry, it is both ironic and humorous that Gill writes, "We can well imagine that, sprung from a race to which the improvisation of poetry is a second nature, the sensitive ear of the le Poer could ill brook the ruder song of the untutored Celt."[23]

Without inventing Catholic ancestors for the writer, suffice it to remark a long-standing pattern of Irish settlers who became, as the phrase goes, more Irish than the Irish. Their complicated patterns of immigration, coexistence, and (sometimes necessarily) shifting religious identities ensured that many Irish, both Protestant and Catholic, were more broadly sympathetic to one another than the convenient binaries of some historical narratives might suggest. Poe might well have been one of their number.

And then there is Sarah Morgan Bryan Piatt (1836–1919), who again demonstrates the biographical complexity of sorting out the exchanges of Irish origins, family culture, and religious persuasion. Her mother's slaveholding ancestors, the Spiers, were probably of Ulster Irish origin. The prolific descendants of her namesake patriarch, Morgan Bryan, have debunked certain theories about his origins but still cannot say with certainty whether his roots traced to Irish Catholic O'Briens or Anglo-Norman Bryans. In any case, Sarah Piatt came from a slaveholding Kentucky family and remained unapologetic about her southern fealties (including her unabashed hatred of Ulysses S. Grant). She would for the rest of her life consider herself a regional expatriate, even as her marriage to an Ohioan took her away from the region and eventually to Ireland. Her husband, John James "J.J." Piatt, an aspiring poet of limited means, followed a career of patronage appointments, including an eleven-year appointment as American consul in Ireland. His fascination with literati brought Sarah Piatt into acquaintance with Henry Wadsworth Longfellow, W. D. Howells, James R. Lowell, Walt Whitman, Bret Harte, Katharine Tynan, Padraic Colum, Lady Wilde, and others.[24]

If Piatt's family ties to Ireland have not been fully established, she seems nevertheless to have given heart and soul to the place, and her deeply felt ties to Ireland are easy to establish in her work and within the legacies of her family. Her poems concerning Ireland were widely published in Ireland and resulted in several Irish-themed collections, including *An Enchanted Castle* (1893). Yeats reviewed that volume and paid her poetry a backhanded compliment, calling "In the Round Tower at Cloyne" "surely perfect after its kind" but adjudging her poems "a little obviously American."[25] This flattens out her work considerably, however, and overlooks her sensitive observations of Irish social hierarchies and social reverses.

If Sarah Morgan Bryan Piatt reinvented herself, to some degree, as "Irish," was she some sort of Irish *Catholic*? She does not appear to have been Catholic in the obvious places where one might examine the record: she married at a relative's home, and the only evidence of her conversion that I have been able to locate is that she is listed as an "American convert from Protestantism" in the index of an 1895 text.[26] If Sarah was a convert, though, she was a rather splendid one. Her poems enter fully into the traditions of Catholic mystery and evince a wide-ranging knowledge of church history and mysteries. Moreover, her poetry was printed and reviewed in the journals *Catholic World* and *New Catholic World* and posthumously reprinted in *Joyce Kilmer's Anthology of Catholic Poets.*[27] Moreover, her family became increasingly involved with Catholicism over the course of her lifetime, with the double conversion of her husband's cousin and his wife.[28] Though the Piatts' ancestry is described as "French Huguenot," the Piatt children were schooled as Catholics, including their daughter Marian, who attended "a convent school in Cincinnati."[29]

Piatt's sons Donn and Fred would remain in Europe. "Marrying into the Sigerson family, Donn carried on his mother's radical politics," notes Paula Bennett, "becoming an ardent supporter of Irish home rule. Donn's son was an active participant in the Gaelic revival."[30] His daughter, Eibhlín Sigerson Piatt, would marry Emmett Humphreys, who had been involved in Fianna Éireann, a quasi-military Irish republican youth movement. Humphreys eventually entered the fray during Easter Week 1916, before being jailed at Kilmainham. Notwithstanding the friendly relations between the English and the Confederates, it is quite an interesting irony that a southern poet of Confederate sympathies would bring her family's blood and fortunes to the Irish republican cause.

Since these ties cannot, as yet, be proven through her family history, it will serve to make her acquaintance here, with the hope that future biographers might tease out her attraction to Ireland and Catholicism. Perhaps the same will be done for Poe and Twain. It will suffice to observe that in each case, proximity to an Irish Catholic Other shaped the version of Scots-Irish identity that the writer ultimately assumed. If we accept that the Irish in America numbered among the "probationary races" of nineteenth-century America, as Matthew Jacobson argues,[31] the plasticity of Irish identity is easier to comprehend. In like vein, southern genealogies have often been simplified in order to expurgate the messiness of a remnant Catholicism or the stigma of the socially undesirable.

William Faulkner, in his typically canny way—one step ahead of the historians, as the historian Don H. Doyle suggests[32]—seems to have intuited some of these complexities. The quiet Mississippian was well acquainted with the work of James Joyce and William Butler Yeats; Joseph Blotner records that Faulkner could recite "An Irish Airman Foresees His Death" from memory.[33] The writer seems to have understood the metanarrative of submerged Catholic identity, but the story of his self-censorship is equally telling. Kieran Quinlan points out (as Cleanth Brooks did not) that Faulkner's awareness of his family's roots in Inverness meant an attendant awareness of Catholicism in the family history.[34] In an annotation in Faulkner's appendix to *The Sound and the Fury,* we learn that the Compson family patriarch "fled to Carolina from Culloden Moor."[35] In a passage ultimately bowdlerized from *Flags in the Dust,*[36] Faulkner explains how the Sartorises, forever enamored of a losing cause, "followed Charles Stuart" in the Jacobites' ill-fated attempt to restore the Catholic line.

Are the Irish to be fully restored to our understanding of regional history, free of misty nationalism? To reiterate, the purpose of this study is not to stake out a special place for the Irish but to show that they too participated in engineering the mindscape of the South. A short list of southern Irish American writers (e.g., Conroy, Mitchell, O'Connor, McCarthy) leaves little doubt of their impact on regional ideology and mythology. Mitchell's Atlanta, Conroy's Citadel, McCarthy's Knoxville, and O'Connor's Andalusia are unmistakable landmarks of the regional imagination, a veritable map of southern mythos. Looking back helps us to understand how these *cairns* dotting the landscape accrued the weight of mutual identification and rose to become landmarks, becoming indispensable to the discourse surrounding what it means to be "southern"—a subject in which the southern Irish had a direct stake.

Looking back might lead to various types of restoration in southern literary history; looking forward is, as usual, a treacherous business. Asked where narrative might go in the twenty-first century, Valerie Sayers suggests,

> We'd better jump in the deep water, in terms of both content and form; i.e.,
> I think Catholic fiction writers should tackle whatever is knocking on their
> doors, whether it's these bizarre sex scandals, if they are so inclined, or the
> hierarchy of the Church, or political and cultural subjects having nothing
> whatsoever to do with Catholicism . . . not to make some statement about
> difficult subjects, but to probe them, meditate on them, illuminate them.
> And we'd better use all the forms at hand, electronic and otherwise.[37]

And the relevance of Irish Catholic identity to the national culture today? "Feeling strong kinship—good secure straight-up unthreatened kinship—seems to me helpful in relating to a broader culture; but otherwise I'd say: pretty irrelevant," responds Sayers.[38]

Perhaps relevance is always preciously ephemeral. Neither terrorism nor Islam is new to the United States or even to the American South (consider the Haymarket Affair, the Confederate plot to set New York afire, and Islamic African American slaves), but because these things seem new, in light of recent events, they are suddenly deemed relevant. The Irish are not new to the South; taking an interest in them is new. At all events, one might hope that the part of southern Irish in creating southern literature would facilitate a deeper understanding of a South that has consistently been defined by its perceived outsiders. Questions linger around the endurance of regional identity, not to mention ethnic persistence, and it is fair to wonder how the terms of the discussion will change. But the South is a region of many reverses, and who knows, but that some son or daughter of Irish wit might come out of the blue and sing to her soul once again?

NOTES

CHAPTER 1

1. The South Carolina priest William Tobin attributed the quotation to John Boyle O'Reilly, but it most likely is derived from the satiric verses of Calvin Brannigan's "The Gathering of the Scotch-Irish Clans": "And we'll join in jubilation for the thing that we are not; / For we say we aren't Irish, and God knows we aren't Scot!" The verses offer an amusing commentary on the dilemmas of misty sectional identity, both Irish and American, and the various societies that play them up. In the Scots-Irish-dominated South, and coming from Father Tobin's tongue, the verses take on yet another register. See Leyburn, *Scotch-Irish* 333–34.

2. Cobb, *Lost Irish Tribes* 3.

3. Ibid. 5.

4. Cobb, *Exit Laughing* 19.

5. Ibid. 25.

6. Cobb, *Lost Irish Tribes* 5.

7. For Jackson, see *Virginia Journal* 2.64 (21 Apr. 1785): 3; for Lougherey, see ibid. 2.67 (12 May 1785): 3.

8. See, for example, *Charleston City [SC] Gazette* 6.855 (26 Jan. 1788): 3.

9. Duncan, "Servitude and Slavery" 52, 56.

10. Meaders, *Dead or Alive* 39.

11. K. Miller, "'Scotch-Irish,' 'Black Irish'" 238.

12. K. Miller, *Irish Immigrants* 103.

13. For an interesting recent study, see Bornstein, *Colors of Zion.* See also Giemza, "Turned Inside Out."

14. "Irvin Cobb Lauds Race."

15. R. Watson, *Normans and Saxons* 86–87. *Celt,* of course, is a catchall term for the British Other and was applied freely to the Scots and Welsh as well.

16. *Southern Literary Messenger* 31 (Nov. 1860): 345–47.

17. R. Watson, *Normans and Saxons* 87.

18. Cobb, *Lost Irish Tribes* 7.

19. O'Hara, *Hibernian Society* 93–95, 112.

20. Mencken, *Prejudices* 76.

21. "Irvin Cobb's Stories," *New York Times* 11 June 1933.

22. See introduction to K. Kenny, *American Irish.*

23. A binary model of Irish history establishes a paradigm of antagonism, as Kerby Miller has observed: in the one column are those described as Catholic, Gaelic, Nationalist, and "Irish"; in the other, Protestant, English/Scottish, Unionist, and "British." See K. Miller, "Ulster Presbyterians."

24. K. Miller, "'Scotch-Irish' Myths" 81.

25. Powell, "North Carolina" 698. *Scotch-Irish* is Connor's term.

26. James Webb's popular book on this topic, *Born Fighting,* gives a latter-day view of the Scots-Irish rampant.

27. K. Miller, *Irish Immigrants* 461.

28. Here and elsewhere, I refer to Native Americans according to their preference, confirmed by census data, to be called "Indians." I generally refer to African Americans as "blacks" for similar reasons, and with the caveat that these terms of convenience, like those used to classify the Irish, are not terribly descriptive and not infrequently misleading.

29. Niehaus, *Irish in New Orleans* 125; O'Brien, *Conjectures of Order* 2:285.

30. K. Kenny, *American Irish* 2–3.

31. Wade, "A United Kingdom? Maybe."

32. Condon, *Irish Race in America* 9. The book includes chapters on the Irish in Maryland and in the South. I am indebted to Maura Burns for sharing it with me.

33. Jacobson, *Whiteness of a Different Color* 49.

34. Ryan, "Thoughts in Solitude."

35. Tinling, *Correspondence of the Three William Byrds* 2:493.

36. K. Miller, *Emigrants and Exiles* 147.

37. Reed, *Minding the South* 254.

38. David Doyle, *Ireland, Irishmen* 51–76.

39. K. Miller, *Emigrants and Exiles* 14–17.

40. John O'Rawe, Charleston, SC, to Mr. and Mrs. Brian O'Rawe, Ireland, 1 Apr. 1809, Manuscripts, South Caroliniana Library, University of South Carolina, Columbia.

41. Paul Muldoon, "Promises, Promises," *Why Brownlee Left* 24. The collection *Madoc: A Mystery* and the poem "Sir Walter" evince the poet's wide-ranging interest in Walter Raleigh and English experiments in colonization.

42. According to the historian Jason Silverman in "Irish."

43. K. Miller, *Emigrants and Exiles* 140.

44. See Woods, *History of the Catholic Church* 347; the percentages of Irish-born are derived from table 10.1 on that page, reprinted as table 1 in the current volume.

45. Ibid. 347.

46. Ibid. 349.

47. Griffin, "Irish Migration to the Colonial South."

48. "Books: Scholar in America."

49. Coakley, Rev. of *Foreigners in the Confederacy* 75.

50. Lonn, *Foreigners in the Confederacy* 210. Lonn meticulously combed through muster rolls, leading her to conclude that "a Cuban or a Peruvian is less striking than an Egyptian or Syrian" and to notice that "several of the West Indian islands were represented: Cuba, St. Thomas, Jamaica and Martinique" (210).

51. See Woods, *History of the Catholic Church* 348 (table 10.2).

52. See Mitchell to Helen and Clifford Dowdey, 13 May 1943, in M. Mitchell, *"Gone with the Wind" Letters* 368.

53. Though the term *American South* is tinged with a hemispheric bias, it is perhaps not altogether unfitting in this study, where the North American "South"—in elements of shared colonial, meridional, and Catholic culture—bleeds into the Atlantic world, down into Mexico and Central

America, and points even further to the south. And yet for the purpose of this study, most of the action takes place in the U.S. South.

54. In a strange but true coda to Confederate flight, these mostly forgotten descendants of disillusioned postbellum immigrants preserved folkways that even today reveal elements of a recognizably Confederate society set, as it were, in amber, though they had mostly intermarried by the third generation.

55. *Racialist* is here used to refer to racial pseudoscience.

56. Rubin and Holman, *Southern Literary Study* 235.

57. Flannery O'Connor, *Mystery and Manners* 208. Of course, O'Connor's statement can be seen as motivated, insofar as she wanted her Irish Catholic progenitors to be seen as fully southern.

58. Haddox, *Fears and Fascinations* 49.

59. Meagher, *Columbia Guide* 83.

60. See J. Kelly, "Charleston's Bishop John England."

61. Wolfe, *Of Time and the River* 161 (hereafter cited parenthetically in the text).

62. Eugene Gant does not consider that the southern Irish too were also mostly city dwellers.

63. Franchot, *Roads to Rome* xvii.

64. Griffin, "Irish Migration to the Colonial South."

65. Quinlan, *Strange Kin* 8.

66. See Snay, *Fenians, Freedmen, and Southern Whites*.

67. Gleeson, *Irish in the South* 182.

68. "Canada-Kingston," *Toronto Globe & Mail* 3 Feb. 1883.

69. Consider Robert William Molloy (1906–1977), whose *Pride's Way* reflects his upbringing in a German and Irish household in Charleston, South Carolina.

70. Brooks, *William Faulkner* 2.

71. Mills, "Dead Mule Rides Again" 15.

72. The editor Shannon Ravenel employs an even more inclusive standard: a southern writer is one who lives in the South. One who subscribes to regional ideology, even one who exults in, to use Michael Kreyling's phrase, the "South that wasn't there," is no less concerned with southernness.

73. Hackney, "Southern Violence" 922. Colbert appeared in the 2010 documentary *Faces of America with Henry Louis Gates, Jr.* on PBS. Colbert's interview is available online through the PBS *Faces of America* website.

74. J. Sullivan, "Watching the oil spill."

75. Conroy, *South of Broad* 420.

76. Gooch, *Flannery* 121.

77. W. Smith, "Southerner and Irish?" 235.

78. Conroy, *My Losing Season* 59.

79. O'Gorman, *Peculiar Crossroads* 108; for an excellent discussion of the topic, see ch. 3, "Toward a Catholic Theory of Fiction." See also Greeley, *Catholic Imagination;* Labrie, *Catholic Imagination in American Literature;* Giles, *American Catholic Arts and Fictions;* and Tracy, *Analogical Imagination*.

80. Simms, *Life of Francis Marion* 60.

81. Cantrell, *Celtic Culture* 89.

82. Guilds, *Simms* 4–13.

83. Bottum, "Gatsby's Epitaph"; Kazin, *F. Scott Fitzgerald* 17.

84. Kazin, *Bright Book of Life* 57.

85. R. Wood, "Such a Catholic" 38.

86. Nevils and Hardy, *Ignatius Rising* 69.

87. Massa, *Anti-Catholicism in America.*

88. Gleeson and Buttimer, "We Are Irish Everywhere" 184.

89. Ferris and Welty, "Visit with Eudora Welty" 164.

90. Brooks, *William Faulkner* 3.

91. McWhiney, *Cracker Culture.* McDonald wrote the prologue for the edition.

92. Berthoff, "Celtic Mist over the South"; Newton, "Review."

93. Horwitz, *Confederates in the Attic* 413.

94. Beagle and Giemza, *Poet of the Lost Cause* 206.

95. McWhiney, *Cracker Culture* xliii.

96. See Cantrell, *Celtic Culture.*

97. Burrison, *Roots of a Region* 88.

98. K. Miller, "Re-Imagining Irish Revisionism" 237.

99. Quinlan, *Strange Kin* 256.

100. Ryan, "Lecture of the Poet."

101. Cobb, *Lost Irish Tribes* 4. Cobb's daughter Elisabeth was also a writer; her daughter Buff Cobb, an actress who was once married to the journalist Mike Wallace, died on 20 July 2010.

102. Smietana, "Nashville Priest."

103. Reed, "Choosing the South" 276–77.

104. Ibid. 277.

105. Gleeson, *Irish in the South* 36.

106. Pyron, *Southern Daughter* 121. Like Kate Chopin, Mitchell was doubly a rebel: apparently, neither woman returned to the Catholic Church after renouncing Catholicism.

CHAPTER 2

1. Fanning, *Irish Voice in America* 212.

2. Crump and Spraker, *Boone Family* 518–19; Wayland, *History of Shenandoah County, Virginia* 598.

3. Wayland, *History of Shenandoah County, Virginia* 598.

4. Jordan Dodd et al., *Virginia Marriages, 1740–1850* (Provo, UT), www.ancestry.com. Database

5. Quoted in Fanning, *Irish Voice in America* 39.

6. John England to Daniel O'Connell, 28 Dec. 1829, later printed in the *Charleston Mercury.* Hammond's speech is reprinted in Rodriguez, *Slavery in the United States* 666.

7. Native Irish also played a significant role in describing the war. William Howard Russell, a pioneering figure in war reportage, was raised by a Catholic mother and a Protestant father in Ireland. His accounts of his wartime experiences as a roving reporter, which display a keen eye for the Irish involvement in the American Civil War, are collected largely in *My Diary, North and South.* Thomas Conolly was a fortune-seeking son of the Protestant Ascendancy who picked the Confederate economy for the winner; his diary also provides an interesting view of various wartime movers and shakers. See Conolly, *Irishman in Dixie.*

8. Fessenden, *Culture and Redemption* 6.

9. Beagle and Giemza, *Poet of the Lost Cause* 258.

10. Fogarty, *Commonwealth Catholicism* 141.

11. Dooley, *John Dooley, Confederate Soldier* 117.

12. A. Douglass, *Irish Emigrant* 1:iii.

13. See K. Miller, "'Scotch-Irish,' 'Black Irish'"; David Doyle, *Ireland, Irishmen;* and K. Kenny, *American Irish.*

14. David Doyle, *Ireland, Irishmen* 51–76. One wonders whether Bill Clinton's great-great-great-grandfather Levi Cassidy, of Chesterfield, South Carolina, might have been one of them.

15. Irish geneticists point to an "O'Neil gene" shared by one in five men in northwestern Ireland: "People with the surname of O'Neil have long been thought to have descended from a line of kings known as the Uí Néill. And the Uí Néill dynasty is thought to have been founded by a fifth-century warrior known as Niall of the Nine Hostages. Studies suggest that Niall bequeathed his Y chromosome to over 2 million Irish men alive today" (you may insert your own quip about big Irish families here). Carl Zimmer, "High-Achieving Genes," *Forbes.com,* 2 Mar. 2007, Web. 7 Oct. 2012.

16. A. Douglass, *Irish Emigrant* 2:199.

17. Chalkley, *Chronicles of the Scotch-Irish Settlement* 2:262–63.

18. 1820 US Census (Lexington, Rockbridge County, VA), National Archives and Records Administration, series M33, roll 130, p. 282. Web.

19. 1830 US Census (Western District, Shenandoah County, VA), National Archives and Records Administration, series M19, roll 200, p. 106. Web.

20. 1830 US Census (Boone, Harrison, IN), National Archives and Records Administration, series M19, roll 27, p. 104.

21. K. Miller, "'Scotch-Irish,' 'Black Irish'" 139.

22. McGreevy, *Catholicism and American Freedom* 51; Thigpen, "Aristocracy of the Heart" 591.

23. K. Miller, "'Scotch-Irish,' 'Black Irish'" 139.

24. Indeed, if one follows Noel Ignatiev's suggestion that Huck is an Irish boy, *Huckleberry Finn* dramatizes these choices. See Ignatiev, *How the Irish Became White* 57–59.

25. Baker, "William Alexander Caruthers."

26. Quoted in Gales and Seaton, *Register of Debates in Congress* 1103.

27. Taney, *Memoir* 9.

28. Cf. J. Tucker, "Oscar Wilde, Roman Catholic."

29. Griswold, *Poets and Poetry of America* 75.

30. E. Tucker, *Richard Henry Wilde* 1.

31. Noonan, *Antelope* 142.

32. E. Tucker, *Richard Henry Wilde* 2.

33. Ibid. 44.

34. References to Byron's *Childe Harold's Pilgrimage* and to Wilde's *Hesperia* are to canto and stanza. This passage might also have influenced the opening chapters of James Joyce's *Ulysses,* which imagines a Scylla across the Channel. Joyce too was an attentive student of Byron's work.

35. On the subject of failed American attempts at epic poetry during this period, see McWilliams, *American Epic* 19. For more on southern writers' attempts at the form, see Beidler, "Meek's Great American Epic Poem."

36. E. Tucker, *Richard Henry Wilde* 110; Richard Henry Wilde Papers, box 1, Manuscript Division, Library of Congress, Washington, DC. For an account of the note, see Gronberg, "Problem

of the Pseudonym." Uhler's book leaves no doubt that within the oral traditions of her family, at least, Wilde was a Catholic.

37. Wilde, *Hesperia* 2.60.

38. Mobley, "Slave Ship's Sad Saga."

39. *Register of Debates* 6 (1829–30): 1088, 1103.

40. Gleeson, *Irish in the South* 111.

41. D. Clark, "South's Irish Catholics" 201.

42. Franchot, *Roads to Rome* 103.

43. Carroll, *Life of Catherine McAuley* 52.

44. For more on southern Irish participants in the American Civil War, see Quinn, *Irish in the American Civil War.* For more on Carroll and Florence O'Connor, see Giemza, "Sisters of Secession."

45. Gleeson, *Irish in the South* 154.

46. This is borne out by the chaplain rolls in Brinsfield, *Faith in the Fight.*

47. "Address to the Patrons of the Review."

48. Rugemer, "Southern Response to British Abolitionism" 221.

49. Ibid. 222.

50. Gleeson, *Irish in the South* 130–31.

51. F. Douglass, *My Bondage and My Freedom* 433.

52. Mitchel, *Jail Journal* 170.

53. C. Watson, *History of Southern Drama* 67–68.

54. Florence O'Connor, *Heroine of the Confederacy* 295.

55. D. Brown, *Planter* 9, 10, 158.

56. J. Page, *Uncle Robin* 10, 30, 33–34, 36.

57. The review is excerpted in the publisher's end matter in Grigsby, *Virginia Convention of 1776.*

58. Wilson and Fiske, *Appleton's Cyclopædia of American Biography* 744.

59. *Graham's Magazine* was edited at one point by George Lippard, whose bestseller *The Quaker City* is rivaled only by *Awful Disclosures of the Hotel Dieu Nunnery* in its weird anti-Catholic machinations. According to Emilio De Grazia, Peterson was consecrated to literary immortality in Poe's satirical writings as Professor Peter Sun. In a letter of 7 June 1843 Poe described him as "a good boy" much given to pseudonyms, who "never puts nothing in his productions except something—really moral." De Grazia, "Poe's Devoted Democrat" 7.

60. C. Watson, *History of Southern Drama* 64–65.

61. Randolph [Peterson], *Cabin and Parlor* 187 (hereafter cited parenthetically in the text).

62. Peterson's friend George Lippard describes some of this mayhem in *The Killers* (1850), one of his typically cabalistic potboilers. For a general treatment of the riots, which spanned decades, see Ignatiev, *How the Irish Became White* ch. 6; and Feldberg, *Philadelphia Riots of 1844.*

63. Reid ultimately found his way to Saint Louis and the American West. In addition to his seminal Westerns, his antislavery novel *The Quadroon* contributed to the development of the tragic mulatto type in American culture.

64. S. Faulkner, "Octoroon War" 36.

65. Fawkes, *Dion Boucicault* 107.

66. Richards, *Early American Drama* 459.

67. For a full treatment, see Brody, *Impossible Purities* 46ff.

68. Fawkes, *Dion Boucicault* 110.

69. "Abolition On and Off the Stage."

70. Roppolo, "Uncle Tom in New Orleans" 214.

71. Fawkes, *Dion Boucicault* 109.

72. Stowe, *Uncle Tom's Cabin* 414, 439, 424.

73. Fessenden, *Culture and Redemption* 130.

74. "The Octoroon," *New York Times* 15 Dec. 1859.

75. Fawkes, *Dion Boucicault* 108.

76. Quoted in "The Octoroon Gone Home," reprinted in *New York Times* 9 Feb. 1860.

77. Miller and Wilmeth, *Cambridge Guide to American Theatre* 72.

78. Roppolo, "Uncle Tom in New Orleans" 214.

79. Ibid. 219–21, quotations from 220.

80. Ibid. 223; C. Watson, *History of Southern Drama* 66.

81. "Octoroon Gone Home."

82. S. Faulkner, "Octoroon War" 37–38.

83. Posters for the play's Canadian run in May 1861 proclaimed for Union and flashed the American flag even as some newspapers faulted Boucicault for his light treatment of slavery.

84. Fawkes, *Dion Boucicault* 109. There is a rich history of the Irish on the New Orleans stage, including visits from notable celebrities such as the Irish actor Tyrone Power, who decried the poor treatment of Irish workers in Louisiana. Earl F. Niehaus's *Irish in New Orleans* devotes a chapter to the subject of the Irish on the southern stage.

85. The section that follows considers a few representative writers, but it is hardly exhaustive. Among the first-person accounts that came from the war period were several accounts by Irishmen, including the reportage of the famed Irish war correspondent William Howard Russell and the wartime diary of Thomas Conolly, a would-be profiteer who sought to forge business alliances with well-connected Confederate leaders and businessmen. For an account of their work, see Bryan Giemza, "On the Uses of Slavery: Irish in the South and Civil War Rhetoric," in Giemza, *Rethinking the Irish in the American South*.

86. John Cantwell, letter of 27 Oct. 1847, John Lucas Paul Cantwell Papers (#03027), Southern Historical Collection, The Wilson Library, University of North Carolina, Chapel Hill.

87. Patrick Cantwell to John Cantwell, 1848 or 1849, ibid.

88. Florence O'Connor, *Heroine of the Confederacy* 42.

89. Tardy, *Living Female Writers of the South* 148.

90. What became of Miss O'Connor, the fire-eating Catholic separatist? Did she have her moment of truth? At the very least, she displayed a nimble adaptivity. The *Manchester Times* of 2 June 1866 ran her wedding notice in its "Marriages and Deaths" section, the last trace of her earthly movements that I have been able to find: "On the 26th April, at [the Episcopal] Christ Church, New Orleans, by the Rev. Dr. Leacock, Col. E. A. Willard, of Illinois, U.S., to Miss Florence J. O'Connor, authoress of 'The Heroine of the Confederacy; or, Truth and Justice.'" I am indebted to Donald Beagle for passing this clipping along.

91. Blackman, *Wild Rose* x–xi.

92. Ibid. 64, xv.

93. Ibid. 62.

94. Ibid. 21.

95. Greenhow, *My Imprisonment* 190 (hereafter cited parenthetically in the text).

96. News clipping (likely from the *Wilmington Sentinel*), Wilmington, NC, 1 Oct. 1864, Alexander Robinson Boteler Papers, David M. Rubenstein Rare Book and Manuscript Library, Duke University, Durham, NC.

97. Bailey, "Anthony M. Keiley and 'The Keiley Incident'" 65.

98. John Keiley's journal and extensive records of his son's wartime service are available at the Virginia Historical Society in Richmond. Nora Keiley became the superior of the Visitation Monastery, while brother Benjamin would eventually became the bishop of Savannah.

99. Fogarty, *Commonwealth Catholicism* 115–16.

100. Ibid. 115.

101. Apart from *In Vinculis*, Keiley's writings survive in scattered newspaper articles, a handful of political tracts (including one broadside reprinting a Manhattan Club speech in which he fiercely defended both the honor and the financial solvency of the Old Dominion), and a short history of the Catholic Church in Virginia since the Revolution, the last being remarkable for the span of its institutional memory (e.g., Keiley interviewed an "old negro" who remembered the altar from a chapel dating from 1812). Keiley, *Memoranda of the History of the Catholic Church in Richmond* 5; Keiley and Ficklin, *Virginia Debt!*

102. Keiley, *In Vinculis* 183 (hereafter cited parenthetically in the text).

103. Still other evidences of Keiley's Irishness are identified in Kelly O'Grady's *Clear the Confederate Way!* 189–90. O'Grady notes Keiley's love of Hennessey and his comparison of bad coffee to Wexford poteen (essentially, Irish moonshine). Keiley does refer to "certain liquid comforts"—and Confederate whiskey that "would make a nun swear"—but submits that "neither Father [Theobald] Matthew [the famed Irish temperance leader] nor John B. Gough" could have withstood wartime deprivations without resort to the milk of mercy (28).

104. J. Shannon, *Catholic Colonization on the Western Frontier* 222–23.

105. Fogarty, *Commonwealth Catholicism* 276; D. Clark, *Irish Relations* 116.

106. Bailey, "Anthony M. Keiley and 'the Keiley Incident'" 69.

107. Fogarty, *Commonwealth Catholicism* 189.

108. *Petersburg Daily News* 16 Jun. 1865, Virginia Historical Society, Richmond.

109. John Keiley also became the organizer of the Southern Immigration Association. Bailey, "Anthony M. Keiley and 'The Keiley Incident'" 66. His daughter Helen married Alexander Sullivan of Dublin, Ireland. See "To Marry in Private Chapel."

110. "Roosevelt's Consistency," *New York Times* 11 May 1902.

111. Quoted in Graham, *Soul of John Brown* 228.

112. Keiley, *"Our Dead"* 7, 13.

113. Bailey, "Anthony M. Keiley and 'the Keiley Incident'" 74.

114. J. O'Grady, "Roman Question in American Politics" 370.

115. Rebecca Davis's politically well connected family would leave its stamp on Virginia politics. See Jacob Rader Marcus Center of the American Jewish Archives, Cincinnati, OH; First American Jewish Families, "Davis."

116. "Chief Justice Keiley Resigns at Cairo."

117. Fogarty, *Commonwealth Catholicism* 206.

118. Dooley, *John Dooley, Confederate Soldier* xiv (cited parenthetically in the text).

119. Bailey, "Anthony M. Keiley and 'the Keiley Incident'" 74.

120. Fogarty, *Commonwealth Catholicism* 204, citing *Richmond Dispatch* 13 June 1868.

121. Franchot, *Roads to Rome* 99–100.

122. Dooley owned that some of his romantic notions of combat had come from the high-spirited sketches of the Dubliner Charles Lever, a master raconteur who authored the very popular *Charles O'Malley* (1841). For a Donnybrook touched off by a toast "to good King William, that saved us from Popery," see *Charles O'Malley* 1:104–5.

123. M. Mitchell, *Gone with the Wind* 1030.

124. Beagle and Giemza, *Poet of the Lost Cause* 162.

125. Kinney, *Flannery O'Connor's Library* 116.

126. Mary D. O'Connor, *Life and Letters of M. P. O'Connor* 37.

127. Henry, *Selected Stories* 300.

128. "Valiant Lives" 19; Bill Woolsey, *Tall Tales,* WSM, Nashville, 11 Jan. 1955, Diocese of Nashville Archives; *The Poetry of Father Abram Ryan,* Channel 1 Records, n.d., LP.

129. Beagle and Giemza, *Poet of the Lost Cause* 2, citing Charles S. Olcott, *William McKinley* (Boston: Houghton Mifflin, 1916) 369; "News Gleanings," *Hartford Daily Courant* 7 Oct. 1886, 1.

130. Undated notes, The Lee Camp Soldiers' Home Vertical File, Virginia Historical Society, Richmond.

131. Thus Ryan is touted on the book's cover.

132. For a hilarious account of how Irish music and American/southern music are two sides of the same coin, see the chapters "Rebel Music" and "The Devil in Disguise" in the Irish novelist Joseph O'Connor's *Sweet Liberty*, 138–50 and 244–69, respectively.

CHAPTER 3

1. Brasch, *Brer Rabbit* 4.

2. Wyatt-Brown, *Hearts of Darkness* 160.

3. Cousins, *Joel Chandler Harris* 26.

4. Ibid. 83.

5. Brasch, *Brer Rabbit, Uncle Remus* 24.

6. Bickley, *Joel Chandler Harris: A Biography and Critical Study* 27.

7. Bain, Flora, and Rubin, *Southern Writers* 208.

8. Bickley, *Joel Chandler Harris: A Biography and Critical Study* 34.

9. Margaret Mitchell to the Honorable Jesse M. Donaldson, 9 Jan. 1948, in M. Mitchell, *"Gone with the Wind" Letters* 409.

10. Writing in 1986, Thomas questioned whether Harris's birth year was 1848 by convention or in fact. His skepticism was vindicated when the Turman-Harris Bible, once owned by Harris's grandmother Ann Mary Turman Harris, surfaced in 1997. That Bible is now a permanent part of the Harris Collection, Manuscript, Archives, and Rare Book Library, Woodruff Library, Emory University, Atlanta. It clarifies the family's official date of his birth (1845) rather than the 1848 persistently stated by biographers. K. Thomas, "Roots and Environment" 45–46.

11. Kenneth H. Thomas Jr., e-mail to author, 6 Apr. 2004.

12. Pyron, *Southern Daughter* 350.

13. K. Thomas, "Roots and Environment" 41, citing Esther LaRose Harris to Julia Harris, 10 Dec. 1917, in the Harris Collection at Emory University.

14. Julia Collier Harris, *Life and Letters of Joel Chandler Harris* 7, 3–4.

15. K. Thomas, "Roots and Environment" 45–46.

16. Ibid. 40.

17. M. Kenny, "Father Ryan's Poems." The paraphrase departs somewhat from the wording of the original in Verot, *General Catechism of the Christian Doctrine* 58. A copy of the rare wartime catechism may be found in the Library of Virginia, Richmond.

18. For a complete account of Harris's Catholicism, see Giemza, "Joel Chandler Harris, Catholic."

19. J. Lewis, *Out of the Ditch* 16.

20. Berkeley, *Works of George Berkeley* 389.

21. W. Thomas, *American Negro* 130.

22. E. Andrews, *War-Time Journal* 340.

23. Portions of this and the preceding paragraph were originally published in Giemza, "Turned Inside Out."

24. O'Neill and Lloyd, *Black and Green Atlantic* xvi–xvii.

25. Joel Chandler Harris, *Dearest Chums and Partners* 367.

26. Wyatt-Brown, *Hearts of Darkness* 163.

27. Wilson, *Patriotic Gore* 562.

28. In Joel Chandler Harris, *"Balaam and His Master."*

29. Ladd, *Nationalism and the Color Line* 52.

30. Joel Chandler Harris, "Anne Macfarland Review."

31. Quoted in Hobson, *Tell About the South* 118. Likewise, Joseph Addison Turner, Harris's mentor, complained: "As an editor, I was once bold as a lion. That was when I had a country. Now, it seems, I have none. . . . I will write upon no subject upon which I cannot freely speak my mind." Brasch, *Brer Rabbit* 16. Ironically, for Turner and for Cable, it was Union victory that had muzzled the South—but southerners were the censors.

32. Joel Chandler Harris, *Joel Chandler Harris, Editor and Essayist* 44.

33. Quoted in Brasch, *Brer Rabbit* 302.

34. Joel Chandler Harris, *Joel Chandler Harris' Life of Henry W. Grady* 167.

35. Joel Chandler Harris to Lilian Harris, 5 June 1897, in Joel Chandler Harris, *Dearest Chums and Partners* 132. Harris's Savannah beat probably gave him some exposure to the Irish community there. In a *Morning News* column on 11 March 1873, he reported the "most cold-blooded and heartless murder" of an Irishman. The victim, "known as 'Fred,'" was a boatman, shot in his sleep by his employer.

36. Harris's choice of name is intriguing. Perhaps the Nagle family was riven by war loyalties: the real-life James Nagle was well known as a Union officer at Sharpsburg. Joel Chandler Harris, *On the Wing of Occasions* 34.

37. Joel Chandler Harris, *Tales of the Home Folks* 148 (hereafter cited parenthetically in the text). The story was originally published in *McClure's Magazine* in June 1893.

38. Julia Collier Harris, *Life and Letters of Joel Chandler Harris* 398.

39. K. Thomas, "Roots and Environment" 41.

40. Quoted in Julia Collier Harris, *Life and Letters of Joel Chandler Harris* 78.

41. Gibert, "Role of Implicatures."

42. For the sake of concision, and because Chopin's short stories are widely and freely available online, I refrain from providing page numbers for particular texts, though I read from Chopin, *Complete Novels and Stories*.

43. For a homoerotic reading of the story see Haddox, *Fears and Fascinations* 90–92.

44. Toth, *Kate Chopin* 75.

45. Chopin, *Kate Chopin's Private Papers* 59.

46. Toth, *Unveiling Kate Chopin* 46.

47. Chopin, *Kate Chopin's Private Papers* 10.

48. "The Shape of the Head," trans. Kate Chopin, ibid. 229–32.

49. Toth, *Unveiling Kate Chopin* 9.

50. Ibid. 13.

51. Ibid. 35.

52. Trent et al., *Cambridge History of American Literature* 334.

53. Haddox, *Fears and Fascinations* 87.

54. Chopin, *Kate Chopin's Private Papers* 131. And as John Reed has established, Kate Chopin's other town, New Orleans, has served as a port of call for self-proclaimed bohemians of various stripes. See *Dixie Bohemia* (and, for that matter, the character Davis McAlary in HBO's *Treme*).

55. Putzel, *Man in the Mirror* 14.

56. Ibid. 6–7.

57. Ibid. 15, 12–13, 19.

58. Ibid. 19.

59. Today the area, about twelve miles outside of Saint Louis, is far from bucolic, and one finds situated at the crossroads of Reedy's old farm a busy road, a restaurant, and a convenience store.

60. Putzel, *Man in the Mirror* 246, 284.

61. Ibid. 12.

62. Toth, *Unveiling Kate Chopin* 27–28.

63. Harriet Monroe, quoted in Putzel, *Man in the Mirror* 293.

64. Chopin, *Kate Chopin's Private Papers* 269.

65. Putzel, *Man in the Mirror* 78. Agnes Baldwin is said to have paid for Reedy's treatment for alcoholism at the Keeley Institute, in its way a forerunner to the Betty Ford Clinic, where he would have been required to take daily injections of "bichloride of gold." Reedy in turn disowned Addie Baldwin Reedy altogether and supposedly instructed his business manager, "Tell her to go back where she belongs" (62).

66. Ibid. 86.

67. Ibid. 147–49.

68. Ibid. 268.

69. Cuoco, *Literary St. Louis* 78.

70. Haddox, *Fears and Fascinations* 95–97. The story bears strange parallels to Joel Chandler Harris's gothic "Where's Duncan?," which also features a canvas caravan, a dark stranger, racial ambiguity, and a numinous, moonlit encounter.

71. I am grateful to Farrell O'Gorman for pointing out this scene.

72. Toth, *Kate Chopin* 122.

73. Elizabeth Fox-Genovese, interview, *Kate Chopin: A Re-Awakening*.

74. Putzel, *Man in the Mirror* 286.

75. Ibid. 21.

76. Ibid. 22.

77. "St. Anthony's Temptation."

78. From the unpaged introduction to Flaubert, *Temptation of St. Anthony*.

79. See E. Thompson, "Little Races."

80. Hearn, *Editorials* 253.

81. Quoted in *Daily City Item* 25 June 1878.

82. Hearn, *Editorials* 5. Hearn also wrote, "I think there will be some day a Russian Mass sung in Saint Peter's," as if he foresaw the continuing reconciliation of eastern Catholic churches that would indeed transpire in the twentieth century. Hearn, *Writings* 15:370.

83. Ronan, *Irish Writing on Lafcadio Hearn and Japan* 1.

84. Charles William Kent, an English professor at the University of Virginia who was the literary editor of the Library of Southern Literature, wrote of "Mrs. Brenans" that she "was a convert to the Roman Catholic Church and was extremely bigoted, being surrounded by fawning priests and converted *protégés*." Alderman et al., *Library of Southern Literature* 6:2342.

85. Quoted in Cott, *Wandering Ghost* 26.

86. See MacWilliams, *Lafcadio Hearn* 40.

87. Cott, *Wandering Ghost* 36.

88. *Cincinnati Enquirer* 22 Jan. 1874.

89. Massa, *Anti-Catholicism in America* 23.

90. Lafcadio Hearn, "Feminine Curiosity," excerpted in Cott, *Wandering Ghost* 71–72. Elsewhere Hearn marveled at an exhibition of woodcraft staged by the Sisters of the Ursuline Convent, including a prie-dieu and a kneeling bench, "both of excellent design and delicate cutting." Hearn was predictably taken with the "symbolic and historical emblems of the Ursuline Order, and of the Catholic Christian Church," which he said rivaled their counterparts from the Middle Ages. "Carving in the Convents," *Cincinnati Commercial* 17 Jun. 1877.

91. Fanning, *Irish Voice in America* 2.

92. Hearn, "A Morning in the Police Court," in Hearn, *Period of the Gruesome* 287.

93. Hearn, quoted in Cott, *Wandering Ghost* 70. Hearn notes that "James' actions in jail, his last farewell to his relations, his sensitiveness in regard to certain reports afloat concerning his past career, and lastly, the very fact that his nerve did finally yield under a fearful and wholly unexpected pressure, all tend to show that his nature was by no means so brutally unfeeling as had been alleged." Hearn, *Period of the Gruesome* 244.

94. Hearn, *Letters from the Raven* 46.

95. Kreyling, "(Patricio) Lafcadio (Tessima Carlos) Hearn."

96. Lafcadio Hearn, "The Streets," in Hearn, *Inventing New Orleans* 18–22, quotation from 20.

97. Hearn and Bisland, *Life and Letters* 1:190.

98. Hearn, "A Conservative" 321.

99. Hearn, *Lafcadio Hearn's America* 214.

100. Hearn, *Occidental Gleanings* 1:146.

101. Kreyling, "(Patricio) Lafcadio (Tessima Carlos) Hearn."

102. Quoted in Cott, *Wandering Ghost* 126.

103. Hearn, *Essays on American Literature* 69.

104. Ibid.

105. Hearn and Bisland, *Life and Letters* 2:488.

106. Quoted in Cott, *Wandering Ghost* 179–80.

107. Ibid. 210.

108. Ibid. 185–86, 180.

109. Hearn, *Lafcadio Hearn's America* 31.

110. Quoted in Cott, *Wandering Ghost* 161.

111. Hearn, *Lafcadio Hearn's America* 33.

112. Hearn, *Occidental Gleanings* 2:125.

113. Some of the documents bearing on Hearn's impressions of Cable are to be found among Edward Larocque Tinker's papers in the Houghton Library at Harvard, many of which have been digitized. Hearn's friendship with Father Adrien Emmanuel Rouquette, a priest who served as a Choctaw missionary, cooled after Rouquette lambasted Cable for *The Grandissimes.* Some suggest that Cable felt slighted by Hearn when Hearn scooped Cable's account of Last Island for the novel *Chita.*

114. Quoted in Cott, *Wandering Ghost* 170.

115. *Cincinnati Commercial* 8 July 1877.

116. LaBarre, *New Orleans of Lafcadio Hearn* xliii.

117. According to Kreyling, the title came from Hearn's friend Henry Farney, who said that Hearn's eye reminded him of a carriage lamp.

118. Quoted in Cott, *Wandering Ghost* 126. The last portion of the line scans almost like the famous concluding lines of F. Scott Fitzgerald's *The Great Gatsby:* "So we beat on, boats against the current, borne back ceaselessly into the past."

119. Haddox, *Fears and Fascinations* 88.

120. Ibid. 87.

CHAPTER 4

1. Momaday, *Man Made of Words* 203.

2. Quinlan, *Strange Kin* 134.

3. De Lorme, "Gunfighter 'Doc' Holliday."

4. Ibid.

5. Roberts, *Doc Holliday* 399.

6. Ibid. 400. The quotation is from M. Mitchell, *Gone with the Wind* 101 (hereafter cited parenthetically in the text).

7. Margaret Mitchell to Julia Collier Harris, 28 Apr. 1936, in M. Mitchell, *"Gone with the Wind" Letters* 4.

8. Mitchell to McAvoy, 20 Mar. 1940, Officers' Files, Hibernian Society of Savannah Records, Georgia Historical Society Library and Archives, Savannah; Mitchell to Michael MacWhite, 27 Jan. 1937, in M. Mitchell, *"Gone with the Wind" Letters* 113–14.

9. Mitchell to Helen and Clifford Dowdey, 13 May 1943, in M. Mitchell, *"Gone with the Wind" Letters* 368.

10. Mitchell to Arthur H. Morse, 24 June 1940, ibid. 309.

11. Mitchell to Harris, 28 Apr. 1936, ibid. 4.

12. Mitchell to MacWhite, 27 Jan. 1937, ibid. 113.

13. See Homer, "Kinship."

14. Yaeger, "Race and the Cloud of Unknowing"; Faust, "Clutching the Chains That Bind."

15. Mitchell to James Montgomery Flagg, 22 Oct. 1936, *"Gone with the Wind" Letters* 79.

16. Haskell, *Frankly, My Dear* 114, 15.

17. Sayers, "Guilt and *Gone with the Wind*" 98.

18. See Jones, *Tomorrow Is Another Day* ch. 8.

19. Haskell, *Frankly, My Dear* 133.

20. Ibid. 117.

21. Mitchell to Very Rev. Mons. Jas. H. Murphy, 4 Mar. 1937, *"Gone with the Wind" Letters* 126–27.

22. Pyron, *Southern Daughter* 252.

23. Ibid. 251.

24. Ibid. 250.

25. Conroy, *My Reading Life* 19.

26. Mitchell to Virginius Dabney, 23 July 1942, *"Gone with the Wind" Letters* 359.

27. Ibid.

28. Ibid.

29. Pyron, *Southern Daughter* 250.

30. Mitchell to Thomas Dixon Jr., 15 Aug. 1936, *"Gone with the Wind" Letters* 52.

31. Mitchell to W. W. Watson, 27 Jan. 1937, ibid. 115.

32. Lyerly, "Gender and Race in Dixon's Religious Ideology" 94–95.

33. Poole, "Margaret Mitchell's Nephew Leaves Estate."

34. By contrast, Mitchell's compliments to Faulkner went unrepaid. Perhaps stung at *Absalom, Absalom!*'s being passed over for the Pulitzer that Mitchell captured, when asked if he had read *Gone with the Wind,* he replied that he had not, because it was "entirely too long for any story," and grumbled that no story takes a thousand pages to tell. See Bledsoe, "Margaret Mitchell's Review of *Soldier's Pay*."

35. Mitchell to Helen Dowdey, 16 Sept. 1938, *"Gone with the Wind" Letters* 231.

36. Mitchell to Herschel Brickell, 20 Oct. 1937, ibid. 173. At the same time, she considered Hemingway's *A Farewell to Arms* her "favorite modern novel" (174).

37. Grandma Veal was old enough to remember the Leonid meteor shower of 1833, which occurred on the augured night that the kid of Cormac McCarthy's *Blood Meridian* is born.

38. M. Mitchell, *Margaret Mitchell: Reporter* 190.

39. Ibid. 254.

40. Mitchell to Dabney, 23 July 1942, *"Gone with the Wind" Letters* 359.

41. Mitchell to Brickell, 25 May 1938, ibid. 205.

42. Mitchell to Helen and Clifford Dowdey, 13 May 1943, ibid. 370.

43. 115 Harv. L. Rev. 1193 (2002) 1209. See also Kirkpatrick, "Writer's Tough Lesson in Birthin' a Parody." Alice Randall's unauthorized, satiric novel *The Wind Done Gone* violated all three stipulations, resulting in a swift lawsuit that buoyed interest in her book. The ensuing litigation settled the point that such a work might be protected by fair-use doctrine's parody exception but left open the door to future controversy about such "re-writings."

44. I am grateful to James Flannery and Geraldine Higgins for relating this to me.

45. Fletcher, *Ken and Thelma* 68.

46. Quoted in Nevils and Hardy, *Ignatius Rising* 69.

47. Fletcher, *Ken and Thelma* 69, 61.

48. Ibid. 61, 181.

49. Ibid. 70, 106.

50. Nevils and Hardy, *Ignatius Rising* 9.

51. Yeats, *Collected Works* 110.

52. Elliott, "Satirist and Society" 237.

53. Toole, *Confederacy of Dunces* 64 (hereafter cited parenthetically in the text).

54. Nevils and Hardy, *Ignatius Rising* 69.

55. Donald Pizer, e-mail to author, 4 July 2009; Nevils and Hardy, *Ignatius Rising* 160, 69.

56. Dahlberg-Acton, *Essays* 146.

57. Letter, 31 Jan. 1961, quoted in E. Morgan, "Roommate with a View."

58. Nevils and Hardy, *Ignatius Rising* 70, 71.

59. Ibid. 70.

60. Quoted in Fletcher, *Ken and Thelma* 113.

61. Toole, *Neon Bible* 46 (hereafter cited parenthetically in the text).

62. Hardin, "Between Queer Performances" 62.

63. Nevils and Hardy, *Ignatius Rising* 32.

64. Quoted in ibid. 143.

65. The backronym of the title tells what the book is: an elaborate cod. Look it up.

66. Flannery O'Connor, "Revelation," in *Complete Stories* 496.

67. For an account of Toole's sources of inspiration, see MacLauchlin, *Butterfly in the Type-writer* 34–37.

68. Quoted in ibid. 36.

69. Nevils and Hardy, *Ignatius Rising* 42. See also Fletcher, *Ken and Thelma* 71.

70. Quoted in Tutwiler, "Lafayette Confederacy."

71. Nevils and Hardy, *Ignatius Rising* 36.

72. Ibid. 137.

73. Ibid. 29.

74. Fletcher, *Ken and Thelma* 126.

75. Burgess, *Conversations with Anthony Burgess* 120–21.

76. Ibid. 121.

77. The review of 16 May 1963 was titled "Poetry for a Tiny Room" (tiny room = asylum). Reprinted in R. Lewis, *Anthony Burgess* 313–14. For more on literary hoaxes and *A Confederacy of Dunces,* see Giemza, "Conspiracy of Dunces?"

78. Nevils and Hardy, *Ignatius Rising* 52.

79. In a review of *Ignatius Rising* I reached a conclusion similar to MacLauchlin's and faulted the Nevils and Hardy biography for speculation and thin documentation. See MacLauchlin, *Butterfly in the Typewriter* 253–54; and Giemza, Rev. of *Ignatius Rising.* A full discussion of the matter plays out, with a subsequent reader response from Joel Fletcher, on the pages of the *Oxford American.* See Whorton, "Ignatius Screamed"; and Fletcher and Whorton, "Reader Response."

80. Quoted in Tutwiler, "Lafayette Confederacy."

81. E. Morgan, "Roommate with a View."

82. Quoted in Fletcher, *Ken and Thelma* 139.

83. Gleeson, *Irish in the South* 105.

84. Niehaus, "Paddy on the Local Stage" 117.

85. In fact, the play's popularity was so enduring that Boucicault engaged an intense, up-and-coming actor, one John Wilkes Booth, for an 1858 production. Samples, *Lust for Fame* 202.

86. The result is a disappointingly disembodied affair that includes a number of scenes that do not appear in the book, including a mob at a lynching.

87. Adapted by Mary Machala and Tom Key, respectively.

88. E. Bruce Kirkham, in Bain, Flora, and Rubin, *Southern Writers* 330.

89. E. P. O'Donnell, *Great Big Doorstep* 365 (hereafter cited parenthetically).

90. 1910 US Census (New Orleans Ward 9), Enumeration District 0132, National Archives and Records Administration, series T624, roll 522, p. 16A. O'Donnell's younger sisters, Claire and Alice ("Nettie"), may have furnished models for some of the young women in his novels.

91. Crew Lists of Vessels Arriving at New Orleans, Louisiana, 1910–1945, National Archives and Records Administration, series T939, roll 22, Arrival: July 10, 1916.

92. World War I Selective Service System Draft Registration Cards, 1917–1918, National Archives and Records Administration, Registration County: Orleans, roll 1684920.

93. Flora, Vogel, and Giemza, *Southern Writers* 303.

94. *Soards' New Orleans City Directory 1927* 1183. "Adv mgr" presumably means "advertising manager."

95. Sherwood Anderson to Gordon Lewis, 26 June 1939, Albert and Shirley Small Special Collections Library, University of Virginia, Charlottesville.

96. E. P. O'Donnell, Boothville, LA, to Bennet M. Augustin, n.d., Bennet M. Augustin Collection (MSS 15), Louisiana and Special Collections Department, University of New Orleans.

97. Bain, Flora, and Rubin, *Southern Writers* 330.

98. E. P. O'Donnell, "Fragments from Alluvia" 402.

99. E. P. O'Donnell to Gordon Lewis, 29 May 1929, Albert and Shirley Small Special Collections Library, University of Virginia, Charlottesville.

100. E. P. O'Donnell to Augustin, Nov. 1932, Bennet M. Augustin Collection (MSS 15), Louisiana and Special Collections Department, University of New Orleans.

101. E. P. O'Donnell to Lewis, 29 May 1929.

102. *Saturday Review* (14 Nov. 1936): 12.

103. E. P. O'Donnell to Augustin, 24 May 1936, Augustin Collection.

104. E. P. O'Donnell, "Fragments from Alluvia" 402.

105. E. P. O'Donnell, *Green Margins* 440.

106. E. P. O'Donnell, "Pretty John" 15.

107. Eudora Welty cites both examples of Cajun pride in her afterword to *The Great Big Doorstep* (356) and sees the humor in Evvie as a stand-in for Evangeline (357). Perhaps in Topal there is a hint of Harriet Beecher Stowe's Topsy; Commodo Crochet grumbles that the landlord is "a ole Midas and a ole Simon Legree" (*Great Big Doorstep* 267).

108. Weddle, *Bohemian New Orleans* 23.

109. Wolfe, *Notebooks of Thomas Wolfe* 2:862.

110. E. P. O'Donnell to Lewis, 29 May 1929. See also Westbrook, "Common Roots."

111. O'Donnell, Boothville, LA, to Bennet M. Augustin, n.d.

112. 1940 US Census (Boothville, Plaquemines Parish, LA), Enumeration District 38-6, National Archives and Records Administration, series T627, roll 1439, p. 15A. The sales figure for O'Donnell comes from Hackett, "What Happens to First Novelists?" 9; for Mitchell, Andriani, "*Gone with the Wind* Going Strong."

113. S. Young, "In a Country of Drowsy Waters." Tributes from the London papers and from Huxley appear on the jacket copy of the first edition of *The Great Big Doorstep*.

114. White, "Books of the Fall" 16.

115. Eastman, "How Decadent Are We?" 626–27.

116. O'Donnell, Boothville, LA, to Bennet M. Augustin, n.d.

117. Flora, Vogel, and Giemza, *Southern Writers* 303.

118. See the entry on M. K. O'Donnell in Lee, *Classics of Texas Fiction*. The coming-of-age

story centers on Quincie, a pubescent girl whose hard-living and hard-loving father works as a mule skinner and oil-rig roughneck and consorts with a Mexican prostitute. Her second book, *Those Other People,* follows a number of French Quarter characters through a summer's day.

119. Quoted in Welty's afterword to E. P. O'Donnell, *Great Big Doorstep* 366.

120. Welty, afterword to E. P. O'Donnell, *Great Big Doorstep* 366.

121. Ibid. 359.

122. Ibid. 355.

123. E. P. O'Donnell, *Green Margins* 21.

124. Hammett, *Selected Letters* 194; Goodrich, Hackett, and O'Donnell, *Great Big Doorstep.*

125. Quoted in "The Theater."

126. And there are more interesting stories to be told of performers such as Emmet, though there is not space enough to tell them here. For example, we might consider the playwright Joseph M. Field (1810–1856), who played a part in bringing Southwest humor to the stage, and his daughter, Kate Field (1838–1896), no less an important literary figure, who would reject her father's southern loyalties.

127. It is not clear to me whether Emmet Kennedy bore any relation to John Kennedy Toole.

128. Reed, *Dixie Bohemia* 192. I am grateful to John Reed for bringing Kennedy to my attention and for sharing his materials pertaining to him.

129. *Chicago News* 12 Dec. 1926.

130. Reed, *Dixie Bohemia* 193.

CHAPTER 5

1. Flannery O'Connor, *Habit of Being* 32 (hereafter *HB*).

2. "Flannery O'Connor's Mother Buried."

3. Gooch, *Flannery* 279; *HB* 231, 263, 365.

4. S. Thompson, "Dublin."

5. Spivey, *Flannery O'Connor* 154.

6. S. Thompson, "Dublin."

7. James Joyce to Miss Harriet Weaver, 15 Nov. 1926, quoted in Ellmann, *James Joyce* 595.

8. *Ulysses* 52, line 343: "O, rocks! she [Molly] said." In context, Molly is saying, euphemistically, balls to her husband's theory of the transmigration of souls.

9. Flannery O'Connor, *Complete Stories* 375 (hereafter *CS*).

10. Gooch, *Flannery* 102.

11. Ibid. 133.

12. The comment on Hemingway is remarkably perceptive. The hunger for Catholic wholeness is evident not just in the attractions of his life but in many of his stories and novels. It is especially pronounced in one of his less appreciated Nick Adams stories, "The Wine of Wyoming."

13. O'Connor appended a note to the inside back cover: "Errors 51 107 109 114?" Page 51, part of the book's four-chapter treatment of Saint Patrick, considers the pagan celebration of Beltane and Samhain, connecting these vaguely to sun and moon worship. O'Connor might have taken issue with the author's consideration there that "it was a harmless kind of religion, but one that possessed great hold on the senses, and one which a warlike, chivalrous people would be inclined to relinquish easily for the stern, self-denying doctrines of Christianity."

14. Kinney, *Flannery O'Connor's Library* 160.

15. Flannery O'Connor, *Collected Works* 1237.

16. Kilgore, Smith, and Tuck, *History of Clayton County* 242, cited in Homer, "Kinship" 27.

17. Pyron, *Southern Daughter* 17.

18. Johnston and Browne, *Life of Alexander H. Stephens* 586. Another possible nod to Locust Grove comes from a speech in Augusta addressed to Stephens's Know-Nothing detractors: "Are not the descendants of Catholic Marylanders as much Americans by birth as the New England descendants of the Puritans that landed on Plymouth rock?" (294).

19. For more on the reception of Irish and Catholics in Georgia, see Fitzgerald, "Root and Branch."

20. D. Clark, "South's Irish Catholics" 208.

21. Fitzgerald, "Root and Branch" 382.

22. Cook, *History of Baldwin County, Georgia* 296–97. According to Bill Sessions, the Clines may have drifted away from Irish identity, since Irishness implied Yankee, and they chose to see themselves as southerners first.

23. Spivey, *Flannery O'Connor* 91.

24. Gooch, *Flannery* 21.

25. Gleeson and Buttimer, "We Are Irish Everywhere" 195.

26. Sacred Heart was Monsignor Bourke's first parish assignment in Savannah.

27. Ibid. 184, quoting the *Savannah Morning News* 5 July 1881.

28. Patricia Persse, telephone interview by author, 30 Aug. 2009.

29. J. B. Murphy, "Wolfe Tone before Parnell," letter, *New York Times* 26 Oct. 1899. Murphy's letter to the editor gives an account of the controversy swirling in Savannah, even as the column printed below his letter reports on the reception for Tallon and Redmond at New York's Catholic Club.

30. Gleeson and Buttimer, "We Are Irish Everywhere" 196.

31. Gooch, *Flannery* 24.

32. De Lorme, "Monsignor Patrick J. O'Connor."

33. Gooch, *Flannery* 370.

34. Persse, telephone interview by author, 30 Aug. 2009.

35. Ashley Brown, "Flannery O'Connor: A Literary Memoir," Brainard and Frances Neel Cheney Papers, Special Collections, Vanderbilt University, Nashville. I am grateful to Ashley Brown for discussing his recollections in a telephone interview with me in 2008.

36. J. Cash, *Flannery O'Connor: A Life* 80.

37. W. J. Cash, *Mind of the South* 88; Kinney, *Flannery O'Connor's Library* 145.

38. Flannery O'Connor, *Mystery and Manners* 32 (hereafter *MM*).

39. R. Wood, "Such a Catholic" 38.

40. Patrick Samway, interview by author, Manchester, NH, 8 Apr. 2010. The quoted language about the airport is included in an earlier draft of the article that became Samway, "Toward Discerning How Flannery O'Connor's Fiction Can Be Considered 'Roman Catholic.'"

41. Pat Conroy, conversation with author, Columbia, SC, 19 Jan. 2007.

42. A less romantic explanation is that Regina had a parting of ways with one of Mary Flannery's teachers there.

43. H. Brown, "Flannery O'Connor, the Savannah Years," emphasis added.

44. Georgia Senate Resolution 261, 4 Mar. 1997.

45. The interviews were conducted by Jimmy Buttimer, of Savannah, and the transcripts are held in a private collection. Monsignor Bourke was interviewed on 4, 11, and 18 October and 18 November 1995; Bill Canty, on 13 November 1996 and 8 January 1998.

46. Stramm, "Bill Canty Nov. 23, 1903–Nov. 18, 2002."

47. Gleeson and Buttimer, "We Are Irish Everywhere" 196.

48. As O'Connor herself observed in her introduction to *A Memoir of Mary Ann,* "When tenderness is detached from the source of tenderness, its logical outcome is terror. It ends in forced labor camps and in the fumes of the gas chamber" (9).

49. Gooch, *Flannery* 37.

50. Flannery O'Connor, *Wise Blood* 156.

51. Southern Historical Association, *Memoirs of Georgia* 2:260; *Atlanta Constitution* 19 Apr. 1912.

52. Harden, *History of Savannah and South Georgia* 624–27.

53. Gooch, *Flannery* 85.

54. Persse, telephone interview by author, 30 Aug. 2009.

55. Gooch, *Flannery* 244.

56. Bill Sessions, telephone conversation with author, May 2008.

57. Gooch, *Flannery* 121.

58. Gleeson and Buttimer, "We Are Irish Everywhere" 198.

59. Fraser, *Savannah in the Old South* 239.

60. James Ragland, an African American writer for the *Dallas Morning News,* pointed to a different perception of the sign: "It didn't say 'whites only,' but to black people conditioned to Jim Crow laws and customs, it didn't have to." Ragland, "White Settlement."

61. Gleeson and Buttimer, "We Are Irish Everywhere" 188. John England, the first bishop of Charleston, gravitated toward "the ethnically-sensitive charity of the mostly Protestant [Hibernian Society]" because "the Hibernians did not dispense charity to save souls from 'idolatrous popery'"—unlike many such charities.

62. Brinkmeyer, *Art and Vision of Flannery O'Connor* 114.

63. Gooch, *Flannery* 153.

64. Ibid.

65. During her later, four-month stay in Manhattan she attended Mass daily at the Church of the Ascension, "a mostly Irish parish." Ibid. 177.

66. Duquin, *Century of Catholic Converts* 156–57.

67. Gooch, *Flannery* 334.

68. J. Williams, "Stranger Than Paradise" 7.

69. Oates, "Parables of Flannery O'Connor" 16.

70. Flannery O'Connor, *Conversations with Flannery O'Connor* 98.

71. See also Gooch, *Flannery* 132.

72. Ibid. 282.

73. For more on Benjamin Keiley, see chapter 2.

74. H. Brown, "Flannery O'Connor, the Savannah Years."

75. Bourke observed that mixed marriages in which the husband was a Catholic seemed to be most successful, because women were simply glad to have a churchgoing man.

76. Caminada, "Freedom of Speech Agitation" 2:238. Caminada's memoir gives a remarkably impartial behind-the-scenes look into the incident.

77. The event was covered widely by American newspapers, from the *Savannah Morning News* to the *New York Times*. For interesting accounts, see Britten, "Slatterys"; and Caminada, "Freedom of Speech Agitation." Slattery's pamphlets, offering a "Complete Refutation of Popish Lies," were distributed in places as far-flung as Melbourne, Australia, where they were printed by the Loyal Orange Institute of Victoria.

78. McDonogh, *Black and Catholic in Savannah, Georgia* 79.

79. J. Williams, "Stranger Than Paradise" 7.

80. See Gooch, *Flannery* 324.

81. Flannery O'Connor, *Violent Bear It Away* 124 (hereafter cited parenthetically in the text).

82. Rice, *Called Out of Darkness* 69.

83. Gooch, *Flannery* 301.

84. For more on Ed O'Connor's speeches, see O'Gorman, *Peculiar Crossroads* 32.

85. Samway, "Toward Discerning" 162.

86. Rice, *Called out of Darkness* 20.

87. R. Wood, *Flannery O'Connor* 29.

88. Rice, *Called Out of Darkness* 35–36.

89. J. Cash, "Flannery O'Connor as Communicant" 155.

90. See O'Connor's introduction to *A Memoir of Mary Ann.*

91. Joseph Mitchell, *Up in the Old Hotel* 105.

92. Gordon, "Joe Gould, Daddy Hall, and Lady Olga."

93. In November 2011 I interviewed Horace Butler Jr., a riverman of Irish ancestry who hails from the same precinct as Joseph Mitchell, the area around Dublin, North Carolina. He had hosted Mitchell on several visits when the writer was passing through Elizabethtown.

94. Spivey, *Flannery O'Connor* 24.

95. Ibid. 92.

96. Ibid. 110.

97. Ibid. 153.

98. H. Brown, "Flannery O'Connor, the Savannah Years" 12.

99. Flannery O'Connor, *Collected Works* 1074.

100. J. Cash, "Flannery O'Connor as Communicant" 154.

101. Thomas Haddox, who terms Finn "the annoying priest" of the story, cites him as an example of the sort of Catholic character who fails to "inspire admiration." Haddox, *Fears and Fascinations* 113. In my view, Finn displays unusual persistence and compassion as an ecumenicist.

102. W. Smith, "Southerner and Irish?" 235.

103. Elie, *The Life You Save May Be Your Own* 136.

CHAPTER 6

1. Woodward, "Cormac McCarthy's Venomous Fiction."

2. Cormac McCarthy to Howard Woolmer, 8 Apr. 1989, Woolmer Collection of Cormac McCarthy, Southwestern Writers Collection, The Wittliff Collections, Alkek Library, Texas State University–San Marcos, box 1, folder 7 (hereafter Woolmer Collection).

3. Cormac McCarthy, interview by Oprah Winfrey.

4. Robert Coles Papers (#4333), Southern Historical Collection, The Wilson Library, University of North Carolina, Chapel Hill (hereafter Robert Coles Papers, UNC). I am grateful to Rob-

ert Coles for providing generous access to his correspondence and for our conversations about McCarthy.

5. Producer and director Mylène Moreno, www.souvenirpictures.net/SouvenirPictures.swf.

6. See www.facebook.com/group.php?gid=17067603966.

7. Palmer, "Balzac of Human Trash."

8. Woolmer Collection, box 1, folder 6.

9. McCarthy's correspondence reveals his habit of acquiring reviews of his books. See Woolmer Collection; and Robert Coles Papers, UNC.

10. McCarthy to Coles, 1970s, Robert Coles Papers, UNC.

11. Woodward, "Cormac Country."

12. Lines 13–18, in Yeats, *Yeats Reader* 108, emphasis added.

13. Cormac McCarthy Papers, Southwestern Writers Collection, The Wittliff Collections, Alkek Library, Texas State University–San Marcos (hereafter McCarthy Papers), box 19, folder 13.

14. McCarthy, *Suttree* 287, emphasis added (hereafter cited parenthetically in th text). The tormented heretic of the chapel-keeper's tale in *The Crossing* admits, after attempting to interrogate God in every imaginable way, that "in the end . . . no man can see his life until his life is done and where then to make a mending?" (156).

15. Cf. Arnold, "Naming, Nothing, and Knowingness" 51–52.

16. McCarthy Papers, box 19, folder 13. When Cormac McCarthy left his tenor voice to a class cut—"To H. Gass a popular choice / C. McCarthy wills his tenor voice"—was life imitating art, or the reverse? Bob Gentry noted the lines recalling Joyce's first vocation as an opera singer in his memoir of high-school experiences in Knoxville. E-mail correspondence with author, 27 Feb. 2011.

17. McCarthy, interview by Oprah Winfrey; Jurgensen, "Hollywood's Favorite Cowboy."

18. Olney, *Metaphors of Self* 5.

19. Woodward, "Cormac McCarthy's Venomous Fiction."

20. "Southern Parable."

21. Gibson, "Knoxville Gave" 33.

22. Grammer, "Thing against Which Time Will Not Prevail."

23. Woodward, "Cormac Country"; Kushner, "Cormac McCarthy's Apocalypse."

24. The chain of title of the McGrails' house is recorded here at gowdey.ppsri.org/gowdey/Eames/28%20EamesStreet-DEXTER_BROWN_FARMHOUSE.pdf.

25. 1910 US Census (Providence Ward 2, Providence County, RI), Enumeration District 0161, National Archives and Records Administration, series T624, roll 1442, p. 15A. Helena McGrail gave her origin as "Ire.English." Perhaps she saw herself as Anglo-Irish, or perhaps she framed her family history in terms of its connections to the United Kingdom.

26. National Archives and Records Administration Passport Applications, 2 January 1906–31 March 1925; ARC Identifier 583830 / MLR Number A1 534; NARA series M1490, roll 1949.

27. 1880 US Census (Providence, Providence County, RI), Enumeration District 14, National Archives and Records Administration, roll 1211, p. 234A.

28. Robert Coles Papers, UNC.

29. Ibid.

30. Woodward, "Cormac McCarthy's Venomous Fiction."

31. Cormac McCarthy Society. *Cormac McCarthy: A Biography;* Potts, "McCarthy, Mac Airt and Mythology" 32; O'Gorman, *Peculiar Crossroads* 207.

32. Cormac McCarthy Society, *Cormac McCarthy: A Biography.* Adding to the confusion over how he went from Charles to Cormac, the Knoxville writer Don Williams adds, "Christened Charles

McCarthy, like his father, McCarthy changed it to Cormac because, according to [the novelist Leslie] Garrett, he didn't like associations with one Charlie McCarthy, the famous wooden dummy that played comedian to ventriloquist Edgar Bergen's straight man. While the motivation to change his name appears obvious enough now, one can see how an already estranged father might have taken the act as a personal affront." McCarthy's high-school friends remember him as "Charlie." D. Williams, "Cormac McCarthy Crosses the Great Divide." See also Gibson, "Knoxville Gave."

33. Woodward, "Cormac McCarthy's Venomous Fiction."

34. With native familiarity, Bob Gentry posted extended reflections on the Catholic dimensions of McCarthy's Knoxville, many in a series of posts to the Cormac McCarthy Society Forums, which were subsequently lost. This entry was dated 15 April 2007. I am indebted to Bob Gentry for generously sharing his archival material and recollections with me.

35. Woodward, "Cormac Country."

36. Gentry, e-mail to author, 24 Feb. 2011. I am grateful to Bob Gentry for sharing his insights as well as an unpublished memoir of his high-school years. See also W. Morgan, "McCarthy's High School Years"; and Luce, "Cormac McCarthy in High School." McCarthy had earlier attended St. Mary's School, on Vine Avenue, next to both Immaculate Conception Church and Knoxville Catholic High School.

37. Cormac McCarthy Society, *Cormac McCarthy: A Biography.*

38. Ibid.

39. Woodward, "Cormac Country."

40. Woolmer Collection, box 1, folder 9.

41. Ibid.

42. McCarthy Papers, box 84, folder 3. I am grateful to Katie Salzmann, the main archivist, who scoured these materials for Irish references and alerted me to new material bearing on McCarthy's Catholicism. I am also grateful to Lydia R. Cooper, who pointed out the existence of some of these Irish materials, including Dublin real-estate records.

43. *Blood Meridian* was then a work in progress, and McCarthy echoes the words of the Judge in his letter to Coles c. 1980: "The mystery is that there's no mystery." Robert Coles Papers, UNC.

44. McCarthy Papers, box 97, folder 6. Since "Whales and Men" is an unpublished manuscript, I do not supply page numbers. Several drafts are available in box 97 of the McCarthy Papers. In keeping with McCarthy's wish not to see it into print, I quote sparingly from it.

45. Ibid. box 97, folder 1. There is also this cryptic note: "Blacks and Tans. The English have always enjoyed a good press. No one is safe."

46. Ibid. box 35, folder 3. For the sake of avoiding confusion, I will part company with McCarthy here and capitalize the character names Kid, Judge, and Expriest.

47. It seems unlikely that McCarthy would endorse the position that race or genetics accounts for violence in the context of *Blood Meridian* and other works. Rather, violence is one manifestation of the mystery of evil.

48. McCarthy to Robert Coles, c. 1986. Robert Coles Papers (MSS 323), Special Collections and Archives, Michigan State University Libraries, East Lansing (hereafter Robert Coles Papers, MSU).

49. Fullerton, *Handbook of Ethical Theory* 280.

50. The Kid will behold celestial fire but not covenantal rainbows. The second of T. S. Eliot's four quartets mentions the connections between the Leonids and *Road*-like apocalypse:

> Scorpion fights against the Sun
> Until the Sun and Moon go down

> Comets weep and Leonids fly
> Hunt the heavens and the plains
> Whirled in a vortex that shall bring
> The world to that destructive fire
> Which burns before the ice-cap reigns.
> (Lines 11–17, Eliot, *Collected Poems* 181)

51. Here and elsewhere I break with McCarthy's convention in capitalizing the character's moniker to indicate that I am referring to a character; hence, *Expriest, Judge,* etc.

52. McCarthy's notes to a French translator of *Suttree* reveal an acute awareness of southern language, products, and expressions, including *bassackwards,* Bruton Snuff (from nearby Nashville), *trotlines,* and *splo.* For *walkabout* he advises his translator to "ask at your local pool hall." McCarthy Papers, box 19, folder 15.

53. The editor Albert Erskine hated the dialect of *Suttree* and felt that secondary characters were poorly delineated. See ibid. box 19, folder 1.

54. The definition is from Joyce, *James Joyce's "Dubliners"* 108. And of course, established populations of Irish Travelers dot the South, with a substantial settlement at Murphy Village, South Carolina, founded in 1966 by the Charleston native Father Joseph Murphy. They retain elements of a cant said to predate the Norman invasion, and their gypsylike culture has been the subject of much speculation and even a little criminal investigation. Duke, "Secret Life Ends for Irish Travellers." Gypsies resurface in many McCarthy works for example, in the gypsy-fortune teller of chapter 7 in *Blood Meridian,* whose auguries the Expriest dismisses as "idolatry," and again in the "signs in gypsy language, lost patterans" of *The Road* (152). A patteran is a gypsy trail sign, made of sticks, leaves, or whatever is on hand, to indicate a direction taken.

55. Annie DeLisle, quoted in Gibson, "Knoxville Gave."

56. Sepich, *Notes on "Blood Meridian"* 119–22. See also N. Shannon, "Cormac McCarthy Cuts to the Bone."

57. McCarthy to Woolmer, 22 June 1981, Woolmer Collection, box 1, folder 4.

58. DeLisle, quoted in D. Williams, "Cormac McCarthy Crosses the Great Divide."

59. Brickman, "Imposition and Resistance in *The Orchard Keeper.*" The standard collection of the Red Branch tales is Gregory, *Cuchulain of Muirthemne.*

60. Potts, "McCarthy, Mac Airt and Mythology" 28.

61. Canfield, "Dawning of the Age of Aquarius" 675.

62. Pope, *Pope's Odyssey of Homer* 172.

63. Ellmann, *James Joyce* 702.

64. Davenport, *Geography of the Imagination* 294.

65. McCarthy Papers, box 19, folder 14. And even if he did not devise such a schema, scholars will be only too happy to supply one.

66. Kushner, "Cormac McCarthy's Apocalypse."

67. McCarthy, interview by Oprah Winfrey.

68. T. S. Eliot would spin *The Waste Land* in part from the stuff of *Ulysses;* section 4, "Death by Water," features a drowned man in Phlebas the Phoenecian. The poem commences with tarot reading (including the reference to belladonna, which appears in McCarthy's marginalia among his papers), an important motif in both *Suttree* and *Blood Meridian.*

69. McCarthy Papers, box 19, folder 13.

70. The Knoxville native and retired professor Wes Morgan has richly documented many of

the people and places of *Suttree*. The real-life characters glossed here are taken from his fascinating project "Sut's Cemetery," photographing the grave sites of many Knoxvillians featured in the novel. To this gallery of the dead must now be added Jim "J-Bone" Long (d. 14 Sept. 2012), friend and rambling companion to McCarthy, a larger-than-life character in *Suttree* and perhaps in McCarthy's own life. See web.utk.edu/~wmorgan/Suttree/SutCemetery.htm. See also Wallach, *Cormac McCarthy Issue;* Neely, "Cormac McCarthy's Knoxville"; and Gibson, "Knoxville Gave."

71. For an enlightening discussion of Joyce's musicality, begin with Anthony Burgess's delightful *Joysprick*.

72. For a complete discussion of how narrative point of view works in *Ulysses* and why it matters, see Thornton, *Voices and Values in Joyce's "Ulysses."* For a useful treatment of narrative point of view in *Suttree,* see Cooper, *No More Heroes.*

73. Durrell and Miller, *Durrell-Miller Letters* 55.

74. Wallach, "Ulysses in Knoxville" 52.

75. Cavanaugh, "Ulysses Unbound." For more on this scatology, if more there need be, see Dianne Luce's analysis, drawn partly from William C. Spencer's work, in Luce, *Reading the World* 231ff.

76. Wallach, "Ulysses in Knoxville" 54–55.

77. W. Morgan, "McCarthy's High School Years" 2.

78. Bloom, *Cormac McCarthy* 2.

79. Wallach, "Ulysses in Knoxville" 52.

80. Eder, "Cormac McCarthy's Next Pilgrimage."

81. Charles McCarthy, "Tennessee Valley" 128–29. I am grateful to Nancy Proctor, of the TVA Library in Knoxville, for helping me to locate materials by Charles McCarthy.

82. Wallach, "Ulysses in Knoxville" 57.

83. McCarthy to Woolmer, 22 June 1981, Woolmer Collection, box 1, folder 4.

84. See Frye, "Yeats' 'Sailing to Byzantium' and McCarthy's *No Country for Old Men*."

85. O'Gorman, "Joyce and Contesting Priesthoods."

86. See also The Hunchback, The Fool, and The Saint in the "Phases of the Moon" section of Yeats's *A Vision*.

87. Wallach, "Judge Holden" 129.

88. Grammer, "Thing against Which Time Will Not Prevail" 33.

89. McCarthy Papers, box 97, folder 1.

90. Of course, not all the poetic influences are Irish either, with T. S. Eliot's notably apparent in McCarthy's works and in his archival notes. Many have pointed to Yeats in McCarthy's work treating falcons and hawks, but his notes on "Whales and Men" suggest a different vector of influence, as they make mention of Robinson Jeffers's "Hurt Hawks." Some poetic allusions are too broad to compass. With the mention of the primrose on page 24 of *The Road,* possible poetic influence might come from Robert Herrick, Patrick Kavanagh, John Donne, Samuel Coleridge, or Thomas Carew, all of whom penned poems on the subject. Or the passage might simply mean that the child must bloom in the endless night to which he was born.

91. Woolmer to McCarthy, 24 Mar. 1994, Woolmer Collection, box 1, folder 8. The address McCarthy furnished for Banville was care of the *Irish Times.* McCarthy's friendships with writers can be difficult to gauge, but it is interesting that in 1989 he reported that he was distraught over the death of two writer friends—Edward Abbey, whom he apparently knew personally, and [Bruce] Chatwin, the English writer. McCarthy might well have encountered Chatwin through his writings

on Patagonia, as McCarthy traveled there as well. "I was very distressed over Chatwin's death. A talented and honest man and a decent human being—the perfect candidate, in other words for the fates to single out. . . . I've lost another writer friend two weeks ago—Ed Abbey. I think he came across in his writing as some thing of a curmudgen [*sic*] but he was a kind and generous man—qualities, sad to say, not common to writers." Woolmer Collection, box 1, folder 7.

92. Arnold, "Naming, Knowing and Nothingness" 56. In *Child of God,* Ballard, like the narrator of "Fern Hill," dreams a pastoral scene of deer in a meadow, a place where he too might be "green and golden," both "huntsman and herdsman." He also rides in his dream, passing through green leaves with "already some yellow," in a novel entirely dedicated to the fall from grace (170–71):

> And nothing I cared, at my sky blue trades, that time allows
> In all his tuneful turning so few and such morning songs
> Before the children green and golden
> Follow him out of grace.
> (D. Thomas, *Selected Poems* 171)

93. Lynch, "Motor Sport."

94. Joyce, *James Joyce's "Dubliners"* 35.

95. Kreilkamp, *Anglo-Irish Novel and the Big House* 22.

96. Ibid. 23.

97. This version matches Douglas Hyde's translation, reprinted in Kenner, *Colder Eye* 72.

98. O'Gorman, "Joyce and Contesting Priesthoods."

99. I am grateful to Raymond Fitzgerald, SJ, of the New Orleans Province of the Society of Jesus, for finding this information.

100. Patrick Samway, interview by author, Manchester, NH, 8 Apr. 2010.

101. McCarthy Papers, box 97, folder 1.

102. O'Gorman, "Joyce and Contesting Priesthoods."

103. Rick Wallach points to another major vector of influence in *Suttree,* one that might help account for its ecclesiology: James Agee's *A Death in the Family.* "We might justifiably regard *A Death in the Family* as the literary Old Testament of Knoxville," writes Wallach, "*Suttree* as the revisionary New" ("Ulysses in Knoxville" 49). Agee's High Church education verged on the Catholic, after all, and might have prepared the way for McCarthy's "alien" Catholic voice.

104. Ambrosiano, "Blood in the Tracks"; C. Campbell, "Resisting the Urge to Believe Terrible Things."

105. Jurgensen, "Hollywood's Favorite Cowboy."

106. McCarthy to Robert Coles, 1970s, Robert Coles Papers, UNC.

107. Woolmer Collection, box 1, folder 3. In an undated letter to Robert Coles, McCarthy praises the work of Brad Dourif, who starred in *Wise Blood* and in the PBS film adaptation of *The Gardener's Son.* Robert Coles Papers, UNC.

108. See Robert Coles Papers, MSU, including Coles's letter to McCarthy of 18 June 1991: "Here are a couple of things on Bernanos. I keep going back to his novels."

109. Materials in the McCarthy Papers, including McCarthy's correspondence and notes, suggest that he has given quite a bit of thought to what constitutes a "real" filmmaker.

110. Lines 27–32, in Yeats, *Yeats Reader* 72–73.

111. In distressingly similar language, in *Blood Meridian* the Judge "shot the wooden barlatch home behind him" (333) when he seized the Kid in the outhouse.

112. In a series of posts to the Cormac McCarthy Society Forums, now lost, Bob Gentry acknowledges some mixed legacies of hovering priests and knuckle-rapping Sisters of Mercy but does much to defend them from their portrayal in *Suttree* ("These were the Mercies who wiped up vomit, weathered countless acts of student crap, dealt with politicking parents, calmed violent-prone striplings who otherwise would have harmed them, offered up their aches and pains and strains to God and taught many times when they didn't feel like it"). Gentry, "The Other Knoxville vs. Suttree et al.," Cormac McCarthy Society Forums post, 2 May 2007. Gentry takes particular issue with the contention that students received only the most rudimentary education: "Over the years, the many achievements of graduates of Knoxville Catholic High School speak for themselves," he writes, pointing out that many regarded parochial schools as superior to their public counterparts.

113. Yeats, "Crazy Jane Talks to the Bishop" lines 5–6. Like Crazy Jane, with her breasts "flat and fallen now," the "small nun with a bitten face" who later rebukes Suttree during his trial fantasy has "dead breasts brailed up in the knitted vest she wore" (457). She also wears "scorched muslin." The singed and starchy clergy of *Suttree* have devilish fumes about them: "the deathreek of the dark and half scorched muslin they wore" clings to them (254). As to scorched muslin, Bob Gentry suggested that "the nuns had little to spend on clothes. They cleaned and re-cleaned habits and collars. No wonder their muslin looked 'half scorched.'" Gentry, "Other Knoxville vs. Suttree et al."

114. Herbermann et al., *Catholic Encyclopedia* 3:527.

115. V. Bell, *Achievement of Cormac McCarthy* 69.

116. The image is reminiscent of "East Coker" in T. S. Eliot's "Four Quartets": "Ash on an old man's sleeve / Is all the ash the burnt roses leave." Eliot's verses too suggest the creation of a new man.

117. A fragment among McCarthy's papers mentions a man who walks Market Street in Knoxville with "an aura of absolutely inviolable spirituality and . . . people felt it, as though he bestows upon them by some unseen aspergillum a balm . . . [that] arrested them at least for a moment in a grip of peace and even of love's vicious gentility." McCarthy Papers, box 19, folder 13.

118. McCarthy's papers contain a note on a dream apparently about communion: "DREAM He said you want to eat too much too [*sic*] bread *every day*. I only eat one slice. On Sunday." Ibid. box 97, folder 2.

119. The *Oxford English Dictionary* defines *clag* as "a clot of wool consolidated with dirt about the hinder parts of a sheep" and *sleech* as "mud deposited by the sea or a river."

120. Gary Wallace, "Meeting Cormac McCarthy" 138.

121. These examples and a small portion of the preceding analysis were originally published in a slightly different form in Giemza, "Toward a Catholic Understanding of Cormac McCarthy's Oeuvre."

122. Moore, "What Bell Leaves Out.".

123. Cumbow, *Once Upon a Time* 225–27. Other Leone touchstones that resonate with McCarthy's work might include male community, sexual sins, the idealization of women (and what Cumbow calls the "Mary-vs.-Eve syndrome"), child murder, and the confessional.

124. Jung, *Mysterium Coniunctionis* 20.

125. McCarthy Papers, box 19, folder 14. As Vladimir Nabokov would have it, in his lecture on Franz Kafka's *Metamophosis:* "Where there is beauty there is pity for the simple reason that beauty must die: beauty always dies, the manner dies with the matter, the world dies with the individual." Nabokov, Bowers, and Updike, *Lectures on Literature* 251.

126. Wes Morgan and others discussed some of these landmarks in the now-defunct "Ulysses and Suttree in Knoxville" thread of the Cormac McCarthy Society Forums, dated 14 Feb. 2006.

Quoth Bob Gentry, "Protestant eavesdroppin was a no-no in them days but we did it anyway and got a bang out of imitating the Mulls between classes, even within earshot of the black habits."

127. Gibson, "Knoxville Gave."

128. Daugherty, "Gravers False and True"; Wallach, "Judge Holden."

129. McCarthy does use the word *gnostic* in *Suttree.*

130. Deresiewicz, "It's a Man's, Man's World."

131. J. Wood, "Red Planet." McCarthy's notes for *Blood Meridian* show him toying with the Athanasian Creed (which demands strict fidelity to Catholicism). McCarthy Papers, box 91, folder 35.

132. Flannery O'Connor, "The Catholic Novelist in the Protestant South," *Collected Works* 854, emphasis added.

133. Kushner, "Cormac McCarthy's Apocalypse."

134. Bells seem to be one of McCarthy's favored symbols; we even have a Sheriff Bell. One is reminded of the duality of bells in Edgar Allan Poe's "The Bells," ringing "in the startled ear of night."

135. Gunn, "McCarthy's *All the Pretty Horses.*"

136. O'Gorman, "Joyce and Contesting Priesthoods" n. 1. Obviously, these are not exclusively Catholic preoccupations.

137. Flannery O'Connor, *Mystery and Manners* 33.

138. Woodward, "Cormac McCarthy's Venomous Fiction."

139. Woodward, "Cormac Country."

140. See Guinn, "Ruder Forms Survive"; and V. Bell, "Ambiguous Nihilism."

141. There is an echo of Stephen Dedalus's "old artificer" in *Portrait of the Artist* in McCarthy's "old hoodwinker," as well as mention of an "Old Execrator" in the *Suttree* composition notes.

142. Flannery O'Connor, *Mystery and Manners* 208.

143. As a student of Dante, McCarthy would know that Judas has a very special place in hell. His Mexican characters regard Judas with reflexive superstition. See *The Crossing* 368, where the fortune-teller explains, idiomatically, that she has been "carried away by Judas."

144. Haddox, *Fears and Fascinations* 86.

145. Thad Sitton's unforgettable book *The Texas Sheriff* demonstrates how true to life McCarthy's Bell is.

146. Gibson, "Knoxville Gave."

147. McCarthy Papers, box 97, folder 1 (cited parenthetically in this paragraph).

148. Lafcadio Hearn rendered perhaps the finest translation of Flaubert's text into English.

149. Davenport, *Geography of the Imagination* 295.

150. Woolmer Collection, box 1, folder 6.

151. Davenport, *Geography of the Imagination* 295, 297.

152. See ibid. 296–97.

153. Introduction to Flaubert, *Temptation of St. Anthony,* unpaginated (hereafter cited parenthetically in the text).

154. Davenport, *Geography of the Imagination* 296.

155. Jurgensen, "Hollywood's Favorite Cowboy." McCarthy's intense interest in the tensions between apophatic and cataphatic theology would make Anthony's temptation appealing indeed.

156. Woodward, "Cormac McCarthy's Venomous Fiction."

157. Gibson, "Knoxville Gave."

158. Yeats, *Yeats Reader* 65.

159. Woodward, "Cormac Country."

160. "Whales and Men," McCarthy Papers, box 97, folder 6.

161. Sepich, *Notes on "Blood Meridian"* 149.

CHAPTER 7

1. William F. Buckley Jr. to author, 17 Nov. 2003.

2. Pat Conroy, conversation with author, Columbia, SC, 20 Jan. 2007.

3. Conroy, *My Reading Life* 19.

4. Austin, "Pat Conroy."

5. M. Mitchell, *Gone with the Wind* xiv.

6. Ibid. xii. With *would,* Conroy demonstrates his genius for poetic license.

7. Pat Conroy to Louis Rubin, 15 Jan. 1982, Louis Decimus Rubin Papers (#3899), Southern Historical Collection, The Wilson Library, University of North Carolina, Chapel Hill.

8. M. Mitchell, *Gone with the Wind* xiv.

9. Ibid.

10. Conroy, conversation with author, 20 Jan. 2007.

11. Conroy, *South of Broad* 507 (hereafter cited parenthetically in the text).

12. Minzesheimer, "Pat Conroy Returns to Familiar Turf."

13. Goldman, "Papal Visit"; Woods, *History of the Catholic Church* 261.

14. Joyce, *Portrait of the Artist* 275–76.

15. Bohjalian, "New Book out by Pat Conroy."

16. John Berendt, "The Conroy Saga," *Vanity Fair* July 1995, quoted in Burns, *Pat Conroy* 13.

17. See Conroy, *My Reading Life* ch. 3.

18. Sayers, "Land's End" 21.

19. Valerie Sayers, e-mail interview by author, 18 Aug. 2010.

20. Sayers, "Land's End, Beaufort, South Carolina."

21. Sayers, e-mail interview by author, 18 Aug. 2010.

22. Ibid.

23. Ibid.

24. Millen Ellis is the basis for the character Ogden Loring in *The Great Santini*. Gene Norris is also remembered in "The Teacher," ch. 3 of Conroy's *My Reading Life*.

25. Sayers, e-mail interview by author, 18 Aug. 2010.

26. Ibid.

27. Ibid.

28. Ibid.

29. See Sayers, *Who Do You Love?* 27; and Sayers, "Guilt and *Gone with the Wind*." Like Pat Conroy, Sayers cites *Gone with the Wind,* a film she experienced with an appropriate sense of guilt, as a major influence. Flannery O'Connor, of course, also reacted to the film's celebrity, which she skewered in "The Enduring Chill" and "The Partridge Festival."

30. Sayers, e-mail interview by author, 19 Jan. 2012.

31. In her review of *The Distance Between Us,* Jill McCorkle wrote that the screenplay portion of the novel amounted to a "digression" that "sometimes strains the reader's patience." The novelist Michael Parker found the narrative voice of *Brain Fever* to be too episodically lucid to represent

an authentic mental breakdown. McCorkle, "One Good, One Bad, One Angry"; Parker, "Crazy in Manhattan."

32. Sayers, "Land's End, Beaufort, South Carolina" 21.

33. Sayers, e-mail interview by author, 18 Aug. 2010.

34. A slightly altered version of this biographical overview and portions of the interviews that follow were first printed in Sayers, "Powers and Prophecy."

35. See Sayers, "Age of Infidelity."

36. Mosby, "Anne Rice."

37. Rice, *Called Out of Darkness* 159 (hereafter *CO*).

38. Rice, *Blackwood Farm* 212.

39. Rice, *Christ the Lord: Out of Egypt* 324.

40. Anne Rice, e-mail to author, 31 Jan. 2012.

41. "How extraordinary it felt to have money in his pockets in his old home town," thinks Michael Curry, the Irish Channel protagonist of *The Witching Hour,* again seeming to channel Rice's own thoughts (830).

42. Rice, "Interview with Anne Rice" 89, emphasis added.

43. Crosby, "Out of Darkness."

44. Snow, "In Defense of Anne Rice."

45. Rice, e-mail to author, 31 Jan. 2012.

46. Rice, *Feast of All Saints* 13 (hereafter cited parenthetically in the text as *FAS*).

47. Hearn, *Chita* 44.

48. Rice, *The Witching Hour* 466 (hereafter cited parenthetically in the text as *WH*).

49. J. Dickinson, *Haunted City* 4.

50. Similarly, when Valerie Sayers writes in *The Distance Between Us* that "they'd none of them had a drink in their lives" (21), one might ask, is this a remnant of Irish American locution, the sort of ethnic trace that Rice fixes on?

51. Snow, "In Defense of Anne Rice."

52. For more on the influence of these orders on the New Orleans Irish, see Giemza, "Sisters of Secession."

53. Rice, *Belinda* 99.

54. "The Impulsive Imp." *Annerice.com.* Web. 18 Oct 2012.

55. Anne Rice, quoted in della Cava, "Passion of the Rices."

56. Rice, "Interview with an Ex-Vampire Novelist."

57. "Writer Anne Rice."

58. Diski, "Review: *Christ the Lord: Out of Egypt*."

59. Cheuse, "'Christ the Lord': An Earnest Mess."

60. Grenier, Rev. of *Christ the Lord.*

61. Maslin, "Telling His Own Tale"; Kuo, "Anne Rice's Jesus Transfixes in *Road to Cana*."

62. McGarvey, "Imagining Jesus."

63. Snow, "In Defense of Anne Rice."

64. Rice, "Interview with an Ex-Vampire Novelist."

65. As Walker Percy claimed in his essay "How to Be an American Novelist in Spite of Being Southern and Catholic," "The intervention of God in history through the Incarnation bestows a weight and a value to the individual human narrative which is like money in the bank to the novelist." *Signposts in a Strange Land* 178.

CHAPTER 8

1. Needless to say, this depends on who is included and how one defines the American South. See Grammich, *Swift Growth and Change.*

2. Ibid.

3. Keysar and Kosmin, "Latino Influx." American Catholics in general have demonstrated much independence of church teaching on a variety of issues. In the matter of gay marriage, for example, they are significantly more likely to support gay marriage than Protestants (39% compared with 24%). See Masci, "Public Opinion on Gay Marriage."

4. See K. Miller, "'Scotch-Irish,' 'Black Irish'" 141–42.

5. Census Bureau, "Race and Hispanic Origin of the Foreign-Born Population." "Europe" includes the countries of the former Soviet Union and Canada. The numbers continue to trend downward in the latest years for which data are available.

6. US Census Bureau data, www.census.gov/newsroom/releases/pdf/cb05-ff03-2.pdf.

7. Meagher, "Discussion on Irish Immigrants."

8. Ibid.

9. Tobin, *Irish in South Carolina* 4. The pamphlet was sufficiently popular that Tobin's second printing ran to six thousand copies.

10. Much of what Burduck labels "Catholic" in Poe's work could equally be Episcopalian in nature and thus attributable to the church of Poe's upbringing. Burduck at times makes a bit much of this circumstantial evidence, especially where Poe's friendships with various Catholic literati are concerned.

11. Burduck, *Usher's Forgotten Church?* 29.

12. Poe, *Edgar Allan Poe: Essays and Reviews,* quoted in Burduck, *Usher's Forgotten Church?* 20.

13. Burduck, *Usher's Forgotten Church?* 20.

14. Flannery O'Connor, *Complete Stories* 201.

15. Flannery O'Connor, *Wise Blood* 18.

16. Flannery O'Connor, *Habit of Being* 28.

17. See Franchot, *Roads to Rome* ch. 8.

18. The existence of the book, long thought to be a literary hoax, was confirmed in the 1960s. Poe's inside joke is that the prayers might have kept one's undead sister at bay. See Bendixen and Nagel, *Companion to the American Short Story* 29.

19. Meyers, *Edgar Allan Poe* 1.

20. See "Poe's Life. Family Tree."

21. See Mabbot, "Poe and *The Philadelphia Irish Citizen.*"

22. Quinlan, *Strange Kin* 191.

23. Gill, *Life of Edgar Allan Poe* 10.

24. Piatt, *Palace-Burner* xxvii.

25. Yeats, *Collected Works of W. B. Yeats, Volume IX* 203–4.

26. A. Young, *Catholic and Protestant Countries Compared* 604.

27. Piatt, *Palace-Burner* lv. Her husband would submit poems to the Boston diocese's *Pilot.*

28. Donn Piatt, like his brother J.J., was a diplomat, described by a biographer as "a national gadfly in the Gilded Age." Bridges, "Don Piatt." A letter from Archbishop William Henry Elder to William J. Onahan, 9 Oct. 1889, mentions Don Piatt as a "practical Catholic for several years." Archives, University of Notre Dame, Notre Dame, IN.

29. Piatt, *Palace-Burner* lii, 172.

30. Ibid. 179.

31. Jacobson, *Whiteness of a Different Color* 8.

32. Don Doyle, *Faulkner's County.*

33. Blotner, *Faulkner* 485.

34. Quinlan, *Strange Kin* 224–25.

35. W. Faulkner, *Sound and the Fury* 318.

36. See Quinlan, *Strange Kin* 224.

37. Sayers, e-mail interview by author, 18 Aug. 2010.

38. Ibid.

SELECTED BIBLIOGRAPHY

ARCHIVES CONSULTED

Albert and Shirley Small Special Collections Library, University of Virginia, Charlottesville
Archdiocese of Mobile Archives
Archives, University of Notre Dame, Notre Dame, IN
DeAndreis-Rosati Memorial Archives, DePaul University, Chicago
Diocese of Charleston Archives
Diocese of Nashville Archives
Diocese of Savannah Archives
David M. Rubenstein Rare Book and Manuscript Library, Duke University, Durham, NC
Division of Library and Archives, Missouri Historical Society, St. Louis
Georgia Historical Society Library and Archives, Savannah
Harry Ransom Center, University of Texas, Austin
Jacob Rader Marcus Center of the American Jewish Archives, Cincinnati, OH
Library of Virginia, Richmond
Louisiana and Special Collections Department, University of New Orleans
Manuscript, Archives, and Rare Book Library, Woodruff Library, Emory University, Atlanta
Manuscript Division, Library of Congress, Washington, DC
McClung Historical Collection, Knoxville, TN
Museum of the Confederacy Archives, Richmond, VA
New Orleans Public Library
North Carolina State Archives, Raleigh
Ryan Archive, Belmont Abbey College, Belmont, NC
South Caroliniana Library, University of South Carolina, Columbia
Southern Historical Collection, The Wilson Library, University of North Carolina, Chapel Hill
Special Collections, Baylor University, Waco, TX
Special Collections, Houghton Library, Harvard University, Cambridge, MA
Special Collections, Vanderbilt University, Nashville
Special Collections and Archives, Loyola University, New Orleans
Special Collections and Archives, Michigan State University Libraries, East Lansing
Spring Hill College Archives, Mobile, AL

Tennessee State Library and Archives, Nashville
Tennessee Valley Authority Library, Knoxville
University of Mobile Archives, Mobile, AL
Virginia Historical Society, Richmond
The Witliff Collections, Alkek Library, Texas State University–San Marcos

PUBLISHED SOURCES

"Abolition On and Off the Stage." *New York Herald* 5 Dec. 1859.

Adams, Bluford. "Reading the Re-Revival: Competing Approaches in U.S. Ethnic Studies." *American Literary History* 15.2 (2003): 34–56.

Adams, Henry. *Mont-Saint-Michel and Chartres.* Boston: Houghton Mifflin, 1904.

Adams, John, Thomas Jefferson, and Abigail Adams. *The Adams-Jefferson Letters: The Complete Correspondence between Thomas Jefferson and Abigail and John Adams.* Ed. Lester J. Cappon. Chapel Hill: U of North Carolina P, 1988.

"Address to the Patrons of the Review, and to the People of the South." *Southern Quarterly* 22 (Apr. 1847).

Akenson, Donald H. *If the Irish Ran the World: Montserrat, 1630–1730.* Montreal: McGill-Queen's UP, 1997.

Alderman, Edwin Anderson, Joel C. Harris, Charles W. Kent, C. A. Smith, and Lucian L. Knight, eds. *Library of Southern Literature, Compiled under the Direct Supervision of Southern Men of Letters.* 16 vols. Atlanta: Martin & Hoyt, 1909.

Allen, Felicity. *Jefferson Davis, Unconquerable Heart.* Columbia: U of Missouri P, 1999.

Allen, Henry. "The Look of the Irish: It's a Heritage as Plain as the Nose on a Face." *Washington Post* 17 Mar. 1995.

Allen, Theodore. *The Invention of the White Race.* New York: Verso, 1993.

Ambrosiano, Jason. "Blood in the Tracks: Catholic Postmodernism in the Crossing." *Southwestern American Literature* 25 (1999): 83–91.

Anderson, Jon W., and William B. Friend. *The Culture of Bible Belt Catholics.* New York: Paulist, 1995.

Anderson, R. Bentley. *Black, White, and Catholic: New Orleans Interracialism, 1947–1956.* Nashville: Vanderbilt UP, 2005.

Andrews, Eliza Frances. *The War-Time Journal of a Georgia Girl, 1864–1865.* Macon, GA: Ardivan, 1960.

Andrews, Kenneth Raymond, Nicholas P. Canny, Paul Edward Hedley Hair, and David P. Quinn. *The Westward Enterprise: English Activities in Ireland, the Atlantic, and America, 1480–1650.* Detroit: Wayne State UP, 1979.

Andrews, William L. *The Literary Career of Charles W. Chesnutt.* Baton Rouge: Louisiana State UP, 1980.

Andriani, Lynn. "*Gone with the Wind* Going Strong at 75." *Publishers Weekly* 25 Apr. 2011. Web. 17 Oct. 2012.

The Antelope. 23 US 66. Supreme Court of the US. 1825.

"The Antelope, or General Ramirez." *The African Observer.* Ed. Enoch Lewis. Philadelphia, 1827. 344–54.

Arnold, Edwin T. "Naming, Nothing, and Knowingness: McCarthy's Moral Parables." Arnold and Luce 45–69.

Arnold, Edwin T., and Dianne C. Luce, eds. *Perspectives on Cormac McCarthy.* Jackson: UP of Mississippi, 1999.

Artuso, Kathryn Stelmach. *Transatlantic Renaissances: Literature of Ireland and the American South.* Newark, DE: U of Delaware P, 2012.

Austin, Jonathan. "Pat Conroy: 'I was raised by Scarlett O'Hara,'" *CNN.com,* Cable News Network, 4 Feb. 2000. Web. 12 July 2012.

Bailey, James Henry. "Anthony M. Keiley and 'The Keiley Incident.'" *Virginia Magazine of History and Biography* 67.1 (1959): 65–81.

Bailly de Barberey, Hélène Roederer, and Mary Coyle O'Neil. *Mother Elizabeth Ann Seton.* Emmitsburg, MD: Mother Seton Guild, 1927.

Bain, Robert, Joseph M. Flora, and Louis Decimus Rubin, eds. *Southern Writers: A Biographical Dictionary.* Baton Rouge: Louisiana State UP, 1979.

Baker, J. Robert. "William Alexander Caruthers." *Dictionary of Literary Biography,* vol. 248. Ed. Kent Ljungquist. Detroit: Gale Research, 2001. 61–68.

"The Banshee." *Washington Post* 25 Nov. 1928.

Barringer, George M. *The American Mission: Maryland Jesuits from Andrew White to John Carroll.* Washington, DC: Georgetown U, 1976.

Barron, James, and Linda Lee. "Public Lives." *New York Times* 13 Dec. 2000.

Bartley, Numan V. *The Evolution of Southern Culture.* Athens: U of Georgia P, 1988.

Bauer, Margaret D. "When a Convent Seems the Only Viable Choice: Questionable Callings in Stories by Alice Dunbar-Nelson, Alice Walker, and Louise Erdrich." *Critical Perspectives on Alice Walker.* Ed. Ikenna Dieke. Westport, CT: Greenwood, 1999. 45–54.

Beach, Patrick. "All the Pretty Sentences; Cormac McCarthy Cleans up His Verbiage—and Gets His Hands Dirty." *Austin American-Statesman* 17 July 2005: K5.

Beagle, Donald Robert. *The Fr. Abram J. Ryan Archive at Belmont Abbey College.* 2011. Web. 3 May 2011.

———. "Integrating Digital and Archival Sources in Historical Research: Recovering Lost Knowledge about a Catholic Poet of the Civil War." *Catholic Library World* 81.3 (2011): 201–9.

———. "Ryan, Beauregard, and Bragg: New Research from the Fr. Abram J. Ryan Archive." *Catholic Library World* 74.3 (2004): 192–295.

Beagle, Donald Robert, and Bryan Albin Giemza. *Poet of the Lost Cause: A Life of Father Ryan.* Knoxville: U of Tennessee P, 2008.

Beckles, Hilary. "Plantation Production and White 'Proto-Slavery': White Indentured Servants and the Colonisation of the English West Indies, 1624–1645." *The Americas* 41.3 (1985): 21–45.

———. "A 'Riotous and Unruly Lot': Irish Indentured Servants and Freemen in the English West Indies, 1644–1713." *William and Mary Quarterly* 47.4 (1990): 503–22.

Beidler, Philip D. "A. B. Meek's Great American Epic Poem of 1855; or, the Curious Career of the Red Eagle." *Mississippi Quarterly* 51.2 (1998): 275–90.

Bell, Madison Smartt. "The Man Who Understood Horses." Rev. of *All the Pretty Horses,* by Cormac McCarthy. *New York Times* 17 May 1992.

Bell, Vereen M. *The Achievement of Cormac McCarthy.* Baton Rouge: Louisiana State UP, 1988.

———. "The Ambiguous Nihilism of Cormac McCarthy." *Southern Literary Journal* 15.2 (1983): 31–41.

Bendixen, Alfred, and James Nagel, eds. *A Companion to the American Short Story.* Oxford: Blackwell, 2007.

Berkeley, George. *The Works of George Berkeley, D.D.* Ed. Alexander Campbell Fraser. Oxford: Clarendon, 1898.

Berlin, Ira. *Many Thousands Gone: The First Two Centuries of Slavery in North America.* Cambridge, MA: Belknap P of Harvard UP, 1998.

Berthoff, Rowland. "Celtic Mist over the South." *Journal of Southern History* 52.4 (1986): 523–46.

Bickley, Robert Bruce. *Joel Chandler Harris.* Boston: Twayne, 1978.

———. *Joel Chandler Harris: A Biography and Critical Study.* Athens: U of Georgia P, 2008.

Bickley, Robert Bruce, Karen L. Bickley, and Thomas H. English. *Joel Chandler Harris: A Reference Guide.* Boston: G. K. Hall, 1978.

Blackman, Ann. *Wild Rose: Rose O'Neale Greenhow, Civil War Spy.* New York: Random House, 2005.

Bledsoe, Erik. "Margaret Mitchell's Review of *Soldier's Pay*." *Mississippi Quarterly* 49.3 (1996): 591–93.

Bloom, Harold. *Cormac McCarthy.* Philadelphia: Chelsea House, 2002.

Blotner, Joseph Leo. *Faulkner: A Biography.* New York: Random House, 1974.

Bohjalian, Chris. "New Book out by Pat Conroy, the Prince of Tears." *Washington Post* 11 Aug. 2009.

Boldrick, Charles C. "Father Abram J. Ryan, the Poet-Priest of the Confederacy." *Filson Club Historical Quarterly* 46.3 (1972): 201–18.

"Books: Scholar in America." *Time* 27 Nov. 1944.

Bornstein, George. *The Colors of Zion: Blacks, Jews, and Irish from 1845 to 1945.* Cambridge, MA: Harvard UP, 2011.

Bottum, Jody. "Gatsby's Epitaph: F. Scott Fitzgerald." *Catholic Dossier* 5.4 (1999): 9–12.

Boucicault, Dion. *The Octoroon.* London: Lacy, 1859.

Bouvier, Jean Baptiste. *Institutiones theologicæ ad usum seminariorum.* Paris, 1873.

Bowers, James. *Reading Cormac McCarthy's "Blood Meridian."* Boise, ID: Boise State U, 1999.

Bowes, John C. "Glory in Gloom: Abram J. Ryan, Southern Catholicism, and the Lost Cause." Diss. Saint Louis U, 1996.

Brady, Ciaran. *The Encyclopedia of Ireland: An A–Z Guide to Its People, Places, History, and Culture.* New York: Oxford UP, 2000.

Brand, C. P. *Torquato Tasso: A Study of the Poet and of His Contribution to English Literature.* Cambridge: Cambridge UP, 1965.

Brasch, Walter M. *Brer Rabbit, Uncle Remus, and The "Cornfield Journalist": The Tale of Joel Chandler Harris.* Macon, GA: Mercer UP, 2000.

Brickman, Barbara. "Imposition and Resistance in *The Orchard Keeper*." Wallach, *Myth, Legend, Dust* 55–67.

Bridges, Peter. "Don Piatt: Diplomat and Gadfly." *American Diplomacy* Feb. 2007. Web. 6 Aug. 2012.

Brinkmeyer, Robert H. *The Art and Vision of Flannery O'Connor.* Baton Rouge: Louisiana State UP, 1993.

———. *The Fourth Ghost: White Southern Writers and European Fascism, 1930–1950.* Baton Rouge: Louisiana State UP, 2009.

Brinsfield, John Wesley. *Faith in the Fight: Civil War Chaplains.* Mechanicsburg, PA: Stackpole, 2003.

Britten, James. "The Slatterys." *Publications of the Catholic Truth Society,* vol. 38. London: Catholic Truth Society, 1898.

Brody, Jennifer DeVere. *Impossible Purities: Blackness, Femininity, and Victorian Culture.* Durham, NC: Duke UP, 1998.

Brooks, Cleanth. *William Faulkner: The Yoknapatawpha Country.* Baton Rouge: Louisiana State UP, 1990.

Brown, David. *The Planter: or, Thirteen Years in the South.* Philadelphia: H. Hooker, 1853.

Brown, Hugh. "Flannery O'Connor, the Savannah Years." MS. Diocese of Savannah Archives, 1994.

Brown, William Wells. *The American Fugitive in Europe.* New York: J. P. Jewett, 1855.

———. *My Southern Home; or, the South and Its People.* Boston: A. G. Brown, 1880.

Brownlow, William Gannaway. *Americanism Contrasted with Foreignism, Romanism, and Bogus Democracy, in the Light of Reason, History, and Scripture; in Which Certain Demagogues in Tennessee, and Elsewhere, Are Shown up in Their True Colors.* Nashville, 1856.

Brownson, Orestes Augustus, and Henry F. Brownson. *The Works of Orestes A. Brownson.* 20 vols. New York: AMS, 1966.

Burduck, Michael Lawrence, and Edgar Allan Poe Society of Baltimore. *Usher's Forgotten Church? Edgar Allan Poe and Nineteenth-Century American Catholicism.* Baltimore: Edgar Allan Poe Society and Library of the U of Baltimore, 2000. Offprint.

Burgess, Anthony. *Conversations with Anthony Burgess.* Ed. Earl G. Ingersoll and Mary C. Ingersoll. Jackson: UP of Mississippi, 2008.

———. *Joysprick: An Introduction to the Language of James Joyce.* New York: Harcourt Brace Jovanovich, 1975.

Burns, Landon C. *Pat Conroy: A Critical Companion.* Westport, CT: Greenwood, 1996.

Burrison, John A. *Roots of a Region: Southern Folk Culture.* Jackson: UP of Mississippi, 2007.

Butsch, Joseph. "Catholics and the Negro." *Journal of Negro History* 2.4 (1917): 393–410.

Buttimer, Brendan J. "Catholic Church." *New Georgia Encyclopedia*. 2005. Web. 3 May 2010.

——. "New South, New Church: The Catholic Public Schools of Georgia, 1870–1917." MA thesis, Armstrong Atlantic State U, 2001.

Caminada, Jerome. "A Freedom of Speech Agitation." *Twenty-five Years of Detective Life.* 2 vols. Manchester, UK: John Heywood, 1895. 2:233–61.

Campbell, Christopher Dallas. "Resisting the Urge to Believe Terrible Things: Cormac McCarthy's Quest." Diss. U of Virginia, 2002.

Campbell, Joseph. *The Hero with a Thousand Faces.* Princeton, NJ: Princeton UP, 1972.

Canfield, J. Douglas. "The Dawning of the Age of Aquarius: Abjection, Identity, and the Carnivalesque in Cormac McCarthy's *Suttree*." *Contemporary Literature* 44.4 (2003): 664–96.

Cant, John. *Cormac McCarthy and the Myth of American Exceptionalism.* New York: Routledge, 2008.

Cantrell, James P. *How Celtic Culture Invented Southern Literature.* Gretna, LA: Pelican, 2006.

Cantú, Carlos H. *Los Colorados del San Patricio.* Monterrey, Mexico: Fondo Estatal para la Cultura y las Artes de Nuevo Léon, 1997.

Cardon, Lauren S. "'Good Breeding': Margaret Mitchell's Multi-Ethnic South." *Southern Quarterly* 44.4 (2007): 61–82.

Carey, Patrick W. "Political Atheism: Dred Scott, Roger Brooke Taney, and Orestes A. Brownson." *Catholic Historical Review* 88.2 (2002): 207–23.

Carroll, Mary Austin. *A Catholic History of Alabama and the Floridas.* New York: P. J. Kenedy & Sons, 1908.

——. *Leaves from the Annals of the Sisters of Mercy.* 4 vols. New York: Catholic Publication Society, 1889.

——. *Life of Catherine McAuley, Foundress and First Superior of the Institute of Religious Sisters of Mercy.* New York: P. J. Kenedy, 1866.

Caruthers, William Alexander. *The Cavaliers of Virginia; or, the Recluse of Jamestown; an Historical Romance of the Old Dominion.* 1834–35. 2 vols. in 1. Ridgewood, NJ: Gregg, 1968.

Cash, Jean W. *Flannery O'Connor: A Life.* Knoxville: U of Tennessee P, 2002.

——. "Flannery O'Connor as Communicant: A Constant Devotion." Gretlund and Westarp, 2006. 149–61.

Cash, W. J. *The Mind of the South.* 1941. New York: Vintage, 1991.

Catechism of the Catholic Church. Libreria Editrice Vaticana. Mahwah, NJ: Paulist, 1994.

Cavanaugh, Tim. "Ulysses Unbound." *Reason* 36.3 (2004): 51–55.

Census Bureau. "Race and Hispanic Origin of the Foreign-Born Population in the United States: 2007." American Community Survey Reports. census.gov. 10 Jan. 2010. Web. 18 Oct. 2012.

Chalkley, Lyman. *Chronicles of the Scotch-Irish Settlement in Virginia, Extracted from the Original Court Records of Augusta County 1745–1800.* 3 vols. Baltimore: Genealogical Publishing, 1965.

Chalmers, David Mark. *Hooded Americanism: The History of the Ku Klux Klan.* Durham, NC: Duke UP, 1987.

Chatterton, Wayne. *Irvin S. Cobb.* Boston: Twayne, 1986.

Cheever, Henry T. *Correspondencies of Faith and Views of Madame Guyon: Being a Devout Study of the Unifying Power and Place of Faith in the Theology and Church of the Future.* London: Elliot Stock, 1887.

Chesnutt, Charles Waddell, and William L. Andrews. *Conjure Tales and Stories of the Color Line.* New York: Penguin, 2000.

Cheuse, Alan. "'Christ the Lord': An Earnest Mess." *All Things Considered.* National Public Radio. 26 Dec. 2005. Web.

"Chief Justice Keiley Resigns at Cairo." *New York Times* 10 Apr. 1902.

Chopin, Kate. *The Awakening.* New York: H. S. Stone, 1899.

———. *Complete Novels and Stories.* New York: Library of America, 2002.

———. *Kate Chopin's Private Papers.* Ed. Emily Toth and Per Seyersted; assoc. ed. Cheyenne Bonnell. Bloomington: Indiana UP, 1997.

———. *A Vocation and a Voice: Stories.* Foreword by Emily Toth. New York: Penguin, 1991.

Ciuba, Gary M. *Desire, Violence and Divinity in Modern Southern Fiction: Katherine Anne Porter, Flannery O'Connor, Cormac McCarthy, Walker Percy.* Baton Rouge: Louisiana State UP, 2007.

Clark, Barrett H. *America's Lost Plays.* Bloomington: Indiana UP, 1963.

Clark, Dennis. *The Irish Relations: Trials of an Immigrant Tradition.* Rutherford, NJ: Fairleigh Dickinson UP, 1982.

———. "The South's Irish Catholics: A Case of Cultural Confinement." Miller and Wakelyn, *Catholics in the Old South* 195–210.

Clinton, Catherine, and Nina Silber. *Battle Scars: Gender and Sexuality in the American Civil War.* Oxford: Oxford UP, 2006.

Cloud, Virginia Woodward. "The Other Man." *Uncle Remus's The Home Magazine* 1.1 (May 1908).

Coakley, R. Walter. Rev. of *Foreigners in the Confederacy,* by Ella Lonn. *William and Mary College Quarterly Historical Magazine* 22.1 (1942): 75–80.

Cobb, Irvin S. *Exit Laughing.* Indianapolis: Bobbs-Merrill, 1941.

———. *The Lost Irish Tribes in the South: An Address Delivered Before the American Irish Historical Society of New York Two Years Ago, Which Is Now Attracting Countrywide Attention.* Washington, DC: Irish National Bureau, Section of Information, 1919.

Cogley, John. *Catholic America.* New York: Dial, 1973.

Cohen, Hennig, and William B. Dillingham. *Humor of the Old Southwest.* Boston: Houghton Mifflin, 1964.

Cohn, Deborah N. *History and Memory in the Two Souths: Recent Southern and Spanish American Fiction.* Nashville: Vanderbilt UP, 1999.

Collum, Danny Duncan. *Black and Catholic in the Jim Crow South: The Stuff That Makes Community.* New York: Paulist, 2006.

Condon, Edward O'Meagher. *The Irish Race in America.* New York: Ford's National Library, 1887.

Conolly, Thomas. *An Irishman in Dixie: Thomas Conolly's Diary of the Fall of the Confederacy.* Ed. Nelson D. Lankford. Columbia: U of South Carolina P, 1988.

Conroy, Pat. *My Losing Season.* New York: Dial, 2006.

——. *My Reading Life.* New York: Doubleday, 2010.

——. *South of Broad.* New York: Random House, 2010.

——. *The Water Is Wide.* Boston: Houghton Mifflin, 1972.

Conyngham, David Power. *Lives of the Irish Saints: From St. Patrick Down to St. Laurence O'Toole.* New York: Sadlier, 1870.

Cook, Anna Maria Green. *History of Baldwin County, Georgia.* Spartanburg, SC: Reprint, 1978.

Cookson, Catharine, ed. *Religious/Freedom, Southern Style: A Collection of Essays from the Spring 2001 Symposium, Held at the Center for the Study of Religious Freedom at Virginia Wesleyan College.* Norfolk: Center for the Study of Religious Freedom at Virginia Wesleyan College, 2002.

Cooper, Lydia R. *No More Heroes: Narrative Perspective and Morality in Cormac McCarthy.* Baton Rouge: Louisiana State UP, 2011.

Corby, William. *Memoirs of Chaplain Life.* Notre Dame, IN: Scholastic, 1894.

Cormac McCarthy Society. *Cormac McCarthy: A Biography.* 2006. Web. 3 May 2011.

Cott, Jonathan. *Wandering Ghost: The Odyssey of Lafcadio Hearn.* New York: Knopf, 1991.

Cousins, Paul M. *Joel Chandler Harris: A Biography.* Baton Rouge: Louisiana State UP, 1968.

Craik, Dinah Maria Mulock. *An Unknown Country.* New York: Harper & Bros., 1887.

Crosby, Cindy. "Out of Darkness: Anne Rice Discusses Her Transformation from Vampire Novelist to Christian Author." *Today's Christian Woman* 1 Nov. 2007. Web. 18 Oct. 2012.

Crump, Jesse P., and Ella Spraker. *The Boone Family: A Genealogical History of the Descendants of George and Mary Boone, Who Came to America in 1717.* Rutland, VT: Tuttle, 1922.

Cumbow, Robert C. *Once Upon a Time: The Films of Sergio Leone.* Metuchen, NJ: Scarecrow, 1987.

Cuoco, Lorin. *Literary St. Louis: A Guide.* St. Louis: Washington U, 2000.

Cushner, Nicholas P. *Soldiers of God: The Jesuits in Colonial America, 1565–1767.* Buffalo, NY: Language Communications, 2002.

Dahlberg-Acton, John. *Essays in the Liberal Interpretation of History.* Chicago: U of Chicago P, 1967.

Daugherty, Leo. "Gravers False and True: Blood Meridian as Gnostic Tragedy." Arnold and Luce 159–74.

Davenport, Guy. *The Geography of the Imagination: Forty Essays.* Boston: Godine, 1997.

Davis, Cyprian. *The History of Black Catholics in the United States.* New York: Crossroad, 1990.

Davis, Richard P. "William Smith O'Brien and the American Civil War." *Canadian Journal of Irish Studies* 19.2 (1993): 45–53.

Dawes, Dorothy, and Charles E. Nolan. *Religious Pioneers: Building the Faith in the Archdiocese of New Orleans.* New Orleans: Archdiocese of New Orleans, 2004.

Day, D. L. *My Diary of Rambles with the 25th Mass. Volunteer Infantry, with Burnside's Coast Division.* Milford, MA: King & Billings, 1884.

De Grazia, Emilio. "Poe's Devoted Democrat, George Lippard." *Poe Studies* 6.1 (1973): 6–8.

della Cava, Marco R. "The Passion of the Rices." *USA Today* 6 Mar. 2008.

De Lorme, Rita H. "Gunfighter 'Doc' Holliday, Sister M. Melanie Holliday, R.S.M.: More Than a Pretty Love Story." *Southern Cross* 9 Dec. 1999.

———. "Monsignor Patrick J. O'Connor Chose Priesthood over Hollywood." *Southern Cross* 20 Apr. 2006.

Deresiewicz, William. "It's a Man's, Man's World." *Nation* 281.7 (2005): 38–41.

Dickinson, Charles. *American Notes for General Circulation.* London: Chapman & Hall, 1842.

Dickinson, Joy. *Haunted City: An Unauthorized Guide to the Magical, Magnificent New Orleans of Anne Rice.* New York: Citadel, 2004.

Dillon, William. *Life of John Mitchel.* London: Kegan Paul, Trench, 1888.

Diski, Jenny. "Review: *Christ the Lord—Out of Egypt.*" *Guardian (UK)* 3 Dec. 2005.

Dixon, Bill. *Last Days of Last Island: The Hurricane of 1856, Louisiana's First Great Storm.* Lafayette: U of Louisiana at Lafayette P, 2009.

Dolan, Jay P. *In Search of an American Catholicism: A History of Religion and Culture in Tension.* Oxford: Oxford UP, 2002.

Dooley, John. *John Dooley, Confederate Soldier, His War Journal.* Ed. Joseph T. Durkin. Washington, DC: Georgetown UP, 1945.

Douglass, Adam. *The Irish Emigrant, An Historical Tale Founded on Fact.* 2 vols. Winchester, VA: J. T. Sharrocks, 1817.

Douglass, Frederick. *My Bondage and My Freedom.* Intro. Philip S. Foner. 1855. New York: Dover, 1968.

Doyle, David Noel. *Ireland, Irishmen, and Revolutionary America, 1760–1820.* Dublin: Mercier, 1981.

Doyle, Don H. *Faulkner's County: The Historical Roots of Yoknapatawpha.* Chapel Hill: U of North Carolina P, 2001.

Dray, Philip. *At the Hands of Persons Unknown: The Lynching of Black America.* New York: Random House, 2002.

Du Bois, W. E. B. *Dusk of Dawn.* Millwood, NY: Kraus-Thomson, 1975.

Duke, Lynne. "Secret Life Ends for Irish Travellers." *Washington Post* 20 Oct. 2002.

Dunbar-Nelson, Alice Moore. *The Works of Alice Dunbar-Nelson.* Ed. Gloria T. Hull. 3 vols. New York: Oxford UP, 1988.

Duncan, John Donald. "Servitude and Slavery in Colonial South Carolina, 1670–1776." Diss. Emory U, 1971.

Duquin, Lorene Hanley. *A Century of Catholic Converts.* Huntington, IN: Our Sunday Visitor, 2003.

Durrell, Lawrence, and Henry Miller. *The Durrell-Miller Letters, 1935–80.* Ed. Ian S. MacNiven. New York: New Directions, 1988.

Dyer, Franklin B., and Mary J. Brady. *The Merrill Readers. Primer.* New York and Chicago: Charles E. Merrill, 1915.

Eagen, Catherine M. "Still 'Black' and 'Proud': Irish America and the Racial Politics of Hibernophilia." *The Irish in Us: Irishness, Performativity, and Popular Culture.* Ed. Diane Negra. Durham, NC: Duke UP, 2006. 20–63.

Eastman, Max. "How Decadent Are We?" *American Mercury* May 1942: 626–30.

Eaton, Clement. *The Growth of Southern Civilization, 1790–1860.* New York: Harper, 1961.

Eder, Richard. "Cormac McCarthy's Next Pilgrimage." *Los Angeles Times* 12 June 1994.

Elie, Paul. *The Life You Save May Be Your Own: An American Pilgrimage.* New York: Farrar Straus & Giroux, 2003.

Eliot, T. S. *Collected Poems, 1909–1962.* New York: Harcourt, Brace & World, 1963.

Elliott, Robert C. "The Satirist and Society." *ELH* 21.3 (1954): 237–48.

Ellis, Jay. "McCarthy Music." Wallach, *Myth, Legend, Dust* 157–70.

———. *No Place for Home: Spatial Constraint and Character Flight in the Novels of Cormac McCarthy.* New York: Routledge, 2006.

Ellis, John Tracy. *American Catholicism.* Chicago: U of Chicago P, 1969.

Ellmann, Richard. *James Joyce.* New York: Oxford UP, 1965.

Emerson, Ralph Waldo. *English Traits.* Ed. Philip Nicoloff, Robert E. Burkholder, and Douglas Emory White. Cambridge, MA: Harvard UP, 1994. Vol. 5 of the *Collected Works of Ralph Waldo Emerson.*

England, John. *Letter of the Late Bishop England to the Honorable John Forsyth, on the Subject of Domestic Slavery.* 1844. New York: Negro UP, 1969.

Escott, Paul D. *Major Problems in the History of the American South: Documents and Essays.* Boston: Houghton Mifflin, 1999.

Faherty, William Barnaby. *Exile in Erin: A Confederate Chaplain's Story; The Life of Father John B. Bannon.* St. Louis: U of Missouri P, 2002.

———. *The St. Louis Irish: An Unmatched Celtic Community.* St. Louis: U of Missouri P, 2001.

Fair, John D. "Parnell and Peaches: A Study in the Construction of Historical Myth." *Alabama Review* 58.2 (2005): 113–35.

Fanning, Charles. *The Irish Voice in America: 250 Years of Irish-American Fiction.* Lexington: UP of Kentucky, 2000.

Faulkner, Seldon. "The Octoroon War." *Educational Theatre Journal* 15.1 (1963): 33–38.

Faulkner, William. *Flags in the Dust.* New York: Vintage International, 2012.

———. *Soldiers' Pay.* New York: Liveright, 1954.

———. *The Sound and the Fury.* New York: Modern Library, 1992.

———. *The Town.* New York: Random House, 1957.

Faust, Drew Gilpin. "Clutching the Chains That Bind: Margaret Mitchell and *Gone with the Wind.*" *Southern Cultures* 5.1 (1999): 6–20.

———. *The Creation of Confederate Nationalism: Ideology and Identity in the Civil War.* Baton Rouge: Louisiana State UP, 1988.

———. *The Ideology of Slavery: Proslavery Thought in the Antebellum South, 1830–1860.* Baton Rouge: Louisiana State UP, 1981.

Fawkes, Richard. *Dion Boucicault: A Biography.* New York: Quartet, 1979.

Fehrenbacher, Don Edward. *Slavery, Law, and Politics: The Dred Scott Case in Historical Perspective.* New York: Oxford UP, 1981.

Feldberg, Michael. *The Philadelphia Riots of 1844: A Study of Ethnic Conflict.* Westport, CT: Greenwood, 1975.

Fellman, Michael. *Inside War: The Guerrilla Conflict in Missouri during the American Civil War.* New York: Oxford UP, 1989.

Fenton, Elizabeth A. *Religious Liberties: Anti-Catholicism and Liberal Democracy in Nineteenth-Century U.S. Literature and Culture.* Oxford: Oxford UP, 2011.

Ferris, William R. "'A lengthening chain in the shape of memories': The Irish and Southern Culture." *Southern Cultures* 17.1 (2011): 9–29.

Ferris, William R., and Ray Lum. *Mule Trader: Ray Lum's Tales of Horses, Mules, and Men.* Jackson, MS: Banner, 1998.

Ferris, William R., and Eudora Welty. "A Visit with Eudora Welty." Welty, *Conversations* 154–71.

Fessenden, Tracy. *Culture and Redemption: Religion, the Secular, and American Literature.* Princeton, NJ: Princeton UP, 2007.

Field, Joseph M. *The Drama in Pokerville: "The Bench and Bar of Jurytown," and Other Stories.* Philadelphia: T. B. Peterson, 1847.

———. *La Déesse, an Elssler-atic Romance.* New York: Carvill, 1841.

———. *The Wery Last Observations of Weller Senior to Boz on his Departure from London.* Boston: W. H. Oakes, 1842.

Field, Matthew C. *Matt Field on the Santa Fe Trail.* Collected by Clyde and Mae Reed Porter. Ed. John E. Sunder. Foreword by Mark L. Gardner. Norman: U of Oklahoma P, 1995.

Fitzgerald, Sally. "Root and Branch." *Georgia Historical Quarterly* 64.4 (1980).

"Flannery O'Connor's Mother Buried From Sacred Heart." *Georgia Bulletin* 18 May 1995. Web. 17 Oct. 2012.

Flaubert, Gustave. *The Temptation of St. Anthony.* Trans. Lafcadio Hearn. New York: Alice Harriman, 1910.

Fletcher, Joel L. *Ken and Thelma: The Story of a Confederacy of Dunces.* Gretna, LA: Pelican, 2005.

Fletcher, Joel, and James Whorton Jr. "Reader Response: *Butterfly in the Typewriter.*" *Oxford American* 11 Sept. 2012. Web. 2 Oct. 2012.

Flora, Joseph M., Lucinda H. MacKethan, and Todd W. Taylor, eds. *The Companion to Southern Literature: Themes, Genres, Places, People, Movements, and Motifs.* Baton Rouge: Louisiana State UP, 2002.

Flora, Joseph M., Amber Vogel, and Bryan Albin Giemza. *Southern Writers: A New Biographical Dictionary.* Baton Rouge: Louisiana State UP, 2006.

Fogarty, Gerald P. *Commonwealth Catholicism: A History of the Catholic Church in Virginia.* Notre Dame, IN: U of Notre Dame P, 2001.

Forkner, Ben, and Patrick H. Samway. *A Modern Southern Reader.* Atlanta: Peachtree, 1986.

Franchot, Jenny. *Roads to Rome: The Antebellum Protestant Encounter with Catholicism.* Berkeley: U of California P, 1994.

Fraser, Walter J. *Savannah in the Old South.* Athens: U of Georgia P, 2003.

Frye, Steven. "Yeats' 'Sailing to Byzantium' and McCarthy's *No Country for Old Men:* Art and Artifice in the New Novel." *Cormac McCarthy Journal* 5.1 (2006): 27–41.

Fullerton, George S. *A Handbook of Ethical Theory.* New York: H. Holt, 1922.

Gale, Robert L. *A Lafcadio Hearn Companion.* Westport, CT: Greenwood, 2002.

Gales, Joseph, and William W. Seaton. *Register of Debates in Congress: Comprising the Leading Debates and Incidents of the Second Session of the Eighteenth Congress.* Washington, DC: Gales & Seaton, 1825.

Gallagher, Gary W., and Alan T. Nolan. *The Myth of the Lost Cause and Civil War History.* Bloomington: Indiana UP, 2000.

Gallier, James. *Autobiography of James Gallier, Architect.* New York: Da Capo, 1973.

Gannon, Michael. *Rebel Bishop: Augustin Verot, Florida's Civil War Prelate.* Gainesville: UP of Florida, 1997.

Genovese, Eugene D. *Roll, Jordan, Roll: The World the Slaves Made.* New York: Vintage, 1976.

Gibert, Teresa. "The Role of Implicatures in Kate Chopin's Louisiana Short Stories." *Journal of the Short Story in English* 40 (Spring 2003): 69–84.

Gibson, Mike. "Knoxville Gave Cormac McCarthy the Raw Material of His Art. And He Gave It Back." Hall and Wallach 23–34.

Giemza, Bryan. "A Conspiracy of Dunces? Walker Percy and the Chance for a Last Laugh." *Southern Cultures* 9.2 (2003): 6–27.

——, ed. *The Irish Issue.* Spec. issue of *Southern Cultures* 17.1 (Spring 2011).

——. "Joel Chandler Harris, Catholic." *Logos: A Journal of Catholic Thought and Culture* 14.3 (2011): 86–103.

——, ed. *Rethinking the Irish in the American South: Beyond Rounders and Reelers.* Jackson: UP of Mississippi, 2013.

——. Rev. of *Ignatius Rising: The Life of John Kennedy Toole,* by René Pol Nevils and Deborah George Hardy. *Southern Cultures* 10:1 (2004): 97–99.

——. "Sisters of Secession: The Unclaimed Legacies of Two Southern American Irish Women." *Irish Studies Review* 18.2 (2010): 199–211.

——. "Toward a Catholic Understanding of Cormac McCarthy's Oeuvre." Wallach, *You Would Not Believe What Watches* 154–72.

——. "Turned Inside Out: Black, White, and Irish in the South." *Southern Cultures* 18.1 (2012): 34–57.

Giles, Paul. *American Catholic Arts and Fictions: Culture, Ideology and Aesthetics.* Cambridge: Cambridge UP, 1992.

Gill, William F. *The Life of Edgar Allan Poe.* New York: Dillingham, 1877.

Glazier, Michael, ed. *The Encyclopedia of the Irish in America.* Notre Dame, IN: U of Notre Dame P, 1999.

Gleeson, David T. "Another 'Lost Cause': The Irish in the South Remember the Confederacy." *Southern Cultures* 17.1 (2011): 50–74.

———. *The Irish in the South, 1815–1877*. Chapel Hill: U of North Carolina P, 2001.

Gleeson, David T., and Brendan J. Buttimer. "'We Are Irish Everywhere': Irish Immigrant Networks in Charleston, South Carolina, and Savannah, Georgia." *Immigrants & Minorities* 23.2–3 (2005): 183–205.

Goldman, Ari. "The Papal Visit." *New York Times* 11 Sept. 1987.

Goluboff, Benjamin. "'If Madonna Be': Emily Dickinson and Roman Catholicism." *New England Quarterly* 73.3 (2000): 355–85.

Gooch, Brad. *Flannery: A Life of Flannery O'Connor*. New York: Little, Brown, 2009.

Goodrich, Frances, Albert Hackett, and Edwin P. O'Donnell. *The Great Big Doorstep: A Comedy in Three Acts*. Chicago: Dramatic Publishing, 1943.

Gordon, Sarah. "Joe Gould, Daddy Hall, and Lady Olga: *The New Yorker*'s Joseph Mitchell and Flannery O'Connor." *Flannery O'Connor Review* 7 (2009): 41–53.

Graham, Stephen. *The Soul of John Brown*. New York: Macmillan, 1920.

Grammer, John M. "A Thing against Which Time Will Not Prevail: Pastoral and History in Cormac McCarthy's South." Arnold and Luce 29–44.

Grammich, Clifford. *Swift Growth and Change: The Demography of Southern Catholicism*. Cincinnati: Glenmary Research Center, n.d. Web. 16 May 2004.

Greeley, Andrew M. *The Catholic Imagination*. Berkeley: U of California P, 2000.

Greenhow, Rose O'Neal. *My Imprisonment and the First Year of Abolition Rule at Washington*. London: Richard Bentley, 1863.

Gregory, Isabella Augusta. *Cuchulain of Muirthemne: The Story of the Men of the Red Branch of Ulster, Arranged and Put into English by Lady Gregory*. New York: Oxford UP, 1970.

Grenier, Cynthia. Rev. of *Christ the Lord: Out of Egypt,* by Anne Rice. *First Things* 1 Feb. 2006. Web. 18 Oct. 2012

Gretlund, Jan Nordby, and Karl-Heinz Westarp, eds. *Flannery O'Connor's Radical Reality*. Columbia: U of South Carolina P, 2006.

Grierson, Francis. *"The Celtic Temperament" and Other Essays*. London: George Allen, 1901.

Griffin, Patrick. "Irish Migration to the Colonial South: A Plea for a Forgotten Topic." Giemza, *Rethinking the Irish*.

———. *The People with No Name: Ireland's Ulster Scots, America's Scots Irish, and the Creation of a British Atlantic World, 1689–1764*. Princeton, NJ: Princeton UP, 2001.

Grigsby, H. B. *Virginia Convention of 1776*. Richmond: J. W. Randolph, 1855.

Griswold, Rufus W. *The Poets and Poetry of America*. Philadelphia: Carey & Hart, 1843.

Gronberg, Douglas C. "The Problem of the Pseudonym and the Fictional Editor in Richard Henry Wilde's *Hesperia: A Poem*." *Georgia Historical Quarterly* 66.4 (1982): 549–54.

Grossman, Lev. "A Conversation between Cormac McCarthy and Joel and Ethan Coen." *Time* 29 Oct. 2007: 62–63.

Guilds, John Caldwell. *Simms: A Literary Life*. Fayetteville: U of Arkansas P, 1992.

Guinn, Matthew. "Ruder Forms Survive: Cormac McCarthy's Atavistic Vision." Wallach, *Myth, Legend, Dust* 108–16.

Gunn, Susan C. "McCarthy's *All the Pretty Horses.*" *Explicator* 54.4 (1996): 250–51.

Gutjahr, Paul C. *Popular American Literature of the 19th Century.* New York: Oxford UP, 2001.

Guyon, Jeanne Marie Bouvier de La Motte, and Benjamin Sahler. *Madame Guyon et Fénelon: La correspondance secrète, avec un choix de poésies spirituelles.* Paris: Dervy-Livres, 1982.

Hackett, Alice. "What Happens to First Novelists?" *Saturday Review* 27.9 (26. Feb. 1944): 8–12.

Hackney, Sheldon. *Magnolias without Moonlight: The American South from Regional Confederacy to National Integration.* Somerset, NJ: Transaction, 2005.

———. "Southern Violence." *American Historical Review* 74 (Feb. 1969): 906–25.

Haddox, Thomas F. *Fears and Fascinations: Representing Catholicism in the American South.* New York: Fordham UP, 2005.

Hague, Euan, and Edward H. Sebesta. "Neo-Confederacy, Culture, and Ethnicity: A White Anglo-Celtic Southern People." *Neo-Confederacy: A Critical Introduction.* Ed. Euan Hague, Edward H. Sebesta, and Heidi Beirich. Austin: U of Texas P, 2008. 97–130.

Hall, A. Oakey. *The Manhattaner in New Orleans; or, Phases of "Crescent City" Life.* New York: J. S. Redfield, 1851.

Hall, Wade H., and Rick Wallach, eds. *Sacred Violence, Volume I: Cormac McCarthy's Appalachian Works.* El Paso: Texas Western P, 2002.

Hammett, Dashiell. *Selected Letters of Dashiell Hammett, 1921–1960.* Ed. Richard Layman and Julie M. Rivett. Washington, DC: Counterpoint, 2002.

Hankinson, Alan. *Man of Wars: William Howard Russell of the Times.* London: Heinemann, 1982.

Hanson, Elizabeth I. *Margaret Mitchell.* Boston: Twayne, 1990.

Harden, William. *A History of Savannah and South Georgia.* Chicago: Lewis, 1913.

Hardin, Michael. "Between Queer Performances: John Kennedy Toole's the Neon Bible and a Confederacy of Dunces." *Southern Literary Journal* 39.2 (2007): 58–77.

Harper, Jared V. "The Irish Travelers of Georgia." Diss. U of Georgia, 1984.

Harris, George Washington. *Sut Lovingood. Yarns Spun by A "Nat'ral Born Durn'd Fool." Warped and Wove for Public Wear.* New York: Dick & Fitzgerald, 1867.

Harris, Joel Chandler. "Anne Macfarland Review." *Uncle Remus's The Home Magazine* (Sept. 1908): 20–21.

———. *"Balaam and His Master," and Other Sketches and Stories.* Freeport, NY: Books for Libraries, 1969.

———. *The Chronicles of Aunt Minervy Ann.* New York: Charles Scribner's Sons, 1899.

———. *Dearest Chums and Partners: Joel Chandler Harris's Letters to His Children; A Domestic Biography.* Ed. Hugh T. Keenan. Athens: U of Georgia P, 1993.

———. *Gabriel Tolliver: A Story of Reconstruction.* New York: McClure Phillips, 1902.

———. *Joel Chandler Harris, Editor and Essayist: Miscellaneous Literary, Political, and Social Writings.* Ed. Julia Collier Harris. Chapel Hill: U of North Carolina P, 1931.

———. *Joel Chandler Harris' Life of Henry W. Grady Including His Writings and Speeches. A Memorial Volume.* New York: Cassell, 1890.

———. *Nights with Uncle Remus: Myths and Legends of the Old Plantation.* Ed John T. Bickley and R. Bruce Bickley. New York: Penguin, 2003.

———. *On the Wing of Occasions.* New York: Doubleday, 1904.

———. *Tales of the Home Folks in Peace and War.* Cambridge, MA: Riverside, 1898.

Harris, Julia Collier. *The Life and Letters of Joel Chandler Harris.* Boston: Houghton Mifflin, 1918.

Haskell, Molly. *Frankly, My Dear: "Gone with the Wind" Revisited.* New Haven, CT: Yale UP, 2009.

Hearn, Lafcadio. *Children of the Levee.* Ed. O. W. Forst. Lexington: U of Kentucky P, 1957.

———. *Chita: A Memory of Last Island.* Ed. Delia LaBarre. Jackson: UP of Mississippi, 2003.

———. *Editorials.* Ed. Charles Woodward Hutson. Boston: Houghton Mifflin, 1926.

———. *Essays on American Literature.* Tokyo: Hokuseido, 1929.

———. *Inventing New Orleans: Writings of Lafcadio Hearn.* Ed. S. Frederick Starr. Jackson: UP of Mississippi, 2001.

———. *Lafcadio Hearn's America: Ethnographic Sketches and Editorials.* Ed. Simon J. Bronner. Lexington: UP of Kentucky, 2002.

———. *Letters from the Raven; Being the Correspondence of Lafcadio Hearn with Henry Watkin.* Ed. Milton Bronner. New York: Brentano's, 1907.

———. *Occidental Gleanings.* 2 vols. London: William Heinemann, 1925.

———. *On Art, Literature and Philosophy.* Tokyo: Hokuseido, 1941.

———. *Period of the Gruesome: Selected Cincinnati Journalism of Lafcadio Hearn.* Ed. Jon Christopher Hughes. Lanham, MD: UP of America, 1990.

———. *The Writings of Lafcadio Hearn.* Ed. Elizabeth Bisland. 16 vols. Boston: Houghton Mifflin, 1922.

Hearn, Lafcadio, and Elizabeth Bisland. *The Life and Letters of Lafcadio Hearn.* 2 vols. Boston: Houghton, Mifflin, 1906.

Helper, Hinton Rowan. *The Impending Crisis of the South: How to Meet It.* New York: Burdick, 1857.

Hennesey, James J. *American Catholics: A History of the Roman Catholic Community in the United States.* New York: Oxford UP, 1981.

Henry, O. *Selected Stories.* Ed. Guy Davenport. New York: Penguin, 1993.

Herbermann, Charles George, Edward A. Pace, Conde B. Pallen, Thomas J. Shahan, and John J. Wynne, eds. *The Catholic Encyclopedia: An International Work of Reference on the Constitution, Doctrine, Discipline, and History of the Catholic Church.* 15 vols. New York: R. Appleton Co., 1907–13.

Heyrman, Christine Leigh. *Southern Cross: The Beginnings of the Bible Belt.* New York: Knopf, 1997.

Higginbotham, A. Leon. *In the Matter of Color: The Colonial Period.* New York: Oxford UP, 1978.

Higgins, Geraldine. "Tara, the O'Haras, and the Irish *Gone With the Wind.*" *Southern Cultures* 17.1 (2011): 30–49.

Hill, Samuel S. *Religion and the Solid South*. Nashville: Abingdon, 1972.

Hobson, Fred C. *Mencken: A Life*. New York: Random House, 1994.

———. *Tell About the South: The Southern Rage to Explain*. Baton Rouge: Louisiana State UP, 1983.

Hodes, Martha. *White Women, Black Men: Illicit Sex in the Nineteenth-Century South*. New Haven, CT: Yale UP, 1999.

Holloway, David. *The Late Modernism of Cormac McCarthy*. Westport, CT: Greenwood, 2002.

Homer, Patricia. "Kinship: Margaret Mitchell's *Gone with the Wind* and the Irish Big House Genre." Diss. Georgia Southern University, 2010.

Horwitz, Tony. *Confederates in the Attic: Dispatches from America's Unfinished Civil War*. New York: Pantheon, 1998.

Hughes, Nathaniel Cheairs, and Thomas Clayton Ware. *Theodore O'Hara: Poet-Soldier of the Old South*. Knoxville: U of Tennessee P, 1998.

Humes, Thomas William. *The Loyal Mountaineers of Tennessee*. Knoxville: Ogden Bros., 1888.

Ignatiev, Noel. *How the Irish Became White*. New York: Routledge, 1995.

Inge, M. Thomas, ed. *The New Encyclopedia of Southern Culture, Vol. 9: Literature*. Chapel Hill: U of North Carolina P, 2008.

Inge, M. Thomas, and Edward J. Piacentino, eds. *Southern Frontier Humor: An Anthology*. Columbia: U of Missouri P, 2010.

"The Irish Sedition—The Method of John Mitchel's Patriotism." *New York Times* 13 Jan. 1859.

"Irvin Cobb Lauds Race in Speech at Paducah." *Cleveland Advocate* 4 Jan. 1919: 8.

Isaac, Rhys. *The Transformation of Virginia: 1740–1790*. Chapel Hill: U of North Carolina P, 1982.

Ives, L. Silliman. *The Trials of a Mind in Its Progress to Catholicism: A Letter to His Old Friends*. Boston: Patrick Donahoe, 1854.

Jacobson, Matthew Frye. *Whiteness of a Different Color: European Immigrants and the Alchemy of Race*. Cambridge, MA: Harvard UP, 1998.

Jarrett, Robert L. *Cormac McCarthy*. New York: Twayne, 1997.

Jenkins, Philip. *The New Anti-Catholicism: The Last Acceptable Prejudice*. Oxford: Oxford UP, 2003.

Johnston, Richard Malcolm, and William Hand Browne. *Life of Alexander H. Stephens*. Philadelphia: J. B. Lippincott, 1878.

Jones, Anne Goodwyn. *Tomorrow Is Another Day: The Woman Writer in the South, 1859–1936*. Baton Rouge: Louisiana State UP, 1981.

Jordan, Don, and Michael Walsh. *White Cargo: The Forgotten History of Britain's White Slaves in America*. Washington Square: New York UP, 2008.

Jordan-Lake, Joy. *Whitewashing "Uncle Tom's Cabin": Nineteenth-Century Women Novelists Respond to Stowe*. Nashville: Vanderbilt UP, 2005.

Josyph, Peter. *Adventures in Reading Cormac McCarthy*. Lanham, MD: Scarecrow, 2010.

Joyce, James. *James Joyce's "Dubliners": An Illustrated Edition.* Ed. John Wyse Jackson and Bernard McGinley. New York: St. Martin's, 1993.

———. *A Portrait of the Artist as a Young Man.* Ed. Seamus Deane. London: Penguin, 1992.

———. *Ulysses: The Corrected Text.* Ed. Hans W. Gabler. New York: Random House, 1986.

Jung, Carl. *Mysterium Coniunctionis: An Inquiry into the Separation and Synthesis of Psychic Opposites in Alchemy.* Ed. and trans. Gerhard Adler and R. F. C. Hull. Vol. 14 of *Collected Works of C. G. Jung.* Princeton, NJ: Princeton UP, 1968.

Jurgensen, John. "Hollywood's Favorite Cowboy." *Wall Street Journal* 20 Nov. 2009: W6. Web. 6 Aug. 2012.

Kate Chopin: A Re-Awakening. Dir. Tika Laudun. Louisiana Public Broadcasting, 1999. Web. 4 Mar. 2011.

Kazin, Alfred. *Bright Book of Life: American Novelists and Storytellers from Hemingway to Mailer.* Notre Dame, IN: U of Notre Dame P, 1980.

———. *F. Scott Fitzgerald: The Man and His Work.* New York: Collier Books, 1951.

Keenan, Hugh T. *The Library of Joel Chandler Harris: An Annotated Book List.* Atlanta: Emory University and the Joel Chandler Harris Association, 1999.

Keiley, A. M. *In Vinculis; or, The prisoner of war, being the experience of a Rebel in two federal pens, interspersed with reminiscences of the late war, anecdotes of southern generals, etc.* New York: Blelock, 1866.

———. *Memoranda of the History of the Catholic Church in Richmond, Va., since the Revolution Reported to the Fourth Annual Convention of the Catholic Benevolent Union of Virginia.* N.p., 1874.

———. *"Our Dead." An Address Delivered at Loudon Park Cemetery, near Baltimore, June 5th, 1879, at the Confederate Graves.* Richmond, VA: Geo. W. Gary, 1879.

Keiley, A. M., and James B. Ficklin. *The Virginia Debt! How Mahone before the Union League Club Deliberately Misrepresented Plain Matters of Fact. Messrs. Keiley and Ficklin at the Manhattan Club Insisting That the Old Dominion Should Pay Her Debts.* N.p., 1881.

Keily, Benjamin J. "Diary, 1869 October 20–1870 January 13." MS. Virginia Historical Society, Richmond.

Keily, Richard, and A. H. Brisbane. *A Brief Descriptive and Statistical Sketch of Georgia, United States of America: Developing Its Immense Agricultural, Mining and Manufacturing Advantages, with Remarks on Emigration.* London: J. Carrall, 1849.

Kelley, William D. *Speeches, Addresses, and Letters on Industrial and Financial Questions.* Philadelphia: H. C. Baird, 1872.

Kelly, George. "A Hibernian in the woodpile." *Salon.com.* Salon Media Group, 17 Mar. 2001. Web. 6 Aug. 2012.

Kelly, Joseph. "Charleston's Bishop John England and American Slavery." *New Hibernia Review* 5.4 (2001): 48–56.

Keneally, Thomas. *The Great Shame: And the Triumph of the Irish in the English-Speaking World.* New York: Nan A. Talese, 1999.

Kennedy, R. Emmet. *Mellows: A Chronicle of Unknown Singers*. New York: Albert and Charles Boni, 1925.

——. *Runes and Cadences, Being Ancestral Memories of Old Heroic Days*. New York: Dodd, Mead, 1926.

——. *Songs of an Alien Spirit*. New York: Poets Press, 1940.

Kenner, Hugh. *A Colder Eye: The Modern Irish Writers*. Baltimore: Johns Hopkins UP, 1989.

Kenney, James. *The Irish Ambassador: A Comedy in Two Acts*. New York: W. Taylor, 1850.

Kenny, Kevin. *The American Irish: A History*. New York: Longman, 2000.

Kenny, Michael, SJ. "Father Ryan's Poems." *America* 40.10 (15 Dec. 1928): 237–39.

Keysar, Ariela, and Barry A. Kosmin. "Latino Influx Bolsters Catholic Church but Young and U.S.-Born Latinos Become More Religiously Diverse." *American Religious Identification Survey 2008*. Web. 3 May 2011.

Kibler, James E., Jr. "A New Letter of Simms to Richard Henry Wilde: On the Advancement of Sectional Literature." *American Literature* 44.4 (1973): 667–70.

Kilgore, Alice Copeland, Edith Hanes Smith, and Francis Partridge Tuck, eds. *A History of Clayton County, Georgia, 1821–1983*. Roswell, GA: Wolfe, 1983.

Kilmer, Joyce, ed. *Joyce Kilmer's Anthology of Catholic Poets*. New York: Liveright, 1939.

King, Edward, and James Wells Champney. *The Great South*. Hartford, CT: American, 1875.

Kinney, Arthur F. *Flannery O'Connor's Library: Resources of Being*. Athens: U of Georgia P, 2008.

Kirkpatrick, David D. "A Writer's Tough Lesson in Birthin' a Parody." *New York Times* 26 Apr. 2001: E1.

Kirn, Walter. "*No Country for Old Men*: Texas Noir." *New York Times* 24 July 2005.

Kneeland, Henry T. "Lafcadio Hearn's Brother." *Atlantic Monthly* 131.1 (1923): 20–27.

Knobel, Dale T. *Paddy and the Republic: Ethnicity and Nationality in Antebellum America*. Middletown, CT: Wesleyan UP, 1986.

Koizumi, Setsu, Paul Kiyoshi Hisada, and Frederick Johnson. *Reminiscences of Lafcadio Hearn*. Boston: Houghton Mifflin, 1918.

Kreilkamp, Vera. *The Anglo-Irish Novel and the Big House*. Syracuse, NY: Syracuse UP, 1998.

Kreyling, Michael. "(Patricio) Lafcadio (Tessima Carlos) Hearn." *Dictionary of Literary Biography*, vol. 12. Ed. Donald Pizer and Earl N. Harbert. Detroit: Gale Research, 1982. 245–33.

——. *The South That Wasn't There: Postsouthern Memory and History*. Baton Rouge: Louisiana State UP, 2010.

Kunst, A. E. *Lafcadio Hearn*. New York: Twayne, 1969.

Kuo, David. "Anne Rice's Jesus Transfixes in *Road to Cana*." *All Things Considered*. National Public Radio. 5 Mar. 2008. Web. 3 May 2011.

Kushner, David. "Cormac McCarthy's Apocalypse." *Rolling Stone* 27 Dec. 2007: 43. Web. 6 Aug. 2012.

LaBarre, Delia. *The New Orleans of Lafcadio Hearn: Illustrated Sketches from the Daily City Item.* Baton Rouge: Louisiana State UP, 2007.

Labrie, Ross. *The Catholic Imagination in American Literature.* Columbia: U of Missouri P, 1997.

Ladd, Barbara. *Nationalism and the Color Line in George W. Cable, Mark Twain, and William Faulkner.* Baton Rouge: Louisiana State UP, 1997.

"The Land League Meeting—Father Ryan to Lecture in Macon." *Macon Weekly Telegraph* 8 Mar. 1881.

Lawson, Anita. *Irvin S. Cobb.* Bowling Green, OH: Bowling Green State U Popular P, 1984.

Lee, James Ward. *Classics of Texas Fiction.* Dallas: E-Heart, 1987.

Leigh, Frances. *Ten Years on a Georgia Plantation since the War.* London: R. Bentley, 1883.

LeMaster, J. R., James D. Wilson, and Christie Graves Hamric, eds. *The Mark Twain Encyclopedia.* New York: Garland, 1993.

Lent, Jeffrey. "Blood Money." Rev. of *No Country for Old Men,* by Cormac McCarthy. *Washington Post* 17 July 2005.

Lever, Charles J. *Charles O'Malley: The Irish Dragoon.* 2 vols. Boston: Little, Brown, 1910.

Levine, Lawrence W. *Black Culture and Black Consciousness: Afro-American Folk Thought from Slavery to Freedom.* Oxford: Oxford UP, 1978.

Lewis, Henry Clay. Odd Leaves *from the Life of a Louisiana Swamp Doctor.* Baton Rouge: Louisiana State UP, 1997.

Lewis, H. H. Walker. *Without Fear or Favor: A Biography of Chief Justice Roger Brooke Taney.* Boston: Houghton Mifflin, 1965.

Lewis, J. Vance. *Out of the Ditch; a True Story of an Ex-Slave.* Houston: Rein & Sons, 1910.

Lewis, Roger. *Anthony Burgess.* New York: Thomas Dunne, 2004.

Leyburn, James G. *The Scotch-Irish: A Social History.* Chapel Hill: U of North Carolina P, 1962.

Lilley, James D. "Of Whales and Men: The Dynamics of Cormac McCarthy's Environmental Imagination." *Southern Quarterly* 38.2 (2000): 111–22.

Lippard, George. *The Killers: A Narrative of Real Life in Philadelphia.* Philadelphia: Hankinson & Bartholomew, 1850.

Longfellow, Henry Wadsworth. *The Letters of Henry Wadsworth Longfellow.* Ed. Andrew R. Hilen. 6 vols. Cambridge, MA: Harvard UP, 1966–82.

Lonn, Ella. *Foreigners in the Confederacy.* Chapel Hill: U of North Carolina P, 1940.

Luce, Dianne. "Cormac McCarthy in High School: 1951." *Cormac McCarthy Journal* 7.1 (2009): 1–6.

———. *Reading the World: Cormac McCarthy's Tennessee Period.* Columbia: University of South Carolina Press, 2009.

Lyerly, Cynthia Ann. "Gender and Race in Dixon's Religious Ideology." *Thomas Dixon Jr. and the Birth of Modern America.* Ed. Michele Gillespie and Randal L. Hall. Baton Rouge: Louisiana State UP, 2006.

Lyons, W. F. *Brigadier-general Thomas Francis Meagher: His Political and Military Career: With Selections from His Speeches and Writings.* New York: D. & J. Sadlier, 1870.

Lynch, Brendan. "Motor Sport." *The Encyclopedia of Ireland.* Ed. Brian Lalor. New Haven, CT: Yale UP, 2003.

Mabbot, Thomas Ollive. "Poe and *The Philadelphia Irish Citizen.*" *Journal of the American Irish Historical Society* 29 (1931): 121–31.

MacLauchlin, Cory. *Butterfly in the Typewriter: The Tragic Life of John Kennedy Toole and the Remarkable Story of a Confederacy of Dunces.* New York: Da Capo, 2012.

MacWilliams, Vera. *Lafcadio Hearn.* Cambridge, MA: Riverside, 1946.

Maréchal, Ambrose. *Pastoral Letter of the Archbishop of Baltimore to the Roman Catholicks of Norfolk, Virginia.* Baltimore: J. Robinson, 1819.

"Marriages and Deaths." *Manchester Weekly Times* 2 June 1866: 7.

Martin, Mariann. "Margaret Skinner Reads at Annual Creative Writing Workshop." *Union [University] News and Information* [Jackson, TN] 8 Apr. 2004. Web. 6 Aug. 2012.

Masci, David. "Public Opinion on Gay Marriage: Opponents Consistently Outnumber Supporters." *Pew Forum on Religion & Public Life,* 2009. Web. 17 Oct. 2012.

Maslin, Janet. "Telling His Own Tale of Passions and Piety." *New York Times* 13 Mar. 2008.

Massa, Mark Stephen. *Anti-Catholicism in America: The Last Acceptable Prejudice.* New York: Crossroad, 2003.

McCafferty, Kate. *Testimony of an Irish Slave Girl.* New York: Viking, 2002.

McCaffrey, Lawrence John. *The Irish Catholic Diaspora in America.* Washington, DC: Catholic U of America P, 1997.

McCarthy, C. J. "A Drowning Incident." *Phoenix* Mar. 1960: 3–4.

———. "Wake for Susan." *Phoenix* Nov. 1959: 3–6.

McCarthy, Charles J. Oral history interview by Mark Winter. May 1983. TVA Employee Series, Tennessee Valley Oral History Collection, Tennessee Valley Authority Library, Knoxville. Transcript.

———. "The Tennessee Valley." *Town Planning Review* 21.2 (July 1950): 116–30.

McCarthy, Cormac. *All the Pretty Horses.* New York: Vintage International, 1992.

———. *Blood Meridian.* New York: Vintage International, 1992.

———. *Child of God.* New York: Vintage International, 1993.

———. *Cities of the Plain.* New York: Vintage International, 1999.

———. *The Crossing.* New York: Vintage International, 1995.

———. Interview by Oprah Winfrey. *The Oprah Winfrey Show.* ABC. 5 June 2007. Television. Available online, oprah.com.

———. *No Country for Old Men.* New York: Knopf, 2005.

———. *The Orchard Keeper.* New York: Vintage International, 1993.

———. *Outer Dark.* New York: Vintage International, 1993.

———. *The Road.* New York: Knopf, 2006.

———. *The Stonemason: A Play in Five Acts.* New York: Vintage International, 1994.

———. *The Sunset Limited.* New York: Vintage International, 2006.

———. *Suttree.* New York: Random House, 1979.

McCorkle, Jill. "One Good, One Bad, One Angry." Rev. of *The Distance Between Us,* by Valerie Sayers. *New York Times Book Review* 20 Feb. 1994: 23.

McDonogh, Gary W. *Black and Catholic in Savannah, Georgia.* Knoxville: U of Tennessee P, 1993.

McGarvey, Bill. "Imagining Jesus." *America* 198.18 (26 May 2008): 26–27.

McGovern, Bryan P. *John Mitchel: Irish Nationalist, Southern Secessionist.* Knoxville: U of Tennessee P, 2009.

McGraw, Eliza Russi Lowen. "A 'Southern Belle with Her Irish Up': Scarlett O'Hara and Ethnic Identity." *South Atlantic Review* 65.1 (2000): 123–31.

McGreevy, John T. *Catholicism and American Freedom: A History.* New York: Norton, 2003.

McWhiney, Grady. *Cracker Culture: Celtic Ways in the Old South.* Tuscaloosa: U of Alabama P, 1988.

McWilliams, John P. *The American Epic: Transforming a Genre, 1770–1860.* Cambridge: Cambridge UP, 1989.

Meaders, Daniel. *Dead or Alive: Fugitive Slaves and White Indentured Servants before 1830.* New York: Garland, 1993.

Meagher, Timothy J. *The Columbia Guide to Irish American History.* New York: Columbia UP, 2005.

———. "A Discussion on Irish Immigrants in America with Timothy Meagher." Interview by Jill O'Neill. *hnn.com.* History News Network. 15 Mar. 2010. Web. 3 May 2011.

Mencken, H. L. *Prejudices: A Selection.* Baltimore: Johns Hopkins UP, 2006.

Metress, Christopher. "*Via Negativa:* The Way of Unknowing in Cormac McCarthy's *Outer Dark.*" *Southern Review* 37.1 (2001): 147–54.

Meyers, Jeffrey. *Edgar Allan Poe: His Life and Legacy.* New York: Charles Scribner's Sons, 1992.

Miller, David C. *Dark Eden: The Swamp in Nineteenth-Century American Culture.* Cambridge: Cambridge UP, 1989.

Miller, Ilana D. *Reports from America: William Howard Russell and the Civil War.* Gloucestershire, UK: Sutton, 2001.

Miller, Kerby A. *Emigrants and Exiles: Ireland and the Irish Exodus to North America.* New York: Oxford UP, 1985.

———. *Irish Immigrants in the Land of Canaan: Letters and Memoirs from Colonial and Revolutionary America, 1675–1815.* New York: Oxford UP, 2003.

———. "Re-Imagining Irish Revisionism." *Re-Imagining Ireland.* Ed. Andrew Higgins Wyndham. Charlottesville: U of Virginia P, 2006.

———. "'Scotch-Irish' Myths and 'Irish' Identities in Eighteenth- and Nineteenth-Century America." *New Perspectives on the Irish Diaspora.* Ed. Charles Fanning. Carbondale: Southern Illinois UP, 2000. 75–92.

———. "'Scotch-Irish,' 'Black Irish' and 'Real Irish': Emigrants and Identities in the Old South." *The Irish Diaspora.* Ed. Andy Bielenberg. New York: Longman, 2000. 139–57.

———. "Ulster Presbyterians and the 'Two Traditions' In Ireland and America." *Making the Irish American: History and Heritage of the Irish in the United States.* Ed. Joseph J. Lee. New York: New York UP, 2006.

Miller, Randall M., Harry S. Stout, and Charles Reagan Wilson. *Religion and the American Civil War.* New York: Oxford UP, 1998.

Miller, Randall M., and Jon L. Wakelyn. *Catholics in the Old South: Essays on Church and Culture.* Macon, GA: Mercer UP, 1983.

Miller, Tice L., and Don B. Wilmeth. *Cambridge Guide to American Theatre.* Cambridge: Cambridge UP, 1993.

Mills, Jerry Leath. "The Dead Mule Rides Again." *Southern Cultures* 6.4 (2000): 11–34.

Minzesheimer, Bob. "Pat Conroy Returns to Familiar Turf with *South of Broad.*" *USA Today* 11 Aug. 2009.

Mitchel, John. *Jail Journal, Or, Five Years in British Prisons: Commenced on Board the Shearwater Steamer.* Glasgow: Cameron & Ferguson, 1876.

Mitchell, Arthur. *South Carolina Irish.* Charleston, SC: History Press, 2010.

Mitchell, Joseph. *"Up in the Old Hotel," and Other Stories.* New York: Vintage, 1993.

Mitchell, Margaret. *Gone with the Wind.* Preface by Pat Conroy. New York: Scribner, 1996.

———. *Lost Laysen.* Ed. Debra Freer. New York: Scribner, 1996.

———. *Margaret Mitchell: Reporter.* Ed. Patrick Allen. Athens, GA: Hill Street, 2000.

———. *Margaret Mitchell's "Gone with the Wind" Letters, 1936–1949.* Ed. Richard Barksdale Harwell. New York: Macmillan, 1976.

Mobley, Chuck. "Slave Ship's Sad Saga Left No Imprint on Savannah." *Savannah Morning News* 29 Feb. 2008. Web. 6 Aug. 2012.

Molloy, Robert William. *Pride's Way.* New York: Macmillan, 1945.

Momaday, N. Scott. *The Man Made of Words: Essays, Stories, Passages.* New York: St. Martin's Griffin, 1998.

Monk, Maria. *Awful Disclosures of the Hotel Dieu Nunnery. Revised, with an Appendix.* New York: Maria Monk, 1836.

Moore, J. Cameron. "What Bell Leaves Out: Moss, Catholicism, and Charity in *No Country For Old Men.*" *Literature and Belief* 31.1 (2011): 83–92.

Morgan, Elemore, Jr. "Roommate with a View: Elemore Morgan Jr. Remembers Toole." Interview by Reese R. Fuller. *Independent Weekly* [Lafayette, LA] no. 97 (2005). Web. 6 Aug. 2012.

Morgan, Wes. "McCarthy's High School Years." *Cormac McCarthy Journal* 3 (2003): 6–9.

Morley, Helena. *The Diary of "Helena Morley."* Trans. and intro. Elizabeth Bishop. New York: Farrar, Straus & Cudahy, 1957.

Mosby, Charmaine Allmon. "Anne Rice: Overview." *Twentieth-Century Young Adult Writers.* Ed. Laura Standley Berger. Detroit: St. James, 1994.

Muldoon, Paul. *Why Brownlee Left.* London: Faber, 1980.

Muldrey, Mary Hermenia. *Abounding in Mercy: Mother Austin Carroll.* New Orleans: Habersham, 1988.

Murphy, J. B. "Wolfe Tone before Parnell." Letter. *New York Times* 26 Oct. 1899.

Murphy, Thomas. *Jesuit Slaveholding in Maryland, 1717–1838.* New York: Routledge, 2001.

Murray, Nicholas. *Romanism at Home: Letters to the Hon. Roger B. Taney, Chief Justice of the United States.* New York: Harper, 1852.

Murray, Paul. *A Fantastic Journey: The Life and Literature of Lafcadio Hearn.* Ann Arbor: U of Michigan P, 1997.

Nabokov, Vladimir V., Fredson Bowers, and John Updike. *Lectures on Literature.* San Diego: Harcourt, 1982.

Neely, Jack. "Cormac McCarthy's Knoxville." Wallach, *Cormac McCarthy Issue* 16–19.

Nelson, Bruce. "'Come Out of Such a Land, You Irishmen': Daniel O'Connell, American Slavery, and the Making of the 'Irish Race.'" *Éire-Ireland* 42.1–2 (2007): 58–81.

Nevils, René Pol, and Deborah George Hardy. *Ignatius Rising: The Life of John Kennedy Toole.* Baton Rouge: Louisiana State UP, 2001.

New Catholic Encyclopedia. 2nd ed. Washington, DC: Thomson/Gale, 2003.

Newton, Michael. "Review, *How Celtic Culture Invented Southern Literature.*" *e-Keltoi* 1 (12 Apr. 2006). Web. 3 May 2011.

Niehaus, Earl F. *The Irish in New Orleans, 1800–1860.* Baton Rouge: Louisiana State UP, 1965.

———. "Paddy on the Local Stage and in Humor: The Image of the Irish in New Orleans, 1830–1862." *Louisiana History: The Journal of the Louisiana Historical Association* 5.2 (Spring 1964): 117–34.

Noonan, John Thomas. *The Antelope: The Ordeal of the Recaptured Africans in the Administrations of James Monroe and John Quincy Adams.* Berkeley: U of California P, 1977.

Nowatzki, Robert. "Paddy Jumps Jim Crow: Irish-Americans and Blackface Minstrelsy." *Éire-Ireland* 41.3 (2007): 162–184.

Oates, Joyce Carol. "The Parables of Flannery O'Connor." *New York Review of Books* 56.6 (2009). Web. 14 Oct. 2012.

O'Brien, Michael. *Conjectures of Order: Intellectual Life and the American South, 1810–1860.* 2 vols. Chapel Hill: U of North Carolina P, 2004.

O'Connell, David. *Furl That Banner: The Life of Abram J. Ryan, Poet-Priest of the South.* Macon, GA: Mercer UP, 2006.

O'Connell, Jeremiah D. *The "Scotch-Irish" Delusion in America.* Washington, DC: American-Irish, 1897.

O'Connell, Jeremiah Joseph. *Catholicity in the Carolinas and Georgia: Leaves of Its History, A.D. 1820–A.D. 1878.* New York: D. J. Sadlier, 1879.

O'Connor, Flannery. *Collected Works.* New York: Library of America, 1988.

———. *The Complete Stories.* New York: Farrar, Straus & Giroux, 1971.

———. *Conversations with Flannery O'Connor.* Ed. Rosemary M. Magee. Jackson: UP of Mississippi, 1987.

———. *The Habit of Being: Letters of Flannery O'Connor.* Ed. Sally Fitzgerald. New York: Farrar, Straus, & Giroux, 1988.

———. Introduction. *A Memoir of Mary Ann.* By the Dominican Nuns of Our Lady of Perpetual Help Home, Atlanta, Georgia. New York: Farrar, Straus & Cudahy, 1961.

———. *Mystery and Manners: Occasional Prose.* Ed. Sally Fitzgerald and Robert Fitzgerald. New York: Farrar, Straus & Giroux, 1969.

———. *The Violent Bear It Away.* 1960. New York: Farrar, Straus & Giroux, 2007.

———. *Wise Blood.* 1952. New York: Farrar, Straus & Giroux, 2007.

O'Connor, Flannery, Brainard Cheney, Frances N. Cheney, and C. R. Stephens. *The Correspondence of Flannery O'Connor and the Brainard Cheneys.* Jackson: UP of Mississippi, 1986.

O'Connor, Florence J. *The Heroine of the Confederacy, or, Truth and Justice.* London: Harrison, 1865.

O'Connor, Joseph. *Sweet Liberty: Travels in Irish America.* Boulder, CO: Roberts Rinehart, 1997.

———. *Star of the Sea.* Orlando, FL: Harcourt, 2002.

O'Connor, Mary Doline. *The Life and Letters of M. P. O'Connor.* New York: Dempsey & Carroll, 1893.

O'Connor, T. P. *My Beloved South.* New York: Putnam, 1913.

O'Donnell, E. P. "Fragments from Alluvia." *Scribner's* Oct. 1931. 401–10.

———. *The Great Big Doorstep, a Delta Comedy.* Afterword by Eudora Welty. 1941. Carbondale: Southern Illinois UP, 1979.

———. *Green Margins.* Boston: Houghton Miffin, 1936.

———. "Jesus Knew." *Harper's* Apr. 1935: 525–32.

———. "Like a Man!" *Collier's Weekly* 23 May 1931: 18–19.

———. "Pretty John." *Menagerie* 1 Oct. 1935: 12–15.

O'Donnell, Mary K. *Quincie Bolliver.* Lubbock: Texas Tech UP, 2001.

———. *Those Other People.* Boston: Houghton Mifflin, 1946.

Oehlschlaeger, Fritz. *Old Southwest Humor from the St. Louis Reveille, 1844–1850.* Columbia: U of Missouri P, 1990.

O'Faoláin, Seán. *The Irish.* West Drayton, UK: Penguin, 1947.

O'Gorman, Farrell. "Irish Catholics." Flora, MacKethan, and Taylor 378–79.

———. "Joyce and Contesting Priesthoods in *Suttree* and *Blood Meridian*." *Cormac McCarthy Journal* 4 (2005): 100–117.

———. *Peculiar Crossroads: Flannery O'Connor, Walker Percy, and Catholic Vision in Postwar Southern Fiction.* Baton Rouge: Louisiana State UP, 2008.

O'Grady, Joseph T. "The Roman Question in American Politics: 1885." *Journal of Church and State* 10 (1968): 365–78.

O'Grady, Kelly J. *Clear the Confederate Way! The Irish in the Army of Northern Virginia.* Mason City, IA: Savas, 2000.

O'Hara, Arthur J. *Hibernian Society, Savannah, Georgia, 1812–1912: The Story of a Century.* Savannah: Baird & Hutton, 1912.

O'Neill, Charles Edwards. "Toward American Recognition of the Republic of Ireland: De Valera's Visit to New Orleans in 1920." *Louisiana History* 34.3 (1993): 639–50.

O'Neill, Peter D., and David Lloyd, eds. *The Black and Green Atlantic: Cross-Currents of the African and Irish Diasporas.* New York: Palgrave Macmillan, 2009.

Olney, James. *Metaphors of Self.* Princeton, NJ: Princeton UP, 1972.

Page, John W. *Uncle Robin, in His Cabin in Virginia, and Tom Without One in Boston.* Richmond, VA: J. W. Randolph, 1853.

Page, Richard Channing Moore. *Genealogy of the Page Family in Virginia*. New York: Jenkins & Thomas, 1883.

Palmer, John-Ivan. "The Balzac of Human Trash: Novelist Cormac McCarthy." *YourFlesh* 31 (1995). Web. 6 Aug. 2012.

Parker, Michael. "Crazy in Manhattan." Rev. of *Brain Fever*, by Valerie Sayers. *Washington Post Book World* 25 Feb. 1996: 7.

"Parnell's Brother Here: What He Says of His Family and the Dead Leader." *New York Times* 8 Oct. 1891.

Payne, Roger. *Among Whales*. New York: Scribner, 1995.

Percy, Walker. *Signposts in a Strange Land*. Ed. Patrick Samway. New York: Farrar, Straus, & Giroux, 1991.

Phillips, Dana. "History and the Ugly Facts of Cormac McCarthy's *Blood Meridian*." *American Literature* 68.2 (1996): 433–60.

Phillips, Ulrich Bonnell. *American Negro Slavery*. New York: Appleton, 1918.

Piatt, Sarah M. B. *Palace-Burner: The Selected Poetry of Sarah Piatt*. Ed. Paula Bennett. Urbana: U of Illinois P, 2001.

Pizer, Donald. *Realism and Naturalism in Nineteenth-Century American Fiction*. Carbondale: Southern Illinois UP, 1984.

Poe, Edgar Allan. *The Annotated Tales of Edgar Allan Poe*. Ed. Stephen Peithman. Garden City, NY: Doubleday, 1981.

———. *Edgar Allan Poe: Essays and Reviews*. Ed. G. R. Thompson. New York: Library of America, 1984.

"Poe's Life. Family Tree." *Poemuseum.org*. Edgar Allan Poe Museum, n.d. Web. 18 Oct. 2012.

Poole, Sheila. "Margaret Mitchell's Nephew Leaves Estate to Atlanta Archdiocese." Ajc .com. Atlantic Journal Constitution, 16 Aug. 2012. Web. 1 Nov. 2012.

Pope, Alexander. *Pope's Odyssey of Homer*. Ed. Alfred J. Church. New York: Cassell, 1907.

Potts, James. "McCarthy, Mac Airt and Mythology: *Suttree* and the Irish High King." *Mississippi Quarterly* 58.1–2 (2006): 25–39.

Powell, William. "North Carolina." Glazier 696–98.

Power, Tyrone. *Impressions of America During the Years 1833, 1834, and 1835*. Philadelphia: Carey, Lea & Blanchard, 1836.

Powers, William F. *Tar Heel Catholics: A History of Catholicism in North Carolina*. Lanham, MD: UP of America, 2003.

Purdy, Jedediah. *A Tolerable Anarchy: Rebels, Reactionaries, and the Making of American Freedom*. New York: Knopf, 2009.

Putzel, Max. *The Man in the Mirror: William Marion Reedy and His Magazine*. Cambridge, MA: Harvard UP, 1963.

Pyron, Darden Asbury. *Southern Daughter: The Life of Margaret Mitchell*. Oxford: Oxford UP, 1991.

Quigley, Paul. *Shifting Grounds: Nationalism and the American South, 1848–1865*. Oxford: Oxford UP, 2011.

Quinlan, Kieran. *Strange Kin: Ireland and the American South*. Baton Rouge: Louisiana State UP, 2004.

Quinn, E. Moore, ed. *The Irish in the American Civil War.* Spec. issue of *Irish Studies Review* 18.2 (2012).

Ragland, James. "White Settlement: Is It Time for a Change?" *Dallas Morning News* 2 Nov. 2005.

Railton, Ben. "'What Else Could a Southern Gentleman Do?': Quentin Compson, Rhett Butler, and Miscegenation." *Southern Literary Journal* 35.2 (2003): 41–63.

Randall, James Ryder. *The Poems of James Ryder Randall.* Ed. Matthew Page Andrews. New York: Tandy-Thomas, 1910.

Randolph, J. Thornton [Charles Jacobs Peterson]. *The Cabin and Parlor; or, Slaves and Masters.* Philadelphia: T. B. Peterson, 1852.

Ranelagh, John. *A Short History of Ireland.* Cambridge: Cambridge UP, 1994.

Reed, John Shelton. "Choosing the South." *Minding the South.* Columbia: U of Missouri P, 2003. 274–83.

———. *Dixie Bohemia: A French Quarter Circle in the 1920s.* Baton Rouge: Louisiana State UP, 2012.

Reid, Mayne. *The Quadroon, Or, Adventures in the Far West.* London: J. & C. Brown, 1856.

Rice, Anne. *Belinda.* New York: Berkley, 2000.

———. *Blackwood Farm.* New York: Ballantine, 2003.

———. *Called Out of Darkness: A Spiritual Confession.* New York: Knopf, 2008.

———. *Christ the Lord: Out of Egypt.* New York: Knopf, 2006.

———. *Christ the Lord: The Road to Cana.* New York: Knopf, 2008.

———. *The Feast of All Saints.* New York: Ballantine Books, 1986.

———. "Interview with an Ex-Vampire Novelist." By Dwight Longenecker. *First Things* 30 July 2008. Web. 14 Oct. 2012.

———. "Interview with Anne Rice." By W. Kenneth Holditch. *Lear's* 2.7 (Oct. 1989): 86–89.

———. *Lasher: A Novel.* New York: Knopf, 1993.

———. *Taltos: Lives of the Mayfair Witches.* New York: Knopf, 1994.

———. *The Witching Hour.* New York: Ballantine, 1991.

Richards, Jeffrey H. *Early American Drama.* New York: Penguin, 1997.

Rickford, John R. "Social Contact and Linguistic Diffusion: Hiberno-English and New World Black English." *Language* 62.2 (1986): 245–89.

Roberts, Gary L. *Doc Holliday: The Life and Legend.* Hoboken, NJ: John Wiley & Sons, 2006.

Rodriguez, Junius P. *Slavery in the United States: A Social, Political, and Historical Encyclopedia.* 2 vols. Santa Barbara, CA: ABC-CLIO, 2007.

Rolston, Bill. "Bringing It All Back Home: Irish Emigration and Racism." *Race & Class* 45.2 (2003): 39–53.

Ronan, Sean G. *Irish Writing on Lafcadio Hearn and Japan: Writer, Journalist & Teacher.* Kent, UK: Global Oriental, 1997.

Roppolo, Joseph P. "Uncle Tom in New Orleans: Three Lost Plays." *New England Quarterly* 27.2 (1954): 213–26.

Rubin, Louis D., and C. Hugh Holman. *Southern Literary Study: Problems and Possibilities.* Chapel Hill: U of North Carolina P, 1975.

Rugemer, Edward B. *The Problem of Emancipation*. Baton Rouge: Louisiana State UP, 2008.

———. "The Southern Response to British Abolitionism: The Maturation of Proslavery Apologetics." *Journal of Southern History* 70.2 (2004): 221–28.

Russell, Richard Rankin. *Poetry and Peace: Michael Longley, Seamus Heaney, and Northern Ireland*. Notre Dame, IN: U of Notre Dame P, 2010.

Russell, William Howard. *My Diary, North and South*. London: Bradbury & Evans, 1863.

———. *William Howard Russell's Civil War: Private Diary and Letters, 1861–1862*. Ed. Martin Crawford. Athens: U of Georgia P, 1992.

Ryan, Abram J. *A Crown for Our Queen*. Baltimore: John B. Piet, 1882.

———. "The Lecture of the Poet, Patriot and Priest—Father Ryan Speaks to the People of New Orleans." *New Orleans Bulletin* 19 Nov. 1874.

———. *Selected Poems of Father Ryan: With Preface and Life of the Poet*. Ed. Francis Boyle. Dublin: Talbot, 1928.

———. "Thoughts in Solitude." *Catholic Mirror* [Baltimore] 9 Dec. 1882: 4.

Samples, Gordon. *Lust for Fame: The Stage Career of John Wilkes Booth*. Jefferson, NC: McFarland, 1982.

Samway, Patrick, SJ. "Toward Discerning How Flannery O'Connor's Fiction Can Be Considered 'Roman Catholic.'" Gretlund and Westarp 162–75.

Sayers, Valerie. "The Age of Infidelity." *Prairie Schooner* 82.2 (2008): 111–24.

———. *Brain Fever*. New York: Doubleday, 1996.

———. *The Distance Between Us*. New York: Doubleday, 1994.

———. *Due East*. New York: Doubleday, 1987.

———. "Guilt and *Gone with the Wind*." *The Movie That Changed My Life*. Ed. David Rosenberg. New York: Viking, 1991. 89–107.

———. *How I Got Him Back: Or, Under the Cold Moon's Shine*. New York: Doubleday, 1989.

———. "Land's End, Beaufort, South Carolina." *Notre Dame Magazine* 34.4 (2005–6): 20–23.

———. *The Powers*. Chicago: Northwestern UP, forthcoming.

———. "Powers and Prophecy: An Interview with Valerie Sayers." By Bryan Giemza. *Flannery O'Connor Review* 10 (2012): 60–74.

———. "The View from O'Connor's Shadow." Still Alive at 60: Flannery O'Connor's Wise Blood. The Francis and Ann Curran Center for American Catholic Studies, the Fordham Center on Religions and Culture, Tognino Hall, Fordham University. 24 Mar. 2012. Address.

———. *Who Do You Love?* New York: Doubleday, 1991.

Scharnhorst, Gary. "The History of a Letter: Edgar Allan Poe to Joseph M. Field in 1846." *ANQ: A Quarterly Journal of Short Articles, Notes, and Reviews* 19.4 (2006): 26–29.

———. *Kate Field: The Many Lives of a Nineteenth-Century American Journalist*. Syracuse, NY: Syracuse UP, 2008.

———. "Kate Field and the *New York Tribune*." *American Periodicals: A Journal of History, Criticism, and Bibliography* 14.2 (2004): 159–78.

Scott, R. N., and Irwin H. Streight. *Flannery O'Connor: The Contemporary Reviews*. Cambridge: Cambridge UP, 2009.

Sepich, John. *Notes on "Blood Meridian": Revised and Expanded Edition.* Austin: U of Texas P, 2008.

Shankman, Arnold. "Black on Green: Afro-American Editors on Irish Independence, 1840–1921." *Phylon* 41.3 (1980): 284–99.

Shannon, James P. *Catholic Colonization on the Western Frontier.* New York: Arno, 1976.

Shannon, Noah Gallagher. "Cormac McCarthy Cuts to the Bone." *Slate.com.* 5 Oct. 2012. Web. 14 Oct. 2012.

Silverman, Jason H. "Irish." *Encyclopedia of the Confederacy.* Ed. Richard Nelson Current. New York: Simon & Schuster, 1993.

Simms, William Gilmore. *The Life of Francis Marion.* Charleston, SC: History, 2007.

Sitton, Thad. *The Texas Sheriff: Lord of the County Line.* Norman: U of Oklahoma P, 2000

Skinner, Margaret. *Molly Flanagan and the Holy Ghost.* Chapel Hill, NC: Algonquin Books of Chapel Hill, 1995.

——. *Old Jim Canaan: A Novel.* Chapel Hill, NC: Algonquin Books of Chapel Hill, 1990.

Slattery, Joseph. *Ex-priest Slattery's Complete Refutation of Popish Lies.* Melbourne: Loyal Orange Institute of Victoria, 1899.

Smietana, Bob. "Nashville Priest May Get in Trouble over Viral Video." *Tennessean* 10 Aug. 2010.

Smith, Christopher J. "Blacks and Irish on the Riverine Frontiers: The Roots of American Popular Music." *Southern Cultures* 17.1 (2011): 75–102.

Smith, William L. "Southerner and Irish? Regional and Ethnic Consciousness in Savannah, Georgia." *Southern Rural Sociology* 24.1 (2009): 223–39.

Snay, Mitchell. *Fenians, Freedmen, and Southern Whites: Race and Nationality in the Era of Reconstruction.* Baton Rouge: Louisiana State UP, 2007.

Snow, Patricia. "In Defense of Anne Rice." *First Things* 4 Feb. 2009. Web. 3 May 2011.

Snowden, Yates, and H. G. Cutler. *History of South Carolina.* New York: Lewis, 1920.

Sokal, Allen. "Transgressing the Boundaries: Towards a Transformative Hermeneutics of Quantum Gravity." *Social Text* 46–47 (1996): 217–52.

Southern Historical Association. *Memoirs of Georgia; Containing Historical Accounts of the State's Civil, Military, Industrial and Professional Interests, and Personal Sketches of Many of Its People.* 2 vols. Atlanta, 1895.

"A Southern Parable." Rev. of *Outer Dark,* by Cormac McCarthy. *Time* 27 Sept. 1968.

Spivey, Ted Ray. *Flannery O'Connor: The Woman, the Thinker, the Visionary.* Macon, GA: Mercer UP, 1995.

"St. Anthony's Temptation: Lafcadio Hearn's Translation of Flaubert's Drama of the Soul at Last Finds a Publisher." *New York Times* 23 Oct. 1910.

Stevenson, Elizabeth. *Lafcadio Hearn.* New York: Macmillan, 1961.

Stokes, Christopher. "Catholics in Beulahland: The Church's Encounter with Anti-Catholicism, Nativism and Anti-Abolitionism in the Carolinas and Georgia, 1820–1845." Diss. Rice U, 2001.

Stokes, Mason Boyd. *The Color of Sex: Whiteness, Heterosexuality, and the Fictions of White Supremacy.* Durham, NC: Duke UP, 2001.

Stowe, Harriet B. *Uncle Tom's Cabin, Or, Life Among the Lowly.* New ed. Boston: Houghton, Mifflin, 1890.

Stramm, Polly Powers. "Bill Canty Nov. 23, 1903–Nov. 18, 2002: The Stones Will All Bow Down." *Savannah Morning News* 19 Nov. 2002.

Stritch, Thomas. *The Catholic Church in Tennessee: The Sesquicentennial Story.* Nashville: Catholic Center, 1987.

Styron, William. *The Confessions of Nat Turner.* New York: Random House, 1967.

Sullivan, John J. *Blood Horses: Notes of a Sportswriter's Son.* New York: Farrar, Straus, & Giroux, 2004.

———. *Pulphead: Essays.* New York: Farrar, Straus, & Giroux, 2011.

———. "Watching the oil spill [letter from our southern editor]." *The Paris Review Daily,* theparisreview.org, 14 June 2010. Web. 7 Oct. 2012.

Sullivan, Walter. "The Last Cowboy Song: Cormac Mccarthy's Border Trilogy." *Sewanee Review* 108.2 (2000): 292–97.

Sweeney, Fionnghuala. *Frederick Douglass and the Atlantic World.* Liverpool: Liverpool UP, 2007.

Taney, Roger Brooke. *Memoir of Roger Brooke Taney, Ll.D., Chief Justice of the Supreme Court of the United States.* Ed. Samuel Tyler. Baltimore: J. Murphy, 1872.

Tardy, Mary T. *The Living Female Writers of the South.* Philadelphia: Claxton, Remsen & Haffelfinger, 1872.

"The Theater: New Plays in Manhattan, Dec. 7, 1942." *Time* 7 Dec. 1942.

Thigpen, Thomas Paul. "Aristocracy of the Heart: Catholic Lay Leadership in Savannah, 1820–1870." Diss. Emory U, 1995.

Thomas, Dylan. *Selected Poems, 1934–1952.* New York: New Directions Books, 2003.

Thomas, Kenneth H., Jr. "Roots and Environment: The Family Background of Joel Chandler Harris." *Atlanta Historical Journal* 30 (Fall 1986–Winter 1987): 37–56.

Thomas, William Hannibal. *The American Negro; What He Was, What He Is, and What He May Become; a Critical and Practical Discussion.* New York: Macmillan, 1901.

Thompson, Edgar T. "The 'Little Races.'" *Plantation Societies, Race Relations, and the South.* Durham, NC: Duke UP, 1975. 162–82.

Thompson, Scott B., Sr. "Dublin." *New Georgia Encyclopedia,* 2005. Web. 6 May 2010.

Thornton, Weldon. *Allusions in Ulysses: An Annotated List.* Chapel Hill: U of North Carolina P, 1982.

———. *The Antimodernism of Joyce's "Portrait of the Artist As a Young Man."* Syracuse, NY: Syracuse UP, 1994.

———. *Voices and Values in Joyce's Ulysses.* Gainesville: UP of Florida, 2000.

Thuente, Mary Helen. *The Harp Re-Strung: The United Irishmen and the Rise of Irish Literary Nationalism.* Syracuse, NY: Syracuse UP, 1994.

Tinling, Marion, ed. *The Correspondence of the Three William Byrds of Westover, Virginia, 1684–1776.* 3 vols. Charlottesville: UP of Virginia, 1977.

Tobin, William. *The Irish in South Carolina.* Florence, SC: W. J. Stricklin, n.d.

"To Marry in Private Chapel." *New York Times* 11 Aug. 1900.

Toole, John Kennedy. *A Confederacy of Dunces*. Baton Rouge: Louisiana State UP, 1980.

——. *The Neon Bible*. New York: Grove, 1989.

Toth, Emily. *Kate Chopin*. New York: Morrow, 1990.

——. *Unveiling Kate Chopin*. Jackson: UP of Mississippi, 1999.

Tracy, David. *The Analogical Imagination: Christian Theology and the Culture of Pluralism*. New York: Crossroad, 1981.

Trent, William P., John Erskine, Stuart P. Sherman, and Carl Van Doren, eds. *The Cambridge History of American Literature: A Short History of American Literature Based Upon the Cambridge History of American Literature*. New York: G. P. Putnam's Sons, 1922.

Tucker, Edward L. *Richard Henry Wilde: His Life and Selected Poems*. Athens: U of Georgia P, 1966.

Tucker, Jeffery A. "Oscar Wilde, Roman Catholic." *Crisis* 19.1 (Apr. 2001). Web.

Tutwiler, Mary. "The Lafayette Confederacy." *Independent Weekly* [Lafayette, LA] 19 July 2005. Web. 6 Aug. 2012.

Twain, Mark. *Life on the Mississippi*. New York and London: Harper & Bros., 1917.

Uhler, Margaret A. *The Floridians*. New York: Writers Club, 2003.

Valéry, Paul. "The Yalu." *History and Politics*. New York: Pantheon, 1962. Vol. 10 of *The Collected Works of Paul Valéry*. 15 vols. 1968–89.

"Valiant Lives." *Catholic News* 16 Mar. 1940.

Verot, Augustin. *General Catechism of the Christian Doctrine on the Basis Adopted by the Plenary Council of Baltimore. For the Use of Catholics of the Diocese of Savannah & Vicariate Apostolic of Florida, with Slight Additions and Modifications*. Augusta, GA: L. J. T. Paterson, 1864.

Wade, Nicholas. "A United Kingdom? Maybe." *New York Times* 6 Mar. 2007.

Wallace, Garry. "Meeting Cormac McCarthy." *Southern Quarterly* 30.4 (1992): 134–39.

Wallach, Rick, ed. *Cormac McCarthy Issue*. Spec. issue of *Appalachian Heritage* 39.1 (Winter 2011).

——. "Judge Holden, *Blood Meridian*'s Evil Archon." *Sacred Violence: A Reader's Companion to Cormac McCarthy*. Ed. Wade H. Hall and Rick Wallach. El Paso: Texas Western P. 125–36.

——, ed. *Myth, Legend, Dust: Critical Responses to Cormac McCarthy*. Manchester, UK: Manchester UP, 2000.

——, ed. *You Would Not Believe What Watches: Suttree and Cormac McCarthy's Knoxville*. Miami: Cormac McCarthy Society, 2012.

——. "Prefiguring Cormac McCarthy: The Early Short Stories." Wallach, *Myth, Legend, Dust* 15–20.

——. "Ulysses in Knoxville: Suttree's Agean Journey." Wallach, *Cormac McCarthy Issue* 52–62.

Watson, Charles S. *The History of Southern Drama*. Lexington: UP of Kentucky, 1997.

Watson, Ritchie Devon. *Normans and Saxons: Southern Race Mythology and the Intellectual History of the American Civil War*. Baton Rouge: Louisiana State UP, 2008.

Wayland, John Walter. *A History of Shenandoah County, Virginia.* Strasburg, VA: Shenandoah, 1927.

Weaver, Richard M. *Ideas Have Consequences.* Chicago: U of Chicago P, 1948.

Webb, James H. *Born Fighting: How the Scots-Irish Shaped America.* New York: Broadway, 2004.

Weddle, Jeff. *Bohemian New Orleans: The Story of the "Outsider" and Loujon Press.* Jackson: UP of Mississippi, 2007.

Welty, Eudora. *Conversations with Eudora Welty.* Ed. Peggy W. Prenshaw. Jackson: UP of Mississippi, 1984.

Westbrook, Laura Renée. "Common Roots: The Godchaux Family in Louisiana History, Literature, and Public Folklore." Diss. U of Louisiana at Lafayette, 2001.

White, William Allan. "Books of the Fall." *Saturday Review* 10 Oct. 1936: 16ff.

Whiting, Lilian. *Kate Field, A Record.* Boston: Little, Brown, 1899.

Whorton, James, Jr. "Ignatius Screamed." Rev. of *Butterfly in the Typewriter,* by Cory MacLauchlin. *Oxford American* 6 June 2012. Web. 2 Oct. 2012.

Wilde, Richard H. *Conjectures and Researches Concerning the Love, Madness, and Imprisonment of Torquato Tasso.* New York: Alexander V. Blake, 1842.

———. *Hesperia; A Poem.* Ed. William Cumming Wilde. Boston: Ticknor & Fields, 1867.

Williams, Don. "Cormac McCarthy Crosses the Great Divide." *New Millenium Writings* 14 (2004–5). Web. 6 Aug. 2012.

Williams, Joy. "Stranger Than Paradise." *New York Times Book Review* 26 Feb. 2009. Web. 1 Mar. 2012.

Wilson, Edmund. *Patriotic Gore: Studies in the Literature of the American Civil War.* New York: Oxford UP, 1962.

Wilson, James Grant, and John Fiske. *Appleton's Cyclopædia of American Biography.* New York: D. Appleton, 1887.

Wolfe, Thomas. *The Notebooks of Thomas Wolfe.* Ed. Richard S. Kennedy and Paschal Reeves. 2 vols. Chapel Hill: U of North Carolina P, 1970.

———. *Of Time and the River: A Legend of Man's Hunger in His Youth.* New York: C. Scribner's Sons, 1935.

Woman's Faith, A Tale of Southern Life. New York: Derby & Jackson, 1856.

Wood, James. "Red Planet: The Sanguinary Sublime of Cormac McCarthy." *New Yorker* 25 July 2005: 88–93. Web.

Wood, Ralph C. *Flannery O'Connor and the Christ-Haunted South.* Grand Rapids, MI: William B. Eerdmans, 2004.

———. "Flannery O'Connor's Racial Morals and Manners." *Christian Century* 111.33 (1994).

———. "Such a Catholic." *National Review* 61.4 (2009): 38–42.

Woods, James M. *A History of the Catholic Church in the American South: 1513–1900.* Gainesville: UP of Florida, 2011.

Woodward, Richard B. "Cormac Country." *Vanity Fair* Aug. 2005: 98–104.

———. "Cormac McCarthy's Venomous Fiction." *New York Times Magazine* 19 Apr. 1992. Web. 31 Oct. 2012.

Wright, Richard. *Black Boy, a Record of Childhood and Youth.* New York: Harper & Bros., 1945.

"Writer Anne Rice: 'Today I Quit Being A Christian.'" *NPR.org.* 2 Aug. 2010. Web. 14 Oct. 2012.

Wyatt-Brown, Bertram. *Hearts of Darkness: Wellsprings of a Southern Literary Tradition.* Baton Rouge: Louisiana State UP, 2003.

Yaeger, Patricia. "Race and the Cloud of Unknowing in *Gone with the Wind.*" *Southern Cultures* 5.1 (1999): 21–28.

Yeats, William Butler. *The Collected Poems of W. B. Yeats.* New York: Macmillan, 1956.

———. *The Collected Works of W. B. Yeats, Volume IX: Early Articles and Reviews.* Ed. John Frayne and Madeleine Marchaterre. Scribner, 2004.

———. *A Vision.* New York: Macmillan, 1938.

———. *The Yeats Reader.* Ed. Richard J. Finneran. New York: Scribner Poetry, 2002.

Young, Alfred. *Catholic and Protestant Countries Compared in Civilization, Popular Happiness, General Intelligence, and Morality.* New York: Catholic Book Exchange, 1895.

Young, Stanley. "In a Country of Drowsy Waters and Drowsy People." Rev. of *Green Margins,* by E. P. O'Donnell. *New York Times* 4 Oct. 1936.

INDEX